Windows 2000
Active Directory
Survival Guide
Planning and Implementation

Windows 2000 Active Directory Survival Guide
Planning and Implementation

Richard Schwartz

Wiley Computer Publishing

John Wiley & Sons, Inc.

NEW YORK · CHICHESTER · WEINHEIM · BRISBANE · SINGAPORE · TORONTO

Publisher: Robert Ipsen
Editor: Carol Long
Managing Editor: Brian Snapp
Text Design & Composition: Benchmark Productions, Inc.

Library of Congress Cataloging-in-Publication Data:

Schwartz, Richard, 1967–
   Windows 2000 active directory survival guide : planning and
   implementation / Richard Schwartz
      p. cm.
   ISBN 0-471-35600-X (pbk. : alk. paper)
   1. Microsoft Windows (Computer File).   2. Operating Systems (Computers)
   3. Directory services (Computer network technology)   I. Title.
   QA76.O63 S4546   2000
   005.7'1369--dc21
                                                        99-049145
                                                        CIP

Printed in the United States of America.
10 9 8 7 6 5 4 3 2

This book is dedicated to my wife Karen, who not only *allowed* me the time to complete this manuscript, but *afforded* me the time as well, and managed to give birth to our beautiful daughter, Rachael, in the midst of it all. You are truly superwoman and I love you. Of course, I must mention my daughter Rachael, who warms my heart with her smile. I will always believe she is smarter than I, as those well-placed cries easily tore me from my keyboard to run and hold her in my arms . . . cunning. And last but certainly not least, I want to thank Carol Long and John Wiley & Sons for giving me the opportunity to write this much-needed book. I could not have done it without their support.

Contents

Preface

It has been said that good things come to those who wait. Almost six years since the first rumors surfaced about the operating system called "Cairo," rumor has become reality with the release of Microsoft's latest operating system: Windows 2000. And while a treasure-trove of new features await those who quietly and diligently (and often without great reward!) make the business world really work, this new operating system is a Pandora's Box as well, filled with uncertainty.

This should not be cause for alarm or panic. Certainly the new features of Windows 2000 will have a learning curve associated with them, but most people with tech blood running through their veins will welcome the chance to learn something new. At the core of the operating system lies the heart of what will become the most welcome change to anyone who has ever served in an administrative or architectural role using the Windows NT product: Active Directory.

While anticipation abounds for the release of true directory services on the Windows NT platform, many will be caught off guard with the complexity of Active Directory, particularly in complicated scenarios. The product is quite adaptive to the existing network topology, which is an asset indeed. However, Active Directory implementation should not be treated like the "kit" we have all torn into, carelessly and without regard throwing the instructions to the wayside. Hence, the reason this book was written. Active Directory implementation is a multifaceted and intricate process in every case when the prospect of future growth is factored.

There is no doubt a slew of books that will hit the market at the time the product rolls out that will try to cover the topic of Windows 2000 intact. Because of the complex nature of the product, Active Directory being only one part (although a large part), such books could not possibly give the topic the time it deserves. Active Directory design and implementation nirvana cannot be accomplished through an overview, just as the same would never be attempted with, say, a nuclear power plant.

In this book, I have attempted to cover all relevant topics related to a successful and rapid deployment of Active Directory with the least amount of tribulation. Masses of documentation were scoured to compile this text, much of which was cryptic at best. Therefore, this text was written in a language that is as down-to-earth as possible, but not condescending, with a touch of humor throughout to keep it interesting. Additionally, the book could have added tons of granular details about the inner workings of every component and filled volumes; instead, the real concepts that are necessary to achieve a solid and rapid deployment are covered. Details at a very granular level are provided in the Windows 2000 Resource Kit Books, a very interesting and thorough knowledge product that comes highly recommended to those looking for intricate knowledge of the product.

This text takes you from the planning stages of an Active Directory implementation, to design principles, to developing skills with hands-on sections using directory tools, and provides plenty of visual examples in order to follow along and reinforce concepts.

It should also be noted that the entire book was written and based upon Beta 3 code, so there may be inconsistencies from time to time. The actual writing began during the Beta 2 release. However, because so many changes were expected in the next release, I decided to wait it out and base the book on the later releases. Updates to this book may be found on Wiley's Web site at www.wiley.com/compbooks, or, alternatively, you may report bugs or request information from the author at rschwartz@technelogic.com.

This book is meant to be a road map to implementation. The following section outlines the process or plan that is involved in a successful rollout of the product. After reading it, it should be easy to understand why this topic alone deserves its own book.

The Road to Active Directory Implementation

The following is an outline format of an Active Directory implementation. You may notice that the outline and accompanying flowchart do not correspond with the Table of Contents in the book—that is intentional. The book is presented in a format that is meaningful from a learning standpoint and organized to better understand all of the stages and concepts involved.

Begin Active Directory Implementation

Here is an outline of planning and implementing the Active Directory. Also take a look at Figure P.1.

I. Develop the Project Plan

   a. Assemble the project team

   b. Develop a meeting schedule

   c. Assess and document the current systems inhouse

   d. Assess and document the current network infrastructure

   e. Assess and document business goals

   f. Assess and document IT infrastructure

   g. Finalize the project plans based on needs assessments

II. Develop Architecture

   a. Register a domain if necessary

   b. Develop DNS architecture

   c. Develop Domain architecture

   d. Develop Site architecture

   e. Develop Upgrade path(s)

III. Testing

   a. Build test environment

   b. Test installation of O/S on current hardware specification

   c. Test the domain controller promotion process/implement root domain

   d. Implement DNS architecture

   e. Check the installation

   f. Implement child domains

   g. Configure sites

   h. Test replication strategies

   i. Test upgrade procedures for NT 4.0 PDCs and BDCs

   j. Test applications

   k. Test client operability

   l. Test queries

IV. Implement Production Environment

   a. Create root domain (or promote PDCs for all domains)

   b. Configure DNS

   c. Create accounts

   d. Create Organizational Units

   e. Create replica domain controllers (or promote BDCs)

   f. Configure DHCP/WINS

   g. Delegate authority over organizational units

   h. Create/promote member servers

   i. Repeat steps ii–viii for child domains

  V. Implementation Complete

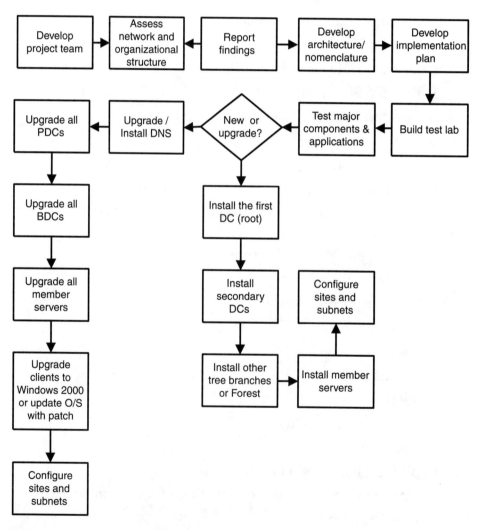

Figure P.1   The Active Directory Implementation Road Map

An Overview of Windows 2000 Active Directory Services

Welcome to Windows 2000 Server Active Directory, Microsoft's next-generation operating system and network management framework. Windows 2000 Server is a completely new breed of operating system. At the heart of Windows 2000 lies Active Directory Services, the latest implementation of directory services for the Windows server line of operating systems. As with any new product in information technology, Active Directory should prove challenging to network architects, IT implementers, administrators, and consultants. Don't get the wrong idea, these changes are welcome and fill the void that was present in previous incarnations of the NT product line. The product is revolutionary in its ability to reduce the burden of operating a Windows-based network while systematically lowering supportability levels.

Before we roll up our sleeves and start under the hood, let's cover a little history on directory services. If you are already familiar with the concepts and theories behind X.500, Lightweight Directory Access Protocol (LDAP), or Novell's Novell Directory Services (NDS), you may want to skip ahead to the section, "Microsoft's Active Directory Services Overview."

This chapter describes the basic and extended feature set of directory services and looks specifically at features indigenous to Microsoft's Active Directory Services.

A Brief History of Directory Services

Directories are not a new idea. In fact, the action of cataloging has been around since recorded history. Perhaps the best and most used analogy for a directory is the telephone book, which is a collection of items provided in a format that allows you to look up the information you desire by referencing an attribute of the object you seek. Items (equated to objects) in this case might consist of phone numbers and addresses. In the case of the Yellow Pages or business index you may need to know only a general attribute of the item you are searching for, such as flowers or florists. The index and alphabetic properties of the telephone book bring order to the directory.

Directory services are a step forward from the basic concept of the directory. Based on the IETF and ISB X.500 directory specification (see RFC 1777 at www.cis.ohio-state.edu/htbin/rfc for more information on this and other Request for Comment documents), directory services offer the end user the ability to find and access resources, be they people, server computers, peer computers, databases, printers, or anything else you can "hang" off a network. Each of these objects has a set of unique properties that allow it to be easily found and distinguished on a network by users or applications.

Directory Services Explained

Microsoft often referred to Windows NT 4.0 as having directory services. These services were defined as:

- A single point of access to network resources
- An adaptive and expandable information source
- A way to set a common policy or set of rules
- A method to query directory objects

Windows NT 4.0 and 3.*x* did offer this functionality to a degree, but not without a great deal of hardship for the administrator and the end user. The method in which the operating system delivered directory services was less than desirable. The concepts of *domains* and *trusts* carry over from Microsoft's LAN Manager product, circa 1989–1993 (see Figure 1.1). Needless to say, the necessity for a new and more robust set of directory services has been a long time coming. Windows 2000 Server Active Directory delivers.

Through the use of Internet standards and protocol, Microsoft has delivered a robust and scalable product that encompasses technology such as Domain Name Service (DNS) and LDAP. DNS is the hierarchical Internet Protocol (IP) to the host name mapping service that allows us to resolve friendly names to host ID numbers on the Internet or intranet. LDAP is the successor to the Directory Access Protocol (DAP), part of the X.500 directory standard. X.500 never reached its full potential largely in part due to DAP's very weighty nature. LDAP provides most of the functionality of DAP with 90 percent less of the overhead associated with it. Figure 1.2 gives an example of how a directory service might look.

The concepts of LDAP and DNS are discussed in greater detail later in this book. As the foundation for Active Directory, it is essential that

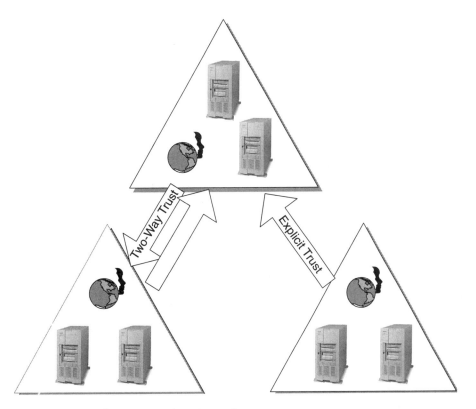

Figure 1.1   Windows NT 4.0 domains and trusts.

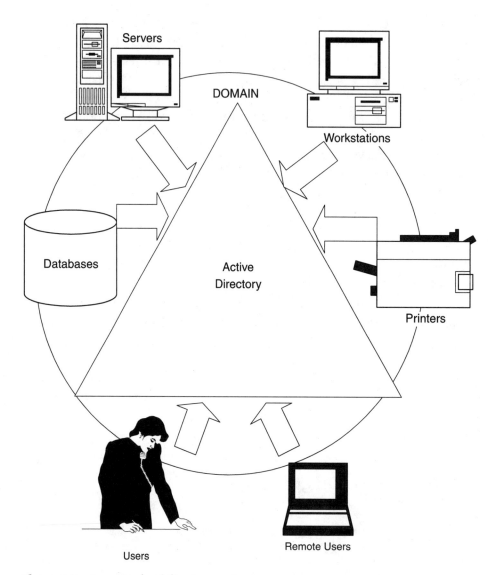

Figure 1.2   An example of directory services.

you fully understand both of these technologies before attempting an Active Directory implementation. Additionally, you must have a firm understanding of the Transmission Control Protocol/Internet Protocol (TCP/IP) specification in order to successfully lay out a Windows 2000 Server network with Active Directory. Microsoft has kept true to their word in promising that the next-generation operating system produced by the company would be fully integrated with the Internet and Internet standards.

Microsoft's Active Directory Services Overview

Active Directory is the directory service packaged with Windows 2000 Server, Windows 2000 Enterprise, and Windows 2000 Data Center. It provides all of the basic functionality of directory services: an information source, a single point of administration, a way to commonly define rules, and a method to query objects in the directory. Let's take a quick look at each of these basic features.

Active Directory Features

A scalable directory. Active Directory serves as the source of information for Windows 2000, and it grows as an organization grows. Windows 2000 introduces the concept of *partitions* that allow a Windows 2000 network to scale to enormous proportions while still maintaining manageability. These partitions are sections of the Active Directory hierarchy and easily allow new additions to the structure. Active Directory features and benefits include a flexible hierarchical structure; security delegation; extensibility through object customization; multimaster replication; scalability; support for resource queries via LDAP, DNS, and Dynamic DNS (DDNS) support; programming interfaces through Active Directory Services interface; and interoperability with existing standards-based directories.

A Windows 2000 network contrasts largely to legacy Windows NT structures as seen in Figures 1.3 and 1.4. Here are the main points we are going to focus on from a planning and integration perspective:

Single point of administration. Because the directory is structured in a hierarchy, and all access to objects is through this hierarchy, the task of administering a Windows 2000 network is much simplified. Support for the new concept of *transitive trusts* further eases administrative burdens, cutting down on the amount of trust relationships that need to be managed by administrators. A transitive trust means simply that if Domain A trusts Domain B, and Domain C trusts Domain B, then Domain A trusts Domain C. For those of you familiar with trust relationships in the Windows NT 4.0 and 3.*x* products, this should come as a huge relief. An example of transitive trusts is shown in Figure 1.5.

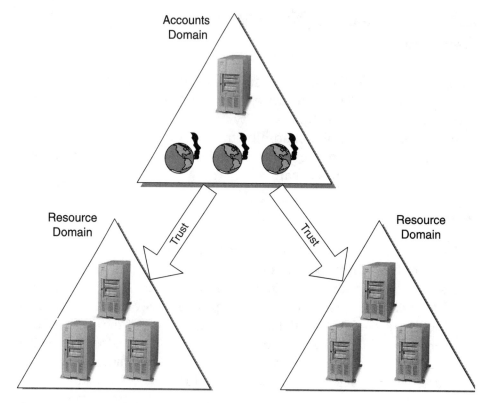

Figure 1.3   NT4 and resource domains.

Defining common rules and policies. The *schema* is a new concept for most. Essentially, the schema provides a way to apply a common set of rules for the way that objects in the directory are described and categorically defined. Further, the schema allows for the creation of custom objects and object attributes within the directory hierarchy. We discuss the schema in greater detail in Chapter 12, "Implementing Administrative Control Over Directory Objects." For now, just remember that the schema provides a mechanism for defining objects and attributes.

Querying objects. Microsoft implemented two Internet standards into Active Directory to provide object location capability. Doing so was part of Microsoft's plan for lowering Total Cost of Ownership (TCO) for Windows-based networks. The concepts of DNS and *namespace* help to define the Windows 2000 network and the objects within by providing a logical naming structure. DNS translates unfriendly host IP addresses to host names. Moreover, DNS provides for the hierarchical structure found in an Active Directory

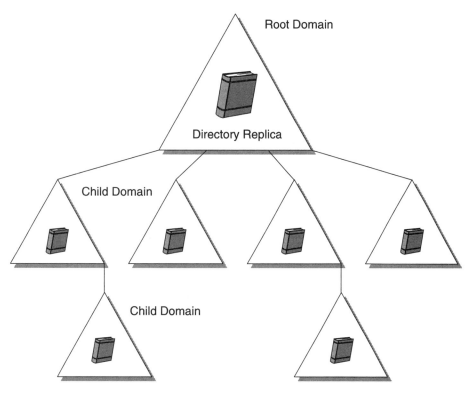

Figure 1.4 The hierarchical structure of a Windows 2000 network.

installation and defines the naming structure of the organization. LDAP is the query and find mechanism used in conjunction with DNS to locate resources on the network. LDAP and DNS are defined as Internet standards and are well defined in Internet RFCs. We discuss LDAP briefly in other chapters; delving into the inner workings of LDAP is beyond the scope of this book. DNS is discussed in great detail in Chapters 3, 4, and 8 due to Active Directory's dependency on this technology to function.

The Extended Feature Set of Active Directory

Active Directory provides several other key features that make it a powerful asset to the core functionality of a network environment. In addition to the basic features, Active Directory provides the following:

- Security definition and control
- Fault tolerance through replication

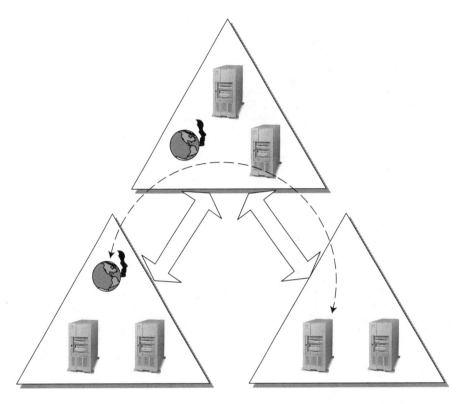

Figure 1.5   Transitive trusts allow resource access throughout the network.

- Interoperability with other directories
- Enhanced query support

In addition to the basic features found in the directory, several extended features provide Active Directory the means for scalability and manageability, and also fault tolerance, tighter security, and interoperability with existing systems. The following is a breakdown of the Active Directory extended feature set:

Security definition and control. The access control list is a feature carried over from Windows NT 4.0, and it is applied to the directory to provide control over access to objects within the directory. The list of permissions is replicated through the hierarchy down to the object level.

Fault tolerance. This feature is provided through replication of the directory. All Windows 2000 sites work off the same copy of the directory, which helps to compensate for limitations or failures in interconnected networks.

Interoperability. As stated earlier in the chapter, Active Directory is closely modeled after Internet standard architecture found in the X.500 specification, DNS, and LDAP. Because of the adoption of these standard technologies, Windows 2000 provides interoperability with legacy NT systems and NDS.

Enhanced query support. With the addition of a global catalog server (GCS), Active Directory supports an enhanced set of query functions and provides a centralized store for directory information. The catalog server is synonymous with an index and supports querying of every object within the directory. Details on the GCS are explained in greater detail later in the book.

You might be asking yourself, "What do all of these features buy you as an administrator or user of a Windows 2000 network?" In a nutshell, you will be able to support more of your network with fewer resources, while lowering overall support costs for the network. As we explore further into the inner workings of Active Directory, you will begin to see how tangible these benefits are.

Active Directory Components

The Windows 2000 Active Directory is an extensible and flexible mechanism for designing your organization from the ground up. The most complex (and consequently, the most important part of implementing this technology) is the planning phase. It may take some enterprise organizations many months to fully plan, test, and institute it. This is due in part to the way Active Directory tightly integrates into your organization. Directory structures may be modeled after business units within the organization or by how the company does business. The main concepts within this framework involve naming standards, logical structures, physical structures, and security.

Remember that Active Directory relies heavily on the concept of the DNS *namespace* (see Figure 1.6). Namespace is a name or group of names that are defined according to some naming convention. A *flat* namespace uses a single, unique name for every device—it is not "stacked," so to speak. For example, a small Windows (NetBIOS) network requires a different, made-up name for each computer and printer. The Internet uses a hierarchical namespace that partitions the names into categories known as *top-level domains,* such as .com, .edu, and .gov, which are at the top of the hierarchy. Active Directory uses the hierarchical model to define the

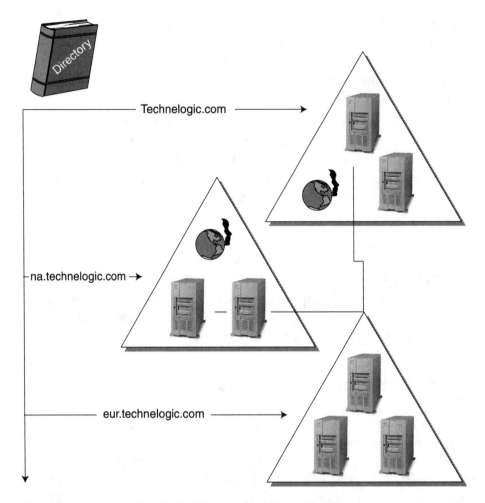

Figure 1.6   An example of Active Directory and the namespace.

network. Those of you already familiar with DNS have a competitive advantage when it comes to Active Directory over those who do not have a working knowledge of name services. Active Directory's use of a hierarchical namespace to define an organization allows for name resolution and queries at the object level and provides a foundation for naming conventions. We cover the DNS and naming conventions in Chapters 3, 4, and 8. Now let's look at a breakdown of the parts that compose Active Directory and the namespace.

Active Directory complements business because of its extensible and flexible nature. This is true regardless of the size of an organization. The logical structure that is Active Directory allows the product to scale

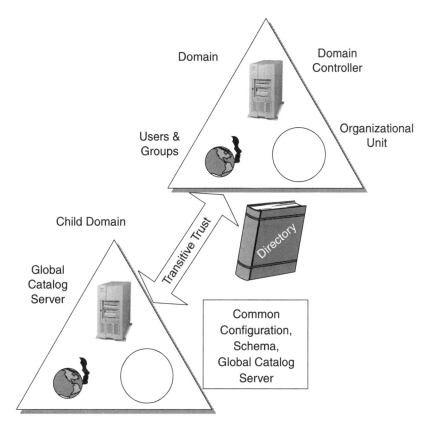

Figure 1.7   Elements that make up Active Directory.

from a single server up to thousands of servers capable of holding literally millions of objects. The concepts that allow for such massive scalability mainly consist of four notions: the naming standards that are defined through DNS (namespace), structural elements that may be both logical or physical, and security elements applied through the directory. Figure 1.7 shows some of the elements that comprise an Active Directory structure.

Namespace and Name Resolution

Remember that Active Directory is structured and defined via a hierarchical naming structure (see Figure 1.8). The entire directory depends on this structure to give it form and organization. At a more granular level, every object contained within the directory is known by a specific name. The Internet concept of *namespace* provides the hierarchical

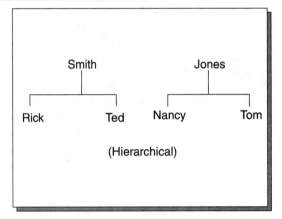

Figure 1.8   Hierarchical namespace versus a flat namespace.

structure and allows enterprises to manage multiple namespaces. This allows Active Directory to integrate other standards-based directories into the organization as well. One of limitations of the legacy NT systems was their inability to provide this hierarchy of names; they allowed only a flat namespace. Simply put, a flat namespace requires a unique name for each object in the directory (Microsoft claims that previous versions possessed directory services).

Name Resolution

Name resolution is the ability to attribute a name to an object, be it a computer, user, or other resource on the network. We can use a telephone directory as an example of a namespace and name resolution. In this simple example, a person's name is resolved to a specific telephone number. Active Directory also provides a namespace and name to object resolution. For example, Bob Jones can be resolved to any number of directory attributes such as his location or the domain in which he resides.

Active Directory, when installed, develops a hierarchy in which each domain, organizational unit, resource, and so on possesses a particular and unique name within the namespace. This nomenclature provides the ability to define an organization from a network perspective, tightly integrating the network infrastructure into a particular business model.

For example, Technelogic's namespace hierarchy is defined by technelogic.com. As with most companies, Technelogic has several divisions within the company: Sales, Corporate, Marketing, Legal, International, Publishing, and IT. These divisions are known within the directory as sales.technelogic.com, corp.technelogic.com, mktg.technelogic.com, legal.technelogic.com, intl.technelogic.com, pub.technelogic.com, and it.technelogic.com, respectively (see Figure 1.9). This naming standard is what defines the hierarchy of Active Directory.

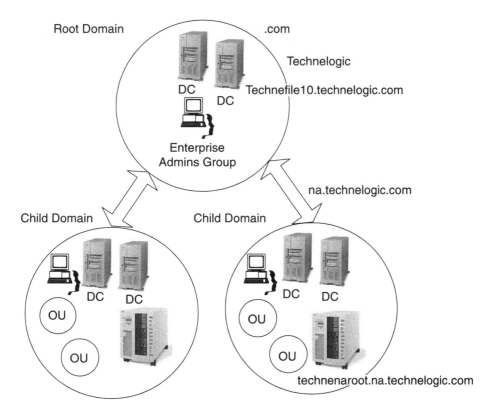

Figure 1.9 The Technelogic.com namespace.

Types of Names

Microsoft made every effort to make Windows 2000 and Active Directory standards compliant. Part of this adaptation includes elements of the X.500 Directory Standard. Active Directory is *not* an X.500 directory, although it borrows traits from this Internet standard and is compliant to the point where it can integrate with X.500 directories. Like Active Directory, every object within must have a name. The X.500 Standard refers to two types of names: the distinguished name (DN) and the relative distinguished name (RDN).

DN and RDN

The RDN identifies an object within a collection of objects with the same parent. Logic would have it then that two objects in the directory can have the same RDN as long as they have a different parent object. A real-world example of this would be two towns named Columbia, one in South Carolina and the other in Maryland.

The DN is a compilation of the RDN of each level in the hierarchy, starting at the root. In other words, traveling downward from the root of the directory from parent to child to object, the DN is formed. Figure 1.10 examines this principle. Think of the way a file system is structured. Using the path to a specific file defines the DN; for example, in c:\winnt\system32\at.exe, the whole path would be considered the DN.

Let's again use our example company Technelogic to inspect the way naming occurs in Active Directory. The user Bob Jones works in the technical division of Technelogic Corporation. The DN of Bob Jones identifies him as a user object. The DN for Bob Jones is expressed as Bob Jones@tech.Technelogic.com. Specifically, "Bob Jones" is the actual name of the object; "tech" is the parent container that represents the Technical division; "Technelogic" is the namespace of Technelogic Active Directory; and "com" is the "root" or top level of the directory that defines Technelogic as a commercial organization on the Internet. If all of this sounds a lot like a DNS namespace, it is—sort of. Remember that Active Directory is based on Internet standards, and the directory itself is a compilation of DNS and X.500. We discuss the role of DNS in Active Directory in greater detail in Chapters 3, 4, and 8. Figure 1.11 shows a typical AD name hierarchy.

User Principal Name (UPN)

In addition to the DN and RDN, Active Directory introduces the concept of the UPN. The UPN may be synonymous with the user's logon name and is a truncated version of the DN (e.g., an alias). This is a sort

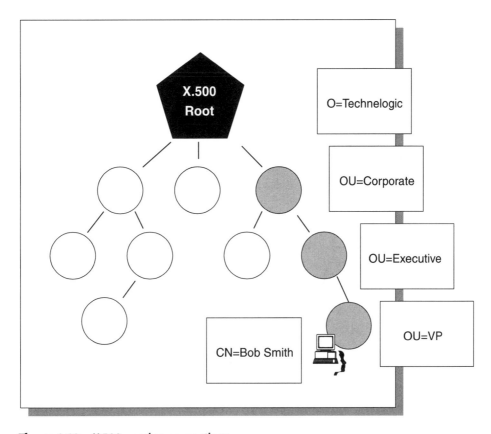

Figure 1.10   X.500 naming conventions.

of shortcut name for the user and is used in conjunction with DNS for user object name resolution. For example, the user Bob Jones in the Technical division of Technelogic logs on to the network as BobJ and is known in the directory by the UPN BobJ@tech.technelogic.com.

Standards

Another asset of Active Directory is built-in query support that offers the ability to locate resources on a Windows 2000 network through the use of LDAP queries to the directory. Two components of the directory make this possible: DNS and LDAP.

DNS

DNS is the Internet standard namespace. As previously mentioned, Microsoft's goal in designing Windows 2000 was integration of adopted Internet standards. Not only does this help Windows 2000 mesh with current mixed networks, it also provides a (somewhat)

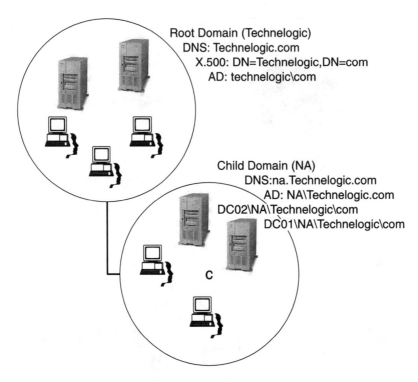

Root Domain (Technelogic)
DNS: Technelogic.com
X.500: DN=Technelogic,DN=com
AD: technelogic\com

Child Domain (NA)
DNS:na.Technelogic.com
AD: NA\Technelogic.com
DC02\NA\Technelogic\com
DC01\NA\Technelogic\com

c

Figure 1.11   The Active Directory name hierarchy.

seamless existence between a company's intranetwork and the Internet. DNS is a set of protocols and services that provide name-to-address resolution. DNS also provides the hierarchical structure inherent to Active Directory. As with most Internet standards, DNS runs in conjunction with the TCP/IP protocol.

LDAP

A subset of protocols used in the X.500 directory standard, LDAP is a streamlined version of the DAP protocol that provides clients the ability to read and query the directory. Versions 2 and 3 of the LDAP protocol are supported in Windows 2000. Please refer to RFC-1777 for further information on the LDAP protocol or Chapter 4 of this book. It is important to note that LDAP is dependent on TCP/IP for functionality .

The Logical Components of Active Directory

Let's now look at the set of concepts that define the Active Directory framework. These encompass the logical elements, structure, and relationships of the directory. The logical organization of directory objects and the extensibility inherent in this relationship mean that Active Directory can be tailored to fit the business model of any company. Another benefit of this logical architecture is the ability to easily find objects within the directory on a Windows 2000 network. Logical structure elements include objects, the schema, domains, containers, organizational units (OUs), trees and forests, sites and domain controllers. Let's look first at the objects that comprise the directory and the attributes that define them.

Logical Elements of the Directory

In examining the logical structure of Active Directory, it is best to start from the bottom of the hierarchy (sometimes called "leaves," a "leaf," or "leaf objects") and work up to the top (technically, the "root") of the tree. The most basic element of the Active Directory logical makeup is the object and its related attributes. The following sections outline the common logical elements found in a typical Active Directory structure.

Objects

An *object* in Active Directory is defined as any item contained in the directory that has a common set of *attributes*. Examples of objects are users, workstations, servers, printers, databases, files, and so on. An object is anything in the directory that has properties or attributes and is further defined by class definitions. An object can exist as a parent container or a child object in a directory hierarchy as well. This relational concept of parent and child is adopted from the X.500 specification discussed earlier (see Figure 1.12).

 A quick word to Novell and Microsoft Exchange administrators: If many of these terms seem familiar to you, this is probably due to the directory standards implemented in these products. NDS and Exchange Server follow the same standards found in the X.500 specification, and consequently, you should feel very much at home with most of the concepts introduced here.

Object Attributes

All objects within the directory have *attributes* or *properties* (Microsoft uses the words "attribute" and "properties" interchangeably, so don't be alarmed if you find the same within this text). An attribute is a categorical set of information or characteristics that define an object. As a

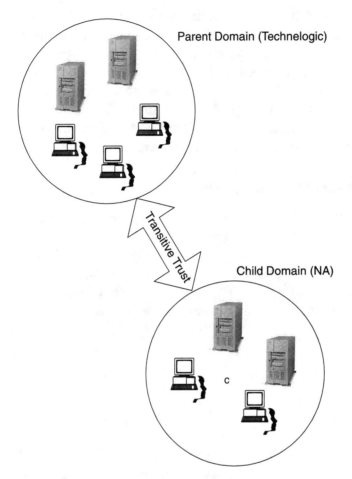

Figure 1.12   The parent-child relationship.

rule, objects that exist in the same parent container have the same attributes. It is the actual *value* of the attribute that provides uniqueness. The UPN is an attribute of the User Account object. The attribute may have any value that conforms to the current logon naming standard currently in place on your network. Therefore, understanding object attributes provides a mechanism for querying the directory for network resources or objects.

Object Classes

Active Directory groups objects by their attributes. All of the aforementioned objects are categorized as users, groups, computers, organizational units, domains, databases, and so forth. These are logical groupings and can help to organize resources in the directory.

Structure Components

Another logical division of Active Directory is the elements that help to organize the hierarchy. The hierarchy is composed of logical units that consist of containers, domains, and organizational units, which in turn house the objects that we discussed previously. These organizational units are integral in defining the network boundaries, security boundaries, and logical divisions within a company's network.

Containers

Simply put, a *container* is a store for other objects in the directory. Containers have attributes just like objects and are crucial to the theory of a hierarchy. Examples of containers are domains and organizational units.

Domains

Domains are the building blocks of a Windows 2000 network (perhaps much to the dismay of many readers) and define the structure of Active Directory. A domain stores objects such as users, computers, servers, and security policies.

While a domain acts as a logical boundary (or container) for the objects within, it also is essential in forming security boundaries on a Windows 2000 network. This means that security settings are contained in the domain and do not cross over the boundary edge of the domain—though it is still possible for domains to interact with other domains. We cover the semantics of this later; for now, just remember that domains are the essence of Active Directory and Windows 2000 Server networks.

Organizational Units (OUs)

OUs help to further subdivide the structure of the directory into manageable partitions. The OU is a container just like a domain and helps to create smaller, more manageable administrative units. This eases administration and allows for delegation of resources.

Relational Components

The last subset of the divisional elements that we will discuss details the relationship between domains. These relationships are defined by trees and forests and further define the hierarchical structure of the directory and the namespace.

Trees

Although not necessary, particularly with a Windows 2000 network, many companies do have a need to create multiple domains in their organization. When using multiple domains in Windows 2000, a hierarchy is formed that creates a contiguous namespace and is formally referred to as a *tree*. Remember that the directory is composed of objects and containers that hold these objects, one of which is the domain. A tree forms a logical top level to a hierarchy of multiple domains that are contained within the same namespace. Within the tree, the domains are interconnected via trust relationships and share three common components: the schema, unified configuration, and a GCS.

Trust relationships are formed when one or more domains are joined in the same namespace in Active Directory and a link between the two is formed. This differs from the way that trusts were implemented in previous versions of the NT legacy where trusts had to be initiated by the administrator. When a domain is grafted into the tree, a trust is automatically generated between the two. A trust forms a singular administrative unit of control over all domains that participate. Trusts are integral to being able to access network resources across multiple domains.

No doubt there are administrators out there who are cringing over all this talk of domains and trusts. These concepts were a nemesis to system administrators of Windows NT networks due to the nightmare of managing multiple trusts between many domains. Microsoft recognized this intrinsic flaw in NT and has implemented the concept of *transitive trusts* in Windows 2000, reducing the number of trusts necessary to manage a unified domain structure. To see how domains and trusts apply in the directory, look at the example of the company Technelogic, Inc., in Figure 1.13.

Forests

In today's business climate, companies very often buy out or merge with other companies to form a more diversified and competitive operation. It is also true that these new divisions or sectors may have an established name in the market in which they do business that precludes them from changing to the name of the parent or sister company. The issue arises within Active Directory as to how to merge the two namespaces into a single manageable network. To address this need, the concept of a *forest* was born, which allows two disjointed namespaces to exist together in the same Windows 2000 network.

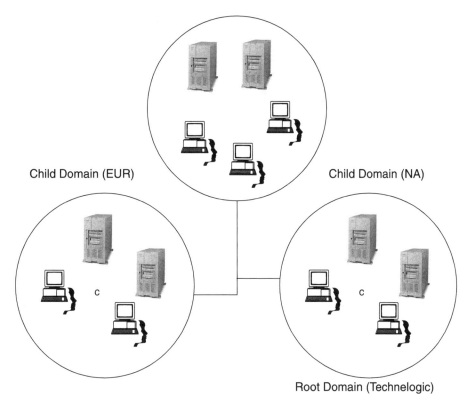

Child Domain (EUR)

Child Domain (NA)

Root Domain (Technelogic)

Figure 1.13   The Technelogic tree structure.

By default, the first tree created in the forest forms the root of the disjointed namespace. Trees in the forest do, however, share a common schema, configuration, and catalog server, just as within a single tree (see Figure 1.14).

The Global Catalog Server (GCS)

The GCS is created by Active Directory replication (we discuss replication and replication theory in greater detail later in the book) and provides a complete view of every object contained in the directory. This catalog is a central repository for objects and their attributes and can be thought of as the index of the entire network. Remember that one of the design goals of Active Directory was to provide access to network objects with as little effort as possible, regardless of the object's location.

The GCS stores a replica of every object in the directory, but only key attribute fields are stored to reduce storage capacity and streamline the query process. This data is referred to as *binding data* and is accessible by administrators and users alike.

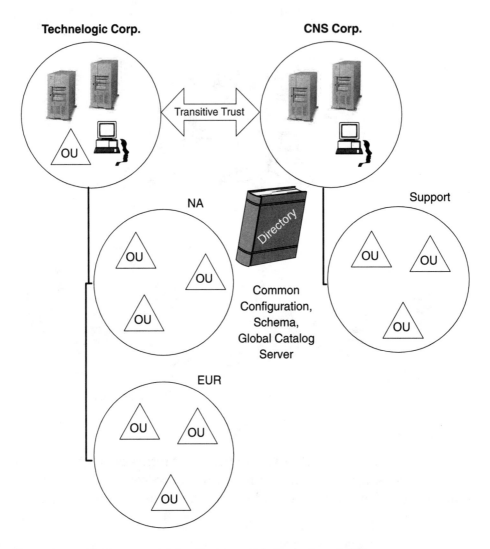

Figure 1.14   The forest containing the trees of Technelogic and CNS.

These elemental, organizational, and relational components join to form the *logical structure* of Active Directory. They provide the framework and organization that makes Active Directory a flexible and extensible solution for businesses that integrates and aligns the network into today's business models.

The Physical Components of Active Directory

The last concept in this discussion of the Active Directory logical framework covers the physical structures present in the interior of the directory and works to define the site topology. The two elements that give physical structure to Active Directory are *sites* and *domain controllers*.

Active Directory Sites

Most businesses today are spread across some territory, regardless of size. *Sites* are physical locations marked by a server that possesses a copy of the Active Directory, which in turn must be a domain controller. There are only two types of servers in Windows 2000: domain controllers and member servers. All servers may be installed as member servers and later promoted to domain controllers should the need arise. In Windows NT you were stuck with the decision of member server or domain controller once the software was installed unless you reinstalled from scratch. This feature on Windows 2000 server offers far greater flexibility when it comes to reorganizing the network, and it saves time and money by not having administrators spending hours reinstalling servers that were member servers as domain servers, or vice versa.

The concept of a site is important in the planning phase of Active Directory for several reasons. First, domain controllers generate considerable traffic on a network due to the amount of data that must replicate to each copy of Active Directory (one copy per domain controller). Logically, then, it is important that domain controllers be interconnected by high-speed connections. Usually a site is on a local area network (LAN) or some other type of fast network. If sites are linked via slow links, the net result is a network that is bogged down, and Active Directory replication will fail.

Windows 2000 also offers the added flexibility of defining your sites by IP subnet, which aids overall integration of Active Directory, even at the network level. Note that sites are part of the physical makeup of Active Directory and do not partake in the namespace.

Domain Controllers

Domain controllers are servers that house a copy of Active Directory and authenticate users to resources on the network. Unlike Windows NT, there is only one type of domain controller in Windows 2000. All changes to the Active Directory hierarchy are replicated to other domain controllers throughout the network. Member servers can be promoted to domain controllers using the upgrade utility Dcpromo.exe.

Operational Functions of Active Directory

Now that you understand the concepts of Active Directory structure and the components that are involved in the physical makeup of directory services, let's look at the way these pieces come together to interoperate with one another. Once sites are created and domains are functioning with a copy of Active Directory, domain controllers work cooperatively to replicate and process Active Directory and updates to it. Each domain stores a copy of local domain object information called a *partition*. The GCS serves to unify all directory object information together in one central database, retaining information from each partition.

Replication

In order for users to access objects across the enterprise, it is imperative that information is shared within and across sites. This process of sharing Active Directory information is known as *replication*. Each time an object in the directory is added or modified, replication takes place instantly. It is quite easy to see how this could add up to quite a bit of network traffic, particularly on larger networks; hence, the reason that sites are typically connected by high-speed network links.

Considering the process of replication, it is logical that the Active Directory database on all domain controllers are writeable copies, which is functionally different from the way that Windows NT domain controllers operate. In Windows NT, only the primary domain controller contained a writeable copy of the security database, and backup domain controllers were instituted for fault tolerance holding a read-only copy of the database. The fact that all domain controllers contain writeable copies of Active Directory means a Windows 2000 network provides greater functionality and flexibility than previous versions. The ability for all domains to write a replica in a given partition is referred to as *multiple-master replication*.

The two key benefits that replication provides are availability of resources to users and fault tolerance of Active Directory information (see Figure 1.15).

Partitions

As previously mentioned, each site houses local Active Directory information. In an environment where there are multiple sites or domains, each site holds a subset of the directory called a *partition*. The primary

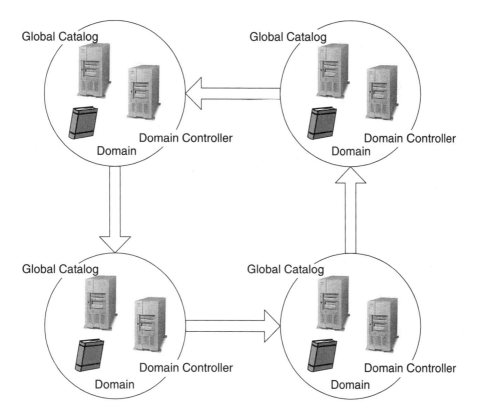

Figure 1.15   The flow of Active Directory replication.

key of an object is the domain name and contains information about the object itself and the object's container (a domain or OU). Domain controllers use domain name information of each object to refer to its location within the directory. Resources can be located through the directory using the domain name because information contained in it (which is replicated to the GCS) has enough information about a specific object's location.

Global Catalog Server (GCS)

GCSs are created when a domain controller is installed and functions as a service and as the storage container of the site's replica of the directory.

Security Features of Active Directory

Active Directory is integral in managing network objects; therefore, it is tightly integrated into the security subsystem of Windows 2000. All access and permission to objects is granted through the directory. This is accomplished through the use of access control lists, trust relationships, inheritance, and delegation of authority. Many of the security ideas adopted by Microsoft for use in Active Directory are part of the X.500 specification.

Access Control Lists

Users are permitted to use a resource on the network by way of *access control lists* (ACL), which determine who can use or manipulate another object (resource). ACLs define rights with a level of granularity down to the object attribute and class level. Each ACL is further broken down into *access control entries* (ACE).

ACE provides rights assigned to each user defined in the directory. An example of ACE functionality would be assigning rights to a particular directory on a file server on a Windows 2000 network. Some users or groups of users may have only read access to the directory, where others can read or write to the directory. This access is provided through the ACE and ACL.

Trusts and Other Relevant Terms

Having the flexibility to create multiple domains and sites would be useless if users from one domain could not access resources in another domain. The establishment of a trust means that the joined domains share a common schema, configuration, and GCS and partake in the namespace of the hierarchy. Two types of trusts exist in a Windows 2000 network: transitive trusts and explicit trusts.

Transitive Trusts

By default, when a new domain is grafted to an Active Directory tree, a *transitive trust* is established between the domains. These are two-way trusts and are authenticated by Kerberos authentication. Users are then able to access resources throughout the network. These implicit trusts allow pass-through access to other domains as previously discussed (refer to Figure 1.5).

Explicit Trusts

Explicit trusts are one-way trusts and are the mechanism of resource access used in tree relationships between forests.

Inheritance

While applying permissions to an object, it may be necessary to apply the same permissions to other objects down the hierarchy. This is accomplished through *inheritance*, where permissions are propagated to all objects in child containers in the directory. This feature eases the administration of applying permissions to objects throughout the directory.

Delegation

A trend long popular with many organizations is allowing business managers or workgroup managers to administer the resources that their respective units use on a daily basis. Through *delegation*, a Windows 2000 administrator can assign other users the ability to manage a set of resources or objects on the network. This helps to offload the administrative load of the administrators so they can focus on higher-level network maintenance and monitoring.

Summary

In this chapter we discussed directories, directory services and nomenclature, Active Directory features and functionality. A directory is a hierarchical database of descriptive information organized for fast and efficient retrieval. Active Directory is comprised of logical and physical components, both of which contain elements critical to the structure and design of the tree hierarchy. A Windows 2000 Active Directory object (such as users, printers, servers, etc.) is defined in the namespace from the bottommost part of the directory where individual objects exist, up through the hierarchy to the root. The directory is flexible and extensible, capable of tremendous scalability, and can contain millions of objects. This flexibility, extensibility, and scalability of Active Directory make Windows 2000 the perfect network operating system for any organization.

CHAPTER

2

Active Directory Architecture

INTRODUCTION

This chapter delves into the inner workings of the Windows 2000 Active Directory. Knowledge of the these concepts helps to better understand how directory components communicate and how certain functions, such as authentication, come to pass within the directory. Topics include:

- The Windows 2000 Security Subsystem
- The Directory Service Module
- Logical Elements Overview
- Best Practices Using Domains and Global Catalogs

A *domain* is a logical grouping of networked computers that share a central directory database that contains user accounts and security information. In lieu of this information, it is logical to assume that Active Directory must exist somewhere within the security subsystem of Windows 2000.

The Windows 2000 security subsystem functions to provide access to resources through authenticating user logons on the local server and throughout a Windows 2000 network. Understanding where Active Directory fits into Windows 2000 architecture provides insight into the way that Active Directory logical and physical components operate. Active Directory is found specifically in a part of the security subsystem called the Directory Service module, which is part of the Local Security Authority (LSA). Figure 2.1 shows the overall architecture of the Windows 2000 showing the components that comprise the ActiveDirectory.

Windows 2000, like most well-designed operating systems, is comprised of modular blocks of code. These individual components are responsible for a given task or function in the operating system. Within the Directory Service module exist subcomponents such as agents, the database layer, the extensible storage engine (ESE), NT File System (NTFS) version 5.0, and logical component information on the schema,

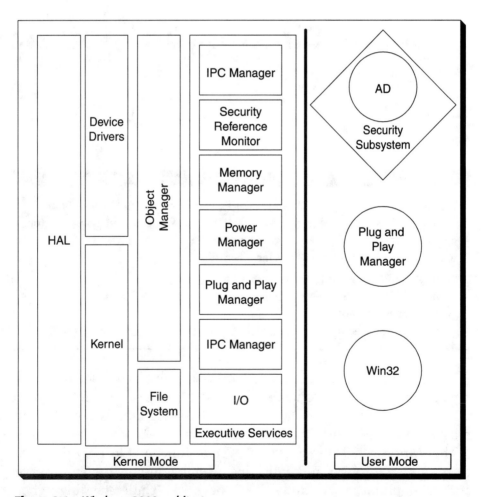

Figure 2.1 Windows 2000 architecture.

sites, partitions, and services. Active Directory and all related elements are contained within the kernel mode layer of the operating system, which means it has direct access to physical memory and executes in an isolated area of memory.

The Windows 2000 security subsystem has four main functions. First and foremost, it operates as a store for security policy and account information, which is accessed by the directory to verify user rights to network objects. Trust information is also stored here. Another function of the security infrastructure is to implement security models for all objects. Finally, all Active Directory authentication takes place through the security subsystem. This core functionality provides the "potential" for tight security for network resources ("potential," as it is up to the administrator to use the tools in Windows 2000 to implement security policy).

The Windows 2000 Security Subsystem

The security subsystem in Windows 2000 is an integral part of directory services as logon and object access functions are provided through the directory with a little help from the Global Catalog. The security subsystem is home to several Active Directory components, including the LSA and related dynamic link libraries (DLLs), which function together to provide access to resources throughout. The following section describes the LSA and its subcomponents. See Figure 2.2 for a schematic of the Windows 2000 subsystem.

The LSA Components

A network would be of little consequence if users could not access resources on the network. Additionally, securing data on a corporate network is a major concern for most companies. The LSA is the component of the security subsystem responsible for checking user permissions. It serves to generate an access token upon user logon to the network, authenticates users, manages the audit policy of the system, and manages local security policy.

An access token is generated by the LSA and contains user and group information. It is this information that is checked against the Access Control List (ACL) of a directory object, which in turn allows or denies access to objects.

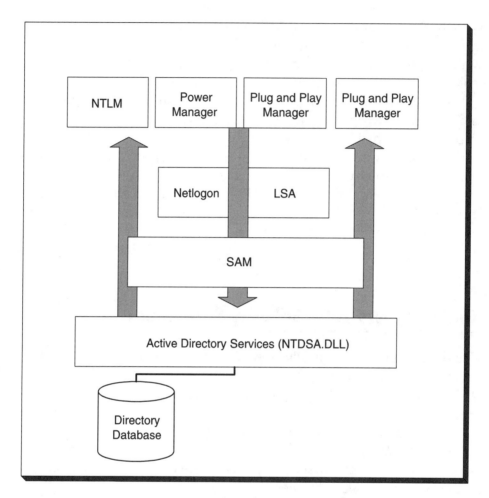

Figure 2.2 Windows 2000 security subsystem components.

The LSA subcomponents include:

NTLM. Windows NT LAN Manager authentication module (provided for backward compatibility).

SSL. Secure Sockets Layer authentication module.

Kerberos. Kerberos v5 authentication module.

Netlogon. Provides secure channel communications to the domain controller and passes Security Identifier (SID) and user rights information to the client.

SAM. Security Account Manager provides legacy NT authentication support (Kerberos is the primary authentication protocol in Windows 2000).

DS. The Directory Services module houses the subcomponents that provide directory service functionality such as queries via LDAP and replication.

It is important to note that legacy authentication facilities such as NTLM are provided strictly for backwards compatibility and coexistence scenarios, and their use is dictated only by integrating legacy Windows NT servers and domains with a Windows 2000 network. Such a configuration is called a *mixed-mode* environment. While it is beyond the scope of this book for a thorough technical description on the various authentication methods and protocols, it is important to consider from a security standpoint whether to integrate legacy systems into a Windows 2000 network due to the weaker nature of these systems. Kerberos v5 security protocol is the preferred protocol of Active Directory authentication and an extremely robust security dynamic. Kerberos should be used in place of legacy systems' methods of authentication if security is of great concern to your organization, particularly when infrastructures are tied into the global public network of the Internet.

The Directory Service Module of the LSA

Within the LSA lies the directory service module in which lies the physical components that provide the basic and extended features we discussed in Chapter 1, "An Overview of Windows 2000 Active Directory Services." The directory service module can be further broken down into the following subcomponents: agents, directory service agent, database layer, extensible storage engine, and Windows NTFS. At the lowest level of the directory service module is the Extensible Storage Engine, and it is there that we start our discussion on this aspect of the architectural aspect of Active Directory. Figure 2.3 outlines the Directory Service Module architecture.

The Extensible Storage Engine (ESE)

ESE technology is widely used throughout Microsoft products. It uses a version of the Jet database engine (the same technology found in the Exchange Serve mail product, part of the BackOffice suite) and is also the underlying technology of the Windows Internet Name Service.

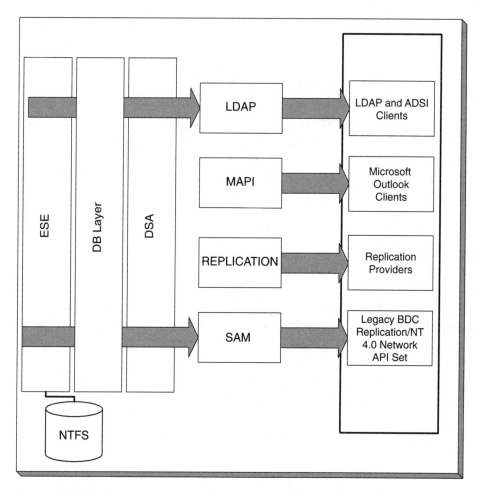

Figure 2.3   Directory Services Module and components.

The "extensible" descriptive is derived from the engine's ability to store up to 17TB (terabytes) of information, which equates to a theoretical maximum of 10 million objects in each domain when divided by the standard set of attributes defined per object by the schema. The design of that database is optimized for storage and retrieval of data. For example, the database can store multiple instances of a value for an attribute, say in the case of phone numbers and address information. The ESE is the bottom layer in the directory service module and has direct dependencies to Windows NTFS v5; therefore, an NTFS volume must be present before installing a domain controller or promoting a domain controller using the dcpromo utility.

The Database Layer

Above the ESE is the database layer. All access to the directory database is filtered through this component, which provides access to the physical database and query services to the database. It is here that data within the tables of the database are presented in a hierarchical manner to Active Directory.

The Directory System Agent (DSA)

Above the database layer is the DSA, which interfaces with the directory agents that ultimately serve applications. The DSA functions to process transactions to and from the database layer on to the five service agents. The DSA is also responsible for enforcing the schema policy of the database and formatting the data for presentation to applications.

Agents

Five agents act as interfaces to the three layers of the directory service module and the programs that request Active Directory services or data.

LDAP (Lightweight Directory Access Protocol). Provides Outlook client, LDAP, and ADSI interface for performing queries to the directory.

REPL (site replication). Provides the replication features for intersite, interdomain, and DC replication via multiple transports.

SAM (Security Accounts Manager). Provides backward compatibility for Windows NT 4.0 security data replication.

NSPI (Name Service Provider Interface). Used primarily by Outlook clients for address book compatibility on older systems.

XDS (Exchange Directory Service). Integrate Exchange Server functionality.

These agents are key in providing directory services to Windows 2000 and are the "diplomats" of the actual database engine. It is important to note that some of these agents provide compatibility and functionality with legacy Windows NT systems as well and are critical to legacy integration. When considering Active Directory physical architecture, it is also helpful to examine the logical structure of these components to further understand interaction and functionality.

Overview of Active Directory's Logical Structures

Several elements of the Active Directory structure aid in defining the overall logical namespace design. These include DNS, partitions, and the schema. Within the DSA lives the rootDSE object. In LDAP 3.0, the rootDSE is defined as the root of the directory information tree (DIT) on a directory server. The rootDSE is not part of any namespace. The purpose of the rootDSE is to provide information about the directory server. The rootDSE then functions as the top of the LDAP search tree. The rootDSE concept is also adopted from Internet standards and can be found in RFC 1777 for LDAP. Contained in the rootDSE is a *configuration container* that houses *metadata* for the network.

Metadata is data about data. Metadata describes how and when and by whom a particular set of data was collected, and how the data is formatted. Metadata is essential for understanding information stored in databases. Remember that Active Directory is a name and further a namespace, the defining standard of which is the naming hierarchy, and so it defines the network. The directory container houses information about Active Directory naming contexts specifically regarding the schema, sites, partitions, and various services that intertwine with Active Directory. Figure 2.4 illustrates how logical elements of the directory transpose to the directory structure.

The schema-naming context contains the attribute and classes for objects in the directory. The sites-naming context contains information on all domain controllers, site lists, and replication information. The partition-naming context identifies partition structure of the directory. Last, services naming context holds configuration information regarding various network-related services, including Remote Access Service (RAS), Routing and Remote Access Service (RRAS), and system volume information.

The rootDSE holds information about the directory tree; specifically, about the top of the LDAP tree. Information about the rootDSE can be viewed using the Active Directory Browser, a tool for locating objects, object attributes, and naming contexts within the directory.

To start the Active Directory browser, click Start, Run, type "adsvw", then click OK. The Active Directory Browser program starts and you are then given a choice of Object Viewer or Query. Choose Object Viewer, and a New Object window will appear asking for path information. Type "LDAP://rootDSE" in the text field and click OK. The rootDSE object is displayed. To view information from the configuration container, select

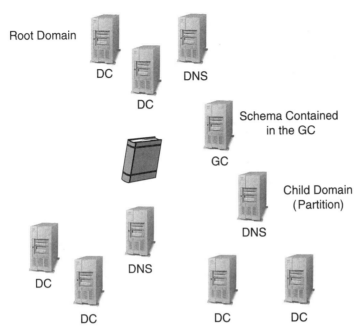

Root Domain

DC

DNS

DC

Schema Contained
in the GC

GC

Child Domain
(Partition)

DNS

DNS

DC

DC

DC

DC

Figure 2.4 Logical elements as they pertain to the directory service architecture.

the configuration-naming context from the properties box and copy the property value. On the File menu, click New and then paste this information *after* the LDAP:// prefix. Click OK and the container information is returned. See Figure 2.5 for an illustration of how the rootDSE is used under Windows 2000.

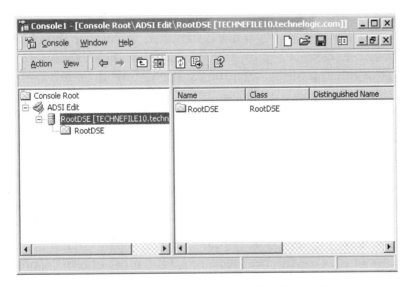

Figure 2.5 Viewing the rootDSE using the Active Directory browser.

Best Practices Considering Active Directory's Architecture

Active Directory was built to scale and ease administrative management and access to network resources. The new management principles inherent in Active Directory are light years ahead of the decentralized management of previous versions of Windows NT. Still, you may encounter a snafu or two along the way. Here are a few things to look out for. Taking time to consider domain structure, server hardware, and network liabilities will help save you from headaches down the road.

Windows 2000 Domain Implementation

As of this writing, there are still some limitations to the domain and child domain relationship that cause excessive administrative cost in Windows 2000. Remember that a Windows 2000 network can be subdivided into child domains and sites to structure an organization as a hierarchy by division or business unit. These child domains are interconnected by transitive trusts that are automatically established when the new domain controller and respective site are grafted to the tree. The administrative limitation to this design is apparent when trying to delegate permissions or authority to child domains in the hierarchy, as permissions do not cross over the natural security boundaries formed when a domain is created. This does not mean that this authority cannot be implemented in child domains; rather, the rights must be applied to *each* of the child domains in the tree. Depending on the size of your organization, this could add up to a rather large task. Figure 2.6 shows how deep level relationships affect overall system performance.

Because of the architectural superiority of Windows 2000 and its ability to scale massively to millions of objects per replica contained on a domain controller, it is Microsoft's recommendation that a *single* domain model be used whenever possible. The catch-22 in this recommendation is that single-site architecture requires that all domain controllers in the domain be connected by high-speed LAN connections or high-speed telecom links. We discuss the different domain architecture best practices later in the book. For now, just remember that the single domain model may be the best way to go for most organizations.

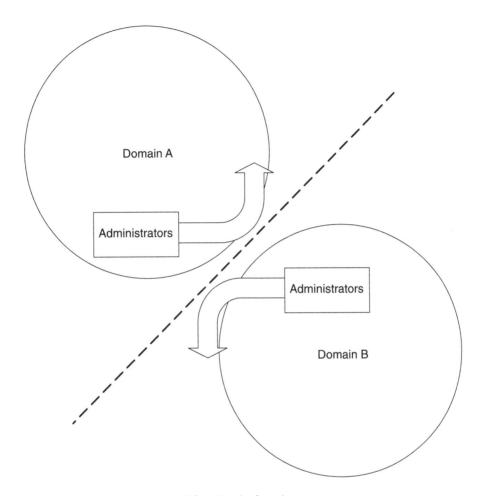

Figure 2.6   Limitations using delegation in domains.

Figure 2.7 illustrates a multi-domain model while Figure 2.8 illustrates a single domain implementation.

Domain Controller and GCS Recommendations

Active Directory is based on Jet database technology and therefore is somewhat hardware intensive. Just as in Exchange Server, planning domain controller hardware needed to support larger Active Directory implementations of the database is critical to the overall success of deploying a fast and functional Windows 2000 network. Hardware I/O, CPU,

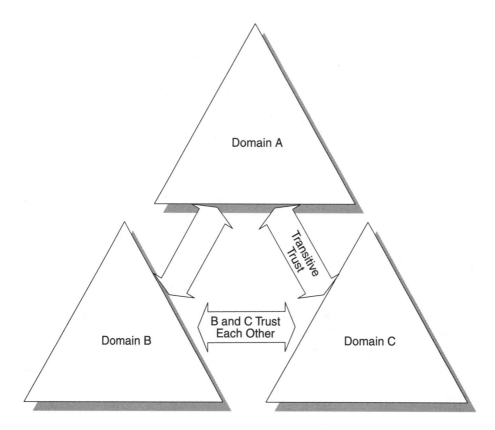

Figure 2.7   Multiple domain relationships in Windows 2000 hierarchy.

and physical memory are all extremely important factors to consider. Do not cut corners when it comes to deploying these key elements.

Network Bandwidth Considerations

A network of 5000 workstations and 5000 users can easily add up to 100 MB of space or greater in an Active Directory deployment. The primary need for high-speed links between sites is due to the replication of such massive data stores between domain controllers. All information updated on one domain controller in a Windows 2000 network is replicated to all other domain controllers; hence, the need for high-speed links. Plan very carefully when designing the structure of your physical network, considering replication issues. More about this later in the book. Figure 2.9 illustrates how AD replication occurs.

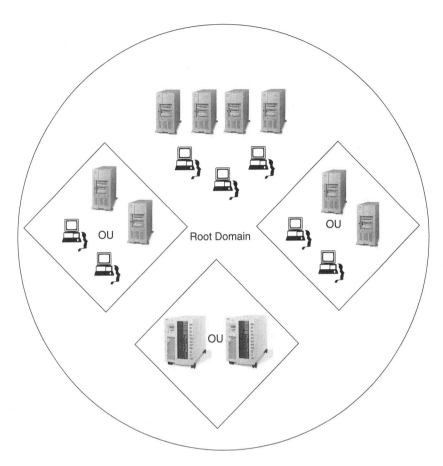

Figure 2.8   A single domain implementation.

Summary

Active Directory serves administrators and end users by unifying directory services into a hierarchical tree. The architectural components of Active Directory provide rapid access to directory features and furnish administrators with a means to control access to network resources and delegation of authority to objects in the hierarchy. In order to command control of such functions, Active Directory must be tightly integrated into the security architecture of Windows 2000.

Active Directory exists in the security subsystem of Windows 2000, a low-level kernel mode service of the operating system. The LSA provides multiple authentication vehicles for the system, which includes modules for Kerberos authentication (new to Windows 2000), Windows NT LAN Manager support (for legacy NT systems), SSL authentication, and Netlogon services for secure channel communication between domains.

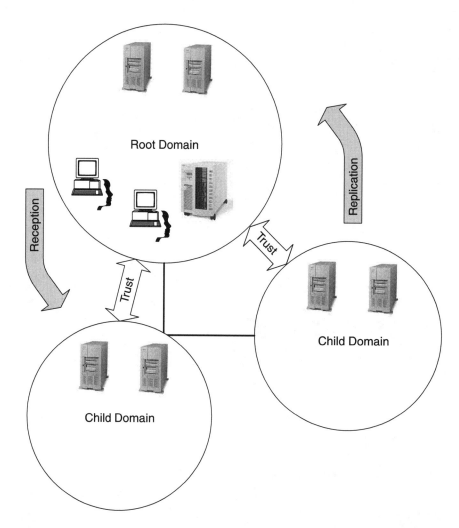

Root Domain

Reception

Replication

Trust

Trust

Child Domain

Child Domain

Figure 2.9   Active Directory replication.

The Directory Services module within the LSA architecture provides directory security, support, and functionality and is comprised of five API elements called *agents* that provide hooks from directory services to application layer programs. Additionally, three sublayers in the Directory Services module—the Directory Service Agent, the Extensible Storage engine, and the Database layer—provide support for directory semantics and transaction processing, replication, and object attribute storage and access.

In the next chapter, we begin looking at the steps necessary in planning a successful implementation of Active Directory. These cannot be overlooked due the restrictions placed on Active Directory network dependencies and the organizational characteristics of the directory itself.

3

Preparing for an Active Directory Implementation

INTRODUCTION

In this chapter, we discuss perhaps the most important aspect of a Windows 2000 and Active Directory implementation: planning the deployment. Many of you reading this book may feel you have enough experience to skip ahead and jump right into the actual installation of Active Directory. I strongly urge you to refrain from doing this and pay particular attention to this chapter. "Hands-on" is by far the "fun" part to this job; however, there are so many factors in the planning phase that are critical to success that this part cannot be sidestepped.

Items covered in this chapter:

- **Planning a Successful Implementation**
- **Examining Your Company's Business**
- **Integrating Windows 2000 into Your Business**

Today's business climate is very different than it was only a few years ago. It was not so long ago that the IBM Selectric, secretaries, and printing calculators were commonplace. Business moved at a steady pace, and companies were comfortable with the pace at which work was done. Today, businesses must plan for every contingency lest they fall prey to the fiercely competitive market of the new millennium. The business of doing business has reached an all-time high. What is driving business so fast and furiously these days? It'simple: technology. The computer revolution has driven most businesses to new highs or out of business all together. The same computer technology that saves one company one year may sink it the next in the hands of the competition.

As business has changed, so has the computer network. The majority of companies with mainframes are now replacing them with multiple smaller, faster, multitiered, Web-based systems. The printed corporate directory has made way for the electronic phone book. Networks span continents and the globe. These technological advances have been integral in shaping this sea change, and business has embraced the new technology, forming a bond between companies and their networks.

If you take a moment to examine your existing network you will find examples of this amalgamation of industry and technology (see Figure 3.1). A good example of this is the way that SAP, BAAN, PeopleSoft, and others have "reengineered" the functional processes of businesses. Another example is the way NT domains have evolved to the "resource domain" model adopted by so many companies today, in which functional and geographic divisions populate their own resources in their own domains. This brings us to the functional and integration issues surrounding the implementation of a Windows 2000 network.

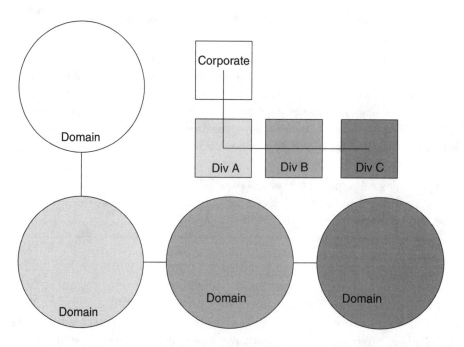

Figure 3.1   Integration of computers and business.

Many of the structure elements of Windows 2000 may resemble legacy NT networks (domains or trusts, for example); however, there are many more design elements to consider with this new operating system. Site replication is one. Sites have conditions placed on them; for example, fast network connections so that directory replication will not bog down the network. Administrative roles may also change with the advent of delegation and organizational units (OUs). Planning for such contingencies ahead of time will prevent headaches down the road. The information-gathering phase of Active Directory implementation is the single most important aspect of the rollout. This chapter focuses on the planning phase of Active Directory and Windows 2000 to help you avoid the common pitfalls associated with an Active Directory deployment.

Organizational Characteristics

The effect an Active Directory deployment will have on your company is profound. Therefore, the best way to plan for Active Directory is to involve all areas of business, from accounting to corporate to IT. Doing so will not only help the deployment, it will also serve to set expectations within the company. Another tangible benefit of involving varying business units is the brain share that evolves from such interaction. Let's face it, most technology people are business neophytes (and happily so!), and vice versa. This type of communication between parties can produce amazing results on *how* to realize this new technology!

The greatest benefit of involving other parts of the company comes in gathering information necessary for a successful installation. Active Directory tightly integrates into your business, starting at the naming hierarchy. Critical tools such as objects queries, or even more important, e-mail, rely on proper naming schemes. It is therefore recommended that a central team be formed to undertake the task of designing the Windows 2000 network. A typical team will consist of upper and middle managers who submit approval to executives; IT members, including those responsible for messaging systems; and DNAs . Systems and operational managers are key, as are members of security if you have such a department. This planning team should task themselves with discovering the technical structure of your organization and business aspects of your company as they pertain to the network (see Figure 3.2).

From a business standpoint, members must gather logistical information on the geographic dispersal of the corporation, administrative models, user locations, user mobility, security policy, and the possibility

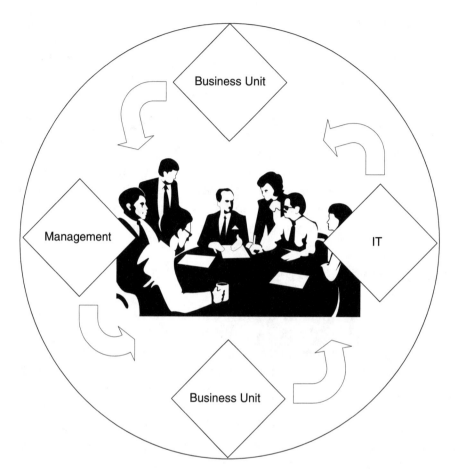

Figure 3.2 A typical planning team.

of future business acquisition or core business changes that may affect implementation.

Technical members should gather as much information on the physical network as possible. Now would be a good time to put together a graphical map of your network topology. Identifying wide area network (WAN) links and their respective bandwidth is exceedingly important in the overall planning for Windows 2000. If you run a network management system such as HP OpenView, Microsoft's Systems Management Server, Compaq Information Manager, or others, generate a report of network resources for review by the group.

The planning team should meet several times to provide updates to the group, and at least one person should act as the scribe, compiling all of the information gathered. This information should then be disseminated up the chain of the organization for approval. Once a complete plan is in place, you will feel far more comfortable moving to the actual implementation phase. Now, on to some of the specific information you will need.

 Having consulted for many corporations, I am shocked by the replies I have received to the simple question, "May I see your network topology map?" Documentation of network resources, while not the most glorious aspect of the job, is not only a time saver in a bind; it serves as an excellent reference tool and planning tool as well. Another caveat to this discussion is the fact that this is a transient business. Documentation helps to alleviate the stress of migrating new IT personnel.

Business Persona

What business is your company in? Why does it matter when planning for your Active Directory implementation? Geographic dispersal, handling of administrative tasks, security, growth, and acquisition all affect the way you will deploy Active Directory. The flexible and diverse capabilities of Active Directory to integrate into a company mean tight integration into a company's framework.

Physical Location

Chances are the company that you work for has more than one location, whether it is in the same building, city, state, country, or around the globe. Knowing the topological layout of your network is critical to the success of Active Directory deployment. During the planning phase, it might be a good idea to consider the following:

- How many physical locations represent your company? Are these connected by LAN, MAN, or WAN connections?
- For every location that represents the company, what is each division's physical layout; for example, the size of the building, multiple buildings, or floors occupied?
  - What are the network connections between those divisions?
  - What do these divisions do functionally?

Refer to your network map and bring multiple copies to planning meetings for strategic placement of your company's domains. Test the link speed between all of your links and make sure you understand the actual link speed. Many times a T1 or fractional T1 may be further subdivided to support voice as well, which reduces the amount of data that can travel over the link. In addition, the reliability of the link may affect decisions on site placement. Check the traffic on local subnets too, as this may ultimately influence site placement.

Administrative Models

Another important consideration when planning for Active Directory is the administrative model that your company uses both for network resource management and departmental supervision. Typically, an organization can classify these three ways; centralized, decentralized, or a combination of both. There are several questions your planning group may want to ask, including:

- How does the company network security?
- Are there central policies in place?
- How are users' computer problems handled by the organization?
- How will the network grow now and in the future?
- What is the current method of handling name resolution?
- How many different administrative units will you need (centralized, decentralized, or both)?
- What functions will other administrators be handling in a decentralized environment?

Centralized organizations usually have a set administrative policy in which all network administration is filtered through the IT department or corporate domain (similar to the way a single master model functioned in previous versions of NT). This model is not limited to small and medium-sized companies. Many larger organizations have adopted this model for the comfort that it offers from a security standpoint and a reduction in support calls (see Figure 3.3).

Decentralized organizations often encompass many business units or company divisions, or they are separated by vast distance where central administration may be impossible (see Figure 3.4). Each of the separate divisions handles administrative functions independently. This model provides challenges presented by the politics that are so often found between different divisions or geographic locations. Face it, business is conducted differently from one part of the country to the next, and certainly around the globe. These politics are often present within a single location, and it is the job of the team, particularly upper managers, to get past such hurdles in rolling out Active Directory.

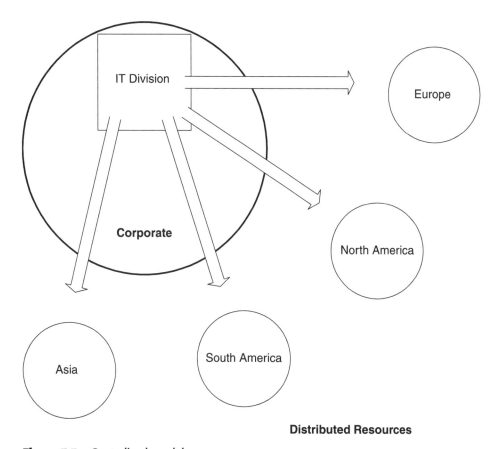

Distributed Resources

Figure 3.3   Centralized model.

Some organizations may find that they use a combination of central-ized and decentralized models in business. Functions such as technical, sales, or manufacturing may be decentralized, and those closer knit

 I have worked for organizations where this type of gridlock effectively shut down projects. One that comes to mind was a decentralized organi-zation comprised of several IT divisions. A massive undertaking was begun to develop a corporate intranet that would house useful tools and applications for the user community. Eight months passed, and after countless meetings and torturous teleconferences, no decision could be reached as to the content and format of the navigation bar that would serve as the header of every page. This senseless barricading can drag a project out for eternity and frustrate even the most patient of team mem-bers. Do everything possible to avoid these fortified positions and work toward the common goal of bringing the project to fruition. It is the job of IT to serve the customer (the end user), and when this situation occurs, it is the customer who suffers the most!

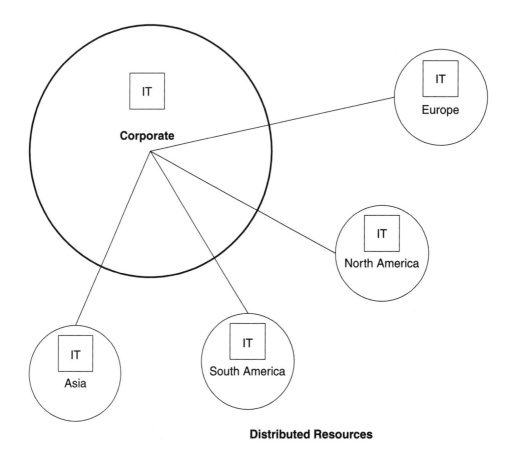

Distributed Resources

Figure 3.4 A decentralized model.

with corporate functions, such as legal or accounting, are nestled in the centralized model.

In the end, there is no right or wrong way to structure a company—each company has a unique identity. You may find that the planning team has very little say in the matter. However, an organization that is flexible may take suggestions from the planning group and embrace recommendations offered. Such open-mindedness will prove a great ally in integrating Active Directory into your network. Overall, most organizations will reflect a combination of these models in order to form a more perfect union (see Figure 3.5). And if this is not the case today, as a company evolves, so too does the IT department.

Security Considerations

A company's security policy may be as unique as the organization itself or nonexistent; it really depends on how business is conducted. Most

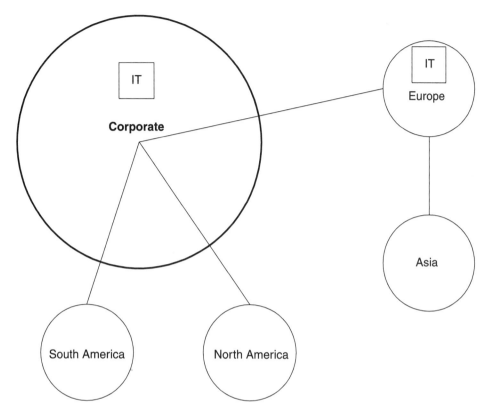

Distributed Resources

Figure 3.5 Combination organizations.

organizations do implement data security, often assigning a single person or a whole department to the task of securing precious information. Security policymakers are a critical asset to the planning team.

When determining the structure of your Active Directory implementation, make sure you consider the following:

- What are the current security policies in place?
- How should data be protected (Windows 2000 offers new security features to protect corporate data)?
- How does the structure of the organization affect security policy?
- Will outside partners be allowed to access network resources (for example, electronic data interchange, remote vendor support, etc.)?
- How is information on the network grouped: by business unit, division, or not at all?
- How does the company interface with the Internet?

Make every effort to map your company's security model in a diagram or flow chart. This will help in applying policies and permissions to network resources after Active Directory is installed. Planning for such things and entering into the implementation phase prepared reduces the time to project completion, and saves money and frustration as well. The majority of companies take data security very seriously, and making any changes to existing policy will almost always have to be run up the ladder for approval.

Preparing for the Future

It goes without saying that in today's competitive environment, all business must conform to the idea of thinking 10 steps ahead. A glitch caused by a lack in planning the network could cause outages resulting in potential revenue lost. Planning for the future growth of the network keeps you one (or more) step ahead of the competition. Mergers and acquisitions are commonplace today, and an organization may grow at explosive rates. Still, an organization may fracture or splinter into decentralized factions or separate billable companies. The participation of upper management in Active Directory planning to provide such details is imperative. Keep the following in mind when in the planning phase:

What is the projected growth rate of the company, and in what divisions can this growth be expected? Failing to plan for future growth will ultimately result in working many extra nights and weekends on your part, not to mention looking bad in the eyes of your superiors. Design the network so that it can be easily expanded.

Is the company poised for restructuring or reorganization? Again, IT organizations should be included in this type of information ahead of time so the necessary planning can take place.

What potential mergers are in store for the company? Merging another company into an existing Windows 2000 network requires careful planning because of the namespace design that must take place (which we discuss in upcoming chapters). Will the company assume the naming identity of the existing organization, will there be multiple namespaces governed, or will the namespace change completely to reflect the new company (for example, the Daimler

Benz and Chrysler Motor Company merger that resulted in Daimler-Chrysler)? (See Figure 3.6.)

Is the company planning any downsizing or splintering? If downsizing, it may become necessary to reorganize parts of the network into existing sites; or in the case of splintering, you may need to develop a new namespace for the new company.

The characteristics that make up your company directly affect the way you architect your Active Directory schematic. Active Directory was built to tightly integrate with your company's business to facilitate better business and reduce support. Gather as much information on company structure during this essential phase, and pay particular attention to security policies, user habits, geographic locales, network layout, and administrative constitution. Several other specific factors

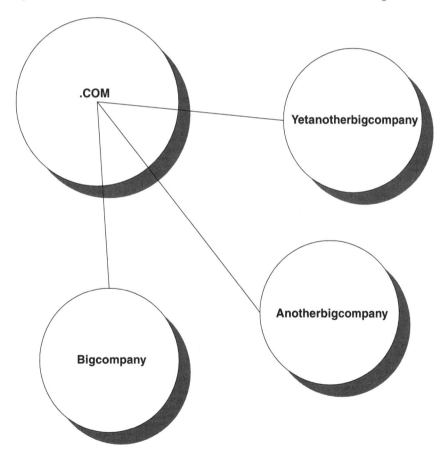

Figure 3.6 Company with multiple namespaces.

that play key roles in the decision-making process as it applies to Active Directory are presented in the following sections.

Assessing Organizational Characteristics

A network is made up of many defining elements that call for particular attention when implementing a Windows 2000 network. These include user considerations, WAN connections, the Internet, remote access to network resources, legacy system integration, mail systems, and integration with existing directories.

Replication of the directory between domain controllers and sites is a major consideration when architecting your Windows 2000 network. Design aspects of the namespace must also weigh heavily in the decision process. The name hierarchy is the defining aspect of Active Directory and the way that your users access network resources. If your company has an Internet presence, this may affect the way you design your naming structure. The existence of non-Microsoft systems that utilize directory services such as Novell Directory Service (NDS) (also available for NT) and Sun's new directory services will also impact overall design.

Physical Network Considerations

As mentioned earlier, a Windows 2000 network is dependent on high-speed links between domain controllers for the replication process to work effectively. Therefore, your physical network, especially wide area links and utilization of all links, should meet several conditions when considering the placement of domain controllers and the construction of sites. A network may contain LAN, MAN, WAN, or a combination of these links (see Figure 3.7). Further, these links may appear to have the bandwidth needed to include all of your domains in a single site where replication takes place instantly, but upon further inspection the utilization on these links might be pegged out.

There are tools for measuring this information, called *network management software*, such as Hewlett-Packard's OpenView, which runs on the Windows platform. Your router manufacturer may offer such tools as well. Gathering statistical information of network utilization and link integrity is not only key to a successful Active Directory implementation, but is a good measure of overall network health. When Active Directory fails to replicate, access to network resources will fail, and dependent

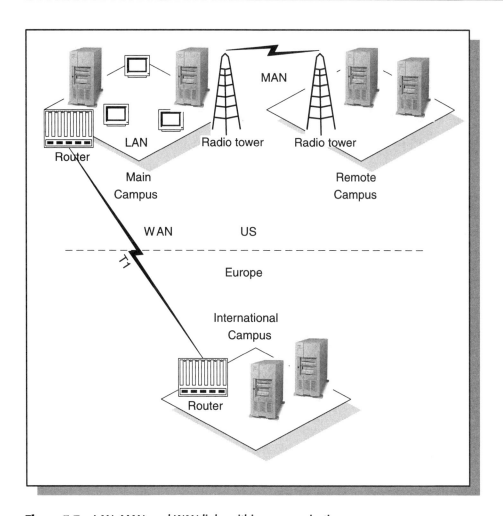

Figure 3.7   LAN, MAN, and WAN links within an organization.

systems such as company mail may fail as well. Keep in mind the following questions when designing your Windows 2000 network:

How much bandwidth will be available for replication between domain controllers during all times: morning logon peaks, normal operation, and even weekends and off-hours? Simply measuring utilization during normal business hours does not give the mean average of network capacity. If utilization is stressed during morning logon and logoff periods, the net result will be slow performance or complete failure of Active Directory replication. This translates into you, the administrator or installer, having to track down these failures later (i.e., more work!).

What is the integrity of each link on the network? What good is a link if it experiences 50-percent downtime? This may be common if you are not partnered with a reputable service provider. This scenario is also common when your network branches out overseas or in developing countries where the telecom infrastructure is not up to par. Consider alternatives such as satellite links rather than leased lines—the prices are often competitive.

User Base Considerations

The way that your user community interacts with the network is just as important when developing network architecture as any other issue we have discussed. Considering the ways in which users are grouped, transient users and user transfers between divisions, and international users, are all integral in the overall design of your network (see Figure 3.8). The following questions will help you to assess your user community and how users might affect overall design:

- How many users are in your user community?
- How many users are in each division?
- How are users grouped within the organization?
- Does the organization span international boundaries, requiring multilingual support?
- Will outside users be using the network (supply chain, vendors, product support, etc.)?
- Will users access the network via dial-up connections?

Integrating the Internet

It is almost unheard of for a company to not participate in the global network community of the Internet. The Internet is not only a rich source of information, it allows a company to interact with business partners through e-mail or even EDI, not to mention an Internet Web presence that serves as a marketing or commerce interface to the rest of the world. The Internet has reshaped the way in which business is conducted in the modern business climate, creating a truly global business interconnect. Microsoft foresaw this inevitability and promised its user

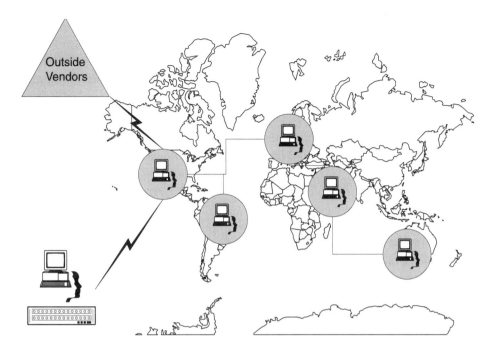

Figure 3.8 User community considerations.

base tight integration of the Internet in all of its systems. Windows 2000 is an exemplary example of the delivery of this promise.

Windows 2000 integrates the Transmission Control Protocol/Internet Protocol (TCP/IP), the Domain Name Service (DNS), X.500, and the Lightweight Directory Access Protocol (LDAP) to provide directory services. The namespace hierarchy provided in Active Directory comes in part from the DNS service, which is the same name registration service used on the Internet.

If your company currently has an Internet presence, chances are it also has a name registered with the Internic (a.k.a. Network Solutions, Inc.). The Internic is a global name registration service that provides domain name to Internet protocol address mappings for the most popular top-level domains (e.g., .com, .net, .org).

With Active Directory, you have the option of integrating (or not) your existing Internet namespace with your Active Directory namespace, providing directory queries and transparent user name to e-mail address registration and resource availability to the outside network. Choosing separate internal and external namespaces may require more stringent security standards in many corporate networks. Regardless of the option you choose, it is necessary to consider the following when implementing Active Directory:

- Is your company currently providing access to the Internet?

- Does your company have an Internet presence (a registered domain name and/or Web site)?

- Will your company use the same or different root domain names for Active Directory and the Internet?

- Will there be multiple root names within the Active Directory namespace?

 While it may be second nature for many to go to work and open up a Web browser for Internet sessions or send Internet e-mail around the globe, many companies today are still precluded from such activities because of security concerns. I have worked in both arenas, and I am typically biased toward the latter because I feel the Internet is a rich source of information if only from a support standpoint. Security aside, Internet browsing open to the entire user community may seem innocent enough. However, the Internet is far from innocent, and many companies do not want to open themselves up to liability because of the potential for users to access noncompany-related material. Whether you fall into one category or the other, the Internet standards offered in the Windows 2000 product line offer the same rich feature set regardless of your Internet connection.

Non-Microsoft Systems Integration with Active Directory

The Windows networking family of operating systems was first introduced in 1992, making it somewhat of a late player in the network operating system game. By 1992 Novell, Unix, and IBM had a stranglehold on the market. Because of the time and money corporations have expended on these systems, they are still resident in many server rooms and data centers. With this in mind, Microsoft has attempted to overcome interoperability issues associated with heterogeneous environments through the use of open standards.

Novell offers directory services through NDS, and several Unix manufacturers offer directory services as well. Prior versions of Windows

NT supported integration options with existing Novell systems through Gateway Services for NetWare (GSNW). However, NDS was not supported, so only Novell Bindery Emulation could be used. Why is this significant? Simple, none of the directory functionality was available using the gateway; essentially, only file sharing was available. In addition, File and Print services were offered as add-ons—for additional cost.

Unix integration with NT (out of the box) has been practically nonexistent until now, although Microsoft recently released a set of add-on tools available for NT 4.0 that allows integration with Unix and Unix file systems.

Many third-party products have emerged to fill the gaps caused by interoperability issues surrounding NT and other network operating systems. Microsoft has made a diligent effort to make the new Windows 2000 product much more data-center friendly through the adoption of open standards. This is true not only for non-Microsoft systems, but for legacy NT systems as well.

In planning your network, try to account for all of the different systems that support your organization, and try to determine if interoperability will be an issue. Do these systems offer directory services, either mail systems such as Exchange or Lotus Notes, or resource directories such as NDS (this product is also available for NT but not supported by Microsoft)? Are DNS, LDAP, or X.500 protocols in use, and if so, are there plans to use them in conjunction with Active Directory? If a DNS namespace already exists, it may be a good idea to adapt or migrate the information stored there for use with Windows 2000 DNS servers (more on this later). Determine if legacy support for NT will occur as well. Many organizations may have a sizable rollout on their hands and will have to plan for legacy coexistence.

Other Considerations

It is also important to consider some of the new features in Windows 2000 that are not open standards but may affect the deployment. Kerberos security is the primary and preferred method of authentication. Other systems may offer Kerberos authentication or a single logon mechanism to multiple systems. Certificates are another authentication method that is commonly used today. Certificate Server is standard issue in Windows 2000 and is widely used in Web-based systems.

Windows 2000 also offers several other protocols, such as IP Security (IPSec) and Quality of Service (QoS), that may affect the overall design of your directory—these are well beyond the scope of this book. Familiarize yourself with these protocols and determine if they have a place in your company. Microsoft also offers the Zero Administration Kit (ZAW) as part of the network operating environment that, if implemented, may have an impact on your network bandwidth and should be considered during planning. While there are currently no metrics to support the exact impact caused by implementing ZAK, allocate sufficient bandwidth to support this feature and never use it over WAN links. For more information on ZAK, see Microsoft's Web site at www.microsoft.com.

Best Practices

While this book can never assume the responsibility of teaching planning strategies, there are some guidelines that you can follow in order to make your Active Directory implementation go smoothly. Here are a few ideas to get you going:

Know your network backward and forward; not just the physical network, everything. While many reading this book may have grown their present network from the ground up, other members of the technical staff may be adoptive parents and will certainly need to come up to speed.

Make sure that everyone from the technical side who will participate on the team is on the same page as far as the network topology and architecture are concerned. This will in the end produce a favorable result.

The main vehicle that will produce desired results is use of the three "Ds": documentation, documentation, documentation. Utilize a network-mapping tool such as Visio to provide visuals not only to the technical people, but also to help the business unit team members visualize what you are verbally trying to articulate. Visuals will serve as a terrific binding agent between these two diverse groups who often speak "greek" to one another.

Organize all information in a clear and concise manner, and store it on a network share to which everyone in the group has access.

Try to pair off technical and nontechnical members of the team. This will help each learn the other's thought processes and jargon while promoting camaraderie and spontaneous brainstorming, not to mention easing any tensions (in most cases!).

Create a distribution list in your mail system for group members to use for mailings to the group.

When forming your team, keep in mind that the rollout of this product will ultimately affect everyone in your organization. It would be wise to diversify your team to include members from all critical areas of the company.

Run all proposals up to the very top of the management chain. These reports should be simple and concise, and they should spell out the pros and cons of each decision.

Know and understand your TCP/IP network infrastructure. This will help in the design of Active Directory; particularly, since there are provisions in Windows 2000 for classifying physical structure components by subnet.

Design a solid administrative model and adhere to it. Designate business unit administrators to oversee the creation of user accounts and resource management. If you are uncomfortable in doing this, implement a change control mechanism by which these changes are approved by an IT administrator or the security department before changes occur, so there is a record of the transaction.

If you haven't already done so, develop a security policy and adhere to it. If your company already has a security policy in place, review it thoroughly and make changes as the Active Directory structure forms.

If you are planning on putting all servers within the same domain and you have links other than LAN connections, test these links over a period of time—say, a month—during all hours of operation. Compile this data into a chart if possible to determine whether you need to break up the network into different sites. If a link is only 128K but supports only two users who run their applications from a local server at that site, chances are that site will work as a member of the domain and replication will not falter. The rule of thumb is to consider both bandwidth and link speed in determining site placement.

Summary

There are many factors that will ultimately decide success or failure in implementing Active Directory. Careful planning is the key to victory. Active Directory impacts the entire company. Pick your team members carefully, and bear in mind that you will be working together for some time to achieve the desired result. The team must document not only the organizational qualities of the network, but those of the organization as well. Administrative models, security, geography, and company growth should all play a part in the final architecture.

CHAPTER

4

Lightweight Directory Access Protocol

INTRODUCTION

In this chapter, we discuss the Lightweight Directory Access Protocol (LDAP) standards and functions, the role of LDAP in a Windows 2000 network, and how queries are processed. The following specific topics are covered:

- **Defining DAP**
- **Defining X.500**
- **Defining LDAP**
- **Standards and Functions**
- **LDAP Versions 2 and 3**
- **Directory Management**
- **Replication**
- **DAP, X.500, and Windows 2000**

LDAP emerged several years ago as a subset of X.500 DAP (Directory Access Protocol). It is a lightweight client used to make queries to X.500 directories, and it is meant to function like DAP without the overhead. Most major messaging, application, database, and operating system vendors are turning to LDAP as the native protocol for directory access in their products. X.500 and DAP were perceived as the long-term solution for directory ills, but it appears now that a large part of the industry considers LDAP the only viable protocol for directory access.

This chapter examines the technical differences between LDAP and X.500 and explores how Microsoft has adopted both in Windows 2000 Active Directory. Further, we discuss the relationship between LDAP and X.500 and how LDAP functions, as both possess a high level of interoperability and interworking features critical to directory functionality (see Figure 4.1).

LDAP is gaining momentum as the Internet directory standard capable of providing open access to directory services on the corporate network or Internet, as well as integrating heterogeneous directories. LDAP was originally conceived as a way to simplify access to a directory service that was modeled according to the X.500 standards. Many of the new features of LDAP go beyond the original specification or definition and identify LDAP as the solution needed to make global directory services a reality. DAP provides this functionality under the original specification, but it is too bulky for use over WAN links. LDAP,

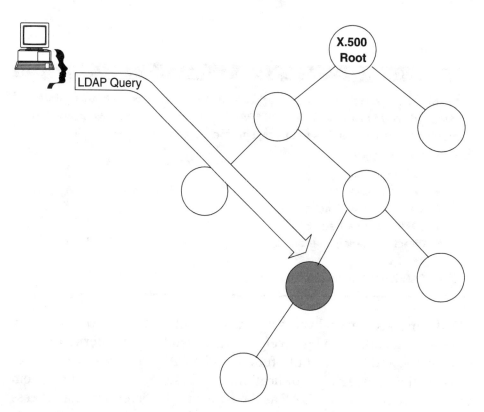

Figure 4.1   X.500 and LDAP interaction.

on the other hand, works quite well over even the slowest links such as those found in analog point-to-point dial-up situations, much like dialing up and using an Internet service provider. Indeed, the LDAP protocol is in use today in many home-based programs such as Microsoft's Outlook Express (see Figure 4.2).

The adoption of LDAP as a standard access protocol has been universally welcomed and endorsed by all the leading industry players. Since its widespread adoption in April 1996, LDAP has gained tremendous momentum in the quest for unified directory functionality—much in the same way as X.500 was perceived in the past. Both offer considerable value, and features of both are integrated in Active Directory. In this chapter, we look at X.500 and LDAP and how both play a large role in directory services functionality.

What Is X.500?

X.500 is the name given to a series of standards produced by the ISO/ITU-T that define the protocols and information model for a global

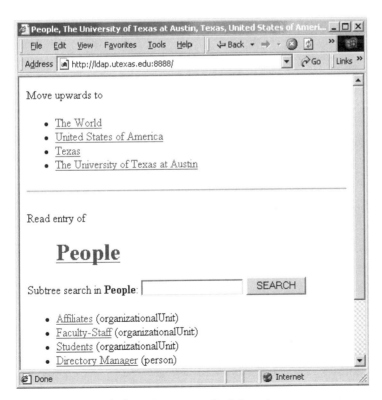

Figure 4.2   A typical LDAP query on the Internet.

directory service independent of computing application and network platform. First released in 1988, the X.500 standards define a specification for a global, distributed directory based on hierarchically named information objects that users can browse and search using specific fields (see Figure 4.3). X.500 uses a model of a set of directory servers, each holding a portion of a global directory information base. In Windows 2000, the directory servers are domain controllers, and the portion of the directory held by each is referred to as a *partition*. These servers cooperate to provide a distributed directory service to users or user applications in such a way that these user applications need not be aware of the location of the information they are accessing. In other words, the user or user applications can connect to any directory server and issue queries to access information anywhere in the global directory.

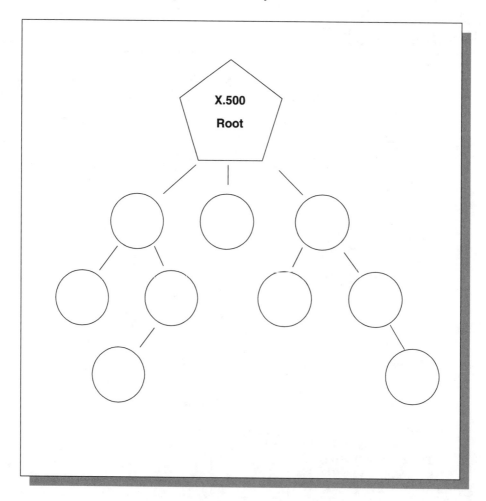

Figure 4.3   X.500 directory structure.

A directory service based on X.500 means that access to data is secure, and data can be distributed or centralized. The 1993 X.500 version incorporates vital features that have significantly increased the desirability of directories based on the X.500 standards and made them more practical for mainstream implementation. An example of this might be that X.500 systems are often deployed to build a single enterprise directory. These possess the access control and security mechanisms necessary to allow unlimited internal and external access, and they can hold a wide variety of data, ranging from databases to network appliance information. Commercial implementations of X.500-based directories are also being used to query individuals' e-mail addresses to ensure that different e-mail directories are synchronized. In addition to these selling points, X.500 is greatly scalable, due in part to the directories nomenclature structure (see Figure 4.4). This scalability makes the X.500 specification the perfect accompaniment to any enterprise class operating system (see Figure 4.5).

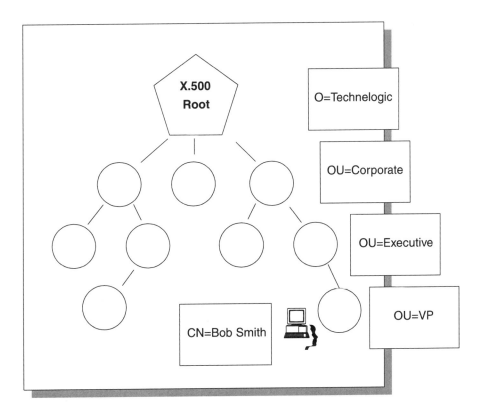

Figure 4.4 X.500 naming conventions.

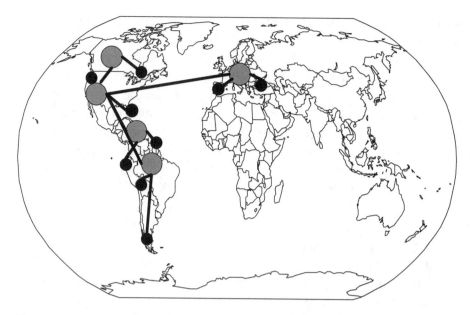

Figure 4.5   An example of a global X.500 implementation.

X.500 and DAP

DAP is the protocol defined by ISO/ITU-T as part of the X.500 directory standards. It provides an open system protocol for *accessing* standardized directory servers for use by users and computer systems . One key feature it provides is a powerful searching facility that allows users to construct arbitrarily complex queries. DAP (and the other X.500 protocols) runs over Internet protocols such as TCP/IP. As previously mentioned, DAP is a very "heavy" protocol that requires much overhead to attain query results; because of this, LDAP was born.

More on X.500 Standards

The definition of an access protocol (DAP) is only one aspect of the X.500 standards. The vast majority of the specification addresses the data and information model and the protocols required to provide a fully distributed service based on a model of cooperating directory servers. Each of these servers is responsible for a portion of the overall Directory Information Base (DIB), linking together to provide a single logical directory for users accessing the service.

To support this model, the X.500 standards address:

- How the directory information is represented in entries (the schema defining, for example, object classes and attributes) (see Figure 4.6)

- How entries are organized and named—the Directory Information Tree and hierarchical naming model, which is used to define a single global namespace

- How information within entries is protected from unauthorized access

- How the global directory information tree is collectively managed, by splitting into management domains

- The protocol needed to chain user requests between directory servers

- The protocol needed to replicate selected information between servers in a managed way such that access control is preserved

The latest version of X.500 introduces more key features such as:

- A standard way to remotely manage directory system components

- International support in the directory model so that multiple languages and character sets can be supported

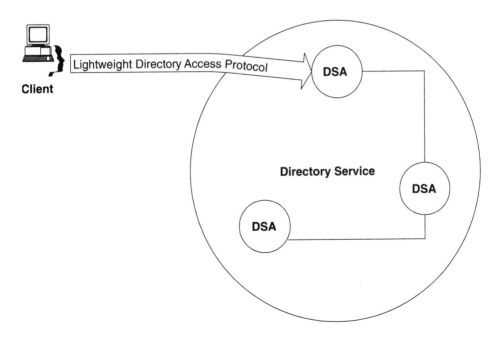

Figure 4.6   LDAP and schema components.

- Further strengthening the use of X.500 as a repository for security-related information through defining encrypted attributes
- Signed attributes
- An encryption mechanism for protocol sessions

Enter LDAP

The LDAP protocol provides a lightweight mechanism for passing text-based queries from an LDAP client to an LDAP server by way of TCP/IP. The query language used is very similar to that found in the DAP specification. The aim is to let users quickly and easily create and query directories of people and information (e.g., user names, e-mail addresses, and telephone numbers).

As a lightweight access protocol, LDAP has become the standard way to access directory services. LDAP was first proposed in the early 1990s when a full OSI solution like DAP did not fit on the desktop technology available at the time. With technology improvements over the last few years, this argument against the use of DAP has receded, and some vendors ship full DAP products that work on all but the oldest desktop systems. LDAP, however, is far more widely used than DAP for access to directories.

LDAP Versions 2 and 3

The current LDAP v2 is defined as a proposed Internet standard in Request for Comments (RFC) 1777. As defined in the RFC, the primary goal of LDAP is to minimize the complexity of the client so as to facilitate widespread deployment of applications capable of utilizing the directory service.

As the RFC itself indicates, the LDAP protocol is "designed to provide access to directories supporting X.500 models, while not incurring the resource requirements of the X.500 Directory Access Protocol (DAP). This protocol is specifically targeted at management applications and browser applications that provide read/write interactive access to directories."

Due to certain limitations in the LDAP v2 specification (including no referral mechanism, no extension mechanism, limited security, and no

Protocols and Directory Models

LDAP allows a user to access a directory that conforms loosely to X.500 because it is a derivative of DAP and X.500. For example, using LDAP you can access any number of directories from any vendor via a Web browser or use your MAPI address book client to access any LDAP-enabled directory such as Microsoft's Outlook. However, LDAP does not specify how the directory service itself operates. This is the distinction between LDAP and the X.500 DAP protocol. LDAP alone does not facilitate for replicating directory data (for redundancy and performance) or updating this data. Any operational directory system needs to provide these components. Microsoft has made provisions for this through directory replication.

Managing the Directory

As mentioned, the LDAP specification does not make a provision for managing the directory. Most of the vendors providing LDAP-based services have their own mechanisms for providing a directory model, access controls, and replication. This is why Microsoft adopted the X.500 model in conjunction with the lightweight query abilities of LDAP to provide the features present in Active Directory. Active Directory functionality is similar to X.500, and it is compliant with the standard and interoperable with products from other vendors. Every attempt was made to interoperate with X.500—these key services are fully defined—ensuring full cooperation among differing directory service implementations.

Replication

There is often confusion between what is defined as an Internet standard protocol (LDAP v2) and the public domain implementations of LDAP. For example, Release 3 of the University of Michigan software implements LDAP v2, which includes a replication server (slurpd). This replication server is one specific implementation that does not follow any standard and has not been widely adopted (see Figure 4.7). These replication processes exchange data in a flat file format known as the Lightweight Directory Interchange Format (LDIF). It is important to

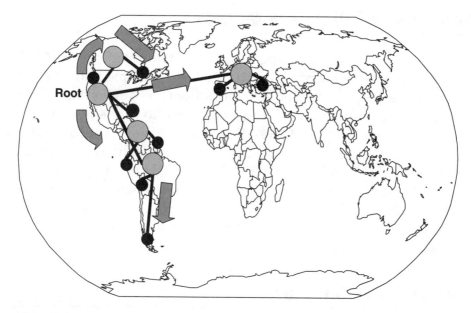

Figure 4.7   X.500 directory replication.

note that interoperation between directory services from different vendors should be tested—particularly replication—for a unified directory across operating system and vendor lines.

The overall design of Active Directory and the directory's ability to segment and replicate data compensate for these limitations of the LDAP Internet standard through adaptation of X.500 qualities. Further, the Global Catalog Server (GCS) contains an agglomeration of these replicated segments (called *partitions*) to provide query support of the entire enterprise.

LDAP and Security

LDAP v2 offers a simple, clear-text password authentication mechanism. LDAP v3 describes a security model based upon the Secure Sockets Layer (SSL) technology (see Figure 4.8). This secures access between the LDAP client and the local LDAP server, which serves systems across the Internet far better.

However, X.500 can offer a higher level of security in the distributed environment. The protocol carried between servers encapsulates the user's query, and the security is carried "end to end." This can be important when corporate intranets are linked over public Internet backbones.

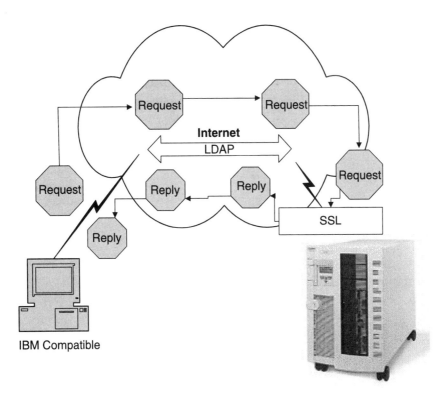

Figure 4.8   An LDAP query from the Internet using SSL.

LDAP does support two security models between protocol versions. Using SSL, LDAP actually achieves strong security and is able to protect the privacy of data as well as its integrity. Using Simple Authentication and Security Layer (SASL), LDAP v3 is able to support an extensible authentication and security framework.

 There are problems with LDAP's handling of X.509 security certificates. The handling of the X.509 attribute userCertificate is based upon a string format and X.500 (88) version 1 certificates. However, this approach does not work with the X.500 (93) version 3 certificates, which are the basis of most security systems. This means these new security fields do not get carried within the LDAP protocol; consequently, the full version 3 certificates cannot be rebuilt in the client.

The solution is found in LDAP v3, which reverts to a binary encoding for userCertificate attributes. This means the certificate is exchanged in its raw ASN.1 form rather than using a string encoding. Consequently, the original, unmodified certificate is carried within the protocol.

In today's distributed network architecture and with more enterprise networks participating in the global Internet, this kind of security support is critical to securing access to directory information. As an HTTPS session supports the authentication and encryption of data, so too does LDAP using version 3 as the provider. Windows 2000 supports both versions 2 and 3 of the LDAP protocol, allowing flexibility in your specific implementation. If you are planning on exposing directory data to outside firms or business partners and security is an issue, make sure that the client supports version 3.

The Global Directory

The X.500 information model uses the concept of a single virtual directory embracing all the countries of the world. This is one of the most powerful aspects of X.500: the ability to distribute data and the management of knowledge across thousands, possibly millions, of directory servers worldwide, thereby creating a logical database of billions of entries. This is why Microsoft chose X.500 to model Active Directory, providing global support for global directories that are often commonplace in corporate networks.

The Future of LDAP

The motivation behind LDAP v2 was to provide lightweight access to directory services that use the X.500 data and information model. While LDAP does not demand a service supporting X.500 protocols, it does require a directory service that uses the X.500 data and information model. This approach is further supported in the LDAP v3 specification as this protocol further supports the features found in the newer X.500 (1993) standards.

LDAP may just end up "reinventing the wheel" if it grows into providing more than just directory access. The X.500 standards provide a solid, proven blueprint for a global distributed directory. The confusion lies between the LDAP protocol itself, specific vendor implementations, and extra functionality beyond the defined LDAP standard they implement. For example, Microsoft has added a host of LDAP features and tools that are far beyond the standard of the original LDAP specification. Novell's NDS is much the same. This may be more harmful because it fails to recognize the requirements of a managed, distributed global directory, moving off-keel for each to fortify their own positions. In the past, such actions have proven only to hurt not only the industry, but the user community as well.

The Future of X.500

X.500 contains the key features that a global distributed directory service needs. LDAP is a lightweight alternative to the X.500 access protocol. It doesn't address how the directory service itself is structured. This is why X.500 is important: It provides an open, standard, proven blueprint for implementing a directory service.

The move within the IETF to de-emphasize the X.500 relationship because of the negative effects of an OSI association is corrosive. If the industry and the Internet need a solution with the power of X.500 (and this section argues strongly that it does), then the substance of these concerns must be addressed. Close analysis shows many of them to be unfounded. The main objections raised against X.500 are:

- It is too complex.
- It is OSI and, therefore, too resource intensive.
- Products are not mature.

To continue to provide maximum benefit to users, standards must be kept open and consistent. One of the Internet arguments against the OSI standardization process is that it takes far too long to ratify required changes. A crucial challenge for X.500 vendors is to consolidate the work that has already taken place in coming to agreement on DSP and DISP. An important test will be the speed of the formal standardization of these protocols running as part of the Internet protocol suite for server-to-server communication, and the subsequent level of acceptance by the Internet community.

Bridging the Gap between Standards

It is already clear that the predominant use of either LDAP or X.500 is the future deployment strategy of products from Lotus, Microsoft, Netscape, and Novell. Despite support for X.500 indicated by all of these companies, it remains to be seen how extensively or how well integrated the X.500 model or protocols will be incorporated into the most commonly deployed software business applications. The same hesitancy cannot be applied to the support promised for LDAP. All of the aforementioned companies, as well as many others, are in the process of providing extensive native LDAP capability in their clients, servers, and applications. By the end of 1999, there will be more products available that support LDAP instead of X.500, and by the end of 2000, it is anticipated there will be more LDAP-enabled servers deployed than X.500 servers.

As has already been noted, LDAP is the best thing that has ever happened to X.500, and this will continue to be the case for the foreseeable future. From the client perspective, the availability of LDAP-enabled applications, mail clients, and Web browsers on most desktops is enormously helpful in legitimizing the deployment of X.500 servers (which in the past have required unpopular, standalone client Directory User Agents (DUAs) access). From a server perspective, it is a matter for conjecture whether LDAP is robust enough to provide production-quality server-to-server connections or replication between two or more disparate standalone LDAP servers (e.g., NDS and Netscape Directory Server). It is also clear that heterogeneous directory environments are not going to go away. Therefore, in the absence of the proven capability of LDAP servers, it appears that the requirement for directory synchronization between directories is going to remain.

The role of X.500 in most corporations deploying X.500-based solutions is to provide the backbone infrastructure, either as a standalone system or with multiple servers replicating with each other (see Figure 4.9). As deployment of X.500 (93) systems and standalone LDAP servers emerges during the course of 2000, it will become clear how far a differentiation of the roles can be determined.

The importance of the definition of LDAP v3 is that it will become the accepted form of the protocol for widespread implementation in the industry over the next two to three years. Individual vendors may choose to make and implement their own extensions (some already have), but these will to all intents and purposes be proprietary. For the vendors who are currently building LDAP servers and clients, there will need to be very compelling reasons to make their directories X.500 compliant. In the absence of such a rationale, it is in everyone's interests to ensure compatibility and coexistence between LDAP and X.500 systems.

Sorting out errors that have already been fixed by X.500 is in no one's best interest, and to a large extent, this is unlikely to happen. One of the

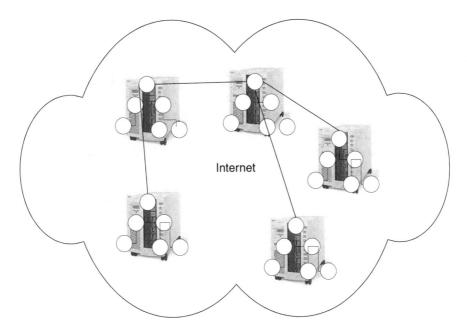

Figure 4.9   Interoperability of X.500-based systems.

ironies of the LDAP movement is that many of the leading vendors either work for X.500 vendors or have been heavily committed to X.500 in the past.

LDAP provides simple access and manipulation of a directory. Some of the lightness of LDAP is achieved by removing rarely used but useful features of X.500. However, the requirement for lightness is much less relevant than it was when LDAP development started. DAP is only a small part of the full X.500 suite. Much of the value of open standards is in providing interoperability.

Active Directory and Adopted Standards

With the nature and origin of LDAP and X.500 in hand, it is time to turn our attention specifically toward how these standards define the way that Active Directory works. As mentioned, many of the features indigenous to X.500 are also found in Active Directory, and LDAP provides the vehicle for access to the directory. While Microsoft may be late in coming to the table with these technologies, the final outcome is a product that extends across operating system boundaries to finally unify the data center model.

In Active Directory, the domain is the logical unit that partitions directory information, and replication takes place between domains as well as the GCS. All objects that partake in the domain tree structure and hierarchical namespace are housed within these containers and are defined and named by existing in them.

Replication, security, fault tolerance, and a robust management model are all features that the X.500 set of protocols brings to Active Directory. With the addition of LDAP as the mechanism for access to information within the directory, Active Directory provides an appropriate set of tools to access and manage an enterprise network (see Figure 4.10).

Summary

X.500 is an overall model for Directory Services in the OSI world. The model encompasses the overall namespace and the protocol for querying and updating it. The protocol is known as DAP (Directory Access Protocol). DAP runs over the OSI network protocol stack; that, combined with its very rich data model and operation set, makes it very weighty. It is rather tough to implement a full-blown DAP client and have it "fit" on smaller computer systems. Thus, the folks at the University of Michigan, with help from the ISODE Consortium,

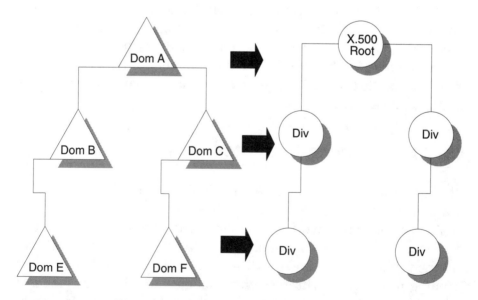

Figure 4.10 How the X.500 model fits into the Active Directory model.

designed and developed LDAP, or the Lightweight Directory Access Protocol. LDAP is, like X.500, both an information model and a protocol for querying and manipulating it. LDAP's overall data and namespace model is essentially that of X.500. The major difference is that the LDAP protocol itself is designed to run directly over the TCP/IP stack, and it lacks some of the more esoteric DAP protocol functions.

A major part of X.500 is that it defines a *global* directory structure. It is essentially a *directory web* in much the same way that HTTP and HTML are used to define and implement the global hypertext Web. Anyone with an X.500 or LDAP client can peruse the global directory just as they can use a Web browser to peruse the global Web. Additionally, with the help of web<->X.500 gateways, you can use your favorite Web browser to peruse both!

Understanding DNS Architecture

INTRODUCTION

In this chapter, we discuss the Domain Name System (DNS) and how it applies to Windows 2000 and Active Directory within an organization. Topics discussed include:

- DNS Concepts
- Planning DNS Naming
- The Root Domain
- DNS Zones
- Server Strategies
- Naming Conventions

 This first section covers the fundamentals of DNS and DNS servers as they pertain to the Internet standard and is not specific to the Microsoft DNS product. If you are already familiar with the principles and architecture of DNS, move on to the section titled "DNS and Windows 2000."

The cornerstone of Active Directory is the *namespace*, which defines the Active Directory organization and the Windows 2000 network. The namespace is the key to defining, locating, and using resources on an Active Directory enabled network. The underlying technologies that allow Active Directory to function are comprised of several Internet standards including DNS, the Lightweight Directory Access Protocol (LDAP), and the X.500 directory service. Windows 2000 Active Directory uses DNS to resolve names to Transmission Control Protocol/Internet Protocol (TCP/IP) addresses on the network. In addition to name-to-IP resolution, DNS in Windows 2000 may be integrated with Active Directory to provide a distributed and replicated DNS model. To fully understand Active Directory architecture and naming, you must also have a solid understanding of DNS functionality and the namespace architecture that it offers. DNS is the element of Windows 2000 that moves the Windows server family from a flat namespace to a hierarchical naming convention, a far more manageable and extensible organization.

 Windows NT 4.0 networks in the past provided two types of name resolution, Windows Internet Name Service (WINS) and DNS. WINS resolution provides a mechanism for dynamically mapping NetBIOS names to IP addresses. WINS could be integrated with Microsoft's static DNS server to provide a makeshift dynamic "host name" to the IP address system. Because of the limited static nature of the DNS product offered with NT 4.0, many companies turned to third-party DNS servers or relied solely upon WINS for name resolution. As we will see, the Windows 2000 version of DNS is far more robust than prior versions and has the option of integrating with Active Directory for dynamically developing a namespace hierarchy.

What Is DNS?

The process of TCP/IP communication occurs between (at least) two computers connected to a network using distinct Internet Protocol (IP) addresses. The IP address can be equated to a postal address of sorts providing a distinct location for the sending and receiving of information. Therefore, it would suffice that all computers that take place in such conversations would also need a distinct address. Where the address 123 Elm St. Houston, TX 77002 describes a U.S. postal address, an IP address is comprised of a complicated number set, or four-octet address, that is not as easy to remember (for humans) as a street address. DNS provides a friendly name to IP address mapping system.

DNS is made up of many elements to provide name resolution for clients on a TCP/IP network, including name servers, domains, zones and zone files, and records.

 The term *domain* in DNS is unrelated to the concept of a Windows network domain or domain controllers that function to authenticate users in the domain, not offer name services.

Hosts and Host Names

DNS is comprised of servers that function to resolve these names; a DNS server may assume several roles in the process of name resolution. Within DNS exist *hosts* and *host names*, which are computers on a TCP/IP network, and the name assigned a host, respectively. The fundamental principals that you should understand up front about DNS are the concepts of *registration* and *resolution* that are part of the DNS naming method and DNS servers in general. See Figure 5.1 for an example of basic name resolution.

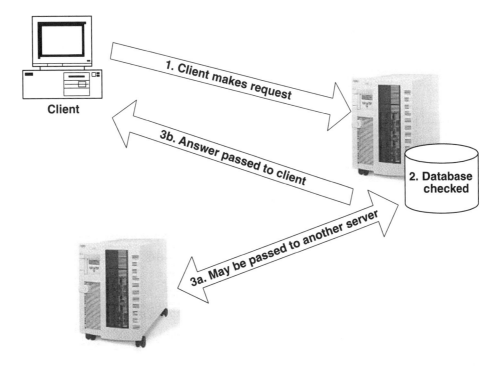

Figure 5.1   Basic name resolution.

Registration, Records, and Resolving Names

Host name registration means simply that a friendly name is mapped to the IP address of a host computer in a directory. Registration can be manual or automatic, static or dynamic. In most cases, this is a manual process, entered at the DNS server console. In addition to this manual process, the addresses are usually static, meaning that when a host name or IP address changes, the record must be updated as well. On a large network the job of keeping such a list updated can be a massive undertaking. To complicate matters more, names within DNS can also be registered dynamically and updated automatically. Nearly all TCP/IP networks use the Dynamic Host Configuration Protocol (DHCP) to automatically configure clients on the network at boot time by passing an IP address, a gateway address in routed networks, and a subnet mask. Additionally, DHCP can be configured to pass WINS and DNS information.

The actual registration process creates what is known as a *resource record* (RR), which may be one of many types that classify the host type entry. It is from these records that *resolution* of the host name occurs. Resolution is the process by which a client initiates a request for a registered name or service to learn the IP address and can then access the given resource. The most common use of this practice is entering a Universal Resource Locator (URL) address in your Web browser to retrieve a Web page from the Internet. Behind the scenes, the browser is initiating a request to resolve the address for a Web site, say www.technelogic.com, and resolving it to the company's registered domain name (the actual name is useless to the computer).

The process of querying for a name to IP address in DNS is functionally supported by a client program called a *resolver*, which functions on a DNS server querying other name servers, or on a workstation attempting to resolve a name. Resolvers forward requests to name servers, which may concatenate the path of the resolved name (many times the result of hops from several servers), to produce the result. See Figure 5.2 for an example DNS path statement.

DNS servers are also capable of resolving names to numbers, called a *reverse lookup*, whereby the IP address is the returned result to the query. A reverse lookup is performed using an "in-addr-arpa" zone on the DNS server that takes the format of an IP address, such as 192.168.1.5, and reverses the first three octets of the address and adds "in-addr-arpa" to the end. The result is 1.168.192.in-addr-arpa. This zone is created on a

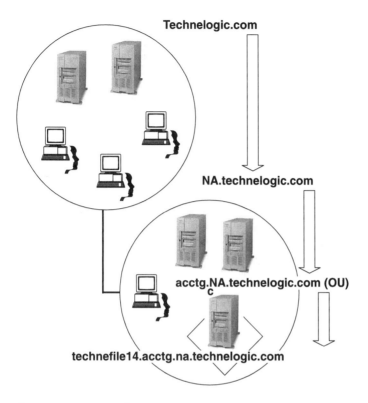

Technelogic.com

NA.technelogic.com

acctg.NA.technelogic.com (OU)

technefile14.acctg.na.technelogic.com

Figure 5.2 DNS path statement.

primary DNS server authoritative only for a particular domain. This functionality is often helpful in troubleshooting DNS services and name resolution.

 Do not become overwhelmed with the terminology at this point if you are unfamiliar with DNS. We will cover all bases as we continue through the chapter.

DNS Search Order

Clients are provided DNS information either manually or automatically via DHCP. Multiple DNS servers are placed on a network to provide fault tolerance, to disperse the load on DNS servers, and because different servers may serve different functions. Networks that have more than one DNS server characteristically provide a primary and secondary DNS entry on client computers, and the client will use the first for name resolution in most cases. The client should be registered in this server's records database. This is the primary server or authoritative server for the client's domain. Secondary entries are provided in case the primary cannot respond to the client's request, or in the event that the address lies beyond the internetwork, say on the Internet.

DNS Hierarchies and Logical Naming Elements

DNS servers may function on their own to resolve names or branch one under the other to form a DNS hierarchy or tree (common in many large organizations with many divisions). This host name distribution is formed from a top-down (visualize it more as an upside-down tree) tree structure for host names (see Figure 5.3). The top of the tree is the root, and the tree may have branches, which in turn have leaves. Typically, a single DNS server will represent a different domain.

 Although difficult, try to make a distinction between the discussion of DNS domains and NT domains. I will attempt to thoroughly confuse you later when we discuss DNS integration in Active Directory. For now put NT domains out of your mind and focus on DNS.

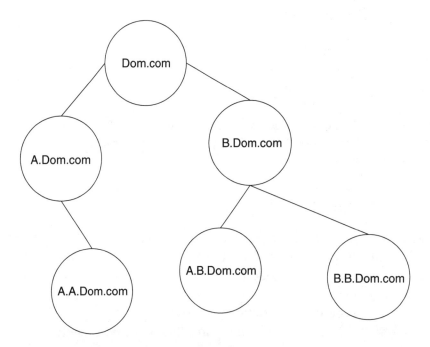

Figure 5.3   A distributed DNS tree hierarchy.

DNS is ideally used to form a hierarchical namespace, which provides logical naming divisions throughout for the network. A host name in a DNS hierarchy is known as a Fully Qualified Domain Name (FQDN), where if you have several branches in a tree, the host name is represented by concatenating the host name to each branch of the tree up to the root. Take the Technelogic domain as an example.

The root of the domain is .com, representing a commercial domain that may or may not be registered with the InterNIC. Technelogic is the company name, so together this forms technelogic.com. Technelogic has several divisions, one of which is finance in the accounting department. A further subdivision of these branches might yield finance.accounting .technelogic.com. Sue Smith's workstation in the finance subdomain has a host name fin845w95, so the result is fin845w95.finance.accounting .technelogic. com (see Figure 5.4). This FQDN encompasses the host name

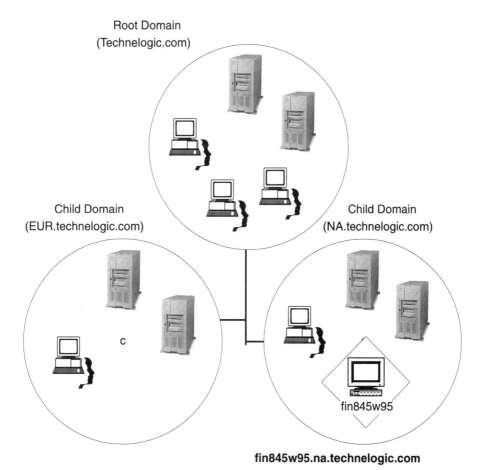

fin845w95.na.technelogic.com

Figure 5.4 The host fin845w95 in the Technelogic DNS tree.

and the names of the subdomain and domain in which it resides. During host name resolution in a DNS hierarchy, the resolver functions to add the elements other than the host name and is further resolved through the concepts of zones. Another example of using an FQDN is illustrated by entering a URL into the address space of a Web browser. Support.Microsoft.com demonstrates the subdomain "support" in the Microsoft commercial domain.

Domains and Zones

A typical DNS arrangement is subdivided into domains and zones, which may seem at first quite identical. On the tree, subdomains and leaves are members of the domains above them. Domains are logical structure components of the hierarchy.

Zones, defined by zone files, set authoritative boundaries that a DNS server is accountable for and are stored as zone files on the DNS server (see Figure 5.5). In other words, a logical boundary is formed that overlays part (or parts) of the hierarchy for which a particular server is responsible for storing names. A zone may encompass only a single domain, a portion of the domain, one or more subdomains, or any combination thereof. This separation of name authority provides a manageable approach to the concept of naming multiple domains in a hierarchy and aids in load balancing the system.

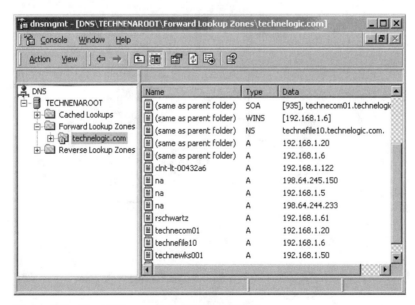

Figure 5.5 The DNS console in Windows 2000.

Primary and Secondary Servers

A primary server is authoritative for names in a domain. When a primary server comes online, zone information comes from local data files on the server that have been either manually entered or stored from dynamic updates. Primary servers may host more than one domain at a time, primary, secondary, or any combination thereof.

 When first implementing a DNS hierarchy for your network, it is good practice to first set up a primary name server that is authoritative for the entire domain. Then create subdomains under this server and migrate data as needed. This provides a good starting point for testing name resolution without adding the complication of multiple child domains.

A secondary server functions to resolve names just like a primary, the difference being that the data comes from a primary server. This data is transferred via a push-pull relationship. Secondary servers are also authoritative for a domain, although the origin of the data is from a primary DNS server and exists mainly for redundancy.

Caching, Forwarder, and Slave Servers

There are three other types of DNS servers that can function in a domain: caching, forwarder, and slaves. Each of these acts as a sort of helper in the quest for resolving host names on the network.

Caching servers are used primarily to enhance the performance of the overall DNS system by providing cached lookups to frequently accessed DNS records. Caching servers are not authoritative for a domain and should not be delegated for domain name resolution. Caching servers are typically configured to forward DNS requests to resolvers from other DNS servers.

DNS servers can be configured to designate another DNS server to be a forwarder, which establishes a path to another name server in the event that the initial server (for whatever reason) cannot answer a query. A slave server makes a server dependent on its forwarder(s) to answer queries by preventing it from being a client to other DNS servers. The fundamental difference between these two types of servers is this: A slave will not try to resolve the query; it waits for the response from other servers. See Figures 5.6 and 5.7 for forwarder and slave name resolutions.

Forwarders and slaves are often found as part of a company's Internet gateway system or firewall, passing on requests for processing by the company's Internet Service Provider (ISP) DNS servers. This reduces administration, offloads local server functions, and provides resolution of Internet addresses.

This model of multiple DNS servers, both primary and secondary, forms a distributed database model from which DNS queries are built. So far, we have discussed the principle elements that compose a typical DNS implementation. With this knowledge in hand, it is time to move to a discussion of the types of records and files found on a DNS server that help provide name resolution.

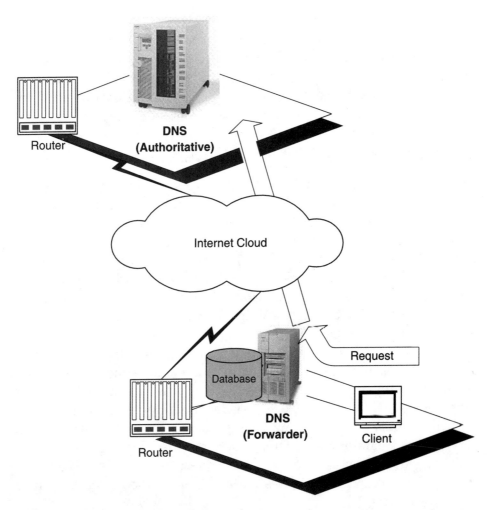

Figure 5.6   Forwarder name resolution.

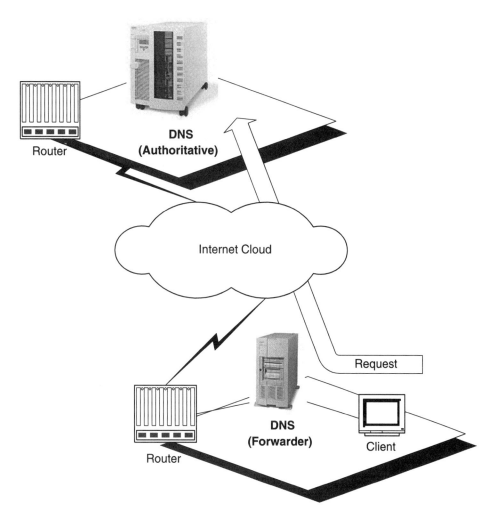

Figure 5.7   Slave name resolution.

Database Resource Records and the DNS Cache File

DNS servers are essentially database servers, and within a database are tables of data that may be queried. These tables are referred to as *zone files* in DNS, and it is this zone file that holds the IP to name address mappings along with other information about the host. The most significant of these files include the Start of Authority (SOA) record, the Name Server (NS) record, the Address (A) record, the Canonical Name (CNAME) record, the Mail eXchange (MX) record, and the Pointer (PTR) record. RRs are parsed (usually as ASCII text files) and are not case sensitive. These records have a specific format, which is explained in Request for Comments (RFC) 1035. The following excerpt from RFC 1035 defines the structure of an RR.

```
<blank> [<comment>]
$ORIGIN <domain-name> [<comment>]
$INCLUDE <file-name> [<comment>]
<domain-name><rr> [<comment>]
<blank><rr> [<comment>]
```

Blank lines with or without comments are allowed anywhere in the file. The first two examples control the formatting and function of returned RRs, while the last two represent the format of an actual RR. Therefore, a generic RR takes the following form:

```
host1 IN A 192.5.29.135 [Host1]
host2 IN A 192.5.29.136 [Host2]
host2 IN A 192.5.29.137 [Host3]
host2 IN A 192.5.29.138 [Host4]
```

The first entry on the row is the name of the host, the second item describes the format of the record (IN=Internet), followed by the record type (A=address record) and the IP address of the host. Comments are optional and follow the record.

For an in-depth discussion of formatting particulars of RRs, please refer to RFCs 1035, 1183, and 1664. The following list describes all record types found on a typical DNS server.

Start of Authority record (SOA). The SOA record (see Figure 5.8) is required as the first entry in all forward and reverse (in-addr) zone files, as it provides key elements the domain needs such as records of the DNS server authority for the domain. SOA records are extremely important to the way a DNS server is defined and functions, and they serve as a sort of configuration file for the primary or secondary server that is authoritative for the domain

Active Address record (A). A records are the most common type of record that you will use or encounter on a DNS server (see Figure 5.9). These are the actual host to IP address records that help in resolving names initiated by client workstations or other DNS servers.

Name Server record (NS). As the name implies, an NS record defines a name server. Specifically, the NS record keeps track of delegated servers for the domain or for subdomains. Delegation is the process in which a server is authorized to answer queries for the given domain. The cascading effect of using forwarder servers and slave servers is applied through such records, as shown in Figure 5.10. NS records

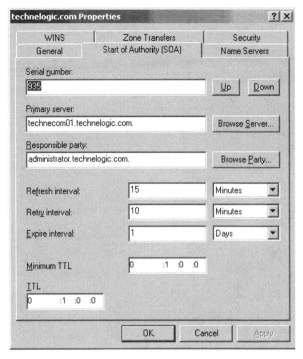

Figure 5.8   An SOA record viewed from Windows 2000 DNS Manager.

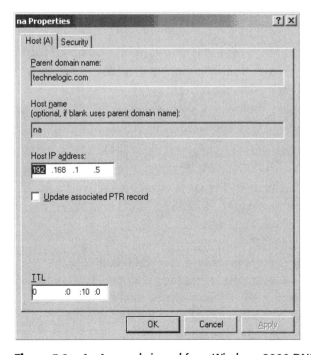

Figure 5.9   An A record viewed from Windows 2000 DNS Manager.

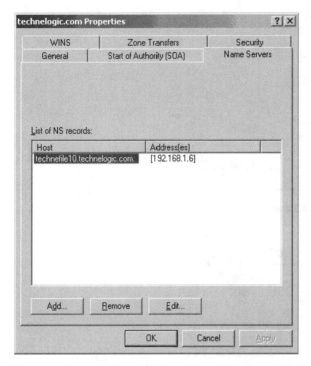

Figure 5.10   An NS record viewed from Windows 2000 DNS Manager.

exist for every name server delegated and are used in both forward and lookup zone files.

Pointer record (PTR). Reverse lookups—that is, the lookup of an IP address from the name—are possible because of the PTR record (see Figure 5.11). Reverse lookups are helpful in resolving names, and the *nslookup* command-line utility provides the mechanism for performing reverse lookups (see Figure 5.12).

Mail Exchange record (MX). Like name servers, mail servers have a record type of their own. MX records provide information about where mail can be routed within the domain (see Figure 5.13). An MX record may function to provide local mail server resolution or to a server hosted by your ISP.

 One common pitfall associated with creating MX records in DNS where there are multiple DNS servers comes in creating a *mail loop*. This is where the Message Transfer Agent (MTA) of the mail server sends to one machine, then it sends to another, and finally, the message "bounces" back to the mail host causing a nondelivery report to the client. This is caused by improperly configuring MX records in DNS. Check to see if your mail server requires the use of MX records before creating them.

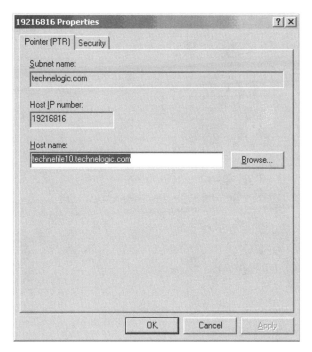

Figure 5.11 A PTR record viewed from Windows 2000 DNS Manager.

Canonical Name record (CNAME). Simply put, a CNAME record (see Figure 5.14) defines an *alias* for a host or host name. An alias is another name that the host is known as. CNAME records are beneficial when the host has an abstract name, a long name, or a nondescript name, and a friendly name needs to be used. Say, for example, a mail server was named houmailserverx4b33.technelogic.com. A CNAME record may be generated so that the friendly name houmail33 or mail33 is used in place of the more abstract name. The resulting IP address is

Figure 5.12 Using the command-line utility nslookup for a reverse lookup.

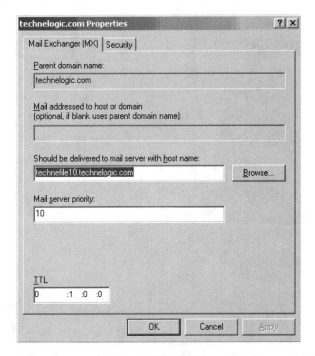

Figure 5.13   AN MX record viewed from Windows 2000 DNS Manager.

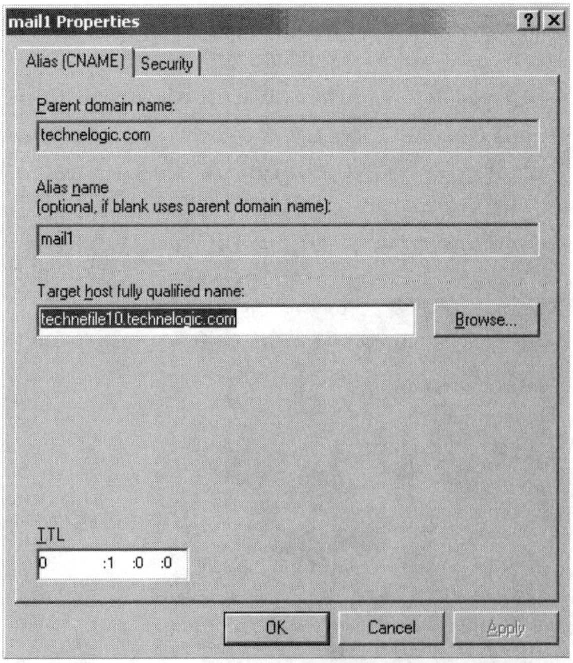

Figure 5.14   A CNAME record viewed from Windows 2000 DNS Manager.

the same if you request houmailserverx4b33.technelogic.com or mail33.technelogic.com. Another instance where a CNAME record might come in handy is if multiple services are being hosted on the same server, such as DNS and a Web server. The server can have only one host name. The alias allows another name for the server to be used for secondary services.

Windows Internet Name Server (WINS, NT Systems only). WINS is commonly used on Windows networks to resolve NetBIOS names to IP addresses. WINS servers are dynamic in their registration process, which poses a problem for reverse name lookup for non-WINS clients. Windows servers (be they NT or 2000) allow for WINS integration with Microsoft DNS for name resolution of these dynamic IP address registrations. The WINS record (see Figure 5.15) is added to Microsoft DNS server(s) to provide a mechanism by which a query that is not resolvable by the DNS server is then passed to the WINS server for resolution.

 WINS is included with Windows 2000 for compatibility of down-level clients, although it is not required in a homogeneous Windows 2000 network.

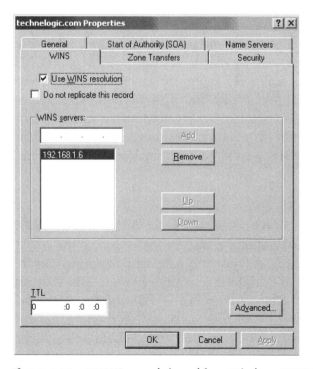

Figure 5.15   A WINS record viewed from Windows 2000 DNS Manager.

Windows Internet Name Server–Reverse (WINS-R, NT Systems only). The WINS-R record is used in a similar fashion to the PTR record, where reverse WINS queries are necessary.

Cache File

The cache file may be thought of as a zone file and holds static addresses and names of the root servers in the domain to use as a last resort for queries. (Although the name would have you believe that cached records are kept here.) The cache file must be present in order for DNS to work. Under Windows 2000 DNS, this file is populated for you and is held in the <system root>\system32\dns\chache.dns. This file may be viewed with any standard text viewer in the event that manual editing or troubleshooting becomes necessary. As with other DNS systems, there are rules that must be followed when naming hosts.

Now that you understand the components of a standard DNS, it is time to focus on DNS on Windows 2000 servers and how it integrates with Active Directory.

DNS and Windows 2000

There are several extended features offered by Microsoft DNS that are nontypical, allowing greater flexibility in the design of a DNS. These features include the ability to integrate DNS zones in Active Directory, specify resource record types, and update the DNS database dynamically. One must also consider legacy system support if Windows 2000 is to be grafted into the existing environment over time, and consider replication of the data in Active Directory integrated systems.

The DNS Namespace

DNS consists of a hierarchical namespace, unlike WINS and NetBIOS networks that are based on a flat namespace. In addition to the namespace, DNS incorporates name servers and resolvers to round out the architecture. A namespace is a database containing records that are used to resolve names. The DNS namespace is a distributed database of records and zones, and it finds its lineage based on the Internet and Unix systems. DNS is constructed from domains, which are synonymous with directories on a file tree. Directories can contain other directories (other domains) and files (records), and domains may contain other domains.

Choosing Names for the Namespace

As previously mentioned, Windows 2000 integrates nicely with the Internet, and DNS is an integral part of this union. Choosing a DNS name for your organization should follow a few simple guidelines. First, a root for the parent domain must be selected. The root is usually determined by the type of business conducted by your organization and is represented most commonly by .com, or .net. While other new root domains exist, it is recommended that you stick with these standard types until the newer roots are accepted as standard. Next, the name of the domain is concatenated to the root and is usually the name of your company (e.g., technelogic.com). Finally, any name of any subdomains may be added to define the name of a child domain (acct.technelogic.com). When defining the namespace, try to stay within the following guidelines:

- Limit the number of child domains. Child domains that are nested too deeply become an administrative burden.

- As a rule, domain names over 63 characters are not valid, including the "." separator.

- The valid character sets in domain naming are A–Z, a–z, 0–9. Underscores are not allowed.

- Each child domain under a parent must have a unique name.

Internal and External Naming Considerations

If your organization already has an Internet presence, you must decide whether to extend this external namespace to incorporate it in the internal namespace. There are several advantages and disadvantages either way. Use Tables 5.1 and 5.2 to weigh both options and then decide which method is best for your organization. The majority of companies, because of manageability issues, commonly implement the use of separate namespaces.

Table 5.1 Same Internal and External Names

ADVANTAGES	DISADVANTAGES
1. Logon and e-mail names may be the same	1. Less secure
2. Administration of a single namespace	2. Harder to distinguish internal and external resources

DNS Zone Types in Windows 2000

In most standard DNS products, there are two types of zones, primary and secondary. Primary zones hold information about the zone that is local to the name server on which it resides, and the data is updated directly. Secondary servers gather information from a primary server, and the data is read-only.

Windows 2000 offers an additional (and preferred) method of zone updates where the DNS zone is created and integrated with Active Directory. This scheme offers several benefits to the network, including a distributed, replicated model updated securely over the network.

Dynamic DNS (DDNS)

Most DNS servers must be updated manually, where records are added to the zone file one at time. On any network with over 100 clients, this becomes an administrative nightmare. Further, if clients are dynamically assigned addresses through DHCP where addresses may change often, the static DNS file quickly becomes outdated. Windows 2000 DNS offers a solution to this dilemma with the option to create DNS zones that are updated dynamically as a client computer comes on the network.

While few changes have occurred in the DHCP service on Windows 2000, the service is now DNS-aware and provides a link for down-level clients to register "dynamically" with the DNS server. If a client is capable

Table 5.2 Different Internal and External Names

ADVANTAGES	DISADVANTAGES
1. Easier to distinguish internal and external names	1. Users may need to be educated on using separate namespaces
2. More secure	2. Administration of multiple namespaces

of leasing an address through DHCP, as most are even down to the DOS level, the two services will work together to update the DNS A record of the client.

DDNS works to solve the administrative overhead associated with keeping up with DNS record registration. When DNS is integrated with Active Directory, it becomes a tremendous asset to the overall machinery of a Windows 2000 network. In Chapter 11, we discuss installing and configuring DNS and integrating the system with Active Directory.

Resource Records Specific to Windows 2000 DNS

Earlier we discussed the many records found on all DNS servers that provide host name information to the resolver. In the Microsoft implementation of DNS, there is yet another record type that exists for the purpose of directing resolvers to services found on a Windows 2000 network. An Service Resource Record (SRV RR) record might be used if a client needs to be validated on the network; the SRV record points to a domain controller. Another example would be resolving LDAP servers on the network for client queries.

SRV records take a different format than most of the other records you find on a typical DNS server.

```
<service>.<protocol>.<domain> IN (or A) SRV <priority> <weight> <port>
    <host>
```

The following is a key to the preceding example:

- "Service" is the type of service being registered (logon, LDAP, DNS).
- "Protocol" is the transport method (TCP/IP).
- "Domain" is the domain where the service is located.
- IN and A carry over from the standard RR format where IN is Internet format indicator and A is the address record indicator.
- "Priority" is a number between 0 and 100 and describes the host's precedence in the domain; 100 is highest and 0 the lowest (a DNS server with weight 100 is tried before a host listed at 49).
- "Weight" is a number between 1 and 10 and is used as a secondary determinant when all "priority" settings for a given service on all hosts are equal.

- "Port" is the TCP or UDP port number that the service communicates through. There are 65,544 available ports on a TCP host.
- "Host" is the host name of the server that hosts the designated service.

The service record allows for fine-tuning of network resources and service redirection. In large networks, this can be a serious ally in resolving service bottlenecks.

Affiliation of DNS Zones and Windows 2000 Domains

Once deployed, there are several options for configuring DNS zones under Windows 2000, namely, primary and secondary text-based zones, or Active Directory integrated zones. The latter is the preferred and recommended alternative because of the distributed nature of Active Directory and replication that occurs between domain controllers. DNS/Active Directory integration provides a fault-tolerant DNS system that is automatically synchronized across domains, reducing the administrative burden of multiple text files.

The distributed DNS architecture resulting from this integration provides read and write capabilities at each domain controller, and when coupled with clients that provide dynamic updates, all data is updated automatically and shared with all domain controllers across the network. Using the Active Directory integration model also means that each DNS zone object stored in the domain's database becomes a primary copy at each domain controller. Refer to Figure 5.16 for a demonstration of how DNS integration with Active Directory flows.

Zone Transfer Considerations

Primary DNS servers replicate information to secondary servers. Depending on the size of the organization, secondary servers may be necessary. The replication of data from primary to secondary provides redundancy of information in the event a primary server goes down, and it helps load balance the entire system. A DNS NOTIFY transaction occurs between primary servers and secondary servers to inform of changes to any of the record types in the database. In dynamic environments dependent on DHCP for IP address assignment, the process of replication is automatically triggered as a new client comes on the network or moves to another subnet.

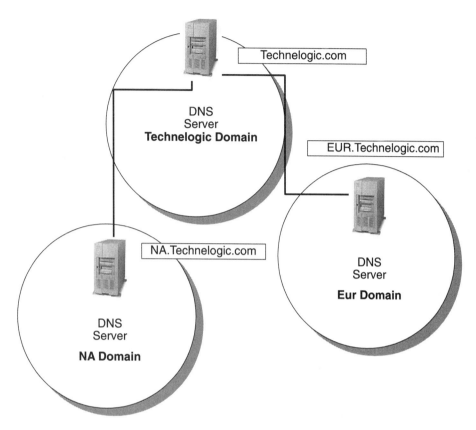

Figure 5.16   DNS integrated with Active Directory.

It is important to consider the impact that DNS replication will have on your network, although less so than with WINS. In routed environments, particularly over a WAN, DNS may have an impact on overall network performance if not carefully architected. Figure 5.17 shows an example of an inadequate design in which client requests must cross over a slow WAN link and back in order to resolve a name. A better arrangement would have been to place a secondary server on the side of the link where the client request initiated and have the client request from the local server. In this model, only changes in the primary server's database are propagated to the secondary server.

 For those familiar with setting up Windows NT in a WAN environment, this example should seem somewhat analogous where Backup Domain Controllers (BDCs) (with a read-only copy of the user accounts database) were often placed at the far side of WAN links in order to limit validation traffic on these links. Replication traffic between the Primary Domain Controller (PDC) and BDC was the only concern.

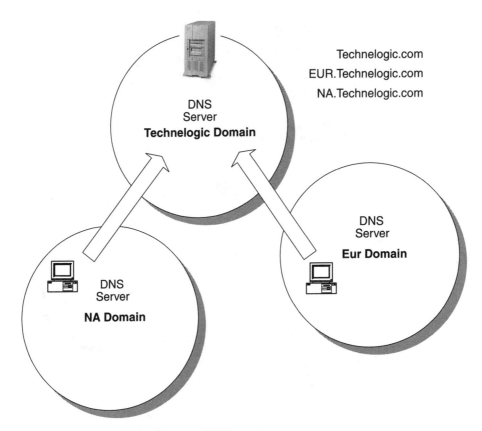

Figure 5.17   A poorly implemented DNS structure.

WINS and DHCP Integration with DNS

As mentioned earlier, the DHCP service on Windows 2000 allows dynamic updates of all legacy clients. However, WINS is still the preferred method of name resolution for down-level clients. DNS zones may be configured to interact with WINS in case the DNS server cannot resolve the request.

DNS Integration with Active Directory

Active Directory depends on DNS as a location service to ascertain the identity of host computers and to make distinctions between domains. In order to log on to a Windows 2000 network, a client will query a DNS server for the location of a directory server (DC). See Figure 5.18 for an example of this process. The SRV record identifies these servers in DNS and further on to the client. The NetLogon service on a Windows 2000 domain controller updates its primary DNS server with an SRV record to make this service accessible to clients.

The <system root>\system32\config\netlogon.dns file is the name of this zone file and may be viewed with any standard text viewer, such as Notepad.

Third-Party DNS Servers

Because Microsoft's previous version of DNS lacked the features of other third-party DNS solutions or Unix-based implementations, many companies are heavily leveraged in these third-party solutions. Use of these products is permissible with Windows 2000, and integrating them with Active Directory is possible. In order to accomplish this, you must identify the server that is authoritative for the root domain. Once this is done, review the documentation to see if the server

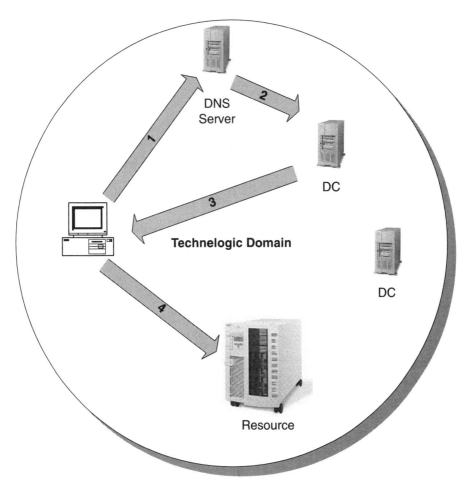

Figure 5.18 The client logon process in a Windows 2000 domain.

supports SRV records, incremental zone transfers, DDNS, and secure DDNS. All but the SRV record are optional, but Microsoft highly recommends the use of these features to guarantee the integrity of the DNS system.

In the event your existing servers do not support SRV records you have three options: upgrade the server to Windows 2000 DNS, upgrade the third-party solution to a version that supports SRV records, or integrate a Microsoft DNS server as a delegated subdomain for the root domain.

 The BIND DNS server by Berkeley version 4.xx does not support SRV records; however, newer versions do. When implementing a third-party solution with Windows 2000, always test the server with other systems in place such as WINS and DHCP. DNS is critical to the NetLogon service (as well as others such as LDAP) in the Active Directory, and therefore the DNS server must support the use of SRV records.

Things to Remember

DNS is a complicated entity to master, and because Active Directory is so dependent on DNS to function (client logons, for example), it is crucial that you take great care in designing the system and configuring zones. The following are recommendations to consider when you implement DNS on Windows 2000:

Set up a test network (on an isolated segment) and work with the new features of Windows 2000 DNS. After you design the system, create a separate network for testing the arrangement of servers. If necessary, join the test segment to another segment over a slower WAN link (e.g., 56K or 115K) with a secondary DNS server on the other end. Make sure that information is replicating between servers, and monitor the bandwidth consumed. If using a third-party DNS product, this is the time to test it with Active Directory integration.

Use Microsoft's DNS server whenever possible. While Active Directory supports the use of third-party DNS servers, there will be no support offered by Microsoft for such an implementation. The Microsoft product is tested with Active Directory and simplifies the integration process by automatically creating the SRV records on the DNS server delegated for the domain. IF you must use third-party solutions, check with the company ahead of time to qualify the product for Active Directory support.

Avoid common pitfalls, and use tools to test when errors occur. There are several tools at your disposal to resolve query failures on any DNS server. First and foremost, if you are using DHCP, make sure that the scope is configured properly, passing the proper DNS credentials to the client. On Windows NT, this may be done from the command line by typing "ipconfig" with the "/all" switch. If you are using Windows 9x clients, there is a graphical version of this program, winipcfg, that may be invoked by clicking Start, then Run, and entering the name of the executable.

The PING utility will verify proper name resolution to IP address. Type "ping <hostname>" at a command prompt. Although not available to Windows 9x clients, the nslookup command-line utility may be used on NT on Windows 2000 clients to test for reverse name lookups.

Also consider very basic troubleshooting when testing any IP network. PING the local adapter first ("ping localhost" or "ping 127.0.0.1") and make sure the adapter and TCP/IP are functioning. Take this a step further by PINGing the near and far sides of the router to ensure that packets are being routed between segments. You may use the tracert utility as well to check the route path from the client to the server.

 A sample DNS file is included with Windows 2000 and can be found in the <system root>\system32\dns\samples directory. This file provides format examples and recommendations and should be reviewed for further study of RR structure. Use Notepad to view the file.

Summary

In this chapter, we covered the Internet standard DNS and further explored the Microsoft extended feature set in their product. DNS is a system comprised of several components, including the namespace, servers, zones, and records, which serve to resolve names at the request of the client resolver. Functionally, Windows 2000 Active Directory depends on DNS as its primary locator service and is integral in the logon process for clients and network services. DNS may involve one server or many servers, forming a hierarchical structure and namespace.

DNS servers may take on several roles, including primary servers, secondary servers, forwarder servers, slave servers, or caching servers. There must be at least one primary server that is authoritative for a given domain. The primary server is a read-write database, and updates are performed at the host, whereas secondary servers get zone information from primary hosts. This is similar to the PDC-BDC server relationship in Windows NT where the BDC relies on the PDC for replication of the user record database.

Zones are created for a given domain, and within these zones are records of each host on the network. Zones may be primary, secondary, or Active Directory integrated, the latter being the recommended method of implementation.

There are eight name record types, each serving a different function within the DNS system. Of the eight types of records, the SRV record is the least ubiquitous. Active Directory depends on this record type to locate services for the client.

Finally, the performance of the system is dependent on the architecture of DNS. WAN links should be considered in the overall design. Planning and testing are key to success.

In the next chapter we begin discussion of the overall design and implementation of Windows 2000 domains and the components that make up these domains.

Naming Strategies for Windows 2000 Active Directory

INTRODUCTION

In this chapter, we discuss the Domain Name System (DNS) namespace and Lightweight Directory Access Protocol (LDAP) naming conventions used in Active Directory. The following specific topics are covered:

- **Elements That Affect Naming Decisions**
- **Namespace Scenarios**
- **Namespace Architecture**
- **Best Practices**

Active Directory functionality is based on names and the naming structure provided by DNS. In order to query or access an object in the directory, a name must be referenced, preferably a meaningful name. Names are defined through the directory and the DNS. These two services are interdependent, relying on each other both for updates to DNS and resolving queries through Active Directory. Various structural elements and design scenarios will affect the outcome of your overall design. Because of the importance of naming in the overall utility of using the directory, it is extremely important to consider the naming of the tree and tree objects.

If you are reading this book, you probably have a little more insight into computing environments than the user to whom you provide service. That point made, have you ever had difficulty locating resources on your network (or other networks) because of the way domains were laid out or because of the name structure used? Take a network printer as an obvious example. When trying to connect to a new or existing printer, all you have to go by is the name. While it is true that some organizations use a highly descriptive naming strategy, the reality is that most administrators assign names that are often cryptic to the end user (QMS1701-22, for example, is a QMS printer model 1701 located on the 22nd floor). These communication gaps are often the single most common reason for support calls by end users (e.g., "I can't find this resource!").

Imagine now that the printer was given a name in the directory that actually made sense to the end user. The same logic holds true for naming the root of the domain on down (see Figure 6.1), and in

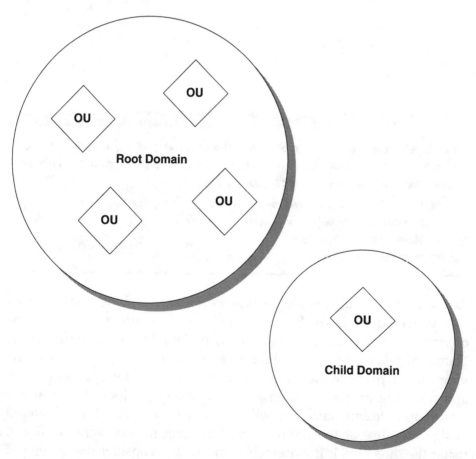

Figure 6.1   Tree elements that affect naming.

Windows 2000 the actual device name matters even less because of the ability to attach attributes to the object (more on this later in the book). The strategy used to name your organizational tree (higher-level directory objects such as domains and organizational units) weighs heavily on the usability of the finished product. In this chapter, we are going to review the best practices for naming structural objects within the directory and strategies to use when connected to the external Internet.

Directory Objects

Active Directory is perhaps the most anticipated change to the NOS line of Windows products. Active Directory offers many new features to navigate a Windows 2000 network that may include many thousands or even millions of objects. The ability to easily find objects within such a network relies heavily on the hierarchical namespace that defines every object within. Components that make up the structure of a Windows 2000 network, and Active Directory, consist of elements such as forests, trees, domains, and organizational units (OU); and all of these units partake in the namespace of the directory. Naming these critical elements properly and with continuity offers the user community a network that is usable and generates less work for the administrator(s) of the network. First let's look at these essential parts of the network structure to better understand why naming is so important.

Domains

The basic building block of a Windows 2000 network is the domain, just as in previous versions of Windows NT (see Figure 6.2). All objects that exist on a Windows 2000 network are contained in a domain, whether they be users, groups, printers, servers, domain controllers, and so on. In order to access any of these objects, an entity must be given access to the object by way of an Access Control List (ACL), which is further comprised of Access Control Entries (ACE). Permissions work much the same as they did in previous versions where access permissions are cumulative. Simply stated, the most restrictive permission is the one that is used to determine access.

Domains are not only a security boundary; they are units of replication as well. In designing a Windows 2000 network with Active Directory as the backbone, it is important to note that a single domain may

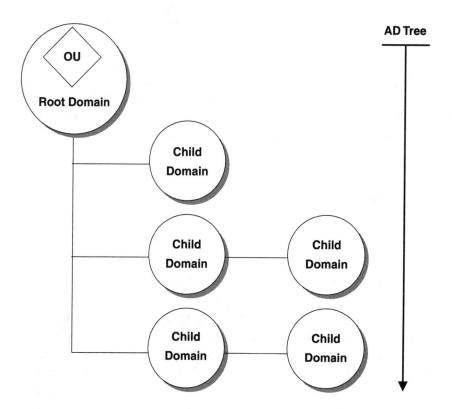

Figure 6.2 Domains are the building blocks of a Windows 2000 network.

encompass the entire network, spanning many different subnets and networks. Within the domain exists a multiple-master scenario where all domain controllers replicate information to other domain controllers. Such a model provides for a more robust authentication and security model where if one domain controller fails, another can take its place without having to promote.

 A word on permissions here for those unfamiliar with rules of persions in a Windows 2000 or Windows NT server. First, when a resource is created, it must be locked down as the global group "everyone (includes anyone accessing the network) has full control." This is the polar opposite of Unix where the resource is created in a locked-down state and only the creator or system administrator can access the file. First, look at this brief explanation of the different permissions that exist at the directory and file levels and each of their meanings.

Directory Level:

No Access (None) (None). A user cannot access the directory in any way, even if he or she is a member of a group that has been granted access to the directory.

List (RX) (Not Specified). A user can list only the files and subdirectories in this directory and change to a subdirectory of this directory. A user cannot access new files created in this directory.

Read (RX) (RX). A user can read the contents of files in this directory and run applications in the directory.

Add (WX) (Not Specified). A user can add files to the directory but cannot view the contents of the directory.

Add & Read (RWX) (RX). A user can add files to the directory and read current files, but cannot change files.

Change (RWXD) (RWXD). A user can read and add files and change the contents of current files.

Full Control (All) (All). A user can read and change files, add new ones, change permissions for the directory and its files, and take ownership of the directory and its files.

File Level:

No Access. A user cannot access the file in any way, even if the user is a member of a group that has been granted access to the file.

Read (RX). A user can read the contents of the file and run it if it is an application.

Change (RWXD). A user can read, modify, and delete the file.

Full Control (All). A user can read, modify, delete, set permissions for, and take ownership of the file.

The following defines the results of applying permissions to a resource. A resource may be accessed in two ways, locally or over the network (share). Local permissions are applied and handled by the NTFS file system. Shared objects that are accessed over the network are given a different "set" of permissions, but bear in mind that the most restrictive permission always works cumulatively. The net result is the use of the most restrictive permission in a situation where more than one set of permissions is in use, and the NTFS permission always takes precedence over share permissions. The following is an example of how this works:

Bob belongs to the group "Remote Admins" which has "full control" permissions to a shared network directory "reports" on an NT server. Later, an administrator of the server sets the NTFS permissions so that a group to which Bob belongs has the "no access" permission. The most restrictive permission is "no access," therefore Bob now will be unable to access the resource.

It is important to understand this functionality, particularly with Active Directory, as changes to permissions are propagated down the tree from the parent container. The result could mean hours of cleanup if you are not careful.

Windows NT used the concepts of Primary Domain Controllers (PDC) and Backup Domain Controllers (BDC) in order to authenticate user logon and access to resources. BDCs contained a read-only copy of the security accounts database, which was replicated from the PDC. Replication in this model was one way and limited the flexibility of the overall design of the network. By eliminating the BDC from the model, all domain controllers are now effectively a PDC, carrying a read/write copy of the accounts database.

If there is more than one domain in a Windows 2000 network, the domains form a tree or hierarchy that shares a common schema, configuration, and Global Catalog Server (GCS). All of the members of the domain are part of the same namespace as well. Beyond these logical connections are the security connections or trusts that allow users across multiple domains to access resources in other domains. These trusts are *transitive*, which means that a user in domain A can access resources in domain C across or through domain B. This was not possible in previous versions. It is important to note that this transitive trust works for users and resources, not for administrative tasks.

Trees and Forests

The concept of trees and forests is new to Windows 2000 (refer to Figure 6.3 for a comparison of the two), whose presence offers a new level of scalability and organization to a Microsoft-based network. A tree consists of two or more domains that share the same namespace. A forest is a collection of one or more trees that form a disjointed namespace, although they share the same schema, configuration, and GCS. The benefits of trees and forests include a concise, consistent, and meaningful naming structure throughout the domain tree(s); support for X.500 naming; and simplification of principal logon. The use of a hierarchy to define domain relationships simplifies the overall use of the network by users and administrators alike because of the logical structure. This logical structure is further defined by the names given to the elements throughout the structure, which follow the trust hierarchy.

Organizational Units

Domain directory service objects may be subdivided further into OUs. These serve as administrative boundaries and are used to organize resources and users within a domain as administrative groups. OUs also help to ease administrative burdens by allowing the delegation of

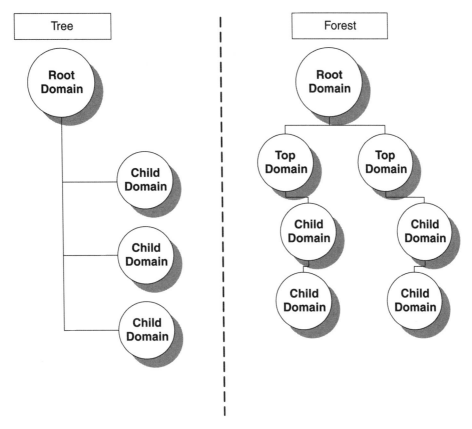

Figure 6.3   A tree versus a forest.

administrators for each OU. As part of the hierarchy, OUs are part of the naming hierarchy as well (see Figure 6.4).

 OUs should not be confused with the OU found in the X.500 naming hierarchy, and they should be thought of as an administrative unit within a domain.

Global Catalog

The new structural elements present in Windows 2000 are an attempt to move away from the domain structures of legacy NT systems where the user was presented with a myriad of domains to sift through to find the resource needed. By presenting the network in a hierarchical manner, this confusing method of resource access has been effectively eliminated. Taking resource location a step farther, the Global Catalog (GC) that serves an entire Active Directory tree structure holds key information about hierarchy

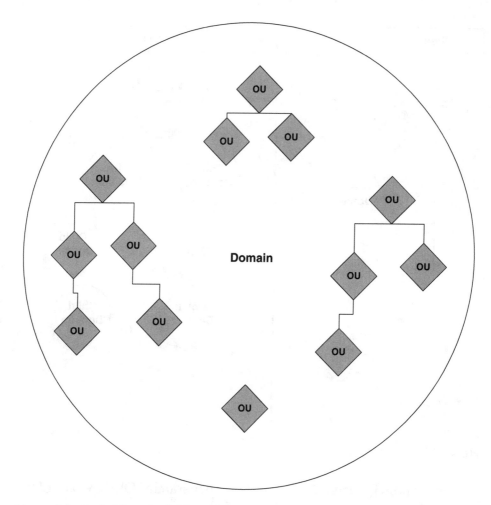

Figure 6.4 Typical domain division using OUs.

objects and resolves these attributes to user queries. See Figure 6.5 for an illustration of how the GC fits into Active Directory architecture.

Think of the GC as directory assistance or the business pages of your phone book. If you know that you need a printer located on the 22nd floor, you can query for all printers on that floor and narrow your search from there. If you have additional information about the printer, such as the make or model, this may further narrow the query results. These types of key attributes form a partial index of directory objects and are the essence of the database found on the GCS.

A query will not work in all cases. A user must have the appropriate rights to the object being queried to have a response returned from

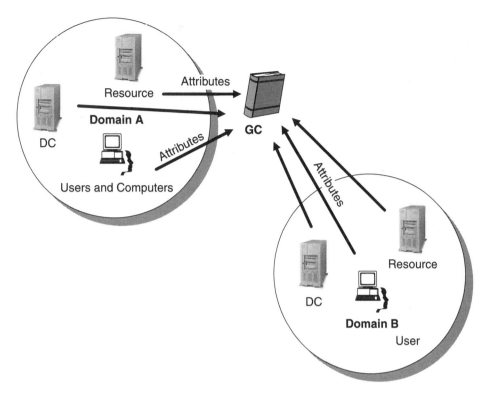

Figure 6.5 How the GC fits into Active Directory architecture.

the GC. In fact, one of the attributes stored by the GC for an object is the ACL and ACE of the object. If a user attempts to query an object where he or she is not a member of the ACL, the query will return a response "query failed."

While the GC is not an overall part of the naming structure, it is the interface between the user of the system and system names and, therefore, an important part of the overall system. For all domain controllers, domains, and members of the tree (and forest, for that matter), there is a single GC that serves a particular Windows 2000 network.

Trust Relationships

Trusts also are not part of the naming structure in Windows 2000, but they do affect access to objects and object discovery, particularly because of legacy support for the Windows NT operating system. There are two kinds of trusts available under Windows 2000, transitive trusts and explicit trusts.

A *transitive* trust is defined as a pass-through trust, where once established allows a domain wide access to resources without the management of multiple two-way explicit trusts. This type of trust is created automatically when a domain joins a tree as a first- or second-level domain. The trust uses Kerberos authentication as the primary security method. Figure 6.6 shows a typical trust hierarchy in Windows 2000.

The second type of trust that exists in Windows 2000 is an *explicit* trust, and it is a carryover from Windows NT legacy. Despite the new features introduced with transitive trusts, they do not work with Windows NT; therefore, the explicit trust must be used. Outside of the domain tree, when a Windows NT domain is added to the tree, users may still browse resources in that domain (provided they have access

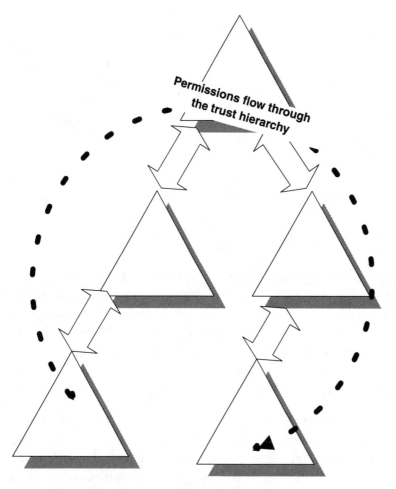

Figure 6.6 A Windows 2000 trust hierarchy.

and the trust is initiated in the right direction), although the domain is not part of the namespace.

Replication

Replication represents a critical system in Windows 2000 Active Directory; without it, changes to the directory would not be propagated to other domain controllers, domains, or other trees in the forest. This essential element is important because as names change at any point in the tree (e.g., the root or a branch) the changes flow down (or across) the entire hierarchical structure (across, as the case may be with a forest of trees) (see Figure 6.7).

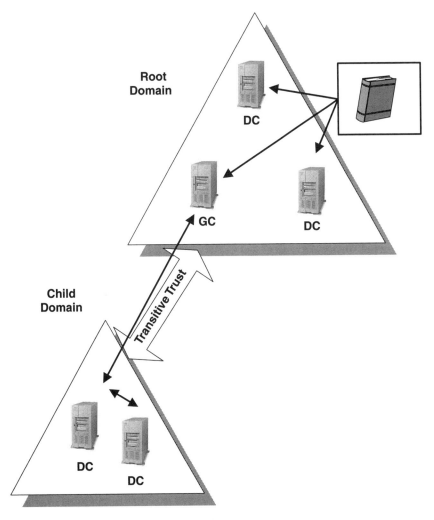

Figure 6.7   A typical replication scenario.

Propagation

The concept of propagation, defined as "the spreading abroad, or extension, of anything," is extremely significant when considered in terms of a hierarchy. Changes made to a parent container are replicated down to the lowest level beneath that object. Therefore, when a name changes at some level in the tree, all subsequent child objects are affected as well, and this must be true to adhere to the concept of a contiguous namespace. Keep this in mind when making any changes to directory objects. Figure 6.8 shows the effect that propagation has on objects in the directory.

Naming Conventions for Trees and Forests

A tree is defined as a set of one or more Windows 2000 domains that share a common schema, configuration, and GC, joined as a contiguous namespace. All domains are interconnected through a system of transitive, hierarchical Kerberos trusts. While a tree may include but a single domain or hundreds, the overall tree and all of its subcomponents are identified by a name. The tree name is always the DNS name given to the root of the tree (see Figure 6.9). The child objects below the root are always contiguous with this name to form the namespace hierarchy we have talked so much about. The DNS names of child objects reflect this as in our example in Chapter 3, "Preparing for an Active Directory Implementation," where we discussed Technelogic Corporation. The root domain is technelogic(.com). Within the company is a Marketing division that has a domain under the root, the child domain mktg. Mktg is known in the namespace hierarchy as mktg.technelogic.com.

The technology behind the namespace hierarchy is DNS; consequently, it is the reason we pay so much attention to DNS in this text. You do have choices as to what naming scheme you use when it comes to naming objects in the tree, although only one type may be used per tree. The classic "DC=" naming convention follows DNS naming structures and is less complicated to master. The more descriptive X.500 method is also available to you, and it may be a good choice if you are integrating Active Directory with other existing or planned X.500 directories.

The complexity that exists in marrying two disjointed networks is made somewhat easier with Windows 2000 networks through the concept of forests. Forests allow the union of two or more tree hierarchies with noncontiguous namespaces to form a single network that shares a

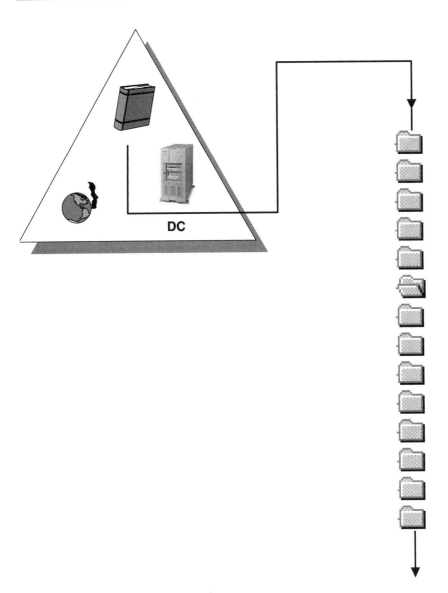

Figure 6.8 The effects of propagation.

common schema, configuration, and GC and are connected through transitive trusts. Despite these common elements, problems do arise from joining dissimilar namespaces.

The resulting disjointed namespace that stems from the union of two or more trees may hamper the intuitive usability of your network that you have worked so hard to create thus far. For example, because search mechanisms are dependent on a contiguous namespace, searching for objects in

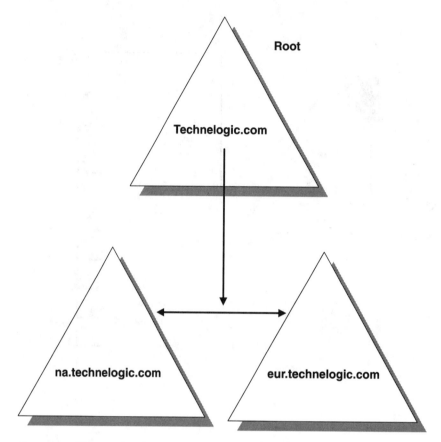

Figure 6.9 The Technelogic Corporation namespace.

the parallel tree will not return results. You must think of trees in the forest as peers; hence, a "forest" was used to symbolize this instead of a larger tree.

Internal and External Naming Strategies

Today's business climate is tightly integrated with the global network known as the Internet. Marketing, Electronic Data Interchange (EDI), electronic mail, fax, and electronic commerce are all examples of how companies use the Internet to improve business processes and stay competitive. When implementing a Windows 2000 network, it is important to make a distinction between internal and external networks and to further formulate a naming strategy for each.

Earlier in the book we discussed reserving a name for your company through the InterNIC in order to use that name as your current DNS root name, or if not connected the Internet, for future use. In actuality, depending on how heavily leveraged your company is in Internet technology and commerce, you may run two separate networks: one internal and one external. The reasons for maintaining separate networks, one private and one public, are primarily based on protecting your internal network from intruders. Network security is beyond the scope of our discussion, but we will assume that most companies are interested in some level of protection between their internal and external networks. There are two naming schemes that you may use, each with its own set of pros and cons. The first scenario describes the use of separate root names for each network.

Separate Namespaces

For this example, assume that Technelogic Corporation is heavily leveraged in Internet technologies and uses two distinct namespaces. The company offers EDI for order processing from customers, WWW and FTP servers, and an e-commerce site that sells products directly to the public. Technelogic maintains an internal and external network, and the two are separated by a firewall. These two networks are set up as separate entities and have two distinct root names (namespaces) to define each. The internal network is defined as tl.com, and the external root name is technelogic.com.

 The more descriptive name was chosen to represent the external network purely from a marketing perspective and to avoid a cryptic domain name for the company. This is not mandatory, and you may opt to call either domain anything you wish. It is, however, good business practice to have a clear and concise name to present to potential customers or business associates when accessing your Web resources. In the preceding example, the full company name drives more of an impact, delivering name recognition and reinforcement to the user of your system. The internal address tl.com is less descriptive, but is easier for day-to-day use for your internal users. It may be that the domain name(s) you want to use are already registered to another company. If this is the case, try to register names that are meaningful as possible.

Externally, there are five servers—"www", "ftp", "edi", "ns1", and "ecomm"—that exist in the domain technelogic.com:

- www.technelogic.com
- ftp.technelogic.com
- edi.technelogic.com
- ns1.technelogic.com
- ecomm.technelogic.com

Internally, there are a number of clients and servers including a domain controller, an intranet server, and a DNS server. Examples of these are:

- dc1.ml.com
- tlcweb.ml.com
- ns1.ml.com
- client1.ml.com
- client2.ml.com

Each side is separated from the other by a firewall, and each is an administrative island. Users on the internal network cannot access resources on the external network for security reasons. In this scenario, two DNS servers exist, one for each network. The main thing to remember here is the distinction of names between the two networks, both of which are registered by an Internet authority such as the InterNIC. Failure to preserve names with a registration authority could prevent internal clients from accessing the namespace on the Internet in the future. Figure 6.10 shows how this scenario might look. Notice the separate DNS zones and namespace.

Like Namespaces

The second option in setting up internal and external resources involves using the same namespace throughout both networks. Using the previous example, both internal and external resources would use the registered domain name technelogic.com. The difference between this model and the other is that internal clients may be allowed to access resources on the external network, although traffic from the Internet and the ability to resolve internal names would not be permitted. Using the same resources, as in the preceding example, the result would look something like Figure 6.11. Notice the different DNS zones for each network. This prevents internal name resolution by external resources.

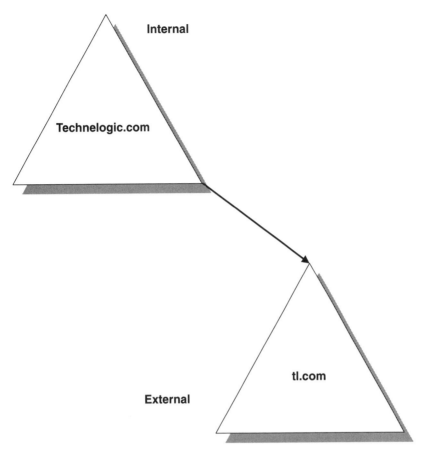

Figure 6.10   Separate internal and external namespaces.

Pros

Of course, any time you are presented with a choice, there are options you must weigh. Seldom is there a perfect fit. The following lists explain the advantages of each naming method to further help you understand how each differs from the other.

Advantages of separate namespaces include the following:

- Operational burdens are eased by having to administer two distinct resources that are clearly defined.

- Web browser support for Internet browsing is made easier as clients' access to the public network may be managed through exception lists.

- If a proxy server is used for Internet access, the distinction of the two names easily defines internal addresses.

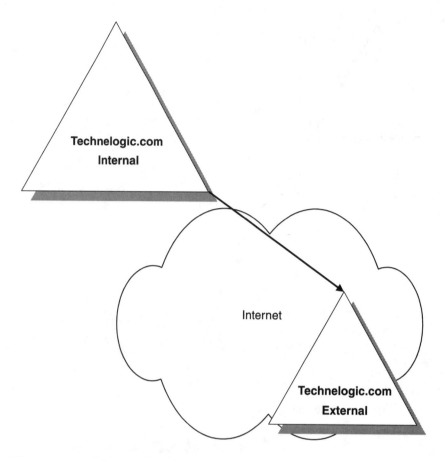

Figure 6.11   Like internal and external namespaces.

- There is a clear distinction between internal resources and external resources, which may help lock down resources and provide a more secure environment.

Advantages of like namespaces:

- The tree name is consistent throughout.
- Users may use the same login name as e-mail address (logon names in Windows 2000 are suggested to follow the format <user>@<domainname.com>).

Cons

There are also disadvantages to each of these naming systems. Review the following list to help you further decide which model will work in your given scenario.

Disadvantages of using different namespaces include the following:

- A level of complexity is added, as the logon name for users will differ from the e-mail address.

- Multiple names must be reserved and managed. Many companies will find that the name they want to use may be reserved.

- A separate workstation on the segment that houses public resources may be necessary in order to manage servers there.

Disadvantages of using like namespaces include the following:

- If your company uses a proxy server for Internet browsing functionality, using like names for both networks may complicate the configuration of the client. The client must be able to make a distinction between internal and external resources; for example, an intranet site versus an Internet site.

- Administrators must take extra care in distinguishing the internal and external networks when performing management tasks.

- Users must be able to distinguish between the private and public resources so as not to publish internal material to the public network.

Namespace Architecture

We have discussed the fact that some thought must go into the overall design of a Windows 2000 network due to directory replication issues and future and present organizational changes and growth. These design principles hold true for naming the infrastructure as well.

Windows 2000 domains consist of many different structural elements such as trees, domains, and organizational units. Your network may contain one, all, or thousands of these elements. In the following sections, we explore the concepts and practices that you should follow when designing the namespace, as well as scenarios and rationale behind each level.

The Domain Tree

Ideally, an Active Directory implementation will mimic in structure the corporate framework that makes up your company. Logically, then, the names given to different elements within the domain tree will also mirror the company's nomenclature. The overall design should include a combination of domains and OUs. If the design dictates the use of multiple domains, there will be the mandatory root domain, followed by first-layer and second-layer domains. As a rule, the first-layer domains should represent geographic or geopolitical boundaries.

The Root Domain

Perhaps the most important naming decision that you will make is giving a name to the root domain, the top of the namespace hierarchy, which represents the entire organization. It is important to note that we are considering an internal architecture here, and the directory should not be exposed to the external network for security reasons. The name given to the root should be registered with a naming authority like the InterNIC (www.internic.net owned by Network Solutions). The name chosen here reflects user logon names and Internet mail addresses. The root domain is an empty Active Directory domain and is used to establish the directory when creating the initial domain and explicitly for the directory namespace. This is true regardless of single- or multiple-domain implementations.

First-Layer Domains

Earlier in the book, we discussed the relevancy of planning for your new Windows 2000 network. That planning now pays off as you start developing the architecture. Depending on the size of your organization and other factors, Microsoft recommends naming first-level domains to represent a high-level overview of the company structure. If we use a geographic model as an example where first-level domains are represented as continents or regions, domains might be named "North America" (NAMER), "South America" (SAMER), "Asia" (PAC OR ASIA), "Europe" (EUR), and so forth. Second-layer domains may be used to further subdivide the domain hierarchy into countries or states. OUs may then be used to further divide the divisional units within those domains.

Second-Layer Domains

Second-layer domains are often called *child* domains and are used to further map out the structure of the company. These domains should represent further logical divisions of the first-layer domains. If you are following the suggested path of the organization following geographic dispersal, the next logical representative domains are named after countries, provinces, or states.

It is important to think and plan in terms of future growth when setting up domains, so be as descriptive as possible and try to avoid conglomerating too many regions or offices together. Changes to the structure after the fact will be very time and resource intensive. It may be helpful to use the ISO 3166 standard naming protocol for countries outside of the United States (a series of internationally standardized two-letter county codes) and U.S. postal codes for inside the United States.

 When using a combination of ISO 3166 standards and U.S. postal codes, be sure to distinguish between the abbreviation for Canada and California, which use the same representative letter combination.

 Many of you reading this may work in small to medium-sized businesses and feel that globalization is far out of reach for your company. Try to disregard this way of thinking and plan your domain structure today for tomorrow. Doing so will allow you to grow with minimal pain should the need arise. If you think that cannot happen, look at companies such as Dell Computer Corporation or Yahoo!.

Organizational Units

OUs are logical administrative units that function similarly to domains but are contained within the domain itself. For the most part, OUs should follow the same basic first-level and second-level implementation and naming guidelines as domains. While OUs may take the place of domains under certain conditions (discussed in Chapter 7), they are also used to further partition or subdivide domains. An example of the use of OUs to subdivide the "NAMER" domain might be to create OUs for "marketing" (MKTG), "research" (RES), "IT," "corporate" (CORP), and "sales." These logical units help to reduce the amount of replication traffic created by domains and may be administered and structured much the same way.

Domain and Divisional Naming Scenarios

To better understand how the namespace overlays the structural components of the directory, let's look at two scenarios of a well-planned architecture. Always try to plan your domain naming scheme with the hierarchy in mind. Future expansion is also key to success when planning a naming model. The first example we examine involves a large organization that spans several continents (see Figure 6.12). The ISO standards for naming are used here.

Notice the way in which all regions are represented by the first-level domains, and the countries within those regions are represented by the second tier. OUs or other child domains are used beneath the second tier to represent the divisions within those countries. Because the namespace represents the organizational structure of the company, the network is presented in a logical manner and is straightforward to use and administer. This model may have easily taken the wrong route, leaving way for administrative complications down the road. Figure 6.13 shows an example of the same namespace incorrectly planned, designed, and implemented.

Notice that there are "dead-ends" and a confusing naming structure.

In our second example the MeDeUm Corporation has set up a network that plans for the future needs of the company. It is presented

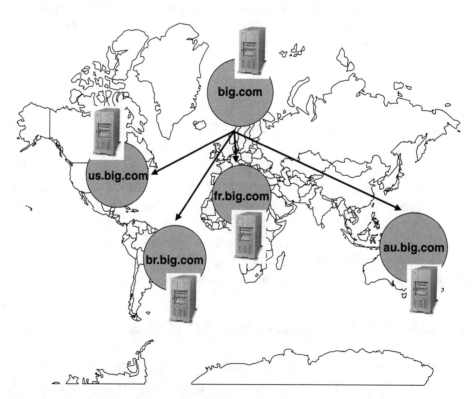

Figure 6.12 Big Corporation's namespace.

Figure 6.13 Big Corporation the wrong way.

in a clear and understandable way to users and administrators (see Figure 6.14). Notice that the same design principles hold true of first-level and second-level domains as was true in the previous example. This "open-ended" design leaves room for the company to grow and reduces the threat of a major outage to reconfigure the entire namespace from poor planning.

Naming Conventions in Active Directory

There are three different naming conventions used in with Active Directory: DNS, LDAP, and NetBIOS for legacy NT and Windows-based clients. By default, Active Directory uses LDAP as its naming standard to refer to objects in the directory. LDAP names are based on the X.500 naming standard of distinguished names (DNs) and relative distinguished

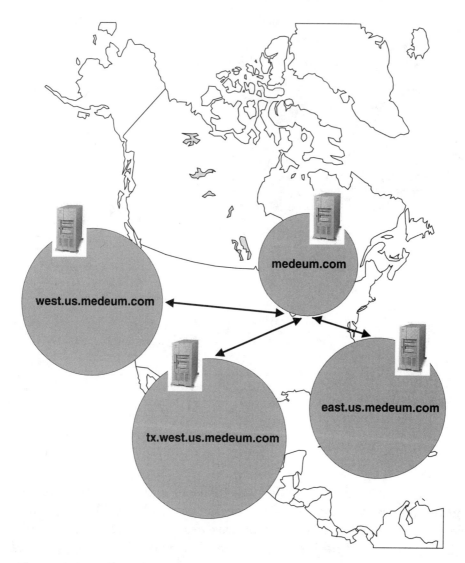

Figure 6.14 MeDeUm Corporation.

names (RDNs). Figure 6.15 shows the X.500 name tree and how DNs and RDNs are comprised from the tree structure.

LDAP Naming Conventions

An object is located through LDAP by its DN, which is comprised of a common name (CN) followed by representations of higher parent containers where the CN is a terminating object (often called a "leaf" of the tree). The DN is always a unique name that is identified by a combination

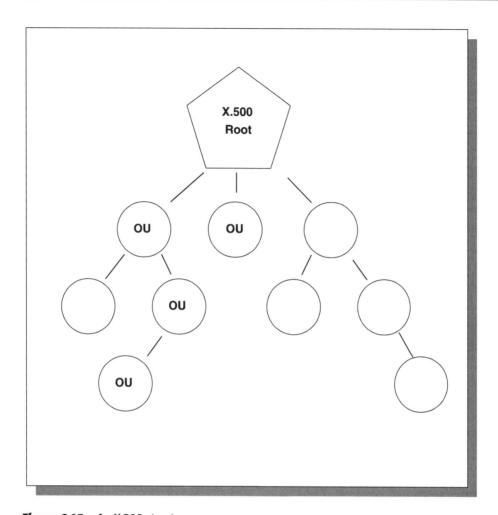

Figure 6.15 An X.500 structure.

of the domain and resulting containers drilled down to the terminating object. In LDAP naming, there are three components: the domain that holds other containers such as domains or OUs, the container that holds objects, and the resulting object. This nomenclature may drill down many levels in order to resolve the object name.

Take the user Bob Smith. The name "Bob Smith" is the CN of the object. That object exists in the "user" container in the directory. The user container is in the domain "technologic" and the root "com". The result looks like this to LDAP:

DC=com,DC=technologic,OU=users,CN=Bob Smith

This resulting statement is a path or directional statement to the object. Another way to think of a DN is a culmination of chained RDNs.

The RDN is really a complex name for the "actual name" of an object at any level, be it a container or terminal object. For example, in the preceding DN statement, the domain RDN is "technelogic", the RDN of the users container is "users".

For a list of other names that are often found in a Windows 2000 implementation, see the Glossary.

Best Practices

There are several rules of thumb that you should use to keep problems to a minimum when defining the Active Directory namespace. First, always use meaningful names to define the structural elements and leaf objects in the directory. It serves no purpose to implement a directory service for your organization if the resulting product delivers nothing but cryptic results. Try not to get into political battles over names. Stick to textbook naming schemes and model the name after your organization. Remember that naming and Active Directory structure go hand in hand, so it is important once again to plan carefully through this exercise.

Summary

Active Directory is based on the principal of names and uses names as the primary means of service and resource location. Naming begins with the creation of the root domain, a mandatory component of all Active Directory installations. From the root, there are infinite combinations of structural elements that may exist. Domains and OUs are the two main structural components. Giving these framework components meaningful names is critical to the overall success of directory functionality.

CHAPTER

7

Building the Network

INTRODUCTION

This chapter takes the concept of the domain learned in earlier chapters and describes the process of building a Windows 2000 network and Active Directory with these essential building elements. Topics in this chapter include:

- **Designing a Domain**
- **Organizational Units in the Overall Design**
- **Best Practices for OU Architecture**
- **Using Delegation in the Domain**

The domain is the core unit or building block of Active Directory and Windows 2000 beginning at the root domain. Active Directory is based on names, so it is important to have developed a naming strategy at this stage. By now, you should have a very good idea of how you are going to name the structure that you are about to architect. If not, I recommend that you review Chapter 6 as this and other chapters require that the namespace design be in place to grasp the concepts addressed.

This chapter addresses building individual domains and further subdividing domains using of organizational units (OUs). It is helpful to think of one domain that you named in the previous chapter, such as the North America domain. The concept of OU hierarchies and design is also addressed, as well as delegation of responsibility in domains. Throughout this chapter and future chapters we will use the Technelogic Corporation as an example. Figure 7.1 shows an example of the North American domain implementation for Technelogic Corporation.

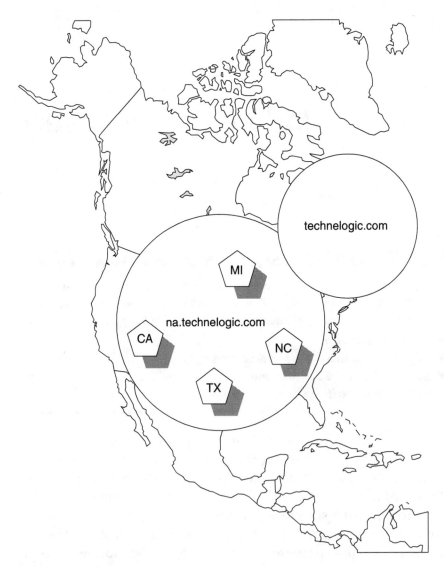

Figure 7.1 The North America domain from the Technelogic example.

Domains in General

There is a great deal of flexibility available when designing your domain with the introduction of OUs within the domain structure. The question then arises, "What criteria do I use to determine the necessity for creating a domain?" More on that subject in a moment. First, the idea behind the introduction of OUs is to avoid endless hordes of domains that can confuse resource management and users, as well as create a tremendous number of trusts to manage. We discuss OUs in detail later in the chapter. For now, keep in mind that OUs exist *within* domains and resemble a domain in that they are container objects that may or may not serve as parent (i.e., OUs can contain other objects or resources). Those of you from the old school of Windows NT should avoid the temptation to create needless domains and embrace and use OUs in the overall design of your network. Doing so will provide a more flexible mechanism for converting domains to OUs, should the need arise.

In order to properly map the design decisions from concept to physical structure and begin domain design, you should have a flowchart that outlines the framework of your company. From this framework, overlay your namespace for each level and you should be in good shape to begin in the process of creating domains. If by chance you bypassed the earlier chapters regarding Active Directory theory and design, or failed to properly map out an organizational structure and namespace, you are urged to do so now.

There is a mandatory domain that must first be created, the root domain. This defines the rest of the organization and serves as the hub for all Active Directory functionality. In larger implementations, it is ill advised to use this domain for creating OUs or adding any structural components. The first-layer domains (below the root) should be used for developing a domain hierarchy that defines the organization. When it comes to designing first-layer domains, you have a certain amount of flexibility in further subdividing domains, as OUs may be promoted to domains later. This model may be used by most organizations, regardless of size. If your organization is a small network comprised of one location and fewer than 200 nodes, a single (root) domain divided into OUs is acceptable, as the OUs may be promoted to first-level domains in the future (see Figure 7.2). On that note, let us further explore the reason for creating domains in the first place.

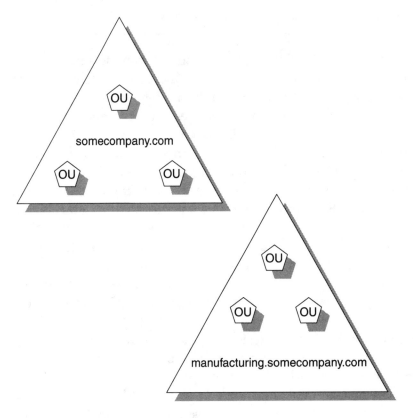

Figure 7.2   A simple domain model.

Factors That Constitute Domain Creation

In order to fully understand why you would create a domain, it is important to understand domains and domain functions within the Active Directory structure. In all Windows 2000 networks that implement Active Directory, there must be at least one domain, the root domain. This initial domain may take on more than one "domain" role depending on the size of your organization. First is the root Domain Name Service (DNS) domain, which defines the top of the namespace hierarchy. In our example of Technelogic Corporation, using the same internal and external naming, the root of the domain hierarchy would be technelogic.com. The second role the initial domain may play is through Active Directory, where the domain is a container for resources such as OUs.

Knowing that the first domain is mandatory, what about subsequent domain creation? Further creation of domains under the root is strictly a preference and should be based on answers to the following questions:

1. Do I have dispersed sites that may necessitate the creation of a domain?

   In many cases, larger sites located in other parts of the country or the world may need to exist within their own domains, handling their own administrative functions. This may stem from a need other than geographic, such as security (often, "corporate" domains that house data and applications of senior officers are islands of data with their own administrator). Domains act as natural security boundaries in Active Directory.

2. What about international locations?

   There is a special provision for multinational, multilingual support in Windows 2000 that makes deploying the international enterprise easier. However, it is unlikely that U.S. administrators will have the capability to support Japanese servers. In this situation, it is best to create separate domains to facilitate the language barrier.

3. My company has a dispersed IT department. How does this affect domain creation?

   In the case that the North American first-layer domain contains several large sites such as manufacturing or production that have their own administrative staff, a new child domain would be created to accommodate this.

4. Our company has a unique manner of managing resources. How does this affect domain creation?

   The administrative model that dictates the way a company manages business operations will have an overall effect on the number of domains and domain creation. Several example models provided by Microsoft are discussed later in this chapter.

There may be several more scenarios not listed that would involve the creation of a domain in your organization. If your company has the resources to do so, a "test" domain may come in handy for developing and deploying new applications to the enterprise. Large-scale mission-critical applications that have rigorous security standards such as SAP, BAAN, or PeopleSoft may need to exist in their own domains as well. Above all, decentralized organizations will reflect far more complex domain models than those that are centralized (see Figure 7.3). The most important thing to consider in the creation of these domains is their place in the Active Directory hierarchy. Once a domain is placed at the first or second level, removing it may be very labor and time intensive. Plan carefully and you can avoid this common pitfall.

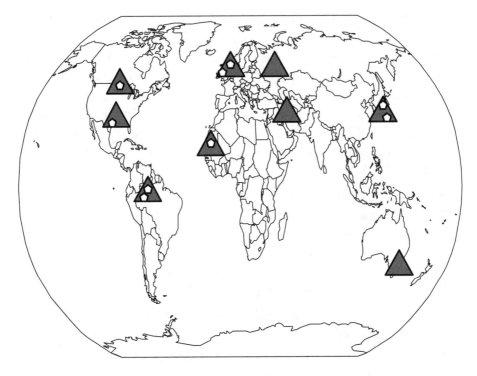

Figure 7.3 A more complex model showing globalization.

The Initial Domain

The most important component to an Active Directory implementation is the creation and naming of the *root domain* because all subsequent additions to the domain and forest will branch from this single point. In order to create the first domain, you should have an available DNS server from which name registration and resolution will occur. Additionally, you will apply the top of the namespace architecture here that you developed earlier. We discuss the hands-on steps of domain creation in the next section. For now, just remember that this is the top of the domain hierarchy as well as the namespace hierarchy (see Figure 7.4).

Organizational Units

There has been much talk of OUs to this point without a proper definition of what an OU is. OUs exists within the boundaries of a domain and provide structure to the domain by organizing logical groups of objects into manageable containers. An OU may represent many different types of

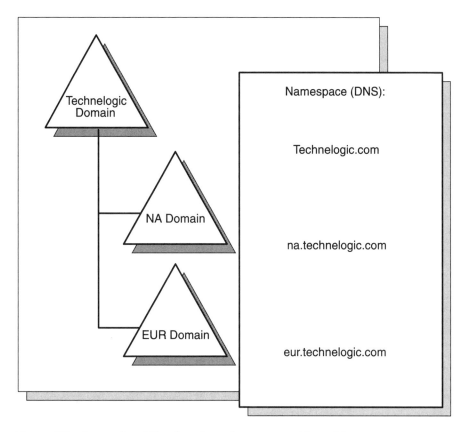

Figure 7.4   An overlay of the domain and namespace hierarchies.

object collections depending on the structure of your organization. For example, a school district will typically be very different in organization from the structure found in a government agency or a corporation.

OUs are similar in function to domains in that they contain a collection of objects manageable through the directory (see Figure 7.5). There are major differences, however, as outlined in Table 7.1. Think of an OU as an administrative unit or grouping, just as exists in your organization. The beauty of this model is that it allows the hierarchy and directory to mimic a company's structure, which benefits the user and administrative staff by presenting a familiar framework. Like domains, the OU is a container, and therefore holds domain objects such as users, groups, servers, workstations, printers, databases, security policies, and even other OUs. Moreover, an OU may hold more than one of the same type of object, such as a group. This comes in handy when applying different permissions to resources in the domain. Additionally, OUs do not require the overhead of a domain controller, or domain for that

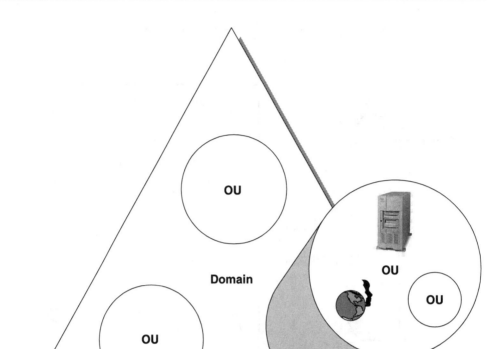

Figure 7.5 OU objects.

matter, which translates into cost savings for the organization. Replication is not an issue as it is with domains.

Choosing Domains or Organizational Units

Whether you choose to use domains or OUs anywhere in the hierarchy, it is always important to remember that the ultimate goal is to try to make the overall structure resemble the framework of your business.

Table 7.1 OUs versus Domains

OU	DOMAIN
Container	Container
Security Unit	Security Unit
Portable	Non-portable
May contain other OUs	May not contain other domains

When you are developing your model, think of every structural component as a hard-coded block of the structure. In thinking this way, the shape of the network will be static and you will avoid costly changes to the arrangement later. Certain models promote a concrete structure that we discuss later in the chapter.

There are also several key points to remember when deciding on an OU or domain. Always keep in mind that an OU can later be promoted to a domain, should the need arise. The following questions should help you decide which is right for your given situation:

1. Is there a need for greater administrative control?

   If your organization has local LAN administrators at remote locations, you may want to create OUs for those sites and delegate control to those individuals or groups.

2. Is there a need to group objects?

   Many organizations use contract labor. Grouping this type of user in an OU and applying the proper security and access to domain objects will help minimize the overall security risk.

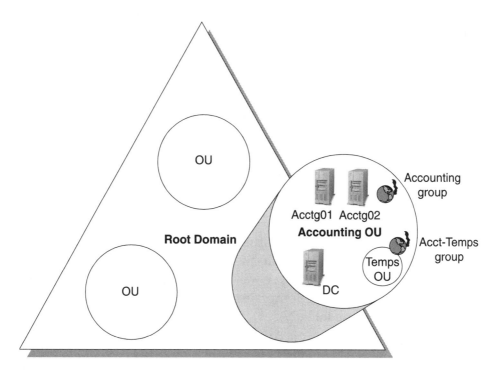

Figure 7.6 Grouping logical objects together.

3. Is there a need to reduce permissions to shares?

   As in Windows NT, managing resources can be a burden. Using OUs to group users and resources reduces the amount of permissions you have to apply to resources (see Figure 7.6).

4. Does the organization use or plan to use policies?

   When users or computers are grouped together in an OU, the administrator can apply a set of policies to that group of objects. An example of this might be restricting Internet access through the Proxy server.

5. Is my company migrating from Windows NT 4.0?

   NT 4.0 resource domains no longer require a separate domain; they can be migrated to Windows 2000 OUs with the same effect. This reduces hardware costs.

With the many benefits introduced to Windows 2000 by using domains, it is easy to lose sight of the reasons for creating domains in the overall structure. There are many situations that dictate the use of domains. It should be noted that domains differ from OUs in that they are a boundary of replication. Replication may affect network links adversely if traffic is heavy, and slow links will affect domain replication where objects and policies fail to replicate. So, when is a domain right for the framework being developed? Use the following questions to decide:

1. What are the security needs at each of my sites?

   Often there are segments of the company that are security islands. Examples of this are research departments or corporate servers that hold sensitive high-level data. These types of groups may need a domain and administrator of their own.

2. What is the projected growth of the company?

   It is important to keep the future of the organization in mind when developing a domain strategy. If first-level domains are poorly implemented today, the tree will be very difficult to build on later. We discuss different templates you may use in creating your domain structure later.

3. How large is my organization?

   Size matters when considering the choice between domains and OUs. If you work in a very large environment and you anticipate that more than 100,000 users or a million objects are a real possibility, then multiple domains are the only logical choice. While Microsoft has tested the preceding numbers, from a practical standpoint your numbers per domain will probably be less due to decentralized IT management and for feasibility reasons (see Figure 7.7).

 I often think of Microsoft Exchange in this situation. As server hardware continues to increase in power, Exchange can support thousands of users on a single server with information stores that exceed 50GB. Great, the company saves money on hardware and all the user mailboxes can be managed from one server.

This is always a poor choice in designing any system. First, there is a single point of failure, and second, if something catastrophic did happen, how would the server be recovered? Even DLT drives would take a considerable amount of time to recover the data.

The beauty of a distributed architecture is reducing the overall impact to the network should something catastrophic happen. Partitioning resources in this manner simply makes good sense.

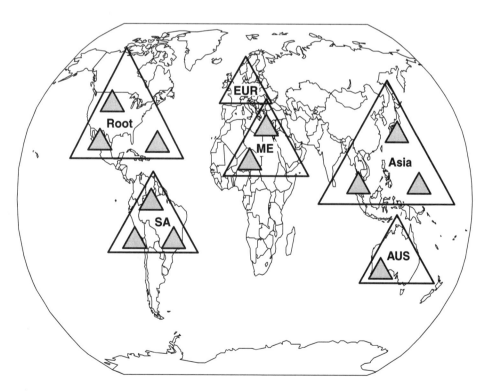

Figure 7.7   An example of a well-planned model for larger organizations.

4. What is the IT model in use?

More and more companies are decentralizing their IT departments, particularly if the company is large or geographically dispersed. In these cases, multiple domains are a necessity.

5. What link speeds exist between all company sites?

Replication of user data may play an important part in your decision to create separate domains for users that are long distances from each other or over slow links. If the Research arm is located in South America, Sales is in North America, and there is little interaction between the divisions, it may be prudent to group these users in their own domains.

6. Does the network span language boundaries?

Unless your IT department is multilingual, it is likely that the non-English speaking (or non-Spanish or non-German speaking, as the case may be) divisions will need a separate resource of their own.

7. Does a particular site have many users or many servers?

The size of a site and the number of users on the network may facilitate the need for a separate domain.

8. Are there servers that need to be grouped logically?

Mission-critical systems that require constant monitoring or attention as well as special security needs deserve a domain of their own. SAP, BAAN, or PeopleSoft are examples of such systems. Servers that run critical operations like plant management or medical systems are examples of this.

There is a tremendous amount of flexibility built into Windows 2000. This may be a new freedom for some and a menace to others. Try to refrain from getting too "loose" with your design. As a rule, focus on creating concrete elements in the hierarchy. If you need the maximum amount of flexibility in designing your framework, try using OUs, which can always be converted to domains later. There are also physical limitations that will affect domain implementation, which are discussed in detail in Chapter 14, "Customizing Active Directory Using the Schema."

 The following section discusses architectural aspects of OU design in the domain. OUs will follow a similar pattern or hierarchical flow as with domains where there should exist several tiers modeled after the structure of the organization. It must be noted that OUs may be stacked many levels deep, although this is ill advised due to performance and query issues.

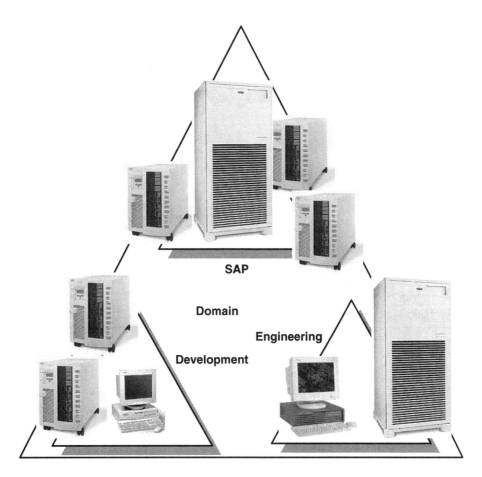

Figure 7.8 Resource division.

The Hierarchy and Organizational Units

Just as in domain creation, the establishment of an OU should be well-planned (see Figure 7.9). First-level OUs should represent concrete structures within the organization. Subsequent OU levels should drill down only two or three levels beyond the first, as deep-level OU hierarchies exponentially affect the overall performance of the Active Directory. OU hierarchies should mimic the structure of the organization, with higher-level OUs representing continents or broad views of the corporate structure. Microsoft has formed several example OU models that an organization might use to build a Windows 2000 network. While some organizations may find one of the following models a perfect fit, more complex organizations will use a mixture of these models to build their Active Directory framework.

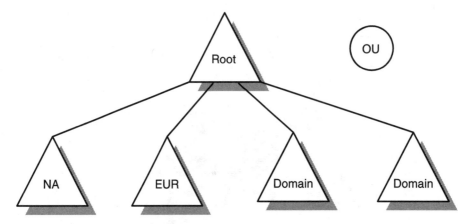

Figure 7.9 A hierarchy of domains compared to a hierarchy of OUs.

Planning the Organization of Organizational Units

Fortunately, as it is with domains, OUs should take on a hierarchical structure. Careful planning should be given to the name structure outlined in the previous chapter. It is also important to note that OUs may be islands of administration in the overall framework of the network through the use of delegation. First-level OUs should represent concrete structures that will not change. Second-level OUs and further should correspond to further divisions of the first-layer containers. Several models define business organization and are recommended by Microsoft when developing a strategy for Active Directory.

Six Organizational Models

No two companies are alike in structure; therefore, no two Windows 2000 networks will be the same. Certainly many companies that are heavily leveraged in Windows NT may have structured their networks into a flat or pseudo-hierarchical model to try to mimic the existing organization. Because Active Directory is based on a hierarchy, it may be difficult to visualize the current structure in a hierarchical manner. Indeed, many organizations may end up restructuring or reinstalling many areas of the network to migrate to Windows 2000. Chapter 18, "Upgrade Issues," goes into detail on upgrading from Windows NT.

In order to help simplify the process of creating a hierarchy, Microsoft recommends six models that will help to develop a hierarchy strategy that closely resembles the corporate structure. These models are based on proven business models that occur in almost any scenario commonplace to today's business climate. As a rule, a company should try to choose a model that is concrete in nature. That is, a model should be founded on principals that enact or anticipate future change based on political or business-unit scenarios that are constantly in a state of flux. These models include geographic, object-based, cost center, project-based, business unit, and administrative models. Of course, in the real world, one model will not fit every organization. Therefore, most companies will not use a model singularly, rather in conjunction with others to best define the company's structure and transpose it to the network. It may serve well to define the *current* network structure and gauge how close the existing structure is to what needs to be accomplished. The first model that we explore, and the founding principal of most Windows 2000 networks, is the geographic model.

Composed of structural elements, the geographic model is based on a company's geographic disbursement across regions, be they cities, counties, states, countries, or continents. It is important to note that a single (root) domain may encompass several high-level OUs that represent regions such as north, south, east, and west. The next level under these may represent cities within those regions, and subsequent levels may represent offices in those cities. This model has the benefit of remaining static (these boundaries likely will not change), and resources are easily cataloged by region. While the geographic model (see Figure 7.10) may seem well suited for most situations, it does not actually imitate corporate structure; therefore, used alone, it could induce confusion to users of the network. The geographic model is well suited for structuring high-level directory objects such as domains and OUs. As we will see, the geographic model used in conjunction with other models is an effective and easy-to-manage way to deliver a network topology to the user community.

Many modern companies use the concept of business units to define their organization, and this is well suited as a model for Active Directory implementation. However, this is dependent on the size, locale, network, and how geographically dispersed the company may be. Business units within an organization refer to divisions within the company such as sales, marketing, IT, corporate, and so on. The business unit model works very well in conjunction with the geographic model, where first-level containers represent geographic domains or OUs and second- or third-level containers represent business units or company divisions. The model that will often be used without any forethought is the business unit model, mainly because of the way it ties into the organizational model of the

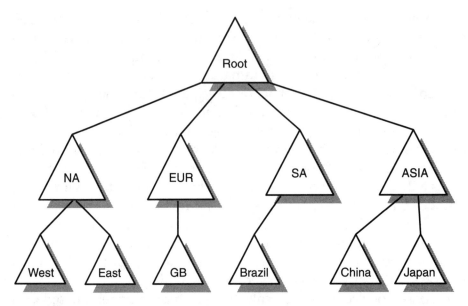

Figure 7.10 An example of the geographic model.

company. Thus far we have discussed how the Windows 2000 Active Directory should mimic the infrastructure of the organization. When discussing design theory as it pertains to Active Directory, however, it is important to note that considering reorganization is just as important in the overall design considerations (unless your IT department likes spending nights and weekends tearing down domains and rebuilding them). Figure 7.11 shows what a business unit model might look like.

An administrative model dictates many organizations, at least from an IT perspective. In this model, the structural components of the network are organized in such a way that the model represents the way that the network is managed, and not so much after the organization itself. Figure 7.12 gives an example of this type of framework. This model is somewhat common in many organizations where the corporate IT department is the top of the structure and domains beneath are child domains. Those familiar with the single master model under NT will find the two somewhat similar in structure; however, management of the directory and directory objects is very different in Windows 2000.

The way companies do business is ever-changing; one seen more frequently is a model based on projects that the company is involved in. Though not a purely static model, the project-based model works well for companies that are involved in long-term contracts with customers

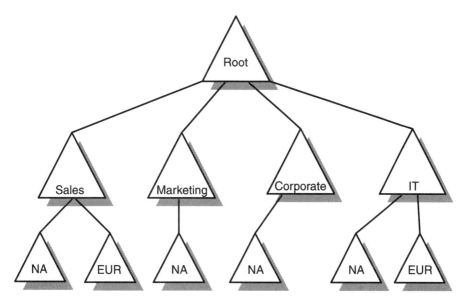

Figure 7.11   The business unit model.

or are based on service offerings for clients. As we see in Figure 7.13, the project-based model is structured like other examples, but the OU represents specific projects that the company is involved in. Organizations that provide IT outsourcing such as EDS or KPMG might find this model attractive to keep track of expenses throughout the life cycle of the project. However, when the project is completed, structural components may have to be torn down and rebuilt, causing administrative overhead.

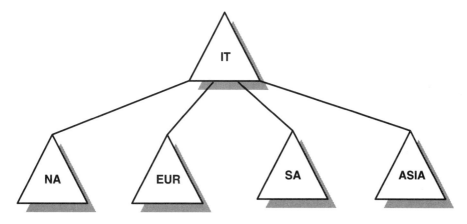

Figure 7.12   Administrative model.

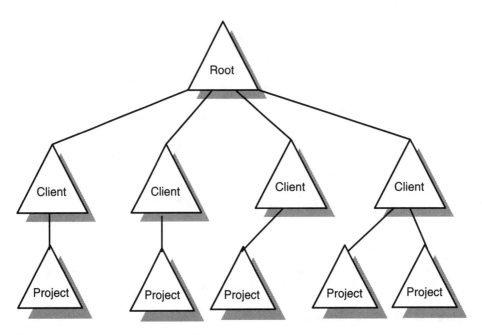

Figure 7.13   Project-based model.

The cost center model may be used favorably when an organization needs to model the network after divisions that are based on the billing framework of the organization. An advantage to this model comes into play when these divisions need to manage their own resources, such as in a decentralized organization. In a decentralized model, such as the project-based scenario, problems may arise when users from other structural groups need to access resources in one or many other domains or OUs. It is therefore advisable to devise a plan for this contingency before implementing such a scheme. Figure 7.14 demonstrates how a cost center model might be arranged.

Finally, the object-based model is an Active Directory structure that is not really based on a business structure at all; rather, it is based on directory objects where key objects are assigned to high-level containers (see Figure 7.15). When we use the term "key elements" we refer to "users," "groups," and so on. From an administrative standpoint, this model eases resource management and assignment of permissions to objects while allowing greater flexibility in the event of reorganization. Downlevel components may then further reflect geographic divisions.

It is important to note again that there is no one right model for most organizations. In most cases, a combination of one or several of these models may be needed to reproduce your specific organizational tree. Use the information from the planning stages to work out the

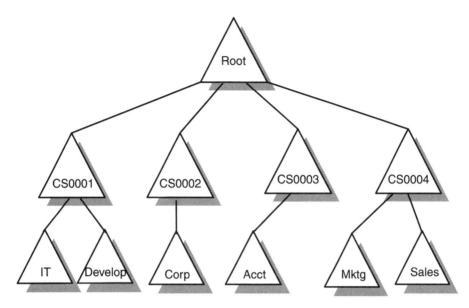

Figure 7.14 Cost center model.

best fit. In order to head off future administrative burden from having to restructure domains and OUs, it is paramount that the structure be developed and implemented correctly on the first pass. Doing so will also avoid confusion in the user community when accessing resources on the network.

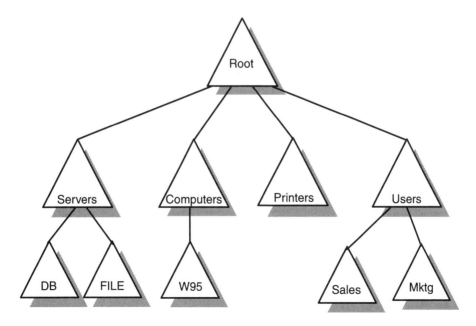

Figure 7.15 Object-based model.

If there was one combination of models that would fit the bill for most organizations, it would be described as geo-political, where first-level domains implement the concrete structure of geographic boundaries and then further subdivide to business unit or political structures (domains or OUs). This combination model represents the strength of a boundary model at the higher level where it is most important, as changes to these structures affect all of the child objects beneath it. Try to work this out on paper or with a visual drawing program such as Visio to iron out the specifics for your organization.

What Is Delegation?

Whether your organization has two servers in a single domain or multiple domains with thousands of users and millions of objects in the directory, the concept of delegating authority will be useful in most organizations to alleviate or disseminate administrative functions to others in the company. In a smaller organization, a higher-ranking employee in the Accounting division might act as the administrative authority for a set of resources that are defined for the Accounting department. In larger organizations, delegation of resources may encompass entire high-level OUs such as North America or Asia, and administrative responsibility will typically be a true administrator. In any case, it is important to mention that discussion of delegation as a whole within this unit applies to organizational units and not domains (see Figure 7.16).

Domains are islands of security within the hierarchy, and delegation of a domain is typically handled by adding groups or users to the global group domain administrators to that domain. By default, the administrators group of one domain is not given rights to other domains in the hierarchy in order to tighten security between them. Why is this useful? The most noted example might come in the creation of a domain that carries extremely sensitive information like that found in R&D, legal, or accounting data. The creation of such a child domain would have its own security for administrators, and root-level administrative functions could be added later if necessary.

Traditionally, there are two different administrative models that an organization may use to manage the network: centralized and decentralized. Do not confuse this with the organizational models discussed earlier. Administrative models dictate the way network resources are managed and by whom. These two models may be associated with

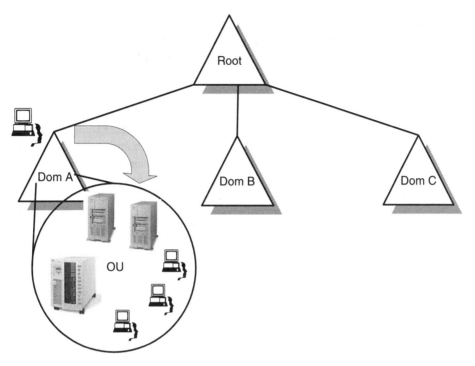

Figure 7.16   Delegation of resources in a typical domain.

tight administrative control or loose administrative control as well; the loose association is often paired with a decentralized environment.

A centralized administrative model is one in which a single group is in charge of security and administration of network resources. Centralized administration is best used in situations where it is imperative that security and administrative duties are maintained and performed by the IT department or some other trusted group. Alternatively, a decentralized administrative model may have several administrators or multiple IT departments that are responsible for their own resources. In a widely distributed enterprise, this model may be implemented in such a way that each geographic location or business unit has its own IT department in charge of local OUs, yet the entire network is interconnected and functions as a single unit.

Again, as all organizations are different, so will be the way the network is managed. There is no right way or wrong way, although the easiest to implement and support from an initial standpoint is a centralized model with a later progressive move toward a mixed model should your situation dictate the need. In medium and large enterprise networks, a strategy of a centralized IT department stationed with the corporate office with a series of LAN administrators at remote locations works quite well. In such

Looking back at Windows NT and the four domain models, the "single master" is a good example of a centralized model where all security and administrative management functions took place through the master domain. The "multiple-master" model leans more toward a decentralized model and further, the "complete trust" model is an example of a completely decentralized example (see Figure 7.17).

It may be common in larger organizations to use a combination of centralized and decentralized models to manage the enterprise, as was true in legacy NT networks. In networks that are migrating to Windows 2000 and Active Directory where both Windows NT and Active Directory exist, it may be beneficial to manage legacy systems through a decentralized model until the entire network is absorbed into Active Directory.

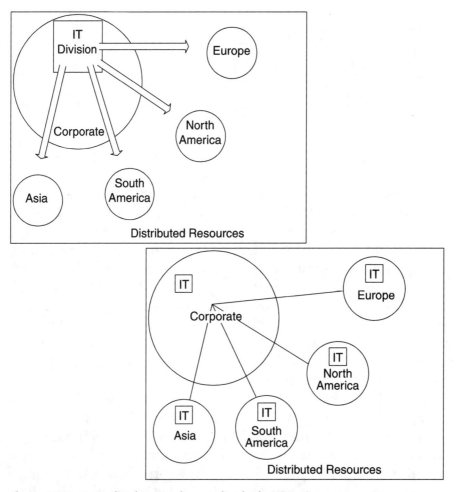

Figure 7.17   Centralized versus decentralized administration.

a model, the distributed administrators should hold to a policy where major changes are added by the main IT department. Tasks such as user or group creation pose security risks if permissions are not properly set and should be left to experienced IT staff, but arbitrary resource management would be left to the local administrator.

Delegated Responsibilities

Just like simple read/write permissions granted to a file system tree, delegation of read/write authority for permissions to resources within OUs is granted by an entity such as an administrator to another individual. This person may be dubbed a "low-level administrator" or "workgroup administrator" over the resources within that particular OU or the OU hierarchy. The user or group delegated to administer a set of resources may possess as many or as few rights as the domain administrator chooses to grant, or may opt to grant total administrative access to the user or group and remove the domain administrators from the ACL altogether. Once delegated, the newly delegated authority might then have the ability to grant or revoke permissions to resources such as databases, printers, or files that exist on file servers in the OU.

Many larger, decentralized businesses already use this management model and have these delegated authorities report to a larger, centralized corporate IT department. This presents many advantages to managing large, dispersed networks, including cost savings from having a person in a dual role on site and keeping corporate IT staff travel to a minimum. Further, delegating administrative tasks outside of the "central" IT department frees up time to allow for new product research and testing, and projects like network design, planning, and documentation. In later chapters, we actually go through the motions of assigning resources and delegation using Console tools. See Figure 7.18 for a further illustration of this type of resource delegation.

Beyond acting as a domain administrator a person or group may be delegated to oversee an OU that is functioning much like a resource domain like those commonplace in previous versions of Windows NT. Often these domains contained logical groups of services such as messaging servers or database servers. These specialized resources require an administrator with a thorough knowledge of the product and operating system expertise. In enterprise networks where there are thousands of printing resources, Internet resources, or remote access

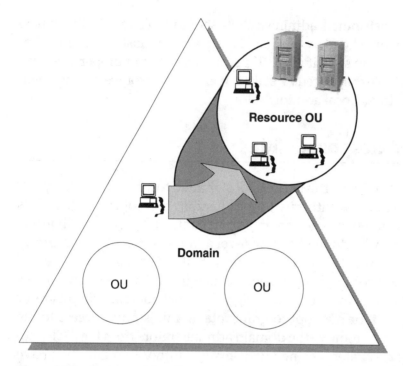

Figure 7.18 Resource delegation.

services, these same logical groupings may exist, and administrative functions will need to be delegated as well. Figure 7.19 shows an example of departmental delegation where a group such as accounting oversees the administrative functions of the OU.

Best Practices

The building blocks of a Windows 2000 network consist of domains and, at a lower level, OUs. The decision to use one over the other should follow some basic principles.

Domains should be created with several factors in mind:

- Security
- Replication
- Migration issues (discussed later in the book)

Many larger, distributed organizations will no doubt choose domain creation to define security policy throughout these dispersed sites where local security is maintained by a local IT group. Additionally,

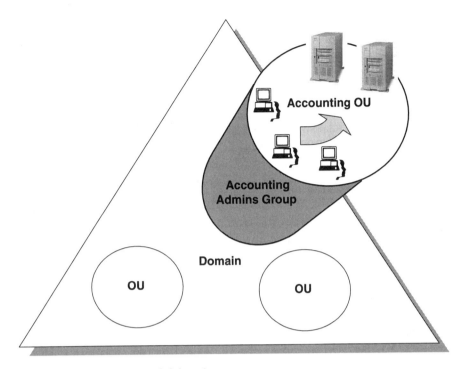

Figure 7.19 Departmental delegation.

domain creation may be used in architecting a Windows 2000 network to limit replication traffic over wide area links that may be metered for bandwidth usage. The use of sites can help in the overall strategy in these instances as well, and it is discussed in detail in the next chapter.

OUs were introduced to help ease administrative control and bring meaning to the overall structure of the Active Directory hierarchical structure.

OUs should be created when:

- Directory structure is critical
- Delegated administration is desired
- Resource management is critical (OUs may replace legacy "resource" domains)

In the case of both domains and OUs, it is paramount to consider the depth to which these structural elements are implemented. Deep structures will seriously affect directory performance and are directly related to CPU load. Deep structures also produce elongated naming structures, such as jsmith@it.seattle.northwest.na.technelogic.com. This can become extremely confusing after eight levels or so! As a rule, considering the CPU load alone, domain or OU hierarchies should not exceed 10 levels.

Summary

In this chapter, we discussed the two elements that make up the primary structure of a Windows 2000 network: domains and OUs. Domains and OUs may exist as a hierarchy or in any combination that best fits the organizational structure of your particular company. Microsoft suggests using concrete structures; in other words, structures modeled after a structure that has little tendency to change, as first-level structures. Microsoft also suggests using a combination of the six structural models to mimic the Active Directory tree and domain structure. These structures may exist in centralized or decentralized environments, and creation and use of both domains and OUs is strictly "open" to the system architect. Lastly, OUs represent a unique presence in the Microsoft server operating system family, helping to ease administration through the use of delegation, while adding structure and meaning to the overall directory structure. In the next chapter we use the concept of domains to bring to light the architectural aspects of domain design and replication, and the use of *sites*.

Directory Traffic Considerations and Management

INTRODUCTION

The way that domain controllers interact through the process of replication is yet another consideration for careful planning when structuring domains and your Windows 2000 network. Replication traffic may be controlled with sites and site connectors, and there are issues such as domain controller placement that will affect replication topology as well. In this chapter, we delve into the uncharted territories of domain functionality and the concept of replication, and controlling that replication process with the creation of *sites*. Topics discussed in this chapter include:

- **Domain Replication**
- **What Is Replicated between Domain Controllers**
- **Site Definition**
- **Site Elements**
- **Domain Controller Placement**

Domains are structural elements of a Windows 2000 network that act as a "logical partition" within an Active Directory structure for security and replication. Replication occurs between domain controllers throughout the directory tree to facilitate changes that occur to objects contained within. For example, when a password is changed on an account, the change is replicated throughout the hierarchy to each domain controller and Global Catalog Server (GCS) in the tree. The concept of directory replication is not new to the Windows NT line of operating systems. In previous versions of the operating system, the Primary Domain Controller (PDC) replicated information contained in its Read/Write SAM to Backup Domain Controllers (BDC) in order for logon and security information to remain consistent across the domain.

This very same behavior is resident in Windows 2000 domains, although more prevalent between Windows 2000 domain controllers. In the new domain model, there are no primary or secondary entities, as all domain controllers possess a read/write copy of directory information. There are, however, differences in the type and amount of information that is passed between domain controllers, as well as the way it is passed or replicated, depending on how domains are logically grouped.

As discussed in previous chapters, Windows 2000 is well suited to work with your existing network topography, especially in the case of wide area network (WAN) links. Many companies are heavily leveraged when it comes to such interconnectivity with all of the remote offices, branches, divisions, or different aggregates that may comprise the whole. Such links, particularly in international locations, are very costly, as are the equipment and staff to support them. This is particularly true in the case where links use a bandwidth on demand or data quotas. The ability to manage resource traffic over such links would be a powerful ally to IT managers and network engineers alike.

Because of the amount of information required to be sent between domain controllers, and considering the overhead that wide area links must maintain with regard to this information, Microsoft implemented the concept of *sites* to logically group structural elements. Connected by high-speed local area network (LAN) technologies, a *site* is defined as a set of IP subnets connected by high-speed network links. It is important to understand that a single domain may encompass many subnets, and so then logically may a site (see Figure 8.1). Within these sites, all replicated information is performed quickly and automatically. When more than one site exists, usually distinguished by a WAN link between the two, the two sites are connected via a *site connector*, a

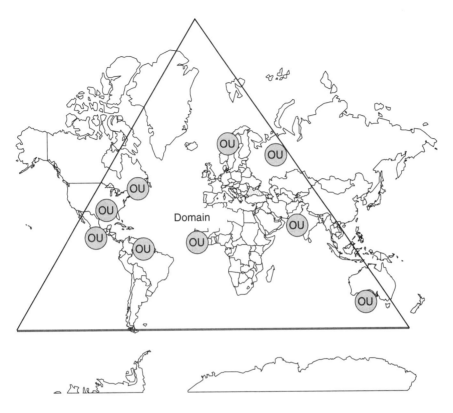

Figure 8.1   A single domain that spans geographic boundaries.

kind of gateway or bridgehead that allows the replication to be controlled through scheduling mechanisms. When scheduled during off-hours or off-peak usage, a site connector can be a very effective tool for load balancing replication traffic between domain controllers. First, it is important to understand what transpires during domain replication, and why such measures are necessary and important in regard to Active Directory.

In order to better understand the information in this chapter and how it applies to your given situation, gather the data recorded earlier that pertains to the physical network itself. A network map that outlines the physical network architecture will aid in visualizing key replication strategies. Additionally, wide area link utilization data should be available to further justify replication decisions. Future growth may also affect the overall outcome of the design.

Network Traffic Considerations

A number of traffic considerations affect the design of domains and sites:

- Replication traffic (directory data)
- Logon (authentication) traffic
- Query traffic
- Network utilization (user/application data)

All three types of traffic affect the overall design of the network. While the use of sites alleviates directory replication issues and logon traffic issues, it does not address the other two, though replication traffic may affect the overall performance of a network link. First then, a discussion of replication and replication traffic patterns, and controlling replication with sites.

Replication

In order for the directory to be unified and conjunct across all boundaries and links, there must be a facility to pass information from one domain to the other. Why is this? The answer lies in what a domain is, particularly in relation to the Active Directory. Domains are structural elements that function as units of replications, islands of resources that have a natural "border," if you will. Each domain and, ultimately, domain controller, is responsible for the information on directory objects contained within the domain itself. A domain controller would have no way of knowing about resources beyond its own boundaries without a vehicle to assist in passing along this information.

Enter domain replication. All domain controllers within a domain replicate information to one another regarding changes to objects in the directory. Again, this could mean anything from permissions, to new objects, to name changes. This matter is further complicated by the fact that domains may reach beyond the high-speed network of the local building across the city, or leased lines may interconnect separate domains across the globe. If directory information cannot successfully replicate across these links, the net result ends in users, services, or systems that cannot authenticate or access other objects on the network. Figure 8.2 illustrates a typical replication scenario.

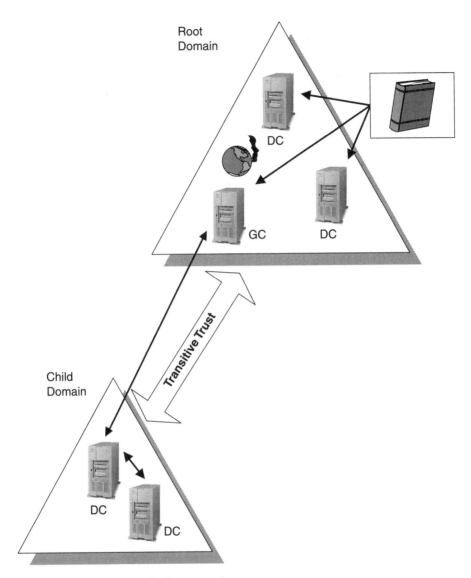

Figure 8.2   A typical replication scenario.

Considering the often geographically dispersed characteristics of most corporate networks, and the links that interconnect these offices, a method for controlling this replication traffic was necessary to overlay the domain model. So, the concept of the *site* was introduced in Windows 2000. In reality, this concept was first adopted in the Microsoft Exchange product several years ago and is based on X.400/X.500 directory standards. As in Windows 2000, connectors between Exchange sites are implemented to pass directory information about users and public folders across network boundaries. Servers within the same site automatically establish connectors, and an administrator creates connectors between different sites to control the replication.

Client logon is facilitated through the Active Directory (see Figure 8.3). Therefore, in order for clients to access objects throughout the network, directory information must be present and consistent on a global level. Replication provides the mechanism that allows logon and SAM information to disseminate all through a Windows 2000 network to every domain controller, allowing the directory to act as a whole. When users log on to

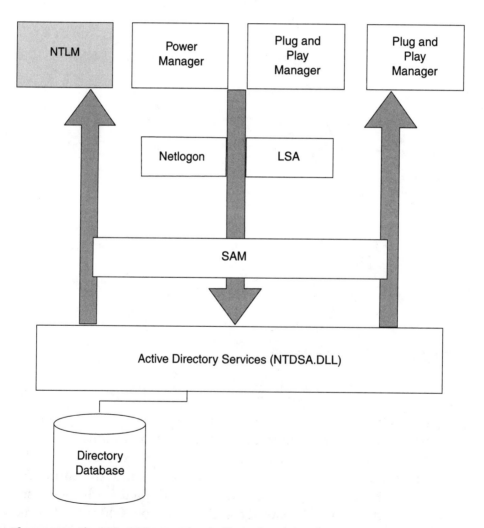

Figure 8.3   The LSA architecture that facilitates logon for native and down-level clients.

the network, the workstation attempts to locate a domain controller (and a GCS) to authenticate the logon. The local domain is the first place clients attempt this act. Upon failing to locate a local domain controller, the workstation will attempt to find another domain controller to validate the logon. Additionally, once authenticated, the user of the workstation may need to locate and access accounting information located in another domain. The ability to do this is in part facilitated by replication.

What Information Is Replicated by the Directory?

Active Directory in any implementation has at least one *domain naming context* otherwise known as a *partition*, which is physically held at each domain in the forest. Partitions represent a unit of replication in the Active Directory tree. Each domain that exists is authoritative, or responsible for, a replica of the domain's naming context, which consists of three types of information:

- Directory object information (naming contexts)
- The replication topology
- The schema

Additionally, each domain tree has a single domain controller within the organization that acts as a GCS used for query support across domains. Information stored on this server is gathered from replica data passed throughout the directory structure by domain controllers. GCS is discussed in depth later in the chapter.

The naming context of the domain consists of the actual container objects that exist in the local domain directory and their respective nomenclature. This information is used in locating directory objects through the use of names. Examples of these containers are:

- Users
- Groups
- Computers
- Organizational Units (OU)

Management of these objects is handled through the Active Directory Users and Computers Console discussed in later chapters. Figure 8.4 shows a typical ADUC console in action.

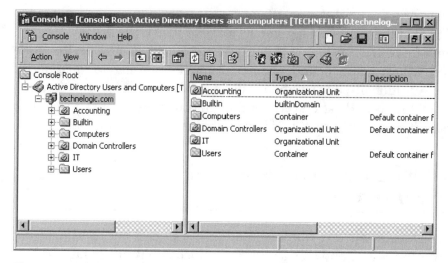

Figure 8.4 The Active Directory Users and Computers Console manages container objects such as users and OUs.

To understand the naming context better, assume that two domains exist in a tree: the parent domain and a child domain. The parent domain is technelogic.com and the child domain is na.technelogic.com. The naming context used to define the "users" container of the parent domain is technologic.com/Users, and in the child domain, na.technologic.com/ Users. The two names are unique within the contiguous namespace of Active Directory. Figure 8.5 illustrates how the naming context looks under the properties page of a user object.

The second data set held in each domain contains configuration information about the directory itself, such as sites, services, and domain controllers. This replica information is used to define the local domain replication topology to all domain controllers both in and outside the domain.

Last, each domain contains a replica of the schema information particular to the domain. Schema information defines (leaf) object attributes that are available in the directory. A leaf object is considered an object at the end of a branch that cannot be further subdivided. Examples of this are users, printers, and so forth.

To further complicate the replication picture, each domain houses a GCS (usually the first domain controller created in the domain), which functions to tie in directory information from the entire forest, and contains a partial replica of all domains' replica information (see Figure 8.6). This service helps to tie in the functionality of the forest and forest-wide

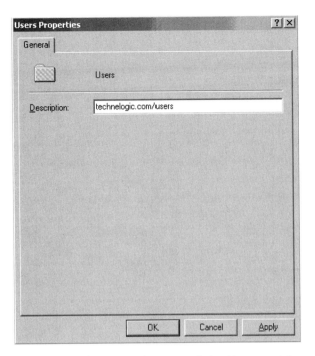

Figure 8.5 The Properties page of the Users container showing the container naming context.

access and query functions by allowing all domains within a contiguous namespace to share the same schema information.

Perhaps the most important of all the information replicated throughout the directory is that contained in the security accounts database. Logon information for users and services and Access Control Lists (ACLs) for resources are all published throughout the directory. Indeed, the very existence of the network and the resources contained within are built on this foundation, and without the proper replication of security information across the directory, access would surely fail. With this in mind, it is a straightforward assumption that directory replication services are a core necessity of Active Directory and the overall function of network services (see Figure 8.7).

Replication Topology

Replication takes place on a polling interval where sequence numbers are used as markers to check that each domain controller has the most current information. If out of date, the domain controller will request an

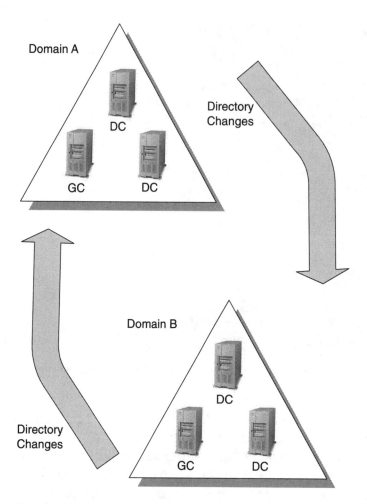

Figure 8.6 Domain replication data.

update with its replication partner, of which it has two for fault tolerance should a domain controller become unavailable. The automated creation of the topology managed by the Knowledge Consistency Checker (KCC) replication topology forms a round-robin approach to replication patterns, in a way like token passing on a Token Ring network.

As the domain (and forest) grows with the addition of new domain controllers, the replication topology will also change, particularly with the added complexity of implementing site boundaries and multiple domains. Built into the operating system is a program that determines the best case routing scenario for a given topology, the KCC. When new domain controllers are added to the domain tree, the KCC will check

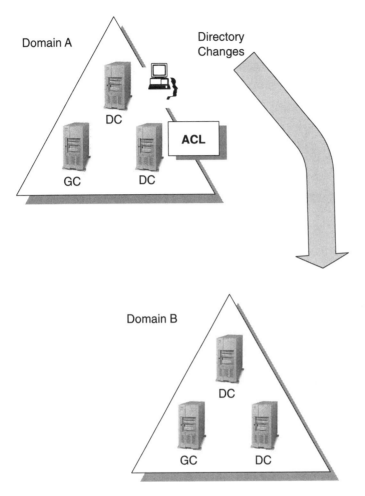

Figure 8.7   Replication of directory security information is a key component of Active Directory and Windows 2000 functionality.

the "cost" assigned between each link and adjust the replication pattern appropriately. The KCC also creates more connectors between domain controllers in the same site to add fault tolerance to the structure, where fewer connections between sites are used with package compression to maximize effectiveness (see Figure 8.8).

The issue of manually implementing a site connector does affect the overall replication topology. The topology must be adjusted to accommodate the new site link. It is important to note that the KCC is still instrumental in implementing the overall strategy regardless of implementation of site connectors. Site connectors allow the scheduling

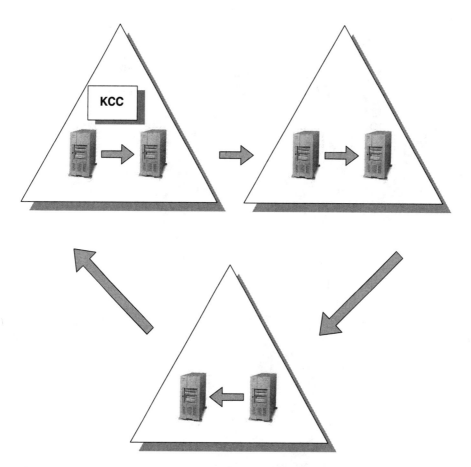

Figure 8.8 The KCC automatically adjusts site replication topology.

of directory replication between IP subnets that have been defined as sites to the directory and are further discussed later in the chapter (see Figure 8.9).

Windows 2000 Sites

The use of sites to control directory replication in Windows 2000 dictates an inherent understanding of the underlying network topology and the TCP/IP addressing scheme that describes each of the network subnets from the backbone to the dial-on-demand router that connects remote offices. In very complex scenarios, it will be crucial to employ the help of infrastructure administrators and architects to design the site replication topology. In smaller implemen-

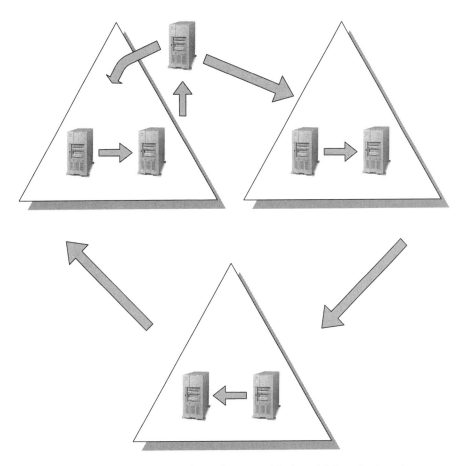

Figure 8.9 Site replication topology changes with the addition of other sites.

tations, a thorough knowledge of the physical network and TCP/IP is invaluable.

It is easy to confuse the concept of sites with the concept of domains and/or tree structure. While sites handle issues related to domains and trees, the two are completely independent entities. A site is more closely related to the underlying network and routing of a network. Wide area links are the starting point in defining site boundaries, and these boundaries are further decided on link size, consistency or reliability, and utilization. Multiple domains are not a prequalification for a site boundary, nor is a single site a disqualification for the need to implement sites. Rather, the most basic defining factor in site creation is simply a slow network link, one that may prevent directory replication from ordinarily occurring. A single domain may span several of these wide area links. Conversely, geographically dispersed domains may be interconnected by sufficient network bandwidth so there is no need for separate sites.

The concept of controlling replication should be thought of not only at the domain level, but also at the domain controller level, where each domain controller is in its own right an island of replication. So you see, replication takes place between domain controllers in the same domain and occurs throughout the Active Directory hierarchy between domains, thereby maintaining consistency throughout. These two distinct types of replication in Windows 2000 are known as *inter-site replication* and *intra-site replication*. Where domain controllers or domains exist on the same LAN or are connected via a high-capacity leased line (we'll discuss that in a minute), replication should not be a concern. Figure 8.10 shows a poorly planned site configuration.

Sites are created and managed through the Active Directory Sites and Services console, which is located in the Administrative Tools group. From this console, the whole replication topology is managed. Monitoring the site replication on a per-server basis is performed through the Performance Monitor console using the NTDS performance object. Monitoring the Inbound sync, Sync requests, KCC reads and writes, and Sync request successful performance counters on remote domain controllers should give a good indication of a healthy or sick system.

What merits the creation of a site is unfortunately not as simple as segmenting the replication topology in every instance there is a WAN link. Microsoft claims that a 99/1 model should be used to determine the replication issues; that is, 99 percent of the traffic to domain controllers will be query information, and 1 percent will be updates. This may or may not be accurate, and as of the writing of this book there was no data to support this model. The only way to really justify this is to perform intensive testing with the aid of a network sniffer. Site creation should be determined by several factors concerning wide area connections. First, what size is the link? If the entire network is connected by T1s, the creation of sites may be a nonissue. Again, this might not suffice either. To further complicate the link issue, if the links are sizable but utilization is at or near capacity during business hours, it is possible that replication will fail and segmentation is necessary. Figure 8.11 illustrates a well-planned site topology and replication system. Without a solid plan, replication may fail and then will user and service logons across the network.

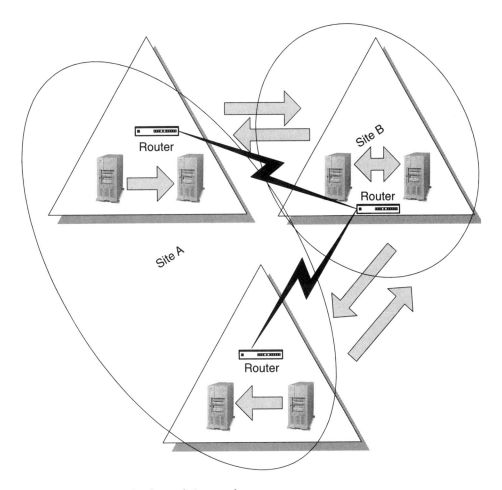

Figure 8.10   A poorly planned site topology.

The size of the organization is another factor that may dictate the creation of separate sites. Network traffic in large organizations is elevated to begin with, amalgamated by the constant changes in user account information, resource addition, and resource modification. It may come down to experimentation and monitoring for many situations. As a rule of thumb, without regard to utilization, if a dedicated 128KB link is installed between sites, it should suffice as the minimum requirement of a high-speed link. If the link is not completely bogged down with other traffic, this site may exist in the inter-site.

For more recommendations regarding the creation of sites, see the Best Practices section of this chapter. Chapter 11, "Installing Active Directory and Using Management Tools," explores the hands-on aspect

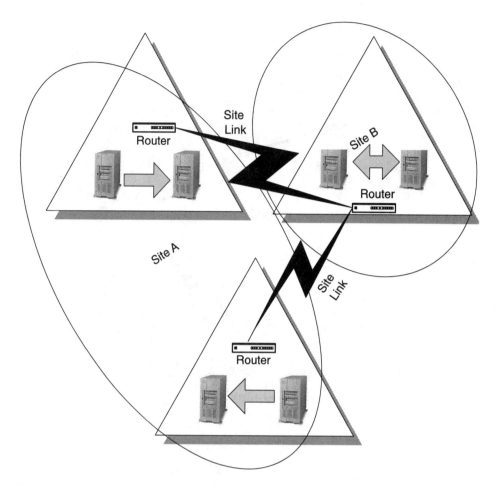

Figure 8.11   A well-planned site topology.

of using the Active Directory tools provided with the operating system and the process involved in creating sites and subnets.

Site Elements

Sites are composed of several elements that lend to replication functionality of the Active Directory in regard to multiple sites. These elements consist of *site boundaries*, *site links*, *site link bridges*, and *bridgehead servers*. The careful planning, configuration, and use of these elements are critical to a healthy replication scheme for the directory and will reduce future replication issues. Those familiar with multiserver Exchange servers will have an easy time understanding the configuration issues surrounding the use of connectors and setting costs. If these concepts are new to you, make a good effort to learn about the issues associated with them.

Site boundaries are really virtual elements (see Figure 8.12) defined by the network topology in any given scenario. Using a copy of your network map, draw these virtual boundaries around the segments of the network that are connected by high-speed links in order to determine site creation and site topology, and where site connectors might be needed.

Site connectors (see Figure 8.13) are technically referenced in inter- and intra-site replication. For the sake of clarity, since the processes involved in inter-site replication are fully automated, in this book a site connector refers to an intra-site connection. Site connectors are created manually using the Active Directory Sites and Services console. Site

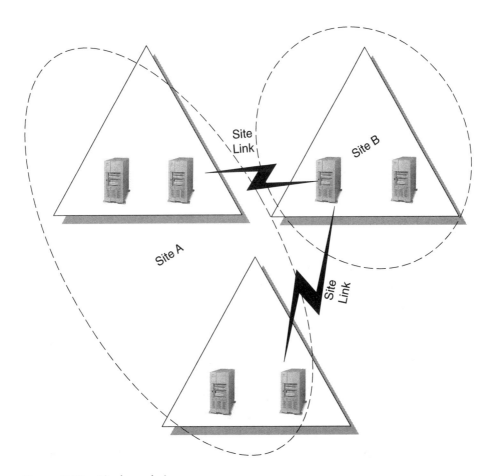

Figure 8.12   Site boundaries.

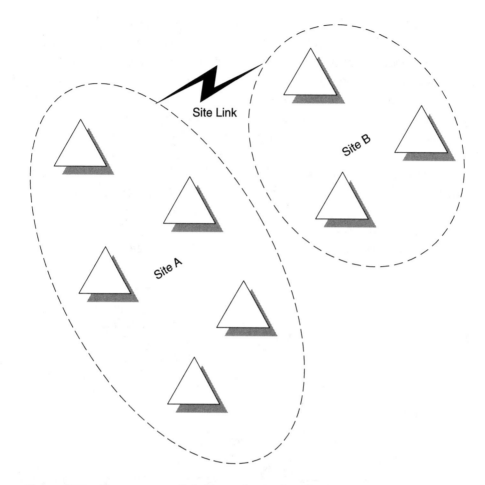

Figure 8.13   Site connectors link sites and control replication.

connectors use IP or SMTP as their primary transport protocol rather than RPC, and replication across these connectors may be scheduled. Additionally, a site connector may have a *cost* associated with it to determine best cost routing between sites.

Site link bridges (see Figure 8.14) are important to the overall replication topology between sites in that they group a set of site connectors, which communicate with the same transport protocol. The nature of these grouped connectors is transitive, where all of the links that are of the same protocol are members of the same site link bridge. These bridges help to optimize the site connector topology and mimic the routing behavior of a network. It is important to consider the underlying network structure before determining the site link bridge configuration.

Site link bridges have a cost value that may be associated with them to control replication routing paths. Chapter 11 outlines this process.

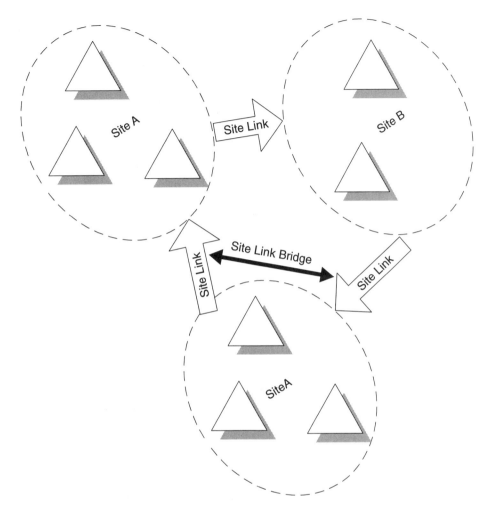

Figure 8.14 Site link bridges group site connectors and determines the routing path.

A bridgehead server (see Figure 8.15) acts as a sort of gateway server, a "hopping-off" point between sites. Say, for example, you have three domains that exist on three separate subnets and are connected via site connectors. Domain A is one site, domain B another (in the middle for the sake of visualization), and domain C is on the other segment. More than one domain controller is located in each of these domains, or at least should be. One server in site A will connect to another domain controller in site B. These two servers act as the bridgehead servers between the sites and function as connecting gateways to each site to handle replication traffic. The same situation exists between site C and site B. These designated servers help to funnel the load and control the replication topology.

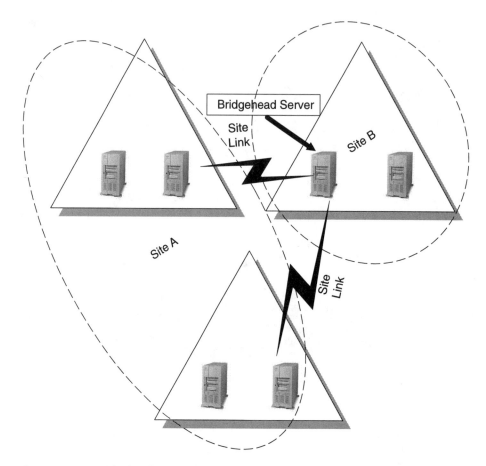

Figure 8.15 Bridgehead servers act as gateways between sites and are part of the topology strategy.

All of these components are critical players in designing a high-quality replication system for replication to occur overall. Sites and site elements have been discussed so far, but what about the differences between replication that occur within sites and between sites? We know that the process is streamlined between sites. The next section describes how this is done.

Inter-Site versus Intra-Site Replication

The replication of directory information may be classified in two categories: inter-site and intra-site. Intra-site replication transpires within a site between replication partners (domain controllers). Inter-site replication occurs between two different sites and is initiated by the creation of a *site connector* (see Chapter 11).

There are several distinct differences between these two types of replication:

- The protocol used
- The package size
- The schedule of transfers

Inter-site replication uses Remote Procedure Call (RPC) as the primary transport provider to pass update packages to other domain controllers in the forest. RPC is a bidirectional protocol popular with client server models for its easy programmability that allows a program running on one host to cause code to be executed on another host. In the case of Windows 2000 and directory updates, the client computer (some domain controller) initiates a call to the remote host (another domain controller) to check the need for directory updates. In this type of polling, a marker is checked against the marker of the previous poll marker sent at the last session. If the marker has changed, directory synchronization begins. If there has been no change, the remote host informs the caller (client). Figure 8.16 illustrates the inter-site replication process.

In regard to the actual package of information that is passed between the client and server during inter-site communication, the data is in an uncompressed format that is sent and processed very quickly by both computers. The downside to this type of communication is the amount of network bandwidth that it uses. This in and of itself is a substantial reason for logically grouping computers connected via high-speed links into sites. This type of communication would be a concern even on networks with a 10MB backbone with high bandwidth usage and no switching. In the majority of today's networks, switches and 100MB backbones are commonplace, so there should be no cause for alarm.

The third attribute of inter-site replication that makes it efficient is the schedule by which updates are processed, or rather the lack thereof. When a change is made to the directory, a sort of trigger is set off that begins the update process across the site, somewhat similar to the way the nervous system fires off synapses. Responses to replication partners are immediate and follow the replication topology that was automatically set by the KCC.

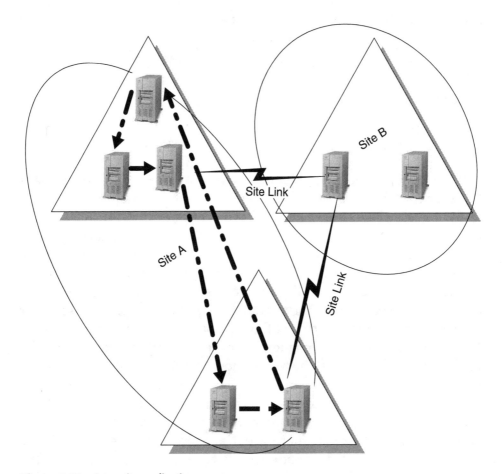

Figure 8.16 Inter-site replication.

Intra-site takes a much different, more streamlined approach to passing information about the directory hierarchy. Precious bandwidth across wide area links must be preserved, and Microsoft developed several innovative ways of accomplishing this (see Figure 8.17).

There is actually a choice of protocols that may be used to transfer directory packages *between* sites, Internet Protocol (IP) or Simple Mail Transport Protocol (SMTP). Either may be used as the vehicle for replication between sites, though IP may be more reliable due to the nature of the protocol itself. Compared to RPC, the use of these transport protocols is far more reliable over slow links.

 Data to support which protocol to use in different situations was not available at the time this book was written. However, testing each did not seem to produce any visible differences.

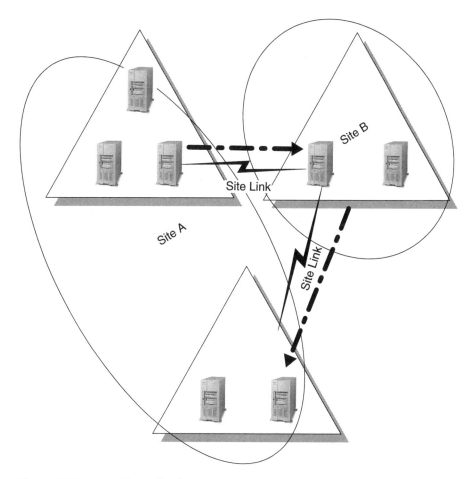

Figure 8.17   Intra-site replication.

Another nuance of the intra-site replication is the format used to transfer the data. Site connectors use compression end to end to reduce the size of the data sent over the wire. This is a tremendous benefit over very slow links or nondedicated links. While the compression and decompression of these packages do require a little more system overhead, the benefit far outweighs the cost. Since the frequency of the operation happens only at scheduled periods, this should not be an issue.

The most noted benefit of using site connectors between sites is the ability to schedule the transfer of data during low network utilization periods. Updates may be set up to occur after business hours or during off-peak hours, reducing the impact of the transfers even further.

Much thought went into the development of a replication system that would adapt to almost any network scenario. Because replication is so critical to the health of the overall directory, the proper use of these technologies is key. Setting up site connectors, scheduling replication, and setting up cost routing are important concepts to master. Chapter 11 details the hands-on of setting up site connectors. Site replication can quickly become very complex, particularly in larger networks that span thousands of subnets. Figure 8.18 shows how a complex replication topology might look like.

Domain Controller Placement

As in previous versions of Windows NT, domain controller placement is still a consideration in the logon process. This is further predicated by the creation of sites and multiple domains. Domain controllers must be

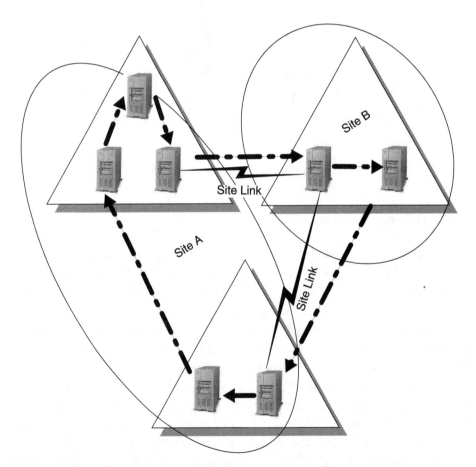

Figure 8.18   A complex replication topology using both replication types.

readily available to validate logon requests. Just as in the case of master or multimaster domain models of old, often a BDC had to be placed on the other end of slower WAN links in order to speed up the logon process for clients. This strategic placement of domain controllers does not necessarily disappear in Windows 2000. In the case of a single domain model under Windows 2000, domains may traverse large geographic regions, and OUs may be used to further subdivide the structure. Logon and domain controller replication traffic becomes a factor in such architecture. If site boundaries are created in these situations, much of this traffic is streamlined to better facilitate the network topology. Figure 8.19 gives an example of an improper DC placement strategy.

As a rule in these types of scenarios, a domain controller should be placed in every instance that multiple client logons may be handled over

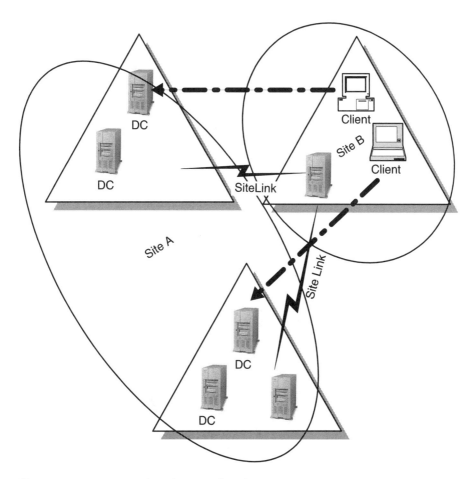

Figure 8.19   Improper domain controller placement.

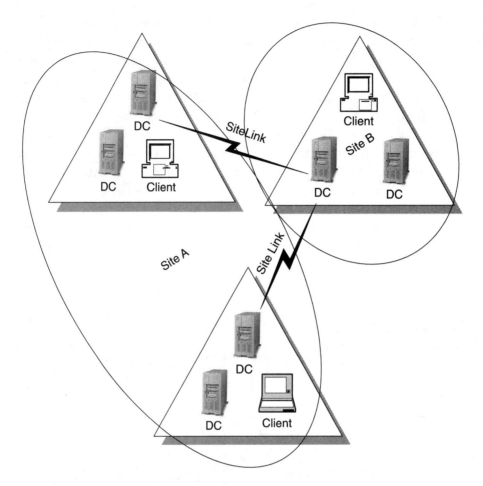

Figure 8.20   Proper domain controller placement.

a low-speed WAN link. In most cases, this may be a multifunctional server that acts as a domain controller, a file server, a mail server, and so forth. The point here is that these servers can exist within the single domain architecture as long as domain controller placement and site replication are configured properly. The benefits of such a structure are many, in that the domain structure is simplified, as is the naming hierarchy. Centralized management of domain resources is also easily facilitated. The placement of domain controllers in a single domain model across WAN links will affect replication strategy and topology, of course, and the use of sites and site connectors is critical to the overall health of the network. Proper DC placement affects the overall health of the network. Figure 8.20 illustrates a proper DC placement.

The Logon Process

Since the action of authentication factors into the overall design of the site topology, a discussion of the logon process and logon traffic is warranted. Logons are provided via several mechanisms in Windows 2000, using a DNS or NetBIOS resolution first to locate a domain controller. Finally, the GCS is used to determine Universal group membership.

Since many corporations will more than likely use a mixed client environment, it is important to grasp the mixed-mode domain logon process of authenticating native Windows 2000 clients and legacy Windows NT, Windows 9x, and Windows 3.x clients.

Two domain locator services are supported by Windows 2000—DNS and NetBIOS—and these locators run on the client (which may be a server or workstation) in the Netlogon service. When a client starts up, the Netlogon service attempts to find a logon server either using DNS (Windows 2000) via a SRV RR, or NetBIOS resolution, which uses WINS or LMHOSTS files (down-level clients) to locate the domain controller. On the server end, the Local Security Authority (LSA) of a Windows 2000 domain controller supports two security providers: NT LanManager authentication for the down-level clients, and Kerberos v5 authentication for native clients.

Traffic figures into this whole process in that the client finds the domain controller in the first place using the locator service. This process is different between native and down-level clients. With native clients, the process is further streamlined using sites, subnets, and the Global Catalog (GC). The IP address and subnet mask are passed by the locator to the DNS server, where associated RRs are checked to determine the location of the domain controller closest to the client and in the same site. The locator is then redirected to the closest domain controller for authenticated logon. The domain controller that performs the authentication queries the GC for Universal group membership and completes the logon process (see Figure 8.21).

In the case of down-level clients, the process is not "controlled." Rather, the process of locating a domain controller occurs during startup and is typically facilitated by the use of a WINS server record. This means down-level clients may attempt to use domain controllers located over WAN links depending on the configuration of the client and the location of the WINS server.

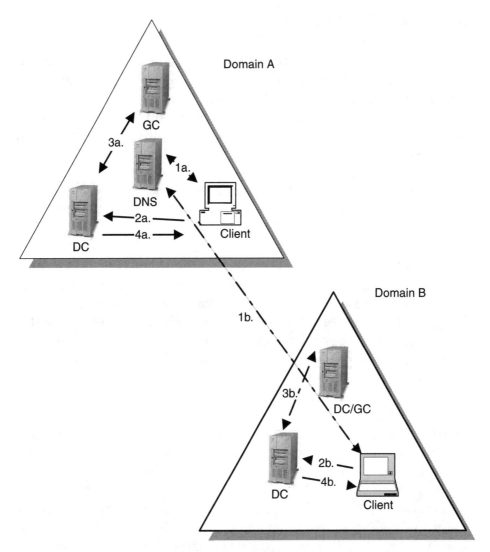

Figure 8.21 The logon and authentication process.

The use of native clients has obvious advantages over the use of legacy clients during the logon process and in distributed environments. Moving to a native-mode system in larger networks will help alleviate the logon and authentication problems inherent in legacy NT networks.

The Global Catalog Server

The GCS within the directory structure serves several functions, including logon, query support, and unifying the directory through the use of replicated directory data and defined schema attributes. By default, this service is created on the first domain controller for the domain/tree/forest. The GCS may be spread around to different domain controllers in different domains. This approach will help to better service the logon process and query support in a multisite scenario. It will also affect the architecture of the site topology, as all GCs that exist in the directory must be in unison lest logon or query problems arise.

Best Practices

The design and implementation of sites in an Active Directory structure can be a complicated commission based on the complexity of the underlying network. Many choices may be made, and a solid understanding of the network and TCP/IP will ensure the design is properly set up. Replication failure of directory information can cause serious problems for the users of the affected segment of the network, including but not limited to logon failure and denial of access to network resources. Object query failure may also result. Therefore, it is important to plan the replication topology carefully and to give great care when modifying existing schemes. Improper placement of network resources such as domain controllers can also negatively affect the user community. A solid architecture planned ahead of time will pay for itself tenfold. Additionally, following the guidelines in this section will also help speed you toward an implementation that is without incident.

Issues Regarding Sites and Site Replication

Several issues determine the need for sites in a Windows 2000 network, the main identifying factor being a slow network link. The mandatory element that determines the need for a site is the absence of a dedicated link. That is, if dial-up links are used in places to connect to remote offices, that office or offices should be placed in a separate site. The goal in site design is to try and create as few sites as possible to limit the amount of sites that must be managed by the IT organization.

The low-speed threshold for a link should be a 128kb dedicated link. Once this low-speed threshold has been determined to qualify the placement of a remote site in an existing site, infrastructure administrators should further qualify the link by determining the utilization of the link. Large remote offices that produce a lot of traffic may have to be segmented.

The use of multiple site connectors is particularly helpful for fault tolerance and can help prevent replication failures in the event a connector fails or the link fails. In Figure 8.22, the North America site and European locations are in the same site because of a robust link between the two domains, but the countries represented in the child domains are linked by slower links and in separate sites. An additional link is implemented between the two countries, and an additional site connector as well. Multiple site connectors exist in the event that a link is dropped between the main site and either of the two country sites (see Figure 8.22).

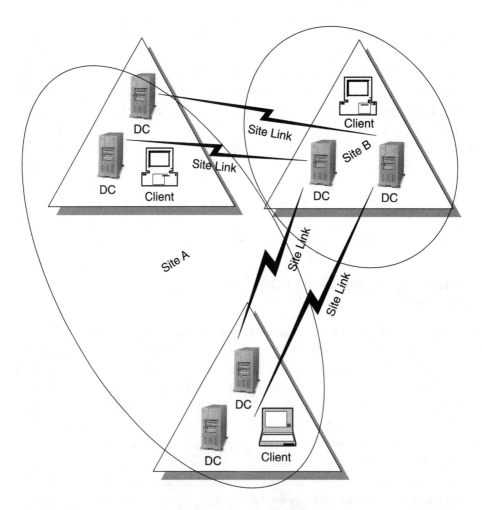

Figure 8.22 Setting up multiple connectors for fault tolerance.

Use cost routing in the case of multiple site connectors to set up a link for which replication will have an affinity. This is also important in the use of site link bridges. Cost associations, and ultimately routing decisions, are based on a number from 1 to 100, where the higher the number, the less likely that link is to be used.

The underlying network dictates the use of site link bridges, where fully routed networks do not need these structures to determine cost basis for routing directory traffic.

Intra-site traffic is multiplied with the addition of domain controllers. Too many domain controllers equate to poor network performance.

Join or split sites as dictated by the changing network topology.

Use IP instead of SMTP for inter-site connectors that have low bandwidth utilization. The use of the (RPC over) IP protocol is synchronous and provides two-way communication between domain controllers. SMTP sends directory information via e-mail messages and requires the use of the SMTP service bundled with IIS, which may result in more server overhead or additional configuration to disable the other services associated with the Web server service.

Issues Regarding Domain Controllers

In single domain models that span WAN links, it is good practice to place a domain controller at remote locations to serve logon requests. This server need not be a dedicated domain controller. In smaller offices, a composite server that acts as a file server, mail server, and domain controller should suffice.

The practice of logically grouping users together that work in close proximity will help reduce logon traffic.

It is important to remember that a GC is also part of the logon and query process in placing domain controllers.

Size all domain controllers according to the amount of data they will contain. More users means more resources needed.

Issues Regarding the Global Catalog

Placing a GC in remote locations that are in separate sites will help to facilitate user logons and return faster queries.

Remote GC servers should be sized properly, as they will contain replica information from every other domain in the tree/forest.

Summary

Active Directory does have a certain cost associated with it in the form of traffic and the domain model used coupled with the integration of a site topology. Replication is a vital aspect of the Active Directory, as it serves as a mechanism for domain-wide logon and query operation. This chapter discussed the idea of replication and what information the directory replicates. The different replication methods were also discussed. A discussion of sites and site objects provided a foundation for managing replication in a distributed environment. Other issues that affect the implementation of sites and network traffic, such as domain controller placement and the logon process, were discussed to better understand how the overall process of logons can affect network design. Finally, best practices help summarize the proper way to design a distribute network. In Chapter 9, "Using Microsoft Management Console," we begin a discussion of the new management shell known as the Microsoft Management Console, from which all administrative functions in Windows 2000 are performed (as well as all new Microsoft server and BackOffice products).

CHAPTER

9

Using Microsoft Management Console

INTRODUCTION

In this chapter, we look at the core management component of Windows 2000 and Active Directory, the Microsoft Management Console (MMC). Topics in this chapter include:

- **Describing MMC**
- **Why MMC Was Developed**
- **MMC and Snap-ins**
- **Configuring and Using MMC**
- **Windows 2000 Tools**

 Many of you may be familiar with the MMC through the use of the product in the Windows NT 4.0 Option Pack. If you are already familiar with the background and general use of MMC, feel free to skip past these sections to the Windows 2000 specific features and use.

Microsoft Management Console (MMC) is an independent and extensible, "common console framework" for Windows management applications. MMC was initially released as part of the Windows NT Option Pack, with the SQL 7.0 interface following soon after, and is a major component of

Windows 2000. This chapter introduces the MMC and provides an overview of the MMC GUI and MMC customization and architecture. It also explains the concept of Snap-ins and how they relate to MMC, as well as general interface guidelines for those who are ambitious enough to create their own. MMC is a core part of Microsoft's management strategy. Microsoft is committed to MMC for all future management applications to provide a unified management interface among all BackOffice products.

MMC itself does not provide any management behavior on its own; rather, it provides a common environment for *Snap-ins,* which are written by both Microsoft and independent software vendors (ISV). Snap-ins provide the actual management behavior within the console. The MMC environment allows for seamless integration between Snap-ins, even those provided by different vendors. Think of the MMC as a framework or shell for common management applications. The tool becomes versatile through the ability to add several different Snap-ins to a single instance of MMC. Administrators create these customized "tools" from various Snap-ins, and they can then save the tools they have created for later use or for sharing with other administrators. This model provides the administrator with efficient tool customization and the ability to create multiple tools of different levels of complexity for task delegation, among other benefits.

How the MMC Came About

Anyone familiar with previous versions of Windows NT knows the administrative cost associated with using multiple tools to manage servers (and clients). MMC is the result of Microsoft's effort to create better tools to administer Windows-based networks. The goal of MMC design was to remove administrative burden by supporting simplified administration through integration, delegation, task orientation, and overall interface simplification. As Microsoft addressed these and other issues, it increased the project's scope to include all Microsoft administration tools and to offer this management framework to ISVs as well. MMC is a core part of Microsoft's future management strategy. Most Microsoft development groups will use MMC for future management applications. An example of this is the new interface used in Microsoft's SQL Server version 7.0, where all administrative tasks are accomplished through a preconfigured MMC.

MMC Defined

MMC is a Windows-based multiple document interface (MDI) application that heavily leverages Internet technologies. "Multiple document" means simply that the structure is capable of housing "child" windows inside the overall structure. Both Microsoft and ISVs extend the console by writing MMC Snap-ins, which are responsible for actually performing management tasks.

The MMC APIs permit the Snap-ins to integrate with the console. These interfaces deal only with user interface extensions; that is, how each Snap-in actually performs tasks is entirely up to the Snap-in. The Snap-in's relationship with the console is a dependency; the MMC provides host environment, and the Snap-in provides the usability function. The MMC itself offers no real behavior; it is the host that gains functionality from its symbiotic relationship with the Snap-in.

Both Microsoft and ISVs have developed management tools to run in the console. MMC is part of the Windows Software Developers Kit (SDK) for Windows 2000 and is available for general use from Microsoft.

MMC Benefits

As previously mentioned, there was a day when NT administrative tools and functions were launched independently and scattered among many different interfaces. The following list defines the benefits that MMC brings to Windows 2000 management:

Simple interface. All tools built for MMC, from any software vendor, will have a similar look and feel, making it easier for users to use all tools after learning one. Because you can mix and match tools from any vendor, you can use the "best of breed" from each management product category. MMC also enables a single piece of software to provide functionality across the interface in a consistent manner.

Extensibility. Tools created to work with MMC are task oriented; that is, each Snap-in performs a certain task. This means that each Snap-in added to the console adds to the usability of the tool being created. Also, because administrators can customize their own tools, using pieces from a variety of vendors, they can create tools that contain only the components needed to manage specific tasks.

Delegation. Administrators can easily modify existing tools to create new tools with reduced functionality and less complex views of the tool namespace, and then give these tools to others. A person who receives such a tool is presented with a simpler, more manageable view of the tasks he or she is being asked to perform.

Integration. The user interface (UI) for all the management tasks an administrator must perform is collected into a single console. As new applications are added to a computer or network, their administration is integrated into the existing administration common console.

The MMC User Interface

Upon first examining the MMC GUI, one may find it looks and operates much like Explorer. A complete MMC console might look like Figure 9.1.

The MMC parent frame has a master menu and toolbar. The master menu offers what is typical of an MDI parent: file and window management, along with Help.

The MDI child windows offer many differing views. Each of these child views includes a command bar, a scope pane, and a result pane. The command bar contains both pop-down menus and buttons. (Note that the screen shots in this chapter do not show command bars—these will be supported in a post-PDC release.) The scope pane (the left pane), is a tree control displaying the tool's *namespace*. The items in this pane contain manageable objects or tasks. The scope pane need not be visible in all views—in this example, it is visible in only the top-left child window.

Each child window's result pane (the right pane) displays the result of selecting a node in the scope pane. In many cases, it's a list of the contents of a folder; in other cases, it's a management-related view (such as the performance graph in Figure 9.2), which can be Web or ActiveX control based.

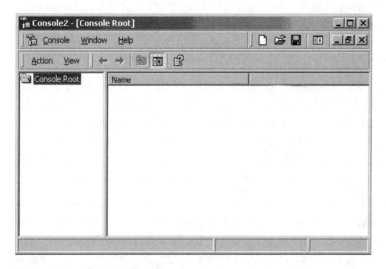

Figure 9.1   The MMC interface.

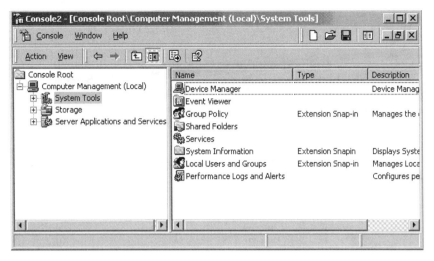

Figure 9.2   A simple MMC view.

MMC can be configured to represent powerful management tools. MMC is also designed to offer a scaled-down view that is much less daunting to less-experienced administrators. In the simplest of cases, it can appear as just a task-oriented taskpad.

Because MMC permits customization, multiple tools can be created and saved; each of the views in the preceding figures can be saved to separate files as different tools. These files may then be shared from the network or mailed to others as self-contained programs that will run on any number of Windows clients. This helps administrators delegate tasks throughout the network. For example, a senior administrator could create the view in Figure 9.2 (a list of services on a computer) and send that view to an operator who will manage only the services on that computer. The operator receives—and can access—only the UI pictured. Figure 9.3 illustrates a complex multiple Snap-in Multiple Document Interface view.

The MMC parent "frame" (or outer container) has a "master menu" and "toolbar" option. The master menu offers what is typical of an MDI parent: file and window management, and Help. You will find these items standard in almost every Windows application. These controls manipulate only overall MMC functions and have no effect on Snap-ins or applications within. Figure 9.4 shows the customization of the MMC console.

MDI child windows offer many different views, each consisting of a command bar, a scope pane, and a result pane. The *command bar* contains both pop-down menus and buttons. *The scope pane* (left side) is a tree control displaying the tool's *namespace*, the tree-formatted listing of

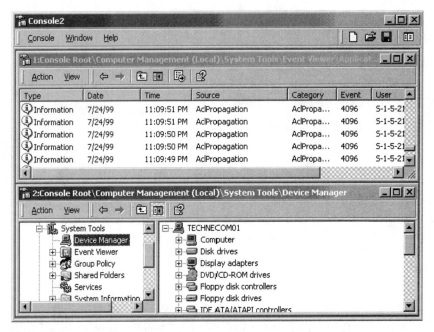

Figure 9.3 A complex MMC view with multiple Snap-ins and MDI.

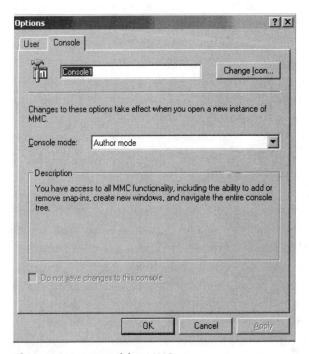

Figure 9.4 Customizing MMC.

all visible segments. Each of these is an object within the tree and can be managed or manipulated, generally with a right mouse click. The scope pane is not always visible, only when it is necessary to display a tree hierarchy. Each child window's *result pane* (right side) displays the result of selecting a node in the scope pane. In many cases, it's a list of the contents of a folder in the scope pane, although it may be any related view as in the case of a Performance Monitor item. Further, it may be a Web or ActiveX control-based view.

The overall customization of the console is simplistic. An administrator can use the GUI Snap-in Manager to load and unload Snap-ins on the fly. Figure 9.5 shows how a computer management Snap-in is added to the current console.

How MMC Works

The MMC console is a Windows-based MDI application that heavily leverages Internet technologies. The console itself has no management behavior; it is a host that contains other software (Snap-ins) that extends the console to offer the actual management capabilities.

The UI elements of the tool interact with the *MMC Snap-in Manager*, which in turn interacts with the various Snap-ins. The Snap-in Manager

Figure 9.5   Adding the File Management Snap-in.

also deals with saving settings into a document (.MSC file). The items at the top of Figure 9.5 (the .MSC file and the UI elements) are all that a user deals with. The items at the bottom (the Snap-in Manager and the two Snap-ins, Router Monitor and Event Viewer) are the elements that the developers deal with.

When an MMC tool document is run, one or more Snap-ins are initialized. These Snap-ins are integrated to create the tool's *namespace*, or the ordered collection of nodes that appears in the tree view in the scope pane. The namespace is a master tree that represents what the tool can do. It appears similar to a tree view of the files and folders on a hard drive in the Windows Explorer program. The namespace can include all manageable aspects of a network, such as computers, users and groups, objects, views, and tasks.

The child windows in MMC are views into this master namespace (see Figure 9.6). This is akin to having multiple instances of Explorer looking at the same hard drive. Each view may be rooted at a different portion of the tree, but they all point to the same master data source. If data is currently displayed in multiple child windows, when that data is deleted in one view, it will also disappear from the other views.

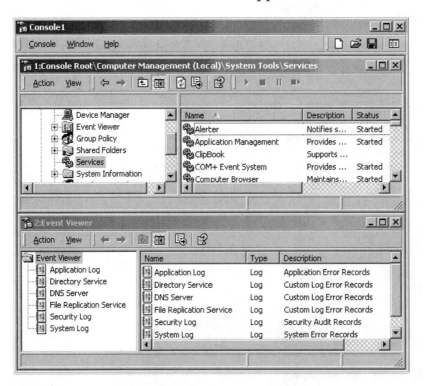

Figure 9.6 How MMC works.

Snap-ins

Each MMC tool is built of a collection of instances of smaller tools called MMC *Snap-ins*. One Snap-in represents one unit of management behavior. A Snap-in is the smallest unit of console extension. Technically, a Snap-in is an OLE in-process server that executes in the process context of MMC. The Snap-in has the ability to call on other supporting controls and DLLs to accomplish its task if necessary.

Snap-ins extend MMC by adding and enabling management behavior. An administrator can assemble multiple Snap-ins into a *tool* (which could also be called an MMC *document*). The tool is the composite of Snap-ins joined within the console by that administrator and is what the administrator actually uses to manage the network. After assembling a tool from various Snap-ins, the administrator can save the tool in a .MSC (Management Saved Console) file. The administrator could then reload the file later to instantly recreate the tool. The .MSC file could also be e-mailed to another administrator, who could then load the file and use the resulting tool. (If the second administrator does not have all the necessary Snap-ins installed on his or her computer, MMC will automatically download the needed Snap-ins when the second administrator loads the .MSC file.) Figure 9.7 shows the installation of a Snap-in.

MMC permits total customization by the end user; a user can construct a custom tool from many different Snap-ins. An administrator

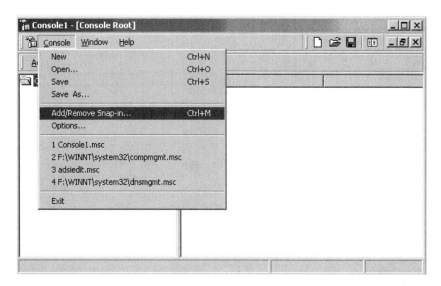

Figure 9.7   Loading Snap-ins from the Console.

can create multiple tools and load and unload them when needed. You can run multiple tools simultaneously on one computer as well, but each tool requires its own instance of the console running.

Note that with MMC, a single "tool" does not necessarily mean that the tool has a single function; for example, Service for the local computer is used only for management of local services. A tool may be constructed to manage server functions, such as security or services, and Web server functions (see Figure 9.8). Construction of a well-rounded tool that the administrator uses regularly will likely contain diversified management functionality for all aspects of the network; for example, the Directory, replication, group and user management, file sharing, and server monitoring. It is called a "tool" because it runs in one instance of MMC and can be saved as an .MSC file. This file may then be distributed among the IT organization for use.

Types of Snap-ins

There are two types of Snap-ins, and each provides some functionality to administrators. Though transparent to the end user, internally each Snap-in is categorized as one or both of the following types:

Stand-alone Snap-in. Provides management functions, even alone in a console with no other supporting Snap-ins. Snap-ins designed for this mode must not have any other Snap-in dependencies.

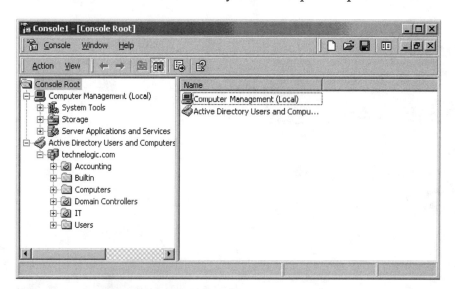

Figure 9.8 A multifunctional tool.

Extension Snap-in. Provides cascaded functionality and is invoked by a parent Snap-in.

An extension Snap-in might be a "Log Corporate Print Functions" Snap-in, providing the user with a way to log corporate print activity to log files (such as the Windows NT Event Log). With this Snap-in installed, every log object in the namespace would be extended with the "Corporate Print" context menu item. Extension Snap-ins can provide a variety of functionality. Some will actually extend the console, while others will simply extend context menus or specific wizards. For more information, see the following section, "Creating a Management Console."

Many Snap-ins support both modes of operation, which offers stand-alone functionality and extends the functionality of other Snap-ins in the tool. Overall, the Snap-in has the option of altering the returned "enumeration" based on the context information passed to it at runtime. This permits Snap-ins to register as extensions and offer conditional behavior. Other than the Create New and Tasks menu extensions, all others are general user interface extension mechanisms. The Create New and Tasks menu extensions are used as a mechanism to group operations in a way to permit integrated command structures throughout. Had the console offered only a generic menu extension interface, there would be little consistency in the usage model. In MMC, each node will have a Create New menu and a Tasks menu. Through this extension registration mechanism, all of these menu items are collected into a single point of usage.

Creating a Management Console

As stated, the MMC offers the administrator the advantage of having all critical tools in one place with multiple views, and complete customization of the tool for different uses. Creating custom consoles consists of only a few straightforward steps, and consoles may be saved as Microsoft Console files with the extension .MSC for future use or distribution. Let's examine the process of creating a custom console, and then we will use that console to set up several views for examination of commonly used data such as log files.

From the Start menu, open a command line from the Run option and type in "MMC" (no quotes please), then press Return or click OK. This will effectively open an empty console shell that is ready to accept Snap-ins (see Figure 9.9).

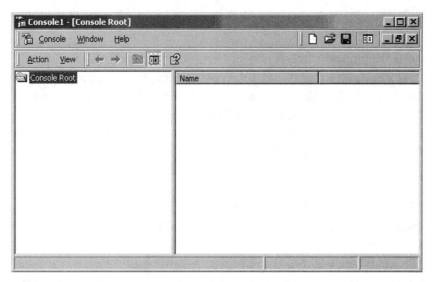

Figure 9.9   The empty console.

From the Console menu (top left), select Add/Remove Snap-in, which will invoke the Add/Remove Snap-in dialog box. You are presented with a drop-down list box that asks *where* (in the console tree) you want to begin adding Snap-ins. Since this a blank console, we are starting at the Console Root (see Figure 9.10).

From here, click the Add button to begin selecting Snap-ins to add to the console. You are presented with a list of Snap-ins that the system has registered. The more packages you install, the more extensive this list will be (see Figure 9.11).

Choose Computer Management from the list of available Snap-ins by double-clicking it, or clicking once and then selecting Add.

A dialog box appears asking you to select the computer you want to manage. Select Local Computer (default) and the "Allow the selected computer to be changed when launching from the command line" check box, then click Finish (see Figure 9.12).

Next, move to the Extensions tab. This is where you select the extension Snap-ins associated with the package. In this case, make sure the "Add all" check box is selected. Click OK to continue. You now have a newly created console that allows you to manage resources and services on the local machine. You will find this is the same as the Computer Management Console found on the Start menu under Administrative Tools. Now, on to using custom views in MMC (see Figure 9.13).

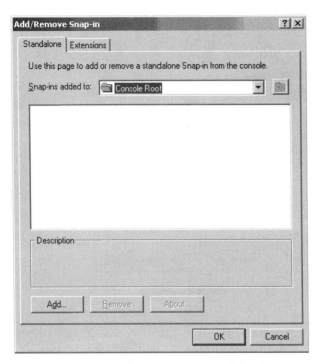

Figure 9.10   The Add/Remove Snap-in dialog box.

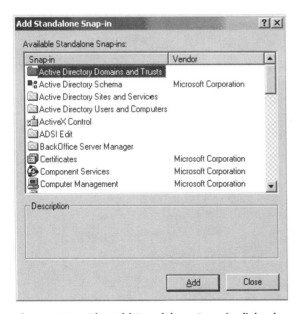

Figure 9.11   The Add Standalone Snap-in dialog box.

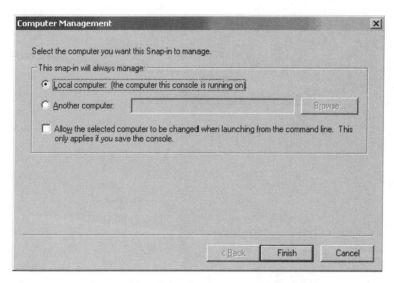

Figure 9.12 The resulting dialog box for computer selection.

The MMC is a multiwindowed environment that allows many of the extension Snap-ins to be viewed succinctly. These custom views are configured from the right-click menu.

First, expand the Computer Management Snap-in to reveal the subtree menu options. In this example, we are going to set up a view that allows an administrator to view the commonly used system tools Event Viewer, Services, and Open Sessions (Sessions) for the server (see Figure 9.14).

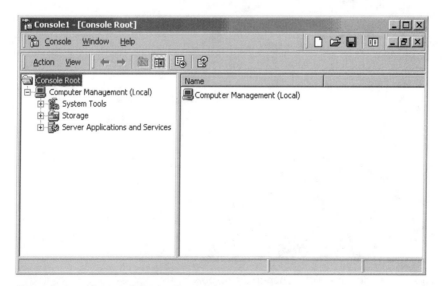

Figure 9.13 The newly created console.

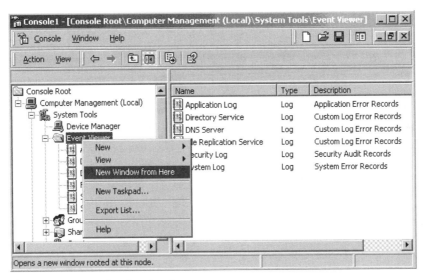

Figure 9.14 Configuring the views.

Right-click the Event Viewer object and select New Window from Here. Follow the same procedure for the other two tools. Close the Computer Management Window, then from the Window menu at the top of the console (appears after the creation of child windows), select Tile Horizontally. Maximize the console if necessary. Critical tools are now at your disposal, all in one place in a single view (see Figure 9.15). In prior versions of Windows NT, this operation would have meant opening three separate applications!

 The Computer Management Console available from the Administrative Tools Group is configured to disallow this type of windowing by default. You are probably better served by creating a custom console and adding it to the menu manually. To do this, create the console as outlined previously and save it in a readily accessible place like the Desktop. Next, right-click the Start button and select Explore All Users. This opens Windows Explorer in the All Users profile where the Administrative Tools group exists for the Start menu. Drop a copy of your console (or shortcut) into this group for easy access to your newly created tool.

Additional customization may be performed on the tool. For example, if the tool was created for distribution and you wanted to lock it down sufficiently so that it would be "idiot proof," you have that option using the Taskpad feature of MMC. To simplify this example, start with a new

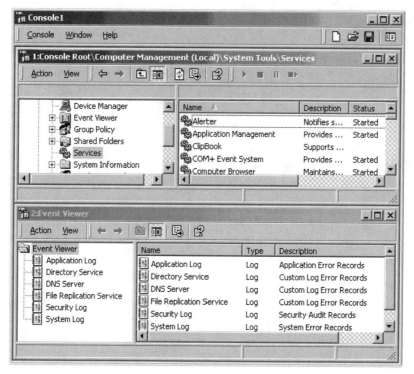

Figure 9.15   The resulting console view.

console and add the Computer Management Snap-in as before. Expand the tree view to show Event Viewer. (Alternatively, if you wanted to remove all of the other dependent Snap-ins to simplify the tool even more, you could remove them on the Extensions tab discussed earlier to reveal only the Event Viewer extension when the tree-view is expanded). Right-click on any of the resulting log options and select New Taskpad.

A Wizard will result. Accept all the defaults and click Finish. This invokes the Task Creation Wizard (see Figure 9.16). Click Next, accept the default on the next page, and click Next again. Now you must choose a command event and click Next. Accept the default on the next page or customize it as you wish, then click Next. Choose an Icon and click Next, then Finish in the next page. The new view is produced in the results pane. (Does this sound like a revamp of the Windows 3.0 PIF Editor?)

Notice that at the top of the console tree a new folder has been created called Taskpads. Expand this object to reveal the newly created view. Now from the View Menu you can remove (uncheck) the console tree option to reveal only the log view. Not idiot proof enough for you yet? There are still plenty of options left to the user to generate a call! Try

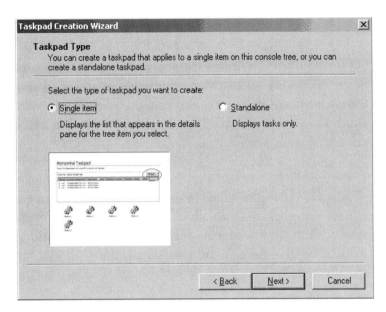

Figure 9.16 The New Taskpad option.

right-clicking the Console Root. From the resulting menu, choose View, then Toolbars. Experiment with removing these items and then hiding the console tree. This simple tool may now be distributed to other users as a simplistic log management tool. Save the tool and distribute as necessary (see Figure 9.17).

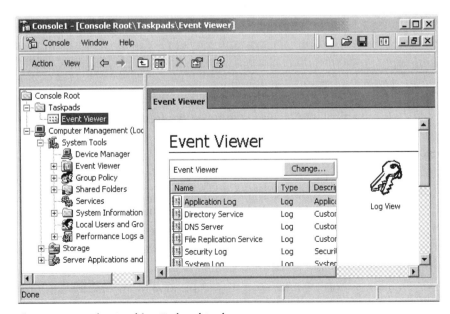

Figure 9.17 The resulting Taskpad tool.

Third-Party Products

Because MMC itself provides the shell, MMC works well in the hands of developers who want to spend more time building real management functionality, and less time building and rebuilding a respectable windowing framework for their tools. Microsoft states that "By writing to the MMC specifications, an ISV will save development time, build in compatibility with other management tools, be able to leverage existing management tools also written for MMC, and offer an integrated look and feel."

Microsoft has made MMC APIs part of the Windows SDK and part of the overall tools strategy for the future. Microsoft is committed to supporting MMC as the way to build Windows-based administration tools and is using the console to build all upcoming Windows NT administration tools.

Comparing MMC to Other Tools

There are a myriad of tools that were developed for Windows NT to provide a unified interface for the express purpose of unifying all administrative controls in one GUI (see www.bhs.com). It is doubtful that these tools will work with Active Directory, and even more doubtful that you would want to use them. Microsoft has done a tremendous job developing MMC as a tool for the next generation of operating systems and applications. MMC offers both UI and APIs that can integrate multiple tools together. MMC was designed specifically to address the issues of integration, delegation, and task orientation, be general enough to be reusable by most tools, and offer simplicity for simple usage scenarios and advanced features for complex management scenarios.

According to Microsoft, the MMC APIs were "designed to the core concept that tools are documents (able to be created, saved, and passed around) and that people should be able to create and customize many new tools." Another key goal was to enable developers to build Snap-ins that can entwine themselves with the Snap-ins provided by others and yet enable the user to experience a single tool. A user using such a tool does not even realize that it is composed of Snap-ins created at different times and possibly by different software vendors.

Microsoft further states that "The MMC interface compensates for both complicated and sophisticated tools" and believes that administration "occurs on a continuous spectrum of levels of experience, rather than a few defined roles (such as user, operator, and administrator)."

MMC allows flexibility in creating tools for delegation of responsibilities and further allows "senior administrators" to create a number of tools to be used by other members of the IT staff. These "tools" may be passed on via e-mail or run from a share once created. MMC possesses the flexibility to build a tool that is perfectly suited for specific users or groups for specific tasks.

MMC and Internet Components

While building management applications using Internet technologies is commonplace (many components of Windows 2000 are built on Web-based technologies, including the "configure server" dialog that appears after logon), there are many aspects of management that are not addressed by the Internet. While many vendors such as Cisco and HP offer Web-based administration for their products, these products still possess external support mechanisms to perform network functions such as browsing for devices. MMC overcomes this shortcoming by combining Snap-in technology and integrating Internet technologies. An example of this is found in the ability of the Results pane (the right-hand pane) to display HTML documents for tool navigation or informational display (Outlook 98/2000 is built on the same principle, where the "Outlook Today" that appears on launch is HTML based).

According to Microsoft, "The implementation of these and other technologies makes it such that Snap-ins can perform the more traditional tasks using well-targeted COM interfaces, and for rendering can use many implementation technologies including traditional list views, HTML, Java, ActiveX, and special purpose ActiveX controls such as a Network Map view like those found in HP's NetView product."

Summary

Microsoft developed MMC to cure the many ills of past network management tools. MMC provides an extensible and powerful environment for creating custom management tools. MMC is the definitive standard for all existing and future management interfaces for all BackOffice products. What this means to the administrator is a simplistic "all-in-one" tool to manage all Microsoft products on a network, including SQL Server, Exchange (soon with the release of Platinum), SMS Server, IIS, Proxy Server, and SNA Server. The benefits of creating a console that allows you to administer all of these resources in one place are obvious. Further, all services indigenous to the server itself such as DNS, DHCP, WINS, Security, User Accounts, and Active Directory may be managed through the same console. By learning to customize MMC and the resulting Snap-ins, you have the ability to create and distribute custom tools to delegated users or groups to manage the enterprise. In the next chapter we will install and explore the Microsoft DNS offering, the first step in an Active Directory installation.

CHAPTER

10

Installing and Configuring DNS

INTRODUCTION

Active Directory functionality is dependent on Domain Name System (DNS) name resolution for object discovery and location. Many may be new to the concepts of DNS; therefore, this chapter focuses on the installation and configuration of DNS services in Windows 2000. Topics include:

- **The DNS Setup Wizard**
- **Installing DNS**
- **Issues**
- **Using the DNS Management Console**
- **Features**
- **Hands-on**

Active Directory objects are based on the hierarchical nomenclature defined through DNS. This means that accessing anything in Windows 2000 and Active Directory is completely dependent on DNS integration. This includes workstations finding logon servers, managing objects, and accessing objects that are contained within the directory structure. The directory itself is, in its simplest form, a name hierarchy based on

X.500 standard format. In Chapter 5, "Understanding DNS Architecture," we discussed how DNS functions and integrates with Active Directory. In this chapter, we focus on the actual installation of DNS under Windows 2000, and how to configure and integrate DNS with Active Directory for name-to-object resolution via queries to the directory. In order to fully grasp this chapter, it is imperative that you understand DNS functionality. If there is any question as to how DNS functions, review Chapter 5 before continuing.

DNS services are a fundamental and necessary service on which Active Directory relies. It is a dependency service of Active Directory, and installing DNS is the first step to installing directory services. Beyond providing name to IP address resolution and service location services, DNS provides a hierarchical naming structure for Windows 2000 objects. As domains are added to the hierarchy, the name of the parent domain is appended to the newly formed child domain or subdomain. As a result, the name given to a subdomain identifies its position in the hierarchy.

Because Active Directory is completely dependent on DNS for functionality, it is also important that the installation process and options along the way are understood. Take great care to note and follow the installation procedures herein lest you botch the installation and find out later that objects in the directory are inaccessible. A DNS server must be present before a server can become the root domain server in an Active Directory hierarchy. If you have a DNS server in place that supports RFC2052, you may opt to skip this chapter and move on to Chapter 11 to install the first domain controller. This is not advised, however, and there are many issues surrounding the use of a third-party DNS server. We begin with a discussion on what choices you have when installing DNS and then move the discussion to the actual installation procedure. Figure 10.1 illustrates how DNS integrates into Active Directory architecture.

Before You Begin

The use of the word "domain" here refers to DNS structure, not Windows 2000 domains. There are several roads to take once you begin your Windows 2000 DNS/Active Directory implementation. By now you should have a good idea of what types of naming conventions you are going use. Have this plan readily available now for reference. If you are facing a large migration implementation, remember to limit your domain levels to no more than five deep, and keep each child

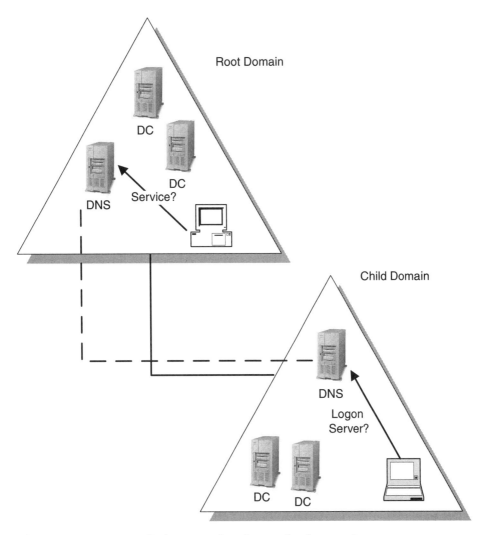

Figure 10.1   How DNS fits into an Active Directory implementation.

domain name unique. Other rules you must abide by are the 63-charac-
ter limit including periods and use of only the character sets a–z, A–Z,
and 0–9. See Figure 10.2 for an illustration.

   This chapter goes into detail to demonstrate the steps to take to configure the Microsoft DNS services on a nondomain controller. Upon
running the DCPROMO utility to create a domain controller, many
events transpire, one of which may be the automatic installation and
configuration of DNS services. In *most* cases, a member server will function as the DNS server to offset the load from the domain controller.

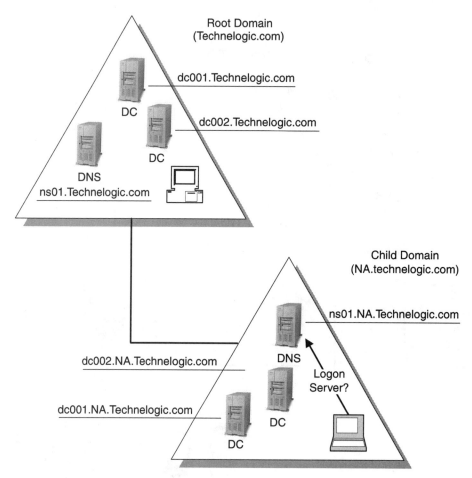

Figure 10.2   Proper DNS nomenclature.

Therefore, the installation of this server is the first step in implementing Active Directory. Certainly, in remote locations, or in the case of networks that consist of only a few servers, it is acceptable for DNS and the domain controller to coexist on the same server.

If your network fits into the latter category, you may skip this chapter. It is advisable to revisit this chapter to better understand the process of running the DNS Wizard and configuring DNS services.

The DNS Setup Wizard

The DNS Wizard is initiated through the Configure Your Server Web-based console that appears after the first logon. Additionally, this interface

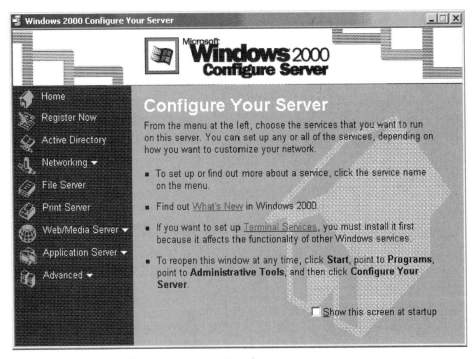

Figure 10.3   The Configure Your Server Wizard.

may be launched from the Administrative Tools group on the Start menu. The Configure Your Server Wizard is shown in Figure 10.3.

From the Networking drop-down link, select the DNS option, as shown in Figure 10.4, and then the Manage DNS link.

On the resulting DNS Wizard frame, click Next. You are presented with an option to create a forward lookup zone or to continue. Select the default to create the zone and click Next. Figure 10.5 illustrates this step.

The next screen presents three options for selecting a zone type: Active Directory integrated, Standard Primary, or Standard Secondary. If this is a stand-alone DNS server, choose the Standard Primary option. This will create a new zone stored in a text file in the <system root>\system32\dns subdirectory. We will worry about the Active Directory integrated part later, as it is a tremendous asset to have DNS interact with Active Directory. Click Next (see Figure 10.6).

The next step is to give the zone a name that takes the form of <child domain>.<domain>.<root>, or as in Figure 10.7, it.corporate.techno-logic.com. Click Next after you have entered a valid name for the zone (see Figure 10.7).

The system will assign a name for the DNS file and append a .dns extension to it. You may accept this default or choose your own name.

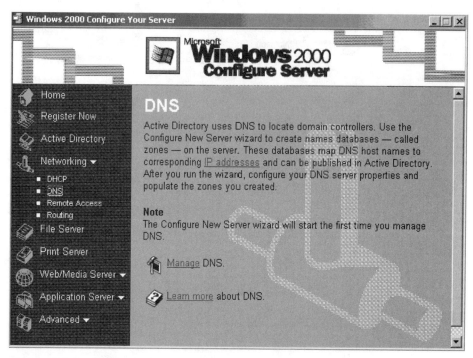

Figure 10.4 Selecting the Manage DNS link to activate the DNS Server Wizard.

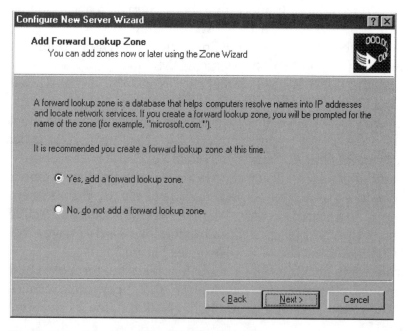

Figure 10.5 Creating a forward lookup zone.

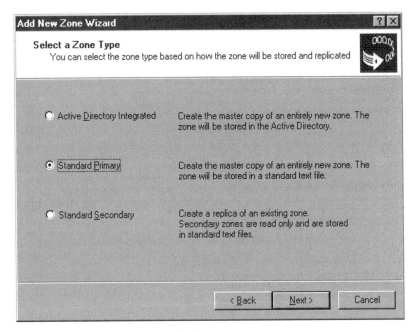

Figure 10.6   The Zone Type selection screen.

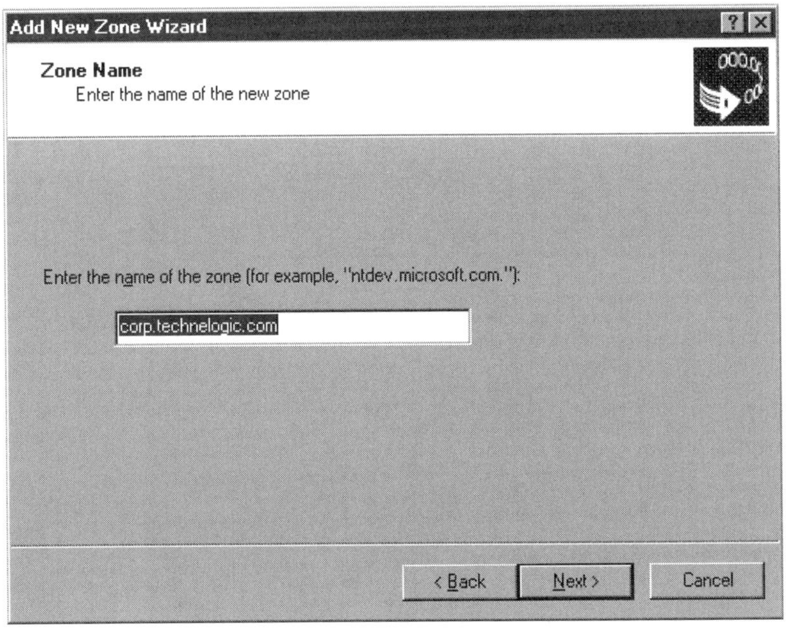

Figure 10.7   Naming the primary zone.

Additionally, you may choose an existing or imported file to use here. Click Next when done (see Figure 10.8).

Adding a reverse lookup zone is next. This step is optional but recommended, as having reverse lookup capability can assist in resolving network and name resolution problems should they occur. Choose the default Yes option, as shown in Figure 10.9, and click Next.

You are then given the option to choose a zone type. Select the default and click Next. The resulting screen asks for the first three octets of the IP address for the server and subnet in order to create the reverse lookup in-addr.arpa zone. The subnet mask should be calculated for you if you click in the subnet mask area. Accept this address and click Next (see Figure 10.10).

Name the file to be created and click Next to bring up the final screen of the Wizard. Review your selections carefully, and then click Finish to complete the installation (see Figure 10.11).

This configuration enhancement should come as a welcome change to those familiar with the Windows NT 4.0 version of DNS, not to mention those unfamiliar with the practice of configuring a DNS server. Now that the installation whizzed right by you, you may be left with some questions about the options selected or those that were not selected. A look at

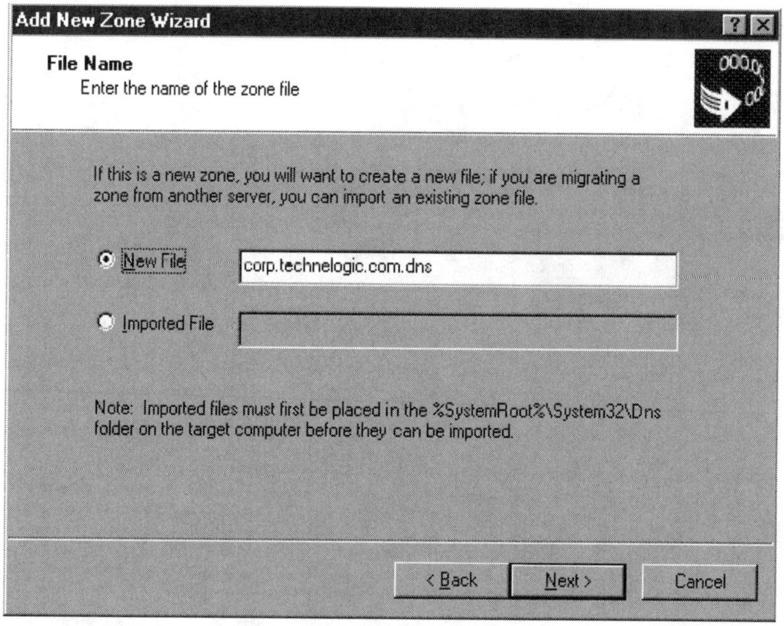

Figure 10.8   Creating the zone file on the server.

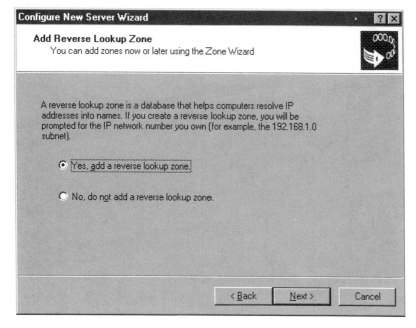

Figure 10.9   Adding the reverse lookup zone.

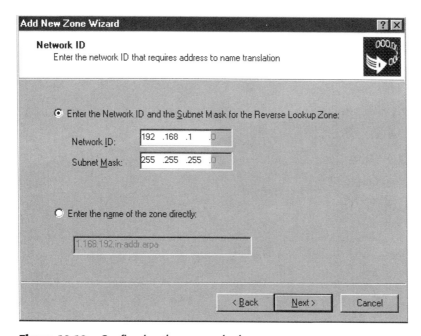

Figure 10.10   Configuring the reverse lookup zone.

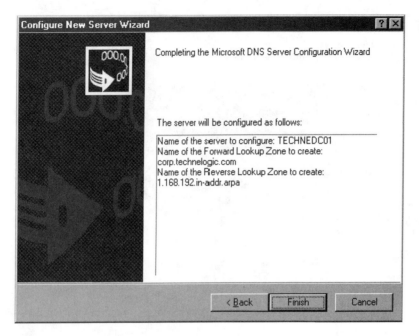

Figure 10.11   Completing the installation.

one of those options now, the zone type, will help you better understand later configuration issues surrounding the design of your DNS infrastructure (see Figure 10.12).

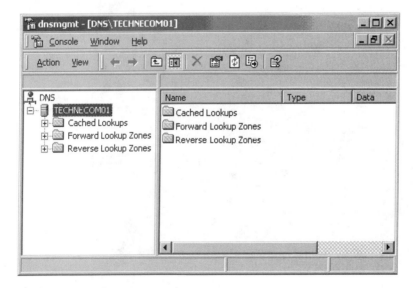

Figure 10.12   The DNS console.

Choosing a Zone Type

The first major choice faced using the DNS Wizard comes in selecting a zone type. Of the three choices presented, Active Directory Integrated is by far the most desirable choice; DNS information is stored in the directory database and therefore the information is replicated throughout the directory. If the server in question is not a domain controller (e.g., you have not run the DCPROMO utility on that server), this option is not available. Regardless of your selection at installation time, you may change this later using the DNS console. Indeed, you do not have to choose a zone type at all when installing DNS. Once the server you are installing or another becomes a domain controller with a copy of the directory database, you may then opt to integrate DNS with the directory and should.

A primary lookup zone will function just as well as an Active Directory integrated zone, although the bonus of replication, and then redundancy, is lost. This is, however, a read/write copy of DNS information, and if Dynamic DNS (DDNS) is enabled, updates to the text file will take place automatically. Figure 10.13 illustrates the zone properties configuration page in Windows 2000.

Secondary zones function as the aforementioned zone types, though in order for name resolution to occur, updated information in the zone file must be obtained through a zone transfer from a primary zone. This is discussed in greater detail in later sections that outline the process of creating or changing the zone types of an installed DNS server.

The DNS Console

So DNS is installed, now what? First, it would be wise to become familiar with the DNS console found under the Administrative Tools group in the Start menu. There are several options available here that will greatly ease the administration of the DNS services on the network.

The DNS console shown in Figure 10.14 allows an administrator to view and manipulate records and server configuration. For those familiar with previous versions of the DNS console, you may find some of the same functionality in the new console, though the structure of the DNS records are different with many new subdirectories created.

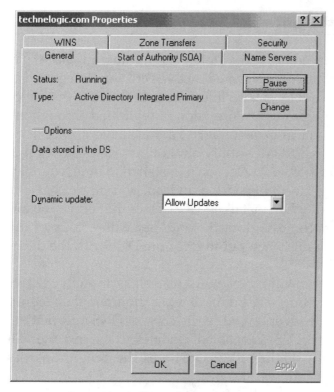

Figure 10.13   Zone properties configuration.

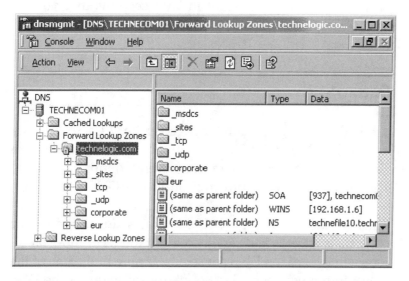

Figure 10.14   The DNS console showing the new DNS service subcategories.

Expand the tree to reveal the newly created zones for the server. Notice that when the zone you created is expanded, several sub-folders are revealed as shown in Figure 10.15. These house the service location records that are so fundamental to client logons, LDAP queries, and other service locations. Drill down through these records and become familiar with them, as they provide core functionality for the directory.

Notice that as in most MMC consoles, you have right mouse-click functionality to perform most tasks. Become familiar with the services offered through these menus, as you will use them often, particularly in larger implementations and situations where legacy NT systems coexist. Try this at the server level of the tree and at the zone level in order to distinguish between the two sets of options.

Fortunately, most of the tedium that existed in configuring the previous version of DNS from Microsoft has been removed, and most processes are now automated. There may, however, come a time where changes to the server become necessary. Let's look at a few of these situations now.

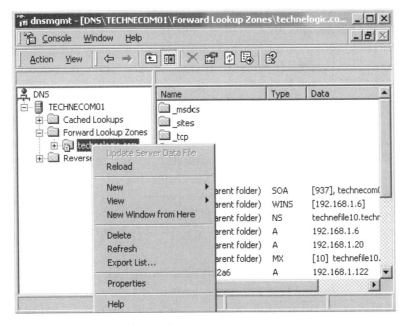

Figure 10.15 Right-click options.

Changing Zone Types

In the future of your organization, it may become necessary to rotate out DNS servers or change their roles in the grand scheme of the namespace. In order to keep the DNS hierarchy flexible, Microsoft allows the zone type to be changed from one form to another; that is, from Active Directory integrated, primary, or secondary. In large, complex DNS implementations, this serves as a powerful ally in an environment where servers often need to be moved or migrated into other roles on the network.

As we discussed in Chapter 5, "Understanding DNS Architecture," zones are based on the concept of server authority, which means that a DNS server is responsible for a particular part of the DNS hierarchy and hosts the zone or zones for it. When a DNS server is configured to load a zone, two types of resource records (RRs) determine these authoritative properties for the zone, the Start of Authority (SOA) and the Name Server (NS).

The SOA RR indicates the name of origin for the zone and contains the name of the server that is the primary source for information for the zone. In short, this record essentially defines the server name as the authority for the zone and provides the IP address mapping as well.

The NS RR is used to state which server is authoritative for the zone, and it can answer name queries for the given zone.

The SOA and NS records are required components for any zone other than secondary. These records should appear as the first and second listings in your DNS console and are often notated in the console as "same as parent folder" followed by the designated type and the data.

Changing zone types is accomplished through the Properties page of the particular zone in question. Open the DNS manager from the Administrative Tools group. Click the plus sign to the left of the forward lookup zones to view the available zones for the local server. Right-click the zone of choice and select Properties from the resulting menu. The Properties page is displayed as in Figure 10.16 with six tabs. The General tab contains the option to change the server's DNS role, as well as an option to stop the particular zone.

Notice the Type for this zone, which should be Primary if the directions in the earlier example were followed. From the General page, click the Change button and notice the options change to Active Directory Integrated or Secondary, as shown in Figure 10.17. The only item that

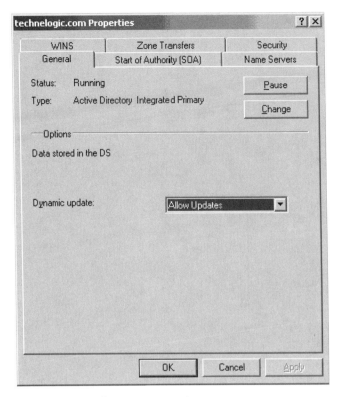

Figure 10.16 The Zone Properties page.

should be noted here is that Active Directory Integrated DNS zones are permitted only on a server that is also acting as a domain controller.

Viewing Other Zone Properties

While in the Properties page for the zone, take a moment to browse the other options contained within. First, notice that directly under the zone type is the Options section that allows the user to change DNS filenames. This actually changes depending on the zone type, where the Standard Primary and Active Directory Integrated options display a selection for dynamic update of the DNS server or Dynamic DNS (DDNS), which we discuss more extensively later in the chapter.

Click the Start of Authority (SOA) tab. Important items to notice here are the Serial number, Primary server name, Responsible party, and the intervals at which information is passed to the local server or secondary zones.

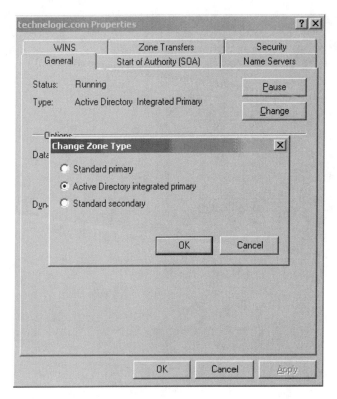

Figure 10.17   Changing zone types.

The serial number reflects the number of times that the zone file has changed (whether Primary or Active Directory Integrated), and this number increments as the file is changed. Secondary zones check for changes to the Primary zone by comparing this number to the number passed at last poll. If the number has changed, the Secondary zone requests an updated copy of the data files.

The Primary server field denotes the host name of the DNS server where the zone was created. The Responsible party field should reflect the e-mail address of the party responsible for the DNS zone. It is important to note that a period is used instead of the @ symbol for the e-mail address.

The interval fields control the refresh intervals of the Secondary zones that poll for new information from a Primary source. Figure 10.18 shows the setup for a Secondary zone where the IP address of other DNS servers is required for the push-pull relationship.

Moving on to the next tab, Name Servers, we see that all name servers registered with the local server are registered here (these are the servers reflected as NS RRs in the zone). You may edit entries here or add name servers if necessary.

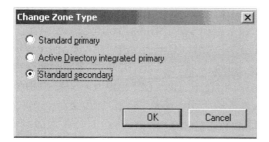

Figure 10.18 Configuring a secondary zone.

The next tab is WINS, or Windows Internet Name Service. Under this section, it is possible to integrate WINS servers in the naming system, which is particularly helpful in mixed Windows 2000/Windows NT environments. Checking the "Use WINS resolution" check box as shown in Figure 10.19 will allow name resolution in case DNS cannot resolve a name. Information is then passed from the DNS server to the WINS server (Windows 2000 still supports WINS, so this may be a

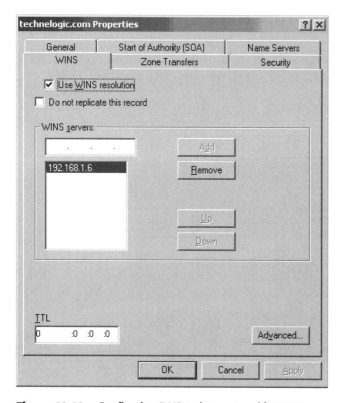

Figure 10.19 Configuring DNS to integrate with WINS.

Windows NT or 2000 server). If a name is not found in the DNS database, the DNS server will pass the request to WINS for resolution. An IP address for at least one WINS server must be furnished if this option is checked, and it may be a Windows 2000 or down-level WINS server.

The Zone Transfers tab allows the configuration of zone transfers from Primary servers to Secondary servers. Security may be tightly integrated from within this dialog box to disallow either all transfers to Secondary servers or only to a select list of servers on the network. This type of configuration will come in handy on large networks or public servers.

The last tab, Security, shows security information for the zone and the rights of the groups that have permissions to the zone.

Unlike its predecessors, the new DNS console allows a straightforward approach to configuring DNS services under Windows 2000. The ability to configure zone properties to a very granular level makes this new breed of DNS and DNS management a welcome change to the Windows 2000 family.

Configuring Server Properties

The server Properties page shown in Figure 10.20 allows configuration of the actual server parameters, such as Forwarders, Root Hints, and so forth.

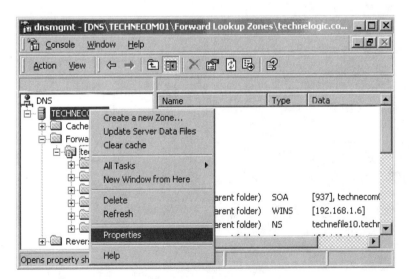

Figure 10.20 Accessing server properties.

The first tab, Interfaces, allows DNS to listen for queries on either all interfaces installed on the server or specific IP addresses. This configuration is beneficial in the case of server load balancing, where more than one network interface resides on the server to handle additional network load from multiple network segments. This will likely be found only in very large enterprise class systems.

The next tab, Forwarders, contains configuration information for entering the IP addresses of servers that will handle forwarded requests. If this is a root server, the option is not available.

In larger DNS implementations, it will become necessary to add DNS servers for fault tolerance and load balancing, not to mention to better follow the network topography and domain hierarchy. As these new DNS servers come online underneath the root, server requests for upstream or cross-stream resources will occur outside of the local DNS zone. Configuring the server with forwarders will point these recursive queries to the proper server for resolve.

To configure a forwarder in the DNS console do the following:

1. In the DNS console, right-click the server icon (not a zone) and choose Properties as shown in Figure 10.21.

2. Check the Enable forwarder(s) check box and then enter the IP address(es) of the DNS servers that will service queries passed from this server for further resolution.

3. The Advanced tab permits enabling or disabling of specific server functions, such as recursion or round robin. For a detailed explanation of configuring round robin, see the DNS help system in Windows 2000.

4. Root hints help the server locate other servers in the hierarchy. If the server is a root server, this option is not available. Enter the domain name and IP address of other servers upstream from the local server.

5. The Logging, Monitoring, and Security tabs provide useful tools to monitor and lock down the DNS server.

Dynamic DNS

Today, most DNS servers must be updated manually to change allocated names and addresses. Most DNS entries are not updated very

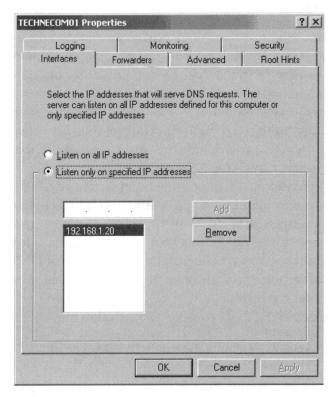

Figure 10.21 Configuring server options.

often, so this isn't a big deal. But it becomes a different story when you're trying to keep up with the constant updates that are incurred by linking DDNS names to Dynamic Host Configuration Protocol (DHCP) leased addresses. If you also have slave DNS servers—servers that have cached their information for a set or lengthy period of time—they most likely won't get the information when it's needed.

The Internet Engineering Task Force (IETF) created RFCs 1996 and 2136 to outline how DDNS should work. DDNS strives to create an environment in which DNS can function without causing a great server load. Because of its interaction with DHCP, as an IP address changes, the DHCP server sends a message to the DDNS server stating the change. The DDNS server then, in turn, sends an update to dependent slave servers. Additionally, a very short cache time-out will enable DNS servers on the Internet to receive changes, while still providing for all the features DNS offers. Further yet, it would be very difficult for a Windows 2000 network to function in such a dynamic environment where the primary location service was static. This is the reason Microsoft recommends using Windows 2000 DDNS in conjunction with DHCP or a viable alternative that supports the aforementioned RFCs. Figure 10.22 shows the interaction between DDNS, DHCP, and the client.

In addition to these RFCs, DDNS servers supporting a Windows 2000 network must also provide a service locator record type, which is defined in RFC 2052 and is known as the SRV RR. SRV records are similar to a mail exchanger MX RR where several different servers advertise a comparable service. SRV resource records are used in locating domain controllers for authentication to the domain as shown in Figure 10.22.

DDNS and Legacy Client Support (DHCP Is DDNS Aware)

We discussed briefly the interaction of DHCP and DDNS earlier in the chapter, which allows support for dynamic client registration with the DNS server.

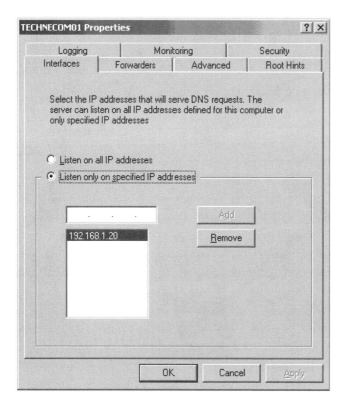

Figure 10.22 SRV RRs.

DHCP is standards based and is defined by IETF RFCs 2131 and 2132. DHCP is used to pass client configuration information about the TCP/IP network in which it will participate. This dynamic method of passing TCP/IP configuration information to the client relieves the tremendous administrative burden of having to manually configure every client on the network individually to partake in an IP network. The key work here is "dynamic," as information such as the IP address or client name may change often.

In situations where there are a large number of clients spanning many subnets using DHCP, the task of manually updating a DNS server would prove to be quite harrowing. Enter DDNS-aware DHCP.

In Windows 2000, a DHCP server will pass first the client configuration information, then the DHCP service-passes updated pointer RR (PTR) and address RR (A) information to the DDNS server, acting on behalf of the client (see Figure 10.23). Additionally, Microsoft states that

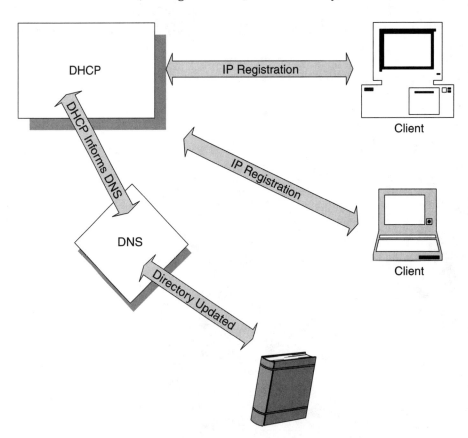

Figure 10.23   DHCP in Windows 2000 integrates with DNS and Active Directory.

"(an) additional DHCP option code (option code 81) (may be entered) that enables the return of a client's fully qualified domain name (FQDN) to the DHCP server. If implemented, this option is then interpreted by the DHCP server, which can then initiate further interaction and updating by using dynamic DNS (DDNS) to modify an individual host's resource records with a dynamic DNS server."

Though covered in more detail later in the book, it is worth mentioning that this interaction allows legacy systems support through the ability to register both A and PTR records. This essentially "lets a DHCP server act as a proxy for clients, such as the Microsoft Windows 9x operating system and Windows NT 4.0, for the purpose of DDNS registration. The DHCP server can differentiate between Windows 2000 Professional and other clients." Windows 2000 clients will automatically attempt to register PTR and A RR's with the DNS server at logon.

Configuring DDNS

Like most of the tasks in this new operating system, setting up the server for dynamic updates is quite easy. Configuring DDNS is done by zone, forward and reverse, one by one. There are two zone types that allow DDNS updates, Primary and Active Directory integrated. Figure 10.24 shows the Properties dialog box for a zone on the DNS server. The General tab houses the option to configure the server for DDNS.

Under the Options section is a drop-down list box titled "Dynamic Update," and it is from here that you "turn on" the DDNS option for the zone. There are three options to choose from: None, Allow Updates, or Allow Only Secure Updates.

Typically, the Allow Updates option will suffice on a local area network or wide area implementations. The secure option only comes into play (although the option is still present in Active Directory integrated zones) in standard primary zones where dynamic updates are not secured and any potential client can update these record types. Active Directory integrated zones automatically enforce secured updates.

As was with WINS clients, the registration process must be refreshed every so often, By default this is 12 hours for Windows 2000 clients. Unlike WINS, the DNS server will not *tombstone* (mark it for deletion) the entry after the expiration of 12 hours or failure to reregister.

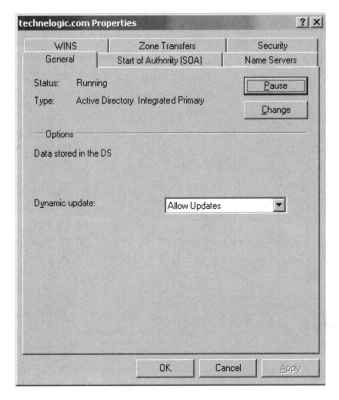

Figure 10.24   The General tab of the Properties page for a zone.

The changes to make the server/zone DDNS capable are instant and require no reboot or restart of the service. Simply click the Apply and/or the OK button to effect the changes.

Testing Name Resolution

Now that the DNS services are properly configured, it is necessary to test and see if the server is actually servicing requests.

 It is assumed that the WINS service is not installed or not running for the following tests, as this may interfere with the results.

There are two Unix-based command-line utilities included with the Windows family of operating systems that are very helpful in determining IP connectivity and name resolution on IP networks: PING and

NSLOOKUP. Let's start by using the PING utility at the server to determine whether TCP/IP services are connected properly.

 This book assumes that the server operating system is installed and functioning properly. Installing and configuring the server and IP services other than those inherent to Active Directory are beyond the scope of this book. Setup instructions for the operating system may be found on the media supplied, or information may be found at www.microsoft.com.

From the Start menu, click Run to open a GUI-based command line. Type in "cmd" and press Return or click OK to open a command prompt. At the prompt, type "ping localhost" and press Return as shown in Figure 10.25. The resulting data should reflect something similar to Figure 10.26.

This test makes sure that the local adapter is configured properly and has an IP and subnet address. Four responses and the statistics are returned. The important data in this test is the information after the PINGING … answer where the output should return the <server-name>.<Windows domain name>.<DNS domain name>.<root>. In our example, the data is techneroot.corporate.technologic.com. If this data was not returned, check that the adapter has at minimum an IP address and subnet mask assigned to the primary adapter. Also, check that the DNS server(s) is listed in network setup as well. This may be the local

```
F:\WINNT\System32\cmd.exe                                          _ □ ×

F:\>ping /?

Usage: ping [-t] [-a] [-n count] [-l size] [-f] [-i TTL] [-v TOS]
            [-r count] [-s count] [[-j host-list] ¦ [-k host-list]]
            [-w timeout] destination-list

Options:
    -t             Ping the specified host until stopped.
                   To see statistics and continue - type Control-Break;
                   To stop - type Control-C.
    -a             Resolve addresses to hostnames.
    -n count       Number of echo requests to send.
    -l size        Send buffer size.
    -f             Set Don't Fragment flag in packet.
    -i TTL         Time To Live.
    -v TOS         Type Of Service.
    -r count       Record route for count hops.
    -s count       Timestamp for count hops.
    -j host-list   Loose source route along host-list.
    -k host-list   Strict source route along host-list.
    -w timeout     Timeout in milliseconds to wait for each reply.

F:\>
```

Figure 10.25 Testing the local interface using the PING utility.

```
F:\WINNT\System32\cmd.exe                                          _ □ ×

F:\>ping 192.168.1.20

Pinging 192.168.1.20 with 32 bytes of data:

Reply from 192.168.1.20: bytes=32 time<10ms TTL=128
Reply from 192.168.1.20: bytes=32 time<10ms TTL=128
Reply from 192.168.1.20: bytes=32 time<10ms TTL=128
Reply from 192.168.1.20: bytes=32 time<10ms TTL=128

Ping statistics for 192.168.1.20:
    Packets: Sent = 4, Received = 4, Lost = 0 (0% loss),
Approximate round trip times in milli-seconds:
    Minimum = 0ms, Maximum = 0ms, Average = 0ms

F:\>_
```

Figure 10.26   The resulting data.

server or another separate DNS server depending on how you installed
these services. The DNS server or domain controller, as the case may be,
should have a static IP address assigned.

Next, try the PING utility again to test name resolution for the local
server, as shown in Figure 10.27. A similar output with name resolution
should occur. If you have other servers or clients on the network at this
point, try this again. Do not fret if you get a "request timed out" or
"unknown host <name>" error. These hosts may not be registered with

```
F:\WINNT\System32\cmd.exe                                          _ □ ×
Microsoft Windows 2000 [Version 5.00.2000]
(C) Copyright 1985-1999 Microsoft Corp.

F:\>ping technefile10

Pinging technefile10.technelogic.com [192.168.1.6] with 32 bytes of data:

Reply from 192.168.1.6: bytes=32 time<10ms TTL=128
Reply from 192.168.1.6: bytes=32 time<10ms TTL=128
Reply from 192.168.1.6: bytes=32 time<10ms TTL=128
Reply from 192.168.1.6: bytes=32 time<10ms TTL=128

Ping statistics for 192.168.1.6:
    Packets: Sent = 4, Received = 4, Lost = 0 (0% loss),
Approximate round trip times in milli-seconds:
    Minimum = 0ms, Maximum = 0ms, Average = 0ms

F:\>
```

Figure 10.27   PINGing a host name to test resolution.

Figure 10.28   Using the NSLOOKUP utility.

the DNS server yet, or another anomaly could be precluding a response. Troubleshooting is covered in detail in following sections. The PING utility returns data about a host name passed from an A type RR on the DNS server. A PTR RR is also created when the client registers with the DNS server and corresponds to a reverse lookup for that client.

 There is yet another assumption here that the server was set up with a reverse lookup zone that corresponds to the forward lookup zone during the DNS setup process.

NSLOOKUP run from the command line allows the reverse function of a name lookup, where the command is issued as NSLOOKUP <host IP address> at the prompt (see Figure 10.28). From the IP address, a reverse lookup is issued to the DNS server and the PTR record accessed, then the host name is returned.

To further test the server, you will want to see if the DNS server is listening for client requests. To do this, use the NSLOOKUP utility with the following syntax:

NSLOOKUP <server ip address> 127.0.0.1

The server should return the local loopback address and server name followed by the name of the local DNS server and IP address. Such a response means that the server is listening (via UDP on port 53) for client requests and is functioning properly.

The NSLOOKUP utility is helpful in many ways. First, it checks the integrity of the reverse lookup zone. Second, it is often necessary to track down hosts that are wreaking havoc on the network or committing other offenses tracked by IP address such as in firewall or proxy server logs. Additionally, this command-line utility may be used to configure DNS server parameters. Type NSLOOKUP at the command prompt and press Return. A prompt is returned without the drive letter designated. You are in the NSLOOKUP command program, which offers many query, database, and configuration options. From here, you may list all records in the database or change the listening TCP/IP port number for the server. Figure 10.28 lists the command-line syntax and was listed by typing "?" at the NSLOOKP program prompt.

It is key that DNS services are working properly before attempting to move forward with the next step of promoting a server to a domain controller. Use these helpful utilities to test the integrity of the server and name resolution. The installation of the service and configuration are fairly straightforward, though there may be snags along the way. The next section outlines steps to take in the event of catastrophic failure.

Manually Updating Database Records

During the course of configuring the DNS server, it may become necessary to manually add, delete, or modify a record in a zone—although the process of RR updates is wholly automated in Windows 2000, regardless of the existence of down-level clients and servers.

In order to add a record manually to a zone, right-click the zone and choose New, and then Host… from the resulting menu. This is the manual insertion of an A RR to the zone. An example of when this type of update might be necessary is in the event that a network is comprised of mixed network members and legacy DHCP servers are in use and not DDNS aware.

Troubleshooting Methods

There are three pieces to the DNS equation that could potentially falter and cause you tribulations on the road to Active Directory Nirvana: the server itself, the DNS zones, and the client. We examine each of these in an attempt to resolve common issues.

Let us assume first that the server is configured correctly and the snag has occurred at the client end, as will most often be the case (unless the IT department is fielding tons of connectivity failure calls, which would obviously be a server issue). As discussed in the previous section, it is important to test that the client actually has network connectivity. Try the following steps:

1. PING the localhost (loopback) address and see if the network adapter is responding.
2. PING the IP address of the client to check that an IP address is bound to the adapter.
3. PING the gateway (router) address for your local subnet, which verifies that packets are being routed.
4. PING the DNS server last to check for a response.

If all of these tests complete successfully, try checking the client's DHCP configuration by typing "IPCONFIG /"all at a command prompt. The returned information should have an entry included that lists one or more DNS servers. If this is not the case, try the same command with the /release option, followed by a reboot. (Note: If the client is of the Windows 9x type, the syntax is "winipcfg /release_all".) Reboot the client and check this configuration information again.

Should the client fail to list DNS servers, then the DHCP scope for that subnet is likely not configured or improperly configured. Check the scope to determine whether it has been set up to pass DNS server information. If your clients are manually configured, check the Network Applet in Control Panel for the existence of the information just discussed.

Check to see if the problem exists for all queries or just a select few, or perhaps just the one. With all of the client-side information confirmed working and DNS problems still in the Help Desk queue, it is time to focus on the server itself. As an intermediary step, first look for reasons why only specific queries fail. Ask the following questions.

Is the server queried authoritative for the name being queried? If the answer is yes, then a DNS server configuration error is probably the culprit. Check that the record exists for the zone (remember you can print the database from a command line using the NSLOOKUP utility!). Also, consider that the FQDN must reflect the parent zone that is loading on the server. Wks1.corporate.technelogic.com reflects the host "Wks1" in domain corporate.technologic.com.

If the server is not authoritative for the name, then the server is likely experiencing recursion problems, whereby the query to another DNS server for the IP address fails. Microsoft DNS servers are set to use recursive queries by default (with the exception of slave servers), and this operation may fail if certain configuration parameters are incorrect. DNS servers use Root Hints to discover other DNS servers in the DNS hierarchy. Root Hints are stored in the cache.dns file located in the <system root>\winnt\system32\Dns folder. It is assumed that your network implementation is a private network, so this file may be populated with the local root server information in order to help the process of discovery. DNS servers that act as Internet resolvers will want to keep this file intact.

Can the server that is authoritative for the record PING the root server? This is important in the grand scheme of your overall DNS design. Child-domain DNS servers authoritative for a zone must be able to move up the hierarchy to resolve names throughout the enterprise. Check for simple IP connectivity using the PING utility from one server to another until a broken link is identified. Often this is a physical network problem and not a configuration issue with the DNS server(s).

For the most part, checking these items should resolve most of the common problems experienced with a DNS system. For advanced troubleshooting and configuration tips, check the DNS help system or Microsoft's Web site for the latest information.

Best Practices

The old days of complicated DNS architectures are far removed from the DDNS hierarchies possible in Windows 2000. Most of the complicated work and administrative tasks are now automated, more so if DNS is Active Directory integrated.

The benefits of DNS Active Directory integration go beyond the simple database replication issues inherent to this type of implementation. Setting up Active Directory integrated DNS offers the added stability of having a one-to-one correspondence of DNS servers to domain controllers, and it eases the configuration issues surrounding third-party DNS solutions or standard primary servers. Use Active Directory integrated zones if possible to simplify administration and configuration.

In situations where server load or bandwidth is an issue, consider the use of additional DNS servers set up as secondary servers. This will help alleviate latency issues that might occur in these situations.

Microsoft suggests limiting the use of CNAME RRs (canonical name resource records) that may be assigned to alias an A RR. The potential exists for duplicate names in the same zone, which further equates to a name resolution or resource access failure. If aliases are to be used, keep a spreadsheet of the aliases and other relevant information to access quickly in the event of a problem.

Use the namespace design drafted in the planning phase of your network implementation to lay out the framework for your DNS infrastructure. Using DNS that is Active Directory integrated is the most straightforward approach if you have limited experience with DNS architecture and best practices.

Summary

This chapter discussed the actual hands-on of installing and configuring DNS, the first step in implementing Active Directory. Installing the service, configuring the server and zones, and best practices were all discussed to better facilitate a smooth DNS installation and further a good foothold to Active Directory installation. The next chapter finally brings the reality of Active Directory to life with the hands-on to installing and configuring Active Directory.

CHAPTER

11

Installing Active Directory and Using Management Tools

INTRODUCTION

This chapter covers the steps one must follow in order to promote a server to a domain controller, the second step in creating an Active Directory hierarchy. Topics include:

- **Requirements for Active Directory Installation**
- **The DCPROMO Command-Line Utility**
- **Installation Scenarios**
- **Checking the Installation**
- **Best Practices**

During the process of running the setup program for Windows 2000 Server, unlike its predecessors, there is no option to choose the role that the server will play. In Windows NT, during the setup process, the setup process asks the person installing the operating system whether the server will act as a Primary Domain Controller (PDC), Backup Domain Controller (BDC), or Standalone server (Member server). This in and of itself was a limitation in previous versions, as the decision between domain controller and Member server was etched in stone.

Once a domain controller was selected, if the server needed to be redeployed as a server in another role, say a Member server, the server would require a reinstallation of the operating system. This was also true if the server acted as a domain controller and needed to be moved to another domain. This concrete nature of server roles is very inflexible, which in turn translates into IT dollars spent redeploying servers. Figure 11.1 outlines a typical Windows NT deployment and the associated inflexibility.

One of the most welcome changes to this new operating system, Windows 2000 Server, is the ability to move servers freely from one role to another, member to domain controller, and vice versa. When running the setup for Windows 2000, you are not asked the role of the server, as the server is brought into its world as a lonely Member server with no affiliation to a domain at all. A conscious, secondary step must be performed in order to *promote* the server to a domain controller. This pro-

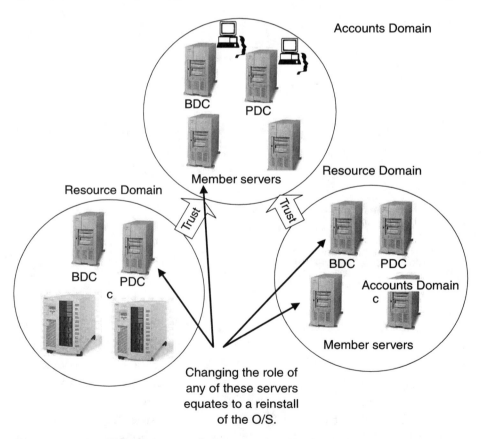

Figure 11.1 A typical Windows NT deployment showing the fixed nature of the operating system.

motion is accomplished through a command-line utility, *DCPROMO*, which invokes a Wizard to guide you through the setup process.

There are forks in the road during the domain controller promotion using the DCPROMO utility. The first step in creating a Windows 2000 network is creating the root domain from which all other domains or organizational or structural elements will follow. It is this first crucial step that determines the success of the rest of the network, as all other domains are dependencies (lest you have decided to take an unorthodox approach to your network architecture).

The act of invoking the DCPROMO utility and converting the Member server to a domain controller will also create either the root of the Active Directory, if this is the first server, or subsequent stores or partitions of the Active Directory hierarchy. Domain controllers provide directory services and are the storage houses of the directory database and replication devices. With directory services in place, clients are then able to authenticate to the domain. When a server is promoted to a domain controller, it becomes the root domain of a tree or a functioning member of the directory services tree. Similarly, when the server is *demoted* from domain controller to a member server, it loses its Active Directory functions and retains only local functions. Figure 11.2 shows the transmutable properties of Windows 2000 Servers.

As with the installation of DNS services, which you will see is also maybe incorporated in this process as well, it is imperative to have your preplanning documentation handy at this stage to use as a guide to naming the domain controller or subsequent domain controllers. First things first, however. Let's look at what is required to promote a server to a domain controller/Active Directory server.

Requirements for Installing a Domain Controller and Active Directory

There are certain requirements that must be fulfilled prior to the installation of Active Directory. Try not to confuse this with the installation of a domain controller, though the two are synonymous. What does that mean? Chapter 10, "Installing and Configuring DNS," discussed the installation of DNS on a level initially where the DNS server acts on an independent server or servers on the network. Later in the chapter, the idea of DNS services coexisting on the same server as the domain

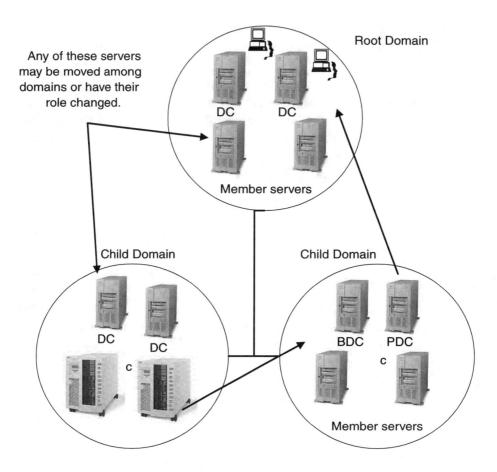

Any of these servers
may be moved among
domains or have their
role changed.

Root Domain

DC   DC

Member servers

Child Domain

DC
    DC

C

Child Domain

BDC   PDC

C

Member servers

Figure 11.2   A typical Windows 2000 deployment with interchangeable servers.

controller is suggested as the recommended approach. In order for Active Directory to function correctly, the dependency services of DNS must be present, even during the setup process. In larger implementations, or in cases where a large DNS infrastructure already exists, DNS will surely not exist on the same server as Active Directory.

In situations where this is not true, or if starting from a clean slate, the recommended option of DNS and Active Directory coexistence is an appealing approach to setting up a Windows 2000 network purely out of the automation of both the DNS and Active Directory installation processes. Part of the setup procedure for promoting a server to a domain controller and installing Active Directory is checking for the existence of a DNS server. If no DNS services are found, the setup program will "auto magically" set up DNS in the same server as well.

In addition to the DNS requirement, the promotion also requires the existence of an NTFS 5 partition in order to install and secure parts of the directory and database. This partition may or may not exist depending on choices made during the installation of the server. Verify that the server does have at least one NTFS partition and that it is large enough to accommodate a decent amount of data. Two gigabytes for this data at the low end per domain controller should suffice. This information may reside on the operating system partition or elsewhere. We will talk more about this later in the chapter.

 This brings up an important consideration for those of you new to Windows Server operating systems. The operating system partition requirements from one version to the next (that is, from 3.51 to 4.0 of Windows NT) changed drastically. To this day, I have seen gross underestimation as to the size of this partition. Often this not the fault of the operator or administrator, rather that certain Microsoft code required that updated versions of programs such as Internet Explorer and the like install to the partition where the operating system lives. Service Packs are another culprit. In sizing your system partitions with Windows 2000, make sure to leave plenty of room for the operating system and supporting utilities. Where 1GB was plenty with version 3.51 of NT, in 4.0 it was not. Similarly, between Windows NT 4.0 and 2000, where 3–4GB may have been enough previously (including additions and Service Packs), it is likely the need will increase under the new operating system in the future. Plan for this so as not to be caught with a host of servers that have to be reinstalled or restored from tape.

Additionally, you must be logged onto the server as the local administrator or have an account with administrative authority in order to run the DCPROMO program. If this is a replica domain controller (other than the original domain controller) for the domain, the domain administrator account is required. The list of names for domain(s) created in the planning stage should also be present. The Active Directory installation may also be run from the Configure Your Server tool that appears on startup of the server. The latter process is completely automated with the exception of a few questions, and much simpler to execute. We will take a look at that process in a moment after taking on the manual process of running DCPROMO, strictly as a learning utility. On to promoting a server.

The DCPROMO Utility

As we discussed earlier, initiating the DCPROMO utility is necessary to promote the server from a Member server to a domain controller. The program is invoked from a command line, either from a command prompt or from the Windows 2000 Run option in the Start menu.

Once the command is run, the Active Directory Installation Wizard is invoked, and a Welcome screen gives information on the process. Next, we'll undergo the step-by-step process of installing Active Directory. The first section on installing Active Directory assumes that this is the initial installation of Active Directory on the network, or more accurately, that a new tree is being created that is not participating in a forest. Subsequent sections and chapters contain the scenarios for creating replica domain controllers and child domains. Figure 11.3 shows a flowchart of the installation process and the paths that may be taken on the

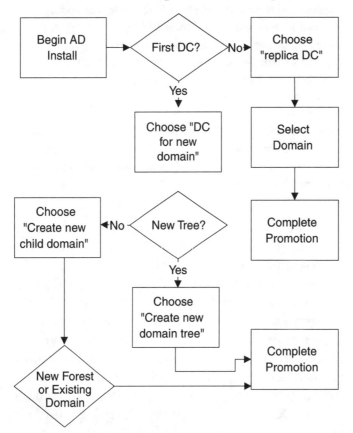

Figure 11.3 Flowchart showing the branches that may be taken during the domain controller promotion.

road to creating an Active Directory hierarchy using the Active Directory Installation Wizard (DCPROMO).

Step-by-Step Installation of the First Domain Controller

The first step to installing Active Directory via the DCPROMO method is through invoking the Active Directory Installation Wizard, which is done by running the DCPROMO command-line function as shown in Figure 11.4.

From the Welcome screen, click Next to begin the process of installing directory services. The next several windows contain a sort of a questionnaire. These questions help the Wizard determine the type of domain controller being installed and where it will sit in the domain tree hierarchy.

You should now be in the Domain Controller Type window, which asks whether you want this domain controller to be a new domain controller for a new domain or a replica domain controller for an existing domain. Since we are assuming that this is the first domain controller in the first domain, select the first option, "Domain controller for a new domain." Figure 11.5 shows this process. Click Next to continue.

The next screen, Create Tree or Child Domain, offers the option to either create a new domain tree using this domain controller as the root server (which, as we will later discuss, may also be used to create a forest of trees), or a child domain using this server as the first domain controller in the branch (this is where you would create first-level domains discussed earlier in the book). Figure 11.6 shows the options on this form. Select the option for "Create a new domain tree" and Next to continue.

Figure 11.7 shows the Create or Join Forest option. Here you are asked if the tree will exist in an existing forest or if this is a new forest altogether. Because this is the first tree in the forest, choose the "Create

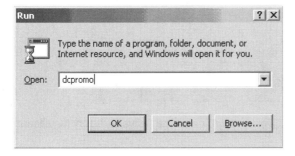

Figure 11.4   Running DCPROMO to invoke the Active Directory Installation Wizard.

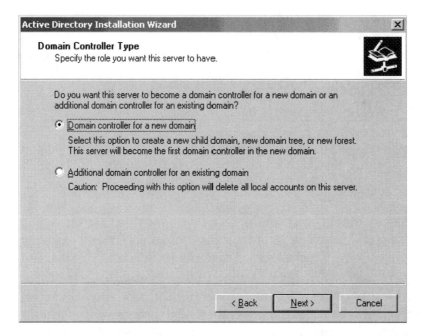

Figure 11.5 Selecting the option for a new domain controller In a new domain.

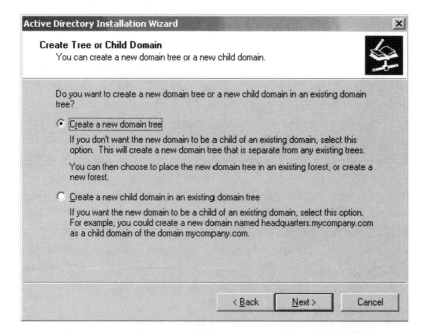

Figure 11.6 The Create Tree or Child Domain window of the Active Directory Installation Wizard.

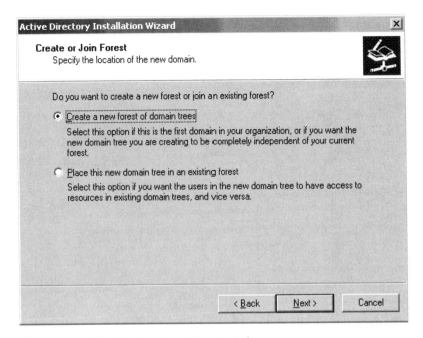

Figure 11.7   The Create or Join Forest window.

a new forest of domain trees" option, and continue. You are asked to provide the name of the domain name next. This should come from your preplanning documentation and will reflect the top-level domain name that you have chosen for the company. In the example shown in Figure 11.8, this is the domain name for the company that is registered with an Internet authority such as the InterNIC. This sets up the possibility for a geopolitical model where the following first-level child domains may be set up as geographical domains, then further subdivided into divisions. Figure 11.8 displays this type of setup in the technelogic.com tree.

Next, select the full DNS for the new domain, and select Next as in Figure 11.9.

A NetBIOS name is required in the next screen (sigh!) for legacy support. This will be the NetBIOS name of the domain. In Figure 11.10, the name for the domain is technelogic, which supports down-level clients on a mixed-mode network. Figure 11.11 shows the way that this would appear in a Windows NT 4.0 Workstation client browse list. The NetBIOS names allow these clients to function on the Windows 2000 network.

The Wizard now asks to verify the location of the directory databases and log files. The default should be acceptable in most situations. In the case of very large enterprise installations where domain controllers will be handling a very large amount of objects in the database, it would be best

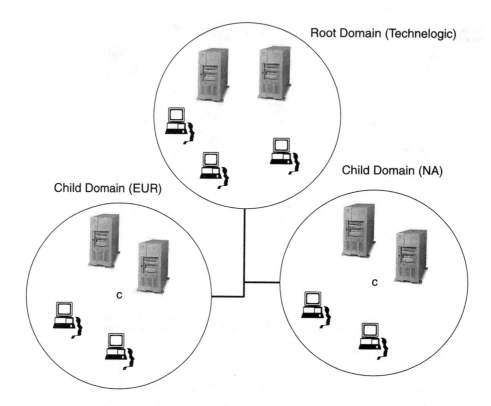

Figure 11.8   The technelogic.com tree.

to relocate these files to dedicated disk or partition (as you would with any database server). Figure 11.12 shows a depiction of this screen.

The next item presented is the location of the "shared system volume," synonymous with the Netlogon directory of old, where logon and replicated items are stored for use by all network clients. Again, the default should be acceptable here. Figure 11.12 shows the Shared System Volume window. The last screen presented in the Wizard confirms all selections. It is a good idea to review these for errors before continuing to avoid having to run DCPROMO twice, once to demote the server, then promote it again. At least that option is available should something go awry, and it is a good idea to be familiar with the process as it will be used in the future.

Installing Replica Domain Controllers

There are conditions that dictate the use of multiple domain controllers in a domain, particularly for fault tolerance. Should the only domain

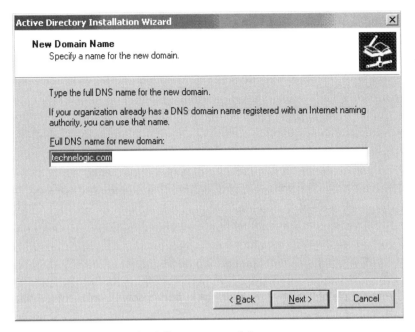

Figure 11.9   Entering the full DNS name of the server.

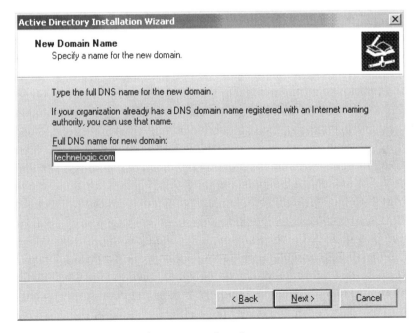

Figure 11.10   Entering the NetBIOS domain name.

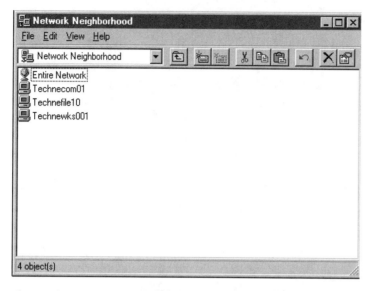

Figure 11.11   An example of how the browse list looks from a down-level client (NT 4.0) perspective.

controller at the root suffer some catastrophic fate without a backup controller in place, the net result is the demotion of all child domains and re-creation of the entire directory structure.

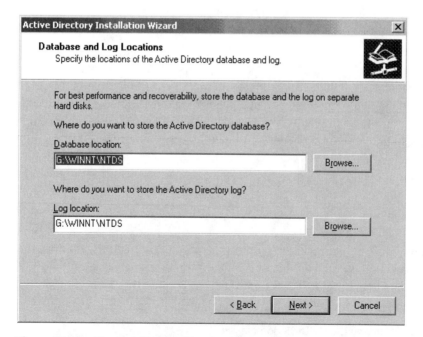

Figure 11.12   The Database and Log Location options.

Other than fault tolerance, larger implementations will certainly call for multiple domain controllers to facilitate a large number of logons within a domain. While it is true that with the implementation of sites that clients will be redirected to other domain controllers (hopefully within the same site if other domain controllers exist) in the event of a situation where a local server cannot provide a reply, this may mean that subsequent logon requests may overrun WAN connections to find a logon server.

The number of logons that a single server can manage depends on the complexity of the server hardware, of course, but the old rules of Windows NT are a good standard to use where there should (roughly) be one domain controller per every 2500 users (dedicated). In all cases, it is recommended that a secondary domain controller exist to contain a replica copy of the root server directory database.

Step-by-Step Installation of Replica Domain Controllers

The installation of replica domain controllers is not so far off the process of installing the initial domain controller. The catch is that you must have an account in the domain that has authority to add a server to the domain. This may be the administrator account, though any account with domain administrative privileges will work.

From the server to be converted, run the DCPROMO utility to begin the Active Directory Installation Wizard, clicking Next to continue to the Domain Controller Type screen. Click on the option for Additional domain controller and click Next as shown in Figure 11.13.

You will need the full DNS name for the domain in which the domain controller will participate. This should be something like domain_name .com. This is shown in Figure 11.14 using the technologic example.

Click Next and enter the administrative credentials necessary to join the server to the domain and partake in the directory. The following options are for database paths and confirmation of the choices made. Once validated, the Wizard will begin installing the directory components and then ask for a reboot.

Creating Child Domains in the Hierarchy

So far, the discussion of creating domain controllers has worked within the confines of a single domain. In order to create the first-level

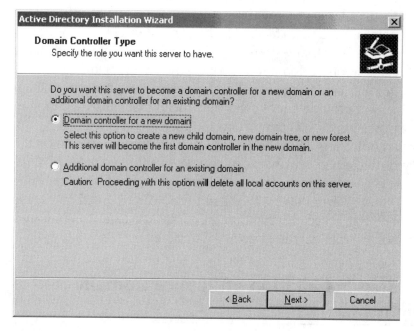

Figure 11.13 Creating a replica domain controller.

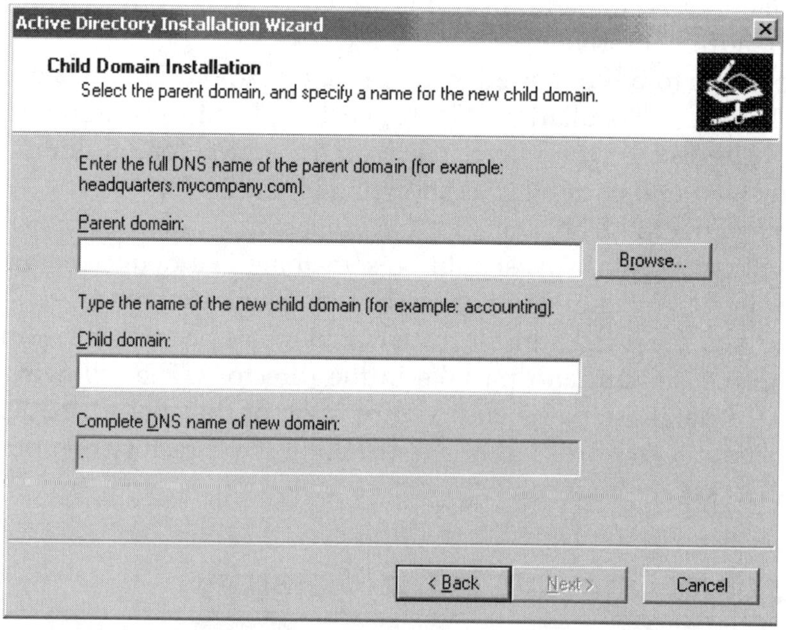

Figure 11.14 Enter the full DNS name.

domains discussed earlier in the book and build a complex Active Directory hierarchy, child domains must be generated. This is accomplished in the same manner as previous installations, with a few twists.

Begin by running the Active Directory Installation Wizard via DCPROMO. At the Domain Controller Type page, choose "Domain controller for a new domain" option and click Next as in Figure 11.15.

On the Create Tree or Child Domain page, choose the option for "Create a new child domain in an existing domain tree," then click Next (see Figure 11.16).

The next set of options on the Child Domain Installation set has not been seen yet. Click on the Browse button to the left of the Parent domain text box to check for the existence of the domain in which you are placing this domain. The Parent domain should appear in a window like the one shown in Figure 11.17.

Select the Parent domain and click OK. The Parent domain text box should now have the name of the Parent domain listed. Add the name of the Child domain in the Child domain text box. This should be the geographic region if this is a first-level domain (providing the geo-political model is being used). Notice that the name of the complete DNS name

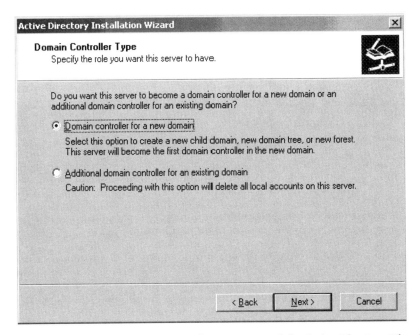

Figure 11.15   The Domain Controller Type page of the Active Directory Wizard.

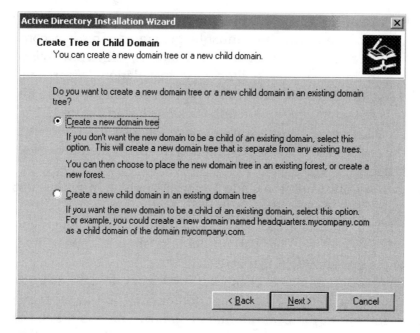

Figure 11.16   The Create Tree or Child Domain page.

is filled in for you beneath. Figure 11.18 shows an example of this. Click Next to continue.

Choose the NetBIOS name and select the database and log paths. Confirm the responses and click Next to install Active Directory.

Figure 11.17   The Browse for Domain window.

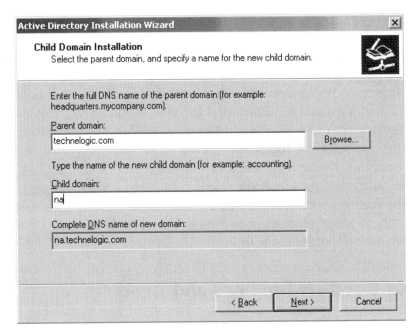

Figure 11.18   The Child domain windows with values completed.

Using the Active Directory Management Tools

Now that the enterprise is forming and child domains are in place, it might be a good time to talk about Windows 2000 management tools used in tuning, configuring, and managing the directory and directory objects. These tools are relevant at this juncture as the creation of directory objects such as user accounts and, more importantly, Organizational Units (OUs) must be carried out to further build the network. As always, have the preplanning documentation on hand for reference before continuing.

There are several management tools provided as MMC consoles that are used in the day-to-day overseeing of the directory:

- The Active Directory Domains and Trusts (ADDT) tool
- The Active Directory Sites and Services (ADSS) tool
- The Active Directory Users and Computers (ADUC) tool

Additionally, you should have a good knowledge of the DNS console in order to check Resource Records (RRs) in the case of failures.

Directory services tools are found beginning from the Start menu, Programs, and then under the Administrative Tools group similar to Figure 11.19. Notice all three of the tools mentioned.

Technically, there are other tools used to manage directory services. Any tool that is used to manipulate objects within the directory would qualify as a directory management tool. However, in order to focus on high-level directory management and to keep confusion to a minimum, these first three tools are the focus in this chapter.

Begin by opening the Active Directory Domains and Trusts (ADDT) console. The console should look like Figure 11.20. In each instance of discussing the Active Directory tool set, we first cover what the console panes and objects are, followed by a functional tour. You must have access permissions to access these tools.

The Active Directory Domains and Trusts Console

The ADDT console provides the user interface by which the branches of the trees are managed. The tool provides a mechanism to manage each domain in the Active Directory from a simple point and click. The functions performed by the ADDT tool are high-level management tasks, such as managing trust relationships, configuring server mode operation (mixed mode or native mode), changing the role of a domain controller to act as Operations Master, and adding UPN suffixes for use in a forest.

Figure 11.20 shows the ADDT console with the Scope pane containing the root directory object and child objects. Objects represented here are the

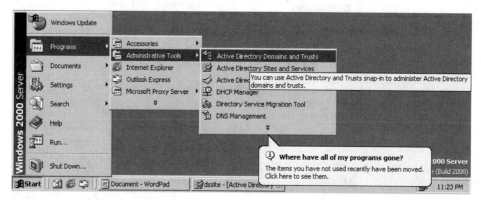

Figure 11.19   Launching the Active Directory consoles from the Administrative Tools group.

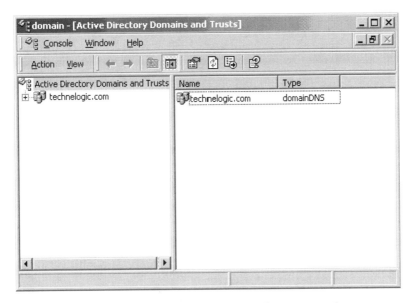

Figure 11.20   The Active Directory Domains and Trusts console.

physical domain objects that make up the directory. Observe the design with the root domain located at the top of the tree and the first-level child domains representing geographic regions beneath. The Scope pane is the main focus of the ADDT console, and the results pane displays little or no information. Object manipulation, as in most console tools, is achieved through the right-click function and resulting menu options.

Right-click the root object to find the following options:

- Manage
- View
- New Window from Here
- Export List…
- Properties
- Help

The two major menu options of concern here are Manage and Properties. Clicking on the Manage menu item of a selected domain object launches the Active Directory Users and Computers console for that domain. More on this tool in a moment.

The Properties menu item is used to configure the mode of the domain and manage trust relationships. There are three tabs on the Properties page:

- General
- Trusts
- Managed By

The General tab shows the down-level domain name and has a place to enter a description of the domain itself. Below these options is the Change Domain Modes selection.

Mixed-mode domain operation allows down-level Windows NT domain controllers to exist in the domain and authenticate user logons. Mixed mode is the default mode at installation, so switching to native mode must be a conscious decision. If your Windows 2000 installation is beginning from scratch, and there are no legacy domains or issues that will coexist, then switching to native mode is perfectly acceptable. It must be noted that this change is irreversible, so the decision must be researched prior to flipping the switch.

The Trusts tab displays trust information (if more than one domain exists in the tree) and permits the addition or removal of trust relationships. Kerberos trusts are automatically built between parent and child domains upon creation of the tree structure. The relationship is shown in the display. It is possible to create lateral trusts or "shortcut" trusts between peer domains; that is, domains that are on that same level. This action may be used to speed up authentication channels between domains instead of using the transitive trust to authenticate users or services to objects, though this may not be necessary in many implementations.

The last tab is an information tab that offers input for the managing party of the domain. Entering the top-level Domain Administrators group here will allow root administrators to manage this domain. The group or person entered here will depend on the structure of hierarchy and the management model used.

The Active Directory Sites and Services Console

Configuring sites and subnets is an integral part of the overall domain strategy. The Active Directory Sites and Services (ADSS) tool allows the creation of sites and subnets to configure domain replication. The Scope pane contains the following objects:

- Sites

- Inter-Site Transports

- Services

Figure 11.21 shows the ADSS console with each of the objects expanded to further display the child objects contained within. Unlike the ADDT console, the results pane does provide further information of console objects.

The Sites object houses all sites created automatically or with user intervention. The right-click menu option of main concern at the Site folder level is New Site, which is the tool used for creating sites to control domain controller replication traffic. In our Technelogic Corporation example used throughout the book, a domain that represents the European branch of the company has been created. The physical location of these servers is connected to the root domain via a T1 link, which for the size of the domain and all of its users may prompt action to create a separate site to control the replication traffic over the WAN link. The following outlines how this is carries out.

To create a new site, right-click the Sites folder and click New Site. In the Create New Object-(Site) window, enter the name of the new site as shown in Figure 11.22. Choose a Site Link Object in the bottom pane and

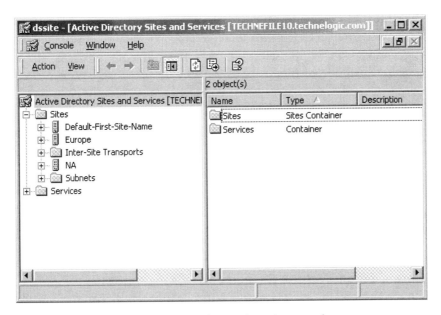

Figure 11.21   The Active Directory Sites and Service console.

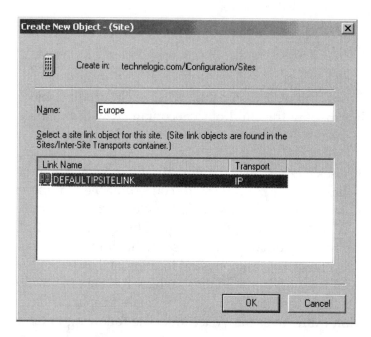

Figure 11.22 The Create New Object–(Site) page.

click OK to continue. The newly created site appears in the results pane under the Site parent folder. Now to create a subnet for the new site.

Once the site is created, a subnet or multiple subnets must be associated to the site. Right-click the Subnet folder and choose the New Subnet option. Type in the name of the subnet, which is the network/bit-masked identifier, as shown in Figure 11.23. This is the network address of the subnet and the number of bits in the network mask. The usage here is as follows:

<network address>/<bits masked> or

192.168.5.0/24 to represents the class C subnet 192.168.5.x with a the first three octets masked.

Click OK to continue. The new subnet is shown in the results pane.

The next and final step is to move the domain into the newly created site object. Right-click on the domain to be moved and choose the Move option. The following window displays a list of sites from which to choose. This process is shown in Figures 11.24 and 11.25. In our example network, the Techneeurroot domain is being moved to the newly created Europe site. Select the site and click OK to continue.

The new site has been created and resources allocated. Site replication between sites is not automatic; hence, it would defeat the purpose of creating the different sites altogether, which is to control replication traffic

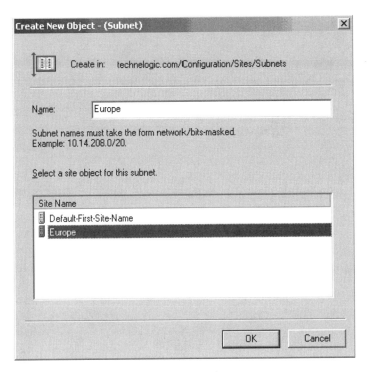

Figure 11.23   Configuring the new subnet.

over wide area links. Logically, the next step is to actually set up a *Site Link Connector* so that directory information may be passed between the newly created sites and, ultimately, the domain controllers within. Once created, the Site Connector replication timetables may be set.

To create a Site Connector, first expand the Inter-Site Transports folder to reveal the IP and SMTP subfolders. Remember from Chapter 8, "Directory Traffic Considerations and Management," that directory information may be passed by either transport protocol.

Right-click on the IP folder and select New Site Link as shown in Figure 11.25. This opens the Create New Object-(Site Link) window where the two site objects to be linked are chosen. In our example, the Europe site and the Default First Site are the link objects, and since there is only one other site, the choice is made for us by default. Click OK to continue. The Site Link is now in place, and replication will occur. In order to actually get a handle on replication traffic, though, a schedule must be implemented.

Right-click on the newly created Site Link and choose Properties for the object. The Site Link Properties page is displayed with options to change the replication partner parameters, schedule the replication frequency, and change time and day of the week. Figure 11.26 shows the Properties page for the Europe Site Link of the Technelogic Corporation example.

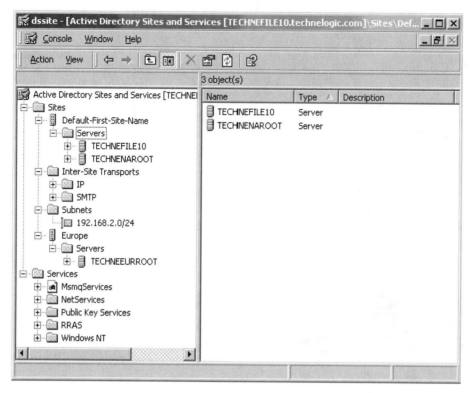

Figure 11.24 Selecting the Move option.

Adjust the frequency of replication as necessary and assign a cost to the connector if there is more than one connector or path for replication. To change the time and day of the week schedule, click the Change Schedule button to launch the weekly/time calendar matrix as shown in Figure 11.27. Highlight the portions of the matrix that you want to disallow replication and click the Replication Not Available radio button to change the parameter.

In the Technelogic example, directory replication should be allowed to occur only during off-peak hours to keep traffic down on the T1 link. Since the other site is located in a time zone that is roughly six to eight hours different, there is an overlapping time frame where the two sites may exchange a large amount of information (business hours). Thus, replication should be inhibited during this time frame to minimize the impact on the WAN link.

Configuring site replication helps to prevent failures caused by overloaded links. Directory information is allowed to pass over dedicated links as small as those found on dial-on-demand analog lines while retaining a consistent directory throughout the hierarchy. Planning site

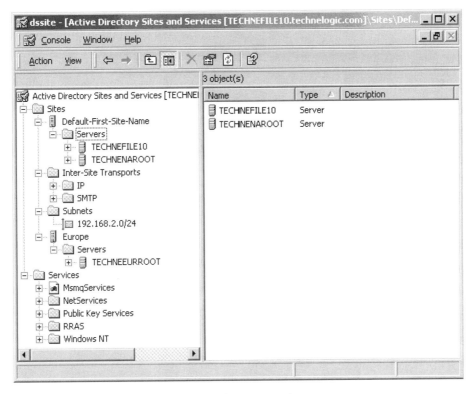

Figure 11.25   Choosing a site to move the resource into.

replication is key to the health of the overall system and should be thought through carefully and with the aid of the preplanning materials developed prior to installation.

Discussion of the ADUC console is reserved for Chapter 15, "Active Directory Management," which explores the use of this console to manage objects within the directory as well as other best practices associated with managing day-to day operations.

Summary

This chapter covered a lot of ground from a hands-on perspective. The long-awaited installation of the directory was covered through the use of the DCPROMO command-line utility. The many options in the Active Directory installation were discussed, including the creation of the initial or root domain, followed by the installation of replica domain controllers and child domains, respectively. The three different directory management consoles and their use were also covered in order to famil-

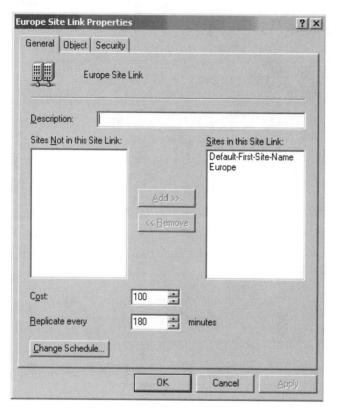

Figure 11.26 The Site Link Properties page.

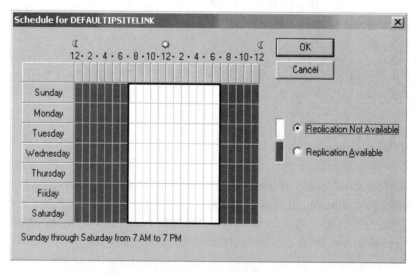

Figure 11.27 The time and week scheduling matrix used to manage replication.

iarize you with the Active Directory tools. The actual creation of sites and management of replication were tied into the discussion of the Active Directory consoles. In order to further facilitate the creation of the directory hierarchy, the chapter covered the creation of Organizational Units (OUs), User accounts, Computer accounts, and groups, as well as how to assign these objects to OU containers. With domains, OUs, and users in place and the directory functioning, the discussion moves to management issues, theory, and actions in Chapter 12 where delegation and group policy in relation to directory objects are discussed.

Implementing Administrative Control over Directory Objects

INTRODUCTION

One of the most useful features available to the Windows 2000 administrator is the ability to delegate authority over directory containers and objects. This deregulated approach to administration is becoming more favorable to many organizations, particularly those that are geographically dispersed. A local user may be given permissions to manage resources locally, offsetting these tasks from the central IT department. This chapter discusses the following objectives in regard to this feature:

- Security Policy
- User and Group Permissions
- Managing Enterprise Resources
- Implementing Control of Objects
- The Delegation of Control Wizard
- Delegation Guidelines

One would be hard pressed to find an argument against the statement "business systems drive business." Networking and business systems are big business. Many companies today are leveraging very large percentages of their budget on these systems and the people that run them to stay competitive in the current business climate.

Two years ago, Microsoft began an initiative to lower the Total Cost of Ownership (TCO) of their products and systems. Indeed, one of the largest selling points of Windows 2000 is the ability of the operating system to ease the administrative burden by implementing technologies such as Intellimirror and remote installation services. This Zero Administration initiative takes the current model of administration and combines common tasks within the operating system, thereby lowering the need for those administrative tasks. One of models used to lower TCO of Microsoft systems is utilizing existing resources to manage network resources. This is known as delegation, the use of users throughout the organization that would not ordinarily act as administrators to perform the mundane tasks often associated with systems management.

Do not fret about losing your job just yet. While this model does ease administrative duties, there is a snafu in all of this, not to mention, wouldn't it be nice to actually have time to focus on projects for the company rather than creating users accounts for the users in Des Moines, Iowa (no offense, Des Moines!)? Perhaps the biggest catch in all of this is the learning curve required to absorb this new operating system and all of its nuances. Delegation is only as strong as the weakest link in the change, that link being the complexity of Windows 2000, compounded by the complexity of many corporate networks. True, once mastered, the Active Directory is a powerful ally to all who embrace it. Further, a personalized console may be created for specific individuals to perform unambiguous tasks. Perhaps the thing to take to heart is not to expect too much up front with this model, with an eye toward the future. As the concept of delegation becomes more widely accepted in organizations, users will become empowered to perform these tasks, perhaps even embrace the opportunity. Figure 12.1 shows a distributed administration model.

One main concern before turning over the network to the user community while you grab your fishing gear and run out the door: Security is typically a very big issue within most organizations. That is, data security. Data is the gold of the new millennium, and protecting it is a very big deal. Delegation has the benefit of easing administrative burden, but in the wrong hands, it can be a tremendous adversary.

A security policy is paramount for any network, regardless of size. There must be some sort of change control policy in place to track mistakes, or worse, hacks. Additionally, a backup and recovery plan should be firmly rooted within the IT organization. Network and data security today means job security tomorrow. Because of the sensitive nature of

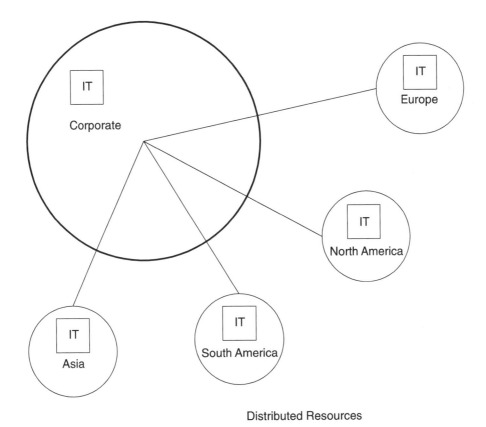

Distributed Resources

Figure 12.1   A distributed administration model.

this topic, and considering the havoc that could befall a network through unleashing unskilled users on the network, we begin with a security primer.

Managing Enterprise Resources

Taking a decentralized approach to the day-to-day operations of the network frees up time for IT managers to allocate resources away from the mundane tasks and refocus on high-level tasks or projects. Earlier in the book, a comment was made about the lack of organization in many IT departments when it comes to network documentation. One reason that many organizations do not possess such a document of network resources is due to the fact that there is no single individual that has the time to sit down and actually do it. It's the old catch-22 of "do more with less." The job of an administrator is often thankless and unglorified. Resources are often tight, and with the day-to-day tasks that must be accomplished along with putting out fires along the way and then meeting deadlines to implement that new product mandated by upper management, it is enough to make one's head spin.

The Total Cost of Ownership (TCO) initiative that burst onto the scene several years ago hurt IT divisions in many ways. Huge pressures are now being felt to reduce the cost of doing business electronically. Managing enterprise resources is challenging enough without having to be under a microscope while doing it. Decentralizing systems management helps to spread out the work across the enterprise, while the idea of utilizing existing resources to carry out commonplace tasks has definite potential in many organizations.

Consider the time it takes in a day to accomplish the task of creating or modifying user accounts. Take this task at one site per day, and then multiply that times by 7 or 20 sites, some maybe with 200+ users. Take that result and compound it by the creation of shares, password resetting, granting access resources, and so forth for all of these sites, and you have one whole resource committed solely to these tasks. What if all of the tedium associated with these types of tasks was removed from the daily task list of the central IT department? Instead, local personnel would fill this role, people who are actually on site. These local resources would also add the benefit of taking care of follow-up requests as well, rather than end users having to call into a help desk somewhere across the country and wait for a response, or worse, track down an administrator via pager.

The benefits of having local resources available to service IT requests are enormous. The sad fact of the matter is that it when it comes back to TCO and doing more with less, management probably is not going to authorize the hiring of local administrators for every site of consequence.

A Word of Caution

This book is not going to attempt to scratch the surface of the wide-ranging topic of security. Rather this is more of a "Before you get started" warning about "empowering" users as part-time administrators in relation to data security.

Systems administrators are hired based on experience and knowledge. The more you know and the longer you have worked in administration, the more likely you are to be hired or promoted elsewhere, and trusted with more sensitive or critical data. A college graduate fresh off the bench is not likely to be hired to a team that manages a large data center of a Fortune 100 company. It takes years of responsibility in a production setting to fully understand concepts like change management or disaster planning.

Entering into the brave new world of delegation will make many administrators uneasy; for others, their companies are doing business like this today. Whatever the situation, Windows 2000, through the use of Active Directory, heavily leverages the possibilities of decentralized administration through the concept of delegation. The delegation model does provide many tangible benefits to an organization, the most important of which is cost savings. On the other hand, pursued the wrong way, delegation can be a nightmare for IT staff.

Imagine what costs would be incurred if a company or organization was heavily geographically dispersed, and remote administrators were inadvertently bringing down servers, and IT staff had to fly to these locations to fix problems. Little would be accomplished from such a poorly implemented delegation model where remote users were improperly trained and unfamiliar with administrative tools. Worse yet, what if sensitive data were compromised or lost altogether? Chances are, the local delegated authority is not the one who is going to get escorted to the door, as the ultimate responsibility falls on the shoulders of the IT staff. Herein lies the bellyache administrators feel when considering such a proposition.

There is a "yellow brick road," however. Through a combination of training and remote management options, these types of matters can be managed or eliminated. The following practices should be followed in order to ensure that delegated authority is properly put into practice:

Education. The best thing you can do for users who also perform administrative functions is educate them. A little bit of the IT staff's time up front will save much more of it down the road. Use resources such as an intranet site to disseminate information or training as well. Press upon delegated users the importance of the role they play, and of the security of the systems and the data they command.

Communication. Delegated users need to feel connected, not hung out to dry. Communicate with this community regularly. Use e-mail as a tool. Have the users send a list of issues in every week. Respond to each with a list of fixes, and encourage the users to fix the problems. This builds confidence and skill.

Response. Accidents will happen, as they do even to the experienced administrator. Be forgiving, but also be ready. Have a disaster plan in place to minimize the impact, and share this plan with delegated users.

Tools. The tools included with Windows 2000 are robust; however, thinking outside of the box when it comes to the tools used can save the day. An investment in a remote control package such as pcAnywhere or Remotely Possible extends the reach of the administrator far beyond the corporate office. If a more robust solution is desired that offers software delivery and inventory features on top of remote help desk features, look into Microsoft's Systems Management Server as a possible solution for the network.

Taking a proactive and interactive approach to rolling out delegation is the only way for it to succeed with minimal downtime and frustration (see Figure 12.2). Develop a project plan for the implementation and get buy-in on it from management. Develop a list of candidates who might fit the bill for such a role. Typically, a person with solid computer skills is a good choice, or, if that option is not available, use a branch manager who will typically exercise good judgment when

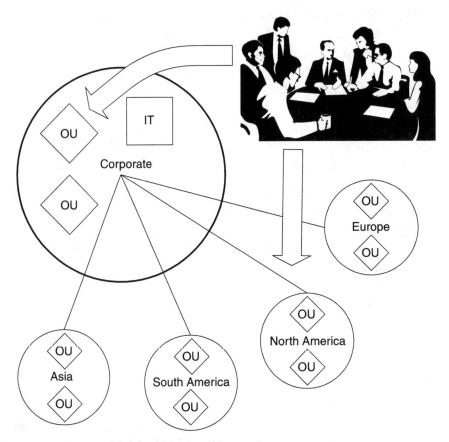

Figure 12.2   A solid delegation plan is imperative.

making decisions. Remember that the corporate data is gold, and decisions such as using delegated roles that could have an impact on that data should be well thought out.

User and Group Permissions

There are some changes in the way business is carried out in the new version of the Windows server operating system in regard to user and group permissions. Group types such as Local and Global still exist, with the addition of the Universal group type. Local groups are local to the server from which the ADUC console is being accessed. Global groups may contain members from anywhere in the domain. Universal groups allow members from anywhere in the forest. This information is kept in the Global Catalog (GC) for reference throughout the domain, and to aid domain controllers in authenticating users in the directory to enterprise-wide resources. These three group attributes are referred to as the *group scope*.

In addition to the group scope, two group types or categories exist: security groups and distribution groups. The distinction between the two is how security is applied: security groups are used in *Access Control Lists*, or ACLs, to authenticate users to resources, and distribution groups are used solely for e-mail applications.

Windows 2000 carries over the following user and groups features from Windows NT, shown in Tables 12.1, 12.2, and 12.3.

New additions to the operating system groups, users, and permissions include a built-in group called Replicator that allows replication of files in the domain. Groups that are (usually) created on promotion of the server and fall into the new category include:

- DNS Admins
- Cert Publishers
- DnsUpdateProxy
- Domain Computers
- Domain Controllers
- Group Policy Admins

No other additional user accounts have been added to the list, with the exception of certain accounts that are added with the installation of particular services; for example, Terminal Services.

Table 12.1   Built-In Groups Carried over from Windows NT

GROUP	FUNCTION
(Local)	
Administrators	May administer system or domain.
Backup Operators	Have the right to override file-level security to back up data.
Guests	Users in this group have "guest" access to the computer/domain.
Replicator	Accounts in this group may perform file replication.
(Domain)	
Domain Admins	Users may administer domain functions.
Domain Users	Users default to this group upon creation.
Domain Guests	Members have guest access domain wide.

Directory objects have a set of permissions that may be applied in regard to delegated tasks, which define action attributes about the object. To clarify, these are the properties that may be attached to an object, say an OU, but apply to all objects contained in the directory. These are:

Read. The right to view the contents on the container or object.

Write. The right to write to the object.

List Contents. The ability to view objects under the parent object.

Write Self. Write-back capability.

Control Access. The right to set permissions on the object.

Delete Tree. Delete the container and all subobjects.

List Object. The container is visible in the directory.

Create Child. The permission to create an object under the specified container.

Delete Child. The ability to remove child objects under the specified container.

Table 12.2   Built-In User Accounts Carried over from Windows NT

USER	FUNCTION
Administrator	May administer the local server
Guest	Guest account for the local server

Table 12.3 Permissions Carried over from Windows NT

PRIVILEGES	GROUP
Act as part of the operating system	-
Add workstations to a domain	-
Back up files and directories	Administrators, B/U Operators
Bypass traverse checking	Everyone
Change the system time	Administrators
Create a token object	-
Create permanent shared objects	-
Create a pagefile	-
Debug programs	Administrators
Force shutdown from a remote system	Administrators
Generate security audits	-
Increase quotas	Administrators
Increase scheduling priority	Administrators
Load and unload device drivers	Administrators
Lock pages in memory	-
Manage auditing and security log	Administrators
Modify firmware environment values	Administrators
Profile a single process	Administrators
Profile system performance	Administrators
Replace a process-level token	-
Restore files and directories	Administrators, B/U Operators
Shut down the system	Everyone
Take ownership of files or other objects	Administrators
Logon Rights:	
Access this computer from network	Everyone
Log on locally	Everyone
Log on as a batch job	-
Log on as a service	-

Mastery of these permissions, groups, and user types by all parties who will be responsible for administering permissions at any point in the directory is vital. Make sure that logging is enabled for OUs that have been delegated to others, particularly in the case where permissions are being applied. This will provide an audit trail in the event of a catastrophe.

Implementing Administrative Control

The OU and delegation are partners in Windows 2000. Delegation is most often applied at the OU level where resources are logically grouped (see Figure 12.3). In the Technelogic example, the directory structure follows the geo-political model. The company is geographically disperse, though the company itself falls into the medium-sized category and only spans two domains. The top of the tree contains the root domain and extends out in two branches, North America (NA) and Europe (EUR). Within these two domains, the organizational model is further subdivided through the use of OUs. Figure 12.4 illustrates this tree structure.

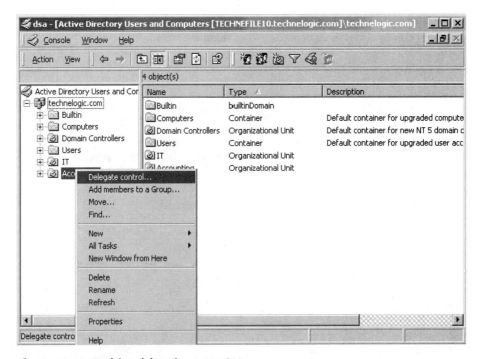

Figure 12.3   Applying delegation to an OU.

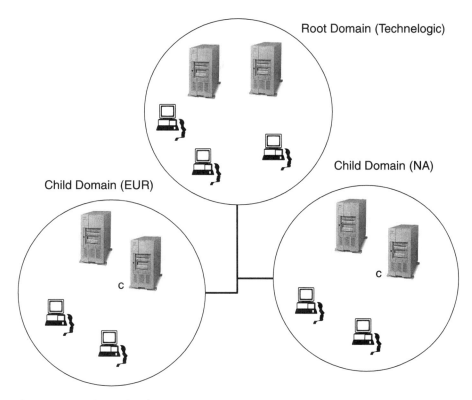

Figure 12.4   The Technelogic Corporation tree structure.

Each of the remote offices has a branch manager who has been tasked with the duties of local administration. This person will be responsible for tasks such as adding users, setting permissions, changing passwords, creating printers, and so forth. This person is responsible for physically changing the tape on the local server and other such functions that would normally be carried out by a local administrator.

Look again at the ADUC console and notice the tree structure of the OUs in the domain North America. The country is divided up into East and West branches under which specific cities exist. It is at the city level that delegation is implemented, and the responsible party is the overseer of all child objects as well. In the case of Austin where there are multiple child objects, the branch manager is responsible for all child object management as well.

 The following exercise assumes that a directory structure is in place, including OUs, and that user accounts have been created in the directory.

Now for a little hands-on, open the ADUC console from the Administrative Tools group. Highlight the OU that will be delegated. Right-click the OU and choose Delegate Control.... This spawns the Delegation of Control Wizard, the tool used to configure delegation in the Active Directory. Figure 12.5 shows the menu option to launch the Wizard, and Figure 12.6 shows the Welcome page.

Click "Next" to continue. The next page of the Wizard simply confirms that the proper container has been selected (see Figure 12.7). Confirm this information and click Next to continue. The next step is to add a user or group account that will function as the delegated authority (see Figure 12.8).

Click the Add button to add a group or user. The Select Users, Computers, or Groups windows is launched (see Figure 12.9). Notice the different options in this window. Beginning from the top, the Look in: drop-down list box permits the focus of the domain to be changed. By default, the local domain is selected. Just beneath this option is a list of all accounts in the domain. To select an account, simply double-click the user or group. Alternatively, a search feature saves time from scrolling

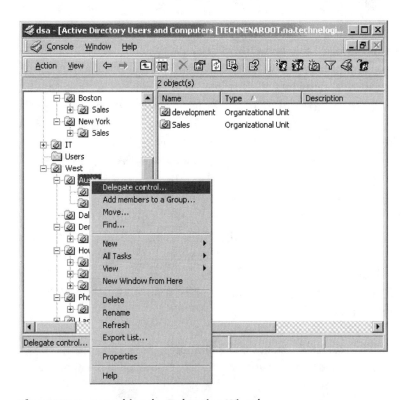

Figure 12.5   Launching the Delegation Wizard.

Figure 12.6   The Delegation of Control Wizard.

through a large list of domain users and groups where the name or logon name can be input into the Name field and then the Check Name feature. Once the account has been selected, choose Add. If additional accounts are required, repeat this step until all accounts are added. Click OK to continue.

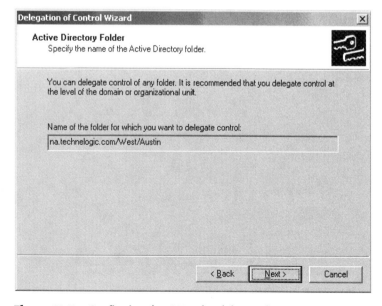

Figure 12.7   Confirming the OU to be delegated.

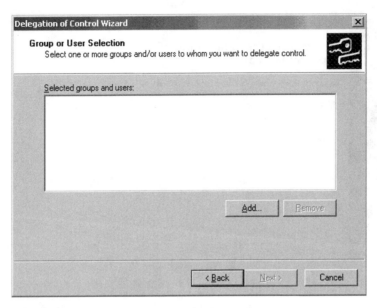

Figure 12.8   The Group or User Selection page.

As shown in Figure 12.10, focus is returned to the Wizard, and the selected account or accounts are displayed. Click Next to continue.

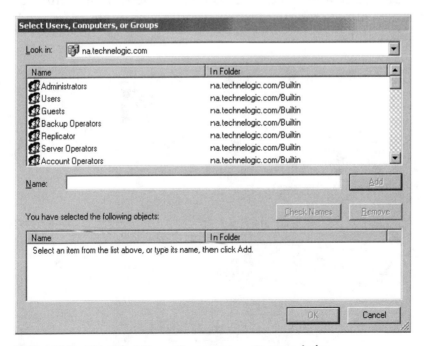

Figure 12.9   The Select Users, Computers, or Groups window.

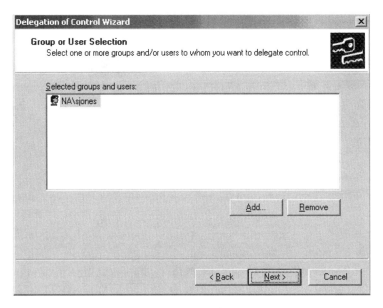

Figure 12.10 Selected groups are displayed.

Now to add a little more complexity. This is where knowing the permissions and their properties comes in handy. On the predefined delegations page, there is a choice between predefined tasks or custom tasks. Certainly, the easy way out is to choose from the predefined set of checklists. That would simply be too easy; therefore, for the express purpose of educating, choose the "Custom task" option and then click Next (see Figure 12.11).

The Active Directory Object Type page shown in Figure 12.12 allows the administrator to fine-tune the delegation experience by allowing or limiting the scope of what may be controlled. There are two options here, "Entire folder," which allows delegation over all folders in the OU, and "Objects in folder," which allows management of specific objects in the OU only.

Choose the "Objects in folder" option and notice that the specific objects that may exist in an OU are displayed. In order to limit control, select only relevant objects to be managed, such as Group Objects, User Objects, Printer Objects, and so forth. This type of fine-tuning what the remote manager can manipulate lessens the chance of something catastrophic happening in the event that permissions or properties to a critical object (for example, site links) are inadvertently changed.

Once the appropriate OU object types have been decided, click Next to select the permissions for these objects. The Permissions page is dis-

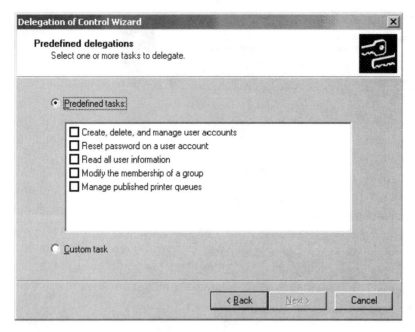

Figure 12.11 Choosing custom or predefined tasks.

played (see Figure 12.13). Scroll through the list of available options. Now click the Filter options checkboxes and scroll through the list again. Take

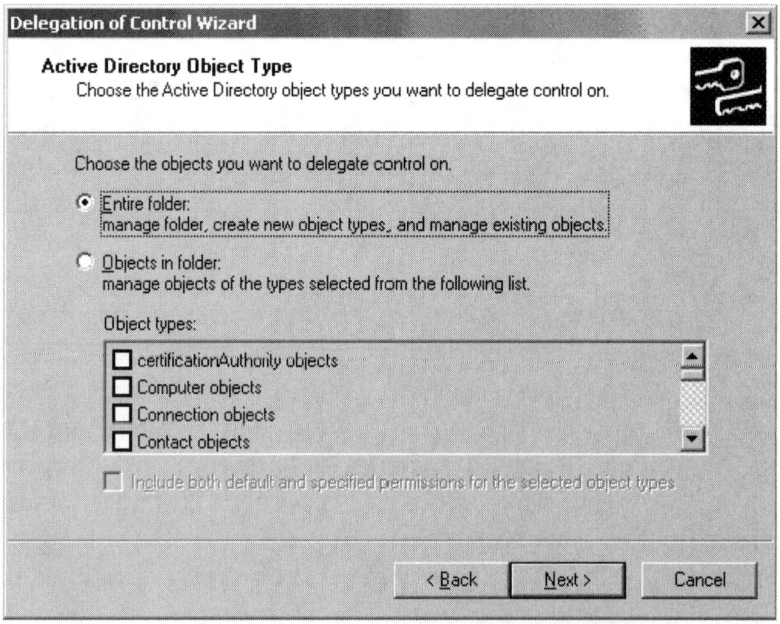

Figure 12.12 Selecting container objects to be managed.

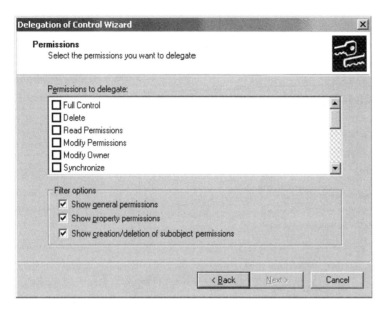

Figure 12.13   Setting permissions for container objects.

note of the permissions that have been added. Select the appropriate permissions for the objects selected and click Next to continue.

The final screen allows for the review of options. Make sure that all options are correct, and then click Finish to complete the Wizard (see Figure 12.14).

Once delegation is completed, it would be prudent to have the user log on to a workstation and test the functionality of the newly created delegation. In order to manage the OU from a workstation, the remote administrator must have the proper tools to manage the directory. Such tools are not available natively on the Windows 9*x*, NT 4.0 Workstation, or Windows 2000 Workstation products. The person functioning in the administrative role could manage all tasks directly from the server every time a change needed to be made, but this would be terribly inconvenient. What is the solution? A custom console is the answer.

Creating Tools for Distribution

In Chapter 9, "Using Microsoft Management Console," we discussed the Microsoft Management Console (MMC), and in Chapter 11, "Installing Active Directory and Using Management Tools," we discussed the tools relevant to the management of the directory. Delegation would be pointless if the tools were not available to delegated users to manage local

Figure 12.14 Completing the Delegation Wizard.

resources. The problem with passing along a tool like the ADUC console is that it is, quite simply, overkill. Not only that, the remote administrator will also need some of the functionality found in the Computer Management tool found in the Administrative Tools group.

Creating custom tools for distribution allows the administrator to distribute just the tool set for the jobs that need to be managed, nothing more. There is also the added security to lock down the tool itself to prevent modification to the console. Now to create a custom console.

From the Start menu, select Run, and at the command prompt type "MMC," and then press OK. A blank console is displayed from which the remote administration tool will be created. From the Console menu, select Add/Remove Snap-in (see Figure 12.15).

The Add/Remove Snap-in page is displayed (see Figure 12.16). Click Add to insert a Snap-in.

From the Add Standalone Snap-in page, select the Active Directory Users and Computers Snap-in and click Add (see Figure 12.17). Repeat this process to add the computer management Snap-in. When prompted by the resulting Computer Management configuration screen (see Figure 12.18), select the computer to which the console will connect. This will be the domain controller at the site where the tool will be used. You may browse to the particular server or simply add the name. Click Finish to continue.

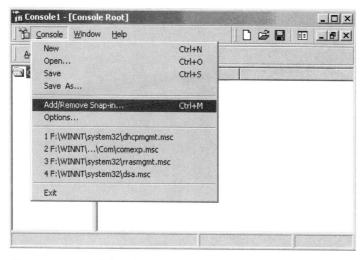

Figure 12.15   Adding the Snap-in.

Click Close on the Add Snap-in page, which brings you back to the ADD/Remove Snap-in page. The two Snap-ins should be listed in the resulting pane. Click on the Extensions tab (see Figure 12.19) to further configure the Snap-ins.

Figure 12.16   The Add/Remove Snap-in page.

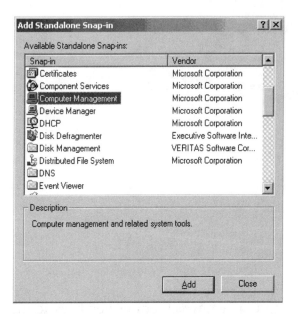

Figure 12.17   Adding the Snap-ins for the delegation console.

Configure the options here that pertain to your particular scenario. For instance, you may want only a couple of features of the ADUC console to be visible while the rest are excluded (Group Policy extensions are a good candidate for removal). Once complete, click OK to return to the main console. Both Snap-ins should be present. Figure 12.20 illustrates this process.

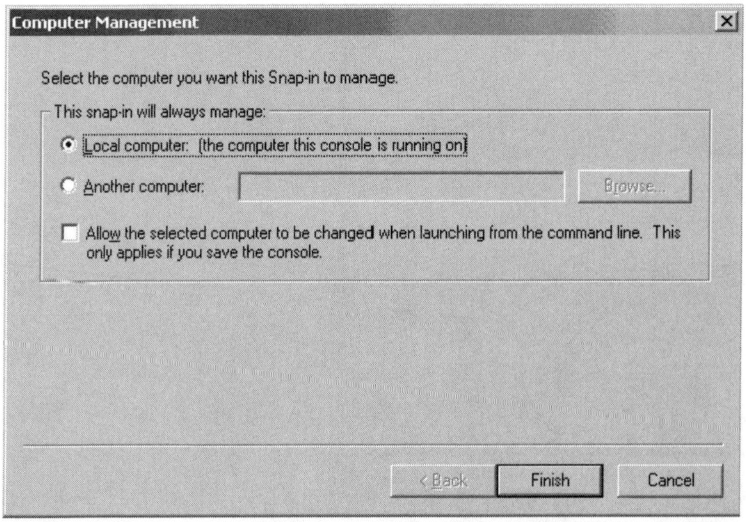

Figure 12.18   The configuration page displayed after adding the Computer Management Snap-in.

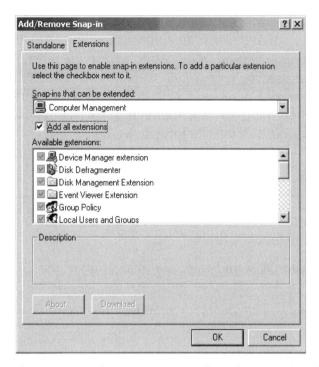

Figure 12.19   The Extensions page allows features to be added or removed from the tool.

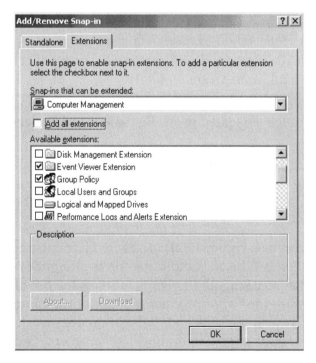

Figure 12.20   Configuring Snap-in extensions.

From the Console menu, use the Save feature to save the console for future distribution. It is likely that one-size-fits-all consoles will work in most situations. The two Snap-ins used in this exercise provide most of the management tools necessary to maintain server and Directory resources. Once saved, the tool may be distributed from a network share or via e-mail. Accompanying documentation that spells out how to perform common tasks would be very helpful as well.

Delegation Guidelines

In order for the delegation process to be successful, use the following guidelines to ensure that all goes smoothly:

- Organize divisions into OUs, and then use delegation at the OU level.
- Track permission changes in order to monitor the progress of delegation.
- Draft a master document that lists delegated users, location, rights, and so on.
- Develop a training program for delegated users.
- When creating any object in the directory, fill in all fields. This helps when querying the directory or information.
- Communicate often with remote administrators, sharing critical updates and other helpful information regularly.
- Try to remember that for the most part, administrative functions are secondary job roles for delegated users. Be patient and understanding.
- Build an access model based on asserting permission instead of denying it, and make this a policy with remote administrators. Debugging failed access due to assigning deny permissions can be lengthy.

Rolling out a decentralized (see Figure 12.21), delegated administration model in an organization can be as complicated or as straightforward as you make it. The key to a smooth implementation is the use of a good plan and documenting the entire process. It takes a little more time up front, but saves plenty on the back end. Delegation does work. Its use is widespread throughout large corporations, government, and universities.

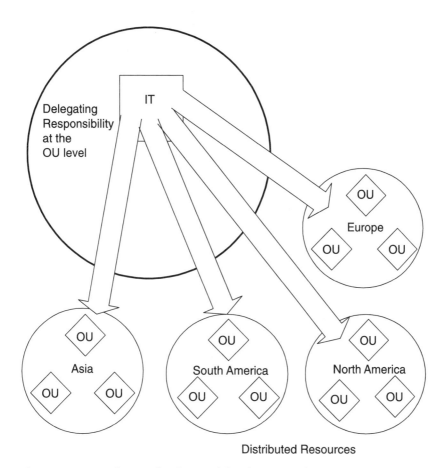

Figure 12.21 A decentralized IT model with positive flow.

Coordination with all administrators, whether in the field or locally, is critical to network health. Also, make a point of passing on informative articles or journals to delegated users. This will encourage them to learn as much as they can about their responsibilities, while lowering the number of support calls to the central IT department.

Summary

Delegation is a good vehicle to take an organization down the road of lower costs and higher productivity, though there are obstacles that can quickly curb the light of success at the end of the tunnel. As with any Active Directory implementation, planning is paramount to success. This chapter discussed the benefits and negatives associated with using a delegation model in any organization, and provided good advice on how to implement it. Additionally, the use of the Active Directory Delegation of Authority Wizard and custom consoles was demonstrated to help in moving toward a delegated system. As stated in the beginning of the chapter, delegation may or may not be a good fit for your situation. Try running a beta or pilot first and get feedback to see if it is feasible for your given implementation. Chapter 13, "Forests and Trees," moves into a discussion of large design considerations as the principles of forests and trees are discussed.

Forests and Trees

INTRODUCTION

In this chapter, the focus turns to the issues of building on the foundation network already in place, and developing complex tree structures and multidomain forests. While many simpler implementations will include only a single domain, larger, more complex, and dispersed organizations will require a complex domain hierarchy that consists of trees and forests of trees. In this chapter, the following subjects are discussed:

- **Definition of Trees and Forests**
- **Joining Trees to Create Forests**
- **Using the Active Directory Domains and Trusts Console**
- **Trusts**
- **Limitations and Issues**
- **Best Practices**

Whether your particular situation dictates the need for a multilevel domain structure or not, the concepts introduced in this chapter are very important to the overall design picture. One cannot discount the likelihood that an organization may grow, and with it, the need for the network to grow and change. While a single domain model provides many conveniences such as a less complex nomenclature and a simpler directory structure to manage, the reality is that most companies that employ a decentralized administration strategy will opt to deploy a multidomain model where domains are units of administration and security.

These larger and geographically dispersed organizations are in a continual state of flux as are the underlying networks. Fortunately, Windows 2000 accommodates such change rather well, where its predecessors fell short. Using Windows 2000, it is entirely possible for two companies to merge their tree structures into one forest, with disjointed namespaces. Information may be shared across these trees via a trust relationship, and the trees may act as a seamless network.

These functional advances accompanied by robust application support, security, directory services, and the numerous standards adopted into the operating system make Windows 2000 an appealing solution for IT managers. Perhaps the one concern voiced by most of these individuals or groups is the scalability of the product. Prior to Windows 2000, former NT domains had a functional limit of 40,000 objects. Large-scale implementations of the NT required numerous domains to support all of the user and computer accounts. The new object support model in Windows 2000 supports a maximum of 1 million objects per domain, more than adequate for most implementations. This scalability, coupled with fail-over capability (Windows 2000 Advanced Server) and massive multiprocessor capability (Windows 2000 Data center), will surely make this latest offering a formidable competitor in the Unix arena, offering IT mangers an alternative to the often cryptic and difficult world of Unix administration while maintaining high availability.

Multidomain structures and multitree structures allow global organizations, or those that aspire to be, the room and flexibility to grow massive tree structures and forests that may encompass many companies under the same canopy. Standards introduced in Windows 2000 means that systems outside of the forest are still accessible by Windows clients (see Chapter 16, "Group Policy and the Active Directory"). Imagine the possibilities where a single-vendor solution were no longer required and NT, Novell, and Unix systems all communicated on the same level. Such a standard is a long time coming in a world community where opinion and harmony coexist, and communication transpires on a seamless, global network. Such a reality would be like dogs and cats living together!

In principle, trees and forests may exist as a single domain in a single location on the map. The really interesting structures, however, are those that span hundreds of routers and communications portals, spanning the globe like an old oak tree whose branches distend out in a massive display of power and functional elegance. This chapter first discusses the what and why of a tree and forest, then moves the discussion to a more theoretical level. There is also a bit on managing the enterprise with the Active Directory Domains and Trusts console.

What Are Trees and Forests?

The definition of a tree is simpler to express due to the context. An Active Directory Tree is a logical structure that provides consistency and links the directory. It comprises many elements, the core of which is the domain, but also includes other physical elements such as trust relationships, Organizational Units (OUs), groups, users, and so forth. Required for the formation of a tree structure is a hierarchical organization of domains that share a contiguous namespace. It is possible to have a collection of domains that are not part of the same namespace, which is not considered a tree at all. Using domains in a hierarchical manner allows the directory to scale, while offering a logical naming structure throughout the organization.

All domains that exist within the same namespace share a common schema and Global Catalog (GC), which define object attributes and provide a common "library" for object attribute queries, respectively. Each domain in the tree is interconnected by two-way, transitive Kerberos trusts. It is the transitive nature of these trusts that allows users in one domain to access resources across the tree (see Figure 13.1) in another domain (providing the appropriate permissions exist).

While the entire tree functions as a seamless unit, each domain is authoritative for information about objects residing within. This logical partition scheme is tied together through the use of trusts and the GC. The ability to search globally is due to this linked structure of which the schema and GC are at the heart. Logically then, it may be stated that all domains that are part of the contiguous namespace also *share the same directory*. Whereas in previous versions of the operating system, searching for directory objects meant drilling up and down through individual domains, Active Directory provides unity to the network and

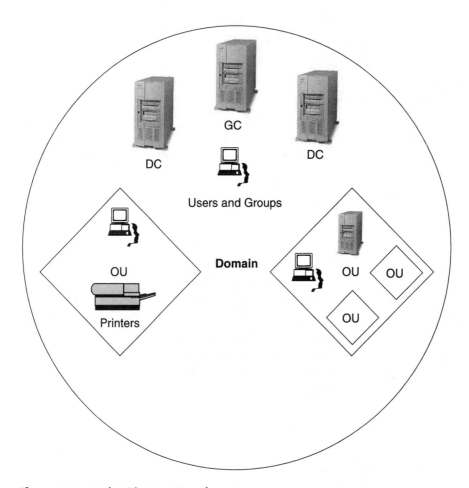

Figure 13.1 Active Directory Tree elements.

all objects that reside within. This ability to query the directory using LDAP provides greater usability to users and administrators.

To recap, an Active Directory Tree is comprised of a multidomain (yes, technically a single domain can be a tree and forest, but it is best to differentiate the two structure types of the single domain model and the multidomain model) hierarchy interconnected by transitive trusts and sharing a common directory, schema, GC, and namespace.

At some point in the life of a company, it may become necessary to join two Windows 2000 Trees together in order to form a unified set of resources. These tree structures are independent in nature with their own set of common schemas, GCs, and namespaces. This being true, how then would two such disjunct structures become unified as a single composition? The answer is through the creation of a *forest*, which allows two Active Directory Trees to exist as a connected formation. Unifying two directories such as this has the technical effect of marrying the schema and GC services of the two directories, though the namespaces remain unique. A Master Schema Server located in the root domain of the tree facilitates searching across forests (see Figure 13.2) for objects. It should be noted that, while objects may be searched across trees in a forest, this is limited to the scope of attributes defined in the GC.

The connection mechanism used in inter-tree trusts and intra-tree communication and authentication is different. While within a tree, transitive trusts are formed upon creation of domain objects, between

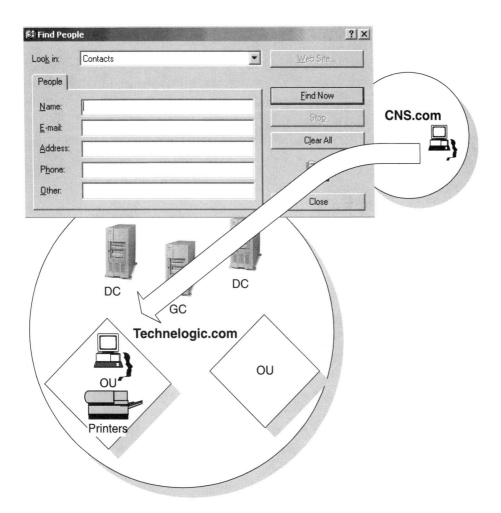

Figure 13.2   Searching across a forest.

trees this is not true. If a two-way trust is desired, one must be explicitly created and therefore agreed upon by the administrative staff of both trees. This situation is ideal for certain "partnership" arrangements and adds an extra level of security. Kerberos v5 is still used as the primary method of authentication.

It is possible to have two distinct forests joined by a trust relationship. In this type of arrangement, the schema and the GC retain separate information databases, and querying across the two forests is not possible. An arrangement such as this is uncommon and serves little purpose in managing resources on a global level.

The creation of a Forest of Trees makes integrating two separate networks a cinch and provides a seamless communication mechanism. It also beats the alternative, having to reinstall one or the other network, or managing a complicated trust arrangement.

The use of trees and forests in Windows 2000 provides a vehicle to logically arrange network resources in a meaningful way and allow the unity of disjointed systems. These new features will certainly weigh favorably in the eyes of large conglomerated organizations (see Figure 13.3) that are searching for a way to unify all corporate networks or sites under one umbrella.

Trust Relationships

A little information on the trust relationships found in Windows 2000 is probably prudent at this stage due to the fact that trusts are so different from previous operating system versions. Transitive trusts are the primary links that exist between domains in this version of the product and are created automatically upon the manufacture of child domains. It may seem at first that the new transitive trust model is so not so far off base from the two-way trust model found in earlier versions. This assumption is quite incorrect. The *transitive* nature of Windows 2000 trusts allows resources in *adjacent domains* to be made available across the tree structure to users in other domains. This is a sort of "trust hopping" that takes place (see Figure 13.4) and was not available in Windows NT.

While it is true that the trusts created between domains in Windows 2000 are bidirectional, in Windows NT three trusts would be required to pull off a configuration similar to Figure 13.4 and achieve a pseudo transitive state. To further complicate this antiquated model, multiply the number of domains by just two and look what happens to the num-

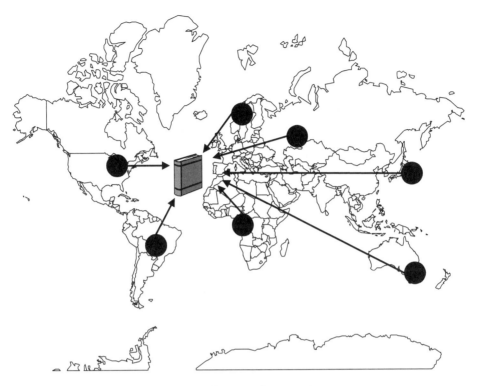

Figure 13.3   The benefit to large conglomerated companies.

ber of trusts to be created and managed (see Figures 13.5 and 13.6). This "complete trust" model is a tremendous administrative burden and makes it extremely difficult to manage security policy.

Like many legacy features (NT LanManager authentication being a prime example), the explicit trust does still exist in Windows 2000. These legacy features do serve the purpose of allowing existing systems to coexist, integrate, and function in a Windows 2000 network, adding value to the product. Use of these options is strictly optional, except in the case of joining two trees in a forest. Now we move the discussion to enterprise domain structures and issues.

Complex Domain Structure Issues

Very large organizations will need to take extra care in the deployment of Active Directory to the enterprise. Other than user education issues, the complex nature of these existing networks will ultimately dictate

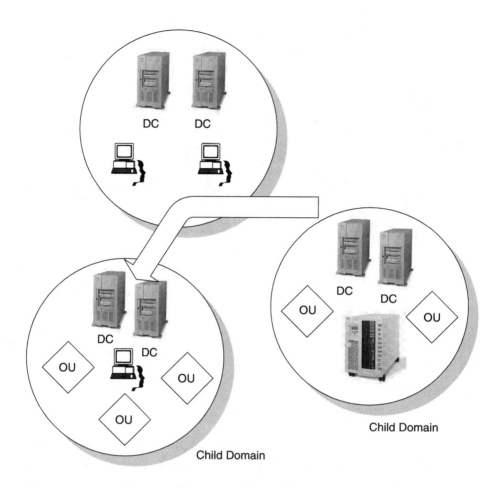

Figure 13.4 Transitive trust flow.

complicated domain, tree, and forest structures, further convoluted by the often decentralized and political nature of the IT infrastructures. Planning stages for such a migration may extend into years and go through many revisions. Drafting and agreeing on a structure will prove challenging, but can be overcome by leaving the politicalities to upper management, and the technical focus in the hands of the experts. If you find yourself in such an environment, work diligently with other administrators and system architects to develop a solid directory model that works well with your organization—sign-off will happen much more quickly. That said, what are the issues regarding the genesis of a Windows 2000 Active Directory hierarchy in a large, global organization?

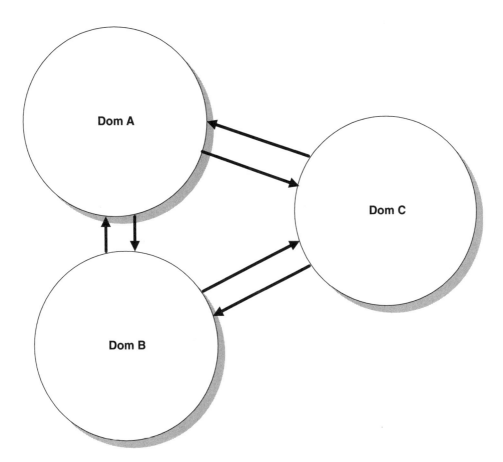

Figure 13.5 Windows NT Explicit trusts (complete trust with three domains and three two-way trusts).

Windows 2000 offers an enterprise directory service that integrates well with other directory services because of the standards built in and is scalable to provide access to a very large amount of objects structures in a single, meaningful system (Figure 13.7 illustrates a large scaled implementation). To facilitate this, a meaningful architecture should be drafted during the planning phase. Even organizations that are not currently global in nature should plan domain structures accordingly if growth and acquisition are likely.

To start, the root domain of an Active Directory tree houses the GC by nature, for it is installed on the first installed domain controller of the root domain. This translates into a single GC for the entire structure of the tree, and if the Microsoft theory of 99 percent query and 1 percent replication is true, this may be a point of failure in large structures. The

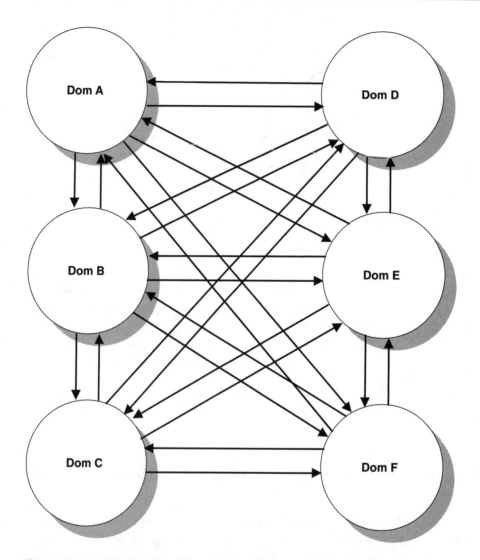

Figure 13.6 Windows NT Explicit trusts (complete trust with six domains and 30 two-way trusts).

GC may become overwhelmed with query requests if the hardware cannot withstand the load. Large numbers of users will require hardware that can handle a large number of queries. Additionally, if the same server is used as the Master Schema server for a forest, there will be an extra cost. A single-processor Pentium-based server with mirrored drives and a single network card could fail-over under the load of 8000 to 10,000 users. This particular server could be the single point of failure if the hardware is not gauged properly. Fortunately, the role of

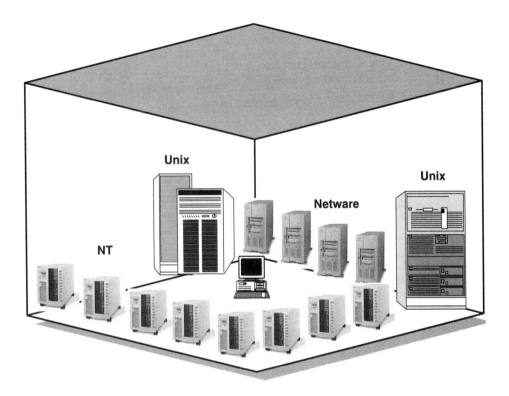

Figure 13.7 An integrated, multiplatform data center.

the GC can be allocated to other servers to spread the load (see the Enterprise Management section later in this chapter for a hands-on example). A good candidate for this server would possess the same sort of qualities that any database server in your organization might have. For fault tolerance, more than one domain controller should exist in any domain. If the root domain is dedicated for directory functions and there are multiple domain controllers, consider spreading the GC role around to all domain controllers for load balancing. If domains exist in other sites, which is likely, GCs should be placed on the other side of WAN links as well. Failure to set up an adequate GC structure will result in logon failures and query dysfunction. Changing the role of a GC is performed through the ADSS console.

Another performance consideration should be noted during domain controller promotion. During this process, it is a good idea to change the location of the directory databases from the defaults to a volume located on a fast drive array (see Figure 13.8). This will improve read/write requests to the database and significantly improve performance.

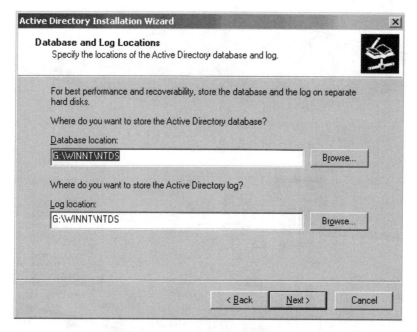

Figure 13.8 Changing the database paths during server promotion.

The depth of domain structures will have a significant impact on overall directory performance. It is therefore considered a good design principal to try and flatten out domain levels as much as possible and use OUs whenever possible in the place of domains. Even in the largest of organizations, it would be frivolous to create more than three or four domain levels, including the root domain. The amount of information that must be truncated to and associated with objects that exist in the very low levels of a domain hierarchy can hamper the performance of domain controllers in the structure and eventually affect logons, replication, and queries. A logical, meaningful domain structure need not take so many levels to make sense to users of the system. Use domains sparingly and with good cause to prevent nested structures.

Make sure that complicated domain architectures are overlaid with a very solid site topology to assist in the smooth replication of directory information between domain controllers and domains. Use Site Links and Site Link Bridges to provide multiple paths with multiple costs. Redundancy never hurts in large-scale implementations (see Figure 13.9). Create multiple connectors if necessary, regardless of the burden of actually creating and managing them.

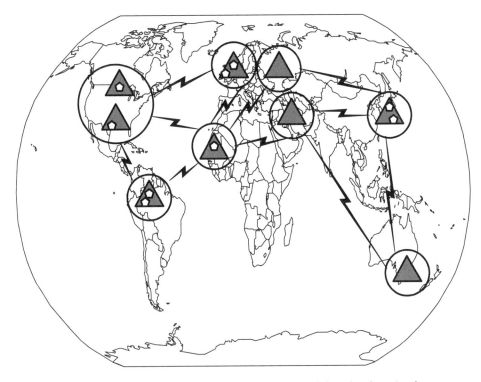

Figure 13.9 The site plan in large forests should be as solid as the domain plan.

Should your organization find itself in a situation where the creation of a forest is eminent, bear in mind that this process may be pursued two-fold. As of the writing of this book, the grafting of one tree to an existing forest is not supported. The option of joining two forests together via a trust relationship is supported, but it is not considered a forest of trees. Rather, it is two distinct forests that function independently of each other with separate schemas and GCs. If joining two forest structures is desired, in order for directory information to be shared across the two structures, a deconstruction and rebuild of the domain controllers on one side or the other is unavoidable. The concept of demotion here will undoubtedly save time rather than completely rebuilding servers from scratch.

The section entitled "Creating a Forest" includes a hands-on for creating such structures. Be sure to assess the structure of the joining tree carefully so that the exact structure may be rebuilt under the existing forest. Also, it is likely that such a marriage of networks will link up via a leased line. If either side has a very large implementation of domains, make sure that the link can accommodate the replication traffic between the two sites. Consider placing the two in separate sites and implementing a site connector.

 Microsoft has stated that the graft and prune operation between forests will be supported in the final release of the product, although it is unclear whether this means it will be an add-on via a Service Pack later or in the gold release of the product. The target date for the release of the product is slated for Q4 of 1999, and there is great pressure to meet this date. The very complex issues surrounding the support of this feature may preclude its release by that time, though there is little doubt that it is very high on the priority list. Should this or any other feature of the operating system change between the writing of this book and the release of the product, check the Wiley Web site for updates at www.wiley.com/compbooks/schwartz.

Implementing forests may mean the union of two IT departments (see Figure 13.10) with very different management practices. Be prepared for this and set up the appropriate communication channels between the two organizations. Attack the creation of a forest of trees the same way you would a new Active Directory installation, with a project plan. The buy-in of all pertinent groups is critical, as the impact is global. A solid project plan is a marketing tool as well.

The management of such massively complex networks certainly benefits from the existence of a unified directory and the robust management tools that accompany it. Having a single view of the entire network coupled with the ability to query for objects in the directory (instead of the old drill-down approach) means that more administrative tasks may be accomplished in less time, therefore requiring less administrative overhead. These robust tools coupled with the use of delegation and third-party remote management tools allow an IT department to reach across the globe in true enterprise class.

Creating a Forest

Windows 2000 domain trees are joined to another domain tree during the Active Directory installation process. As discussed in Chapter 12, "Implementing Administrative Control Over Directory Objects," during the installation of a new Windows 2000 server the following options are presented:

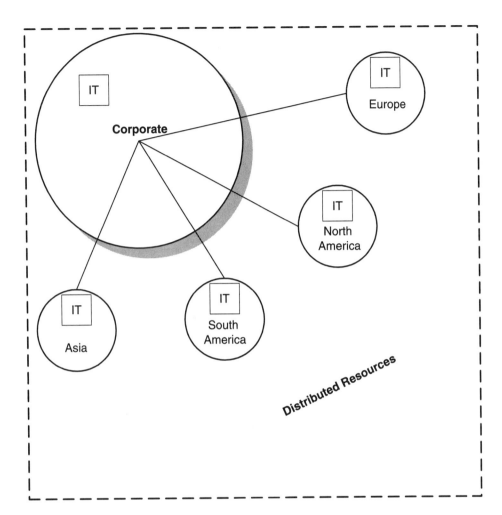

Figure 13.10   A decentralized IT model.

- Create the first tree in a new forest
- Create a new tree in an existing forest
- Create a new replica domain controller
- Install a child domain

The one function that was overlooked in Chapter 11, "Installing Active Directory and Using Management Tools," was the "Create a new tree in an existing forest" option of the Active Directory Wizard. To join an Active Directory Tree structure, choose the install option "Create a new tree in an existing forest."

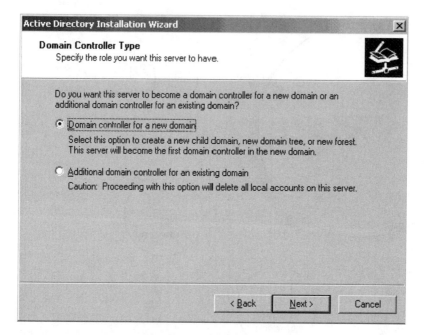

Figure 13.11 Start the Active Directory Installation Wizard using DCPROMO.

Begin now by starting the Active Directory Installation Wizard by running DCPROMO from the command line as in Figure 13.11.

The first option to choose after bypassing the Welcome screen is "Domain controller for a new domain." Click Next to continue (see Figure 13.12).

Next, choose the "Create a new domain tree" (see Figure 13.13) and continue to the following page.

A quick explanation here: The first option (shown in Figure 13.14) "Create a new forest of domain trees" will create a separate forest that is disjointed from the forest that you are trying to hitch. Rather, choose second option, "Place this domain tree in an existing forest," and continue.

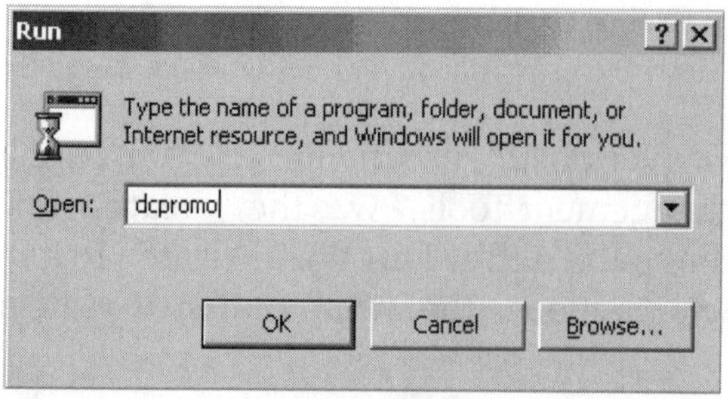

Figure 13.12 Create a new domain.

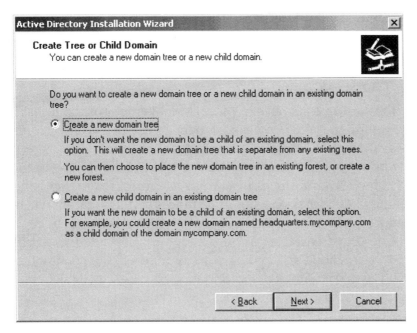

Figure 13.13   Select the new tree option.

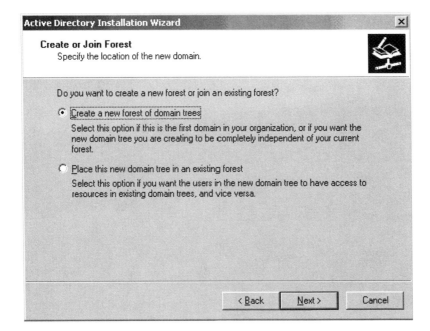

Figure 13.14   Adding the domain to an existing forest.

You are prompted to add the name of the root domain for the existing forest and administrative credentials. Enter this information, and click Next to continue the grafting process (see Figure 13.15).

Finish the installation as carried out in previous installations, relocating the directory database files, logs, and system volume if desired.

The new forest of trees is now in place. Management of the forest is performed through the ADDT console, where a view of the entire forest structure is available.

A quick word here about the grafting of trees. As of the writing of this book, the pruning and grafting of trees from one forest to another is not supported, though there are constant reassurances that this feature will be implemented in the final release. If this is true, then it will surely be an addition to the Active Directory Wizard program, presented as a fifth option. Consider this book an ongoing work; updates to the book will be placed on the Wiley Web site as the information becomes available.

Enterprise Management Using the Active Directory Consoles

There are two consoles used for the management of Active Directory trees and forest: the ADDT console from which connections to trees

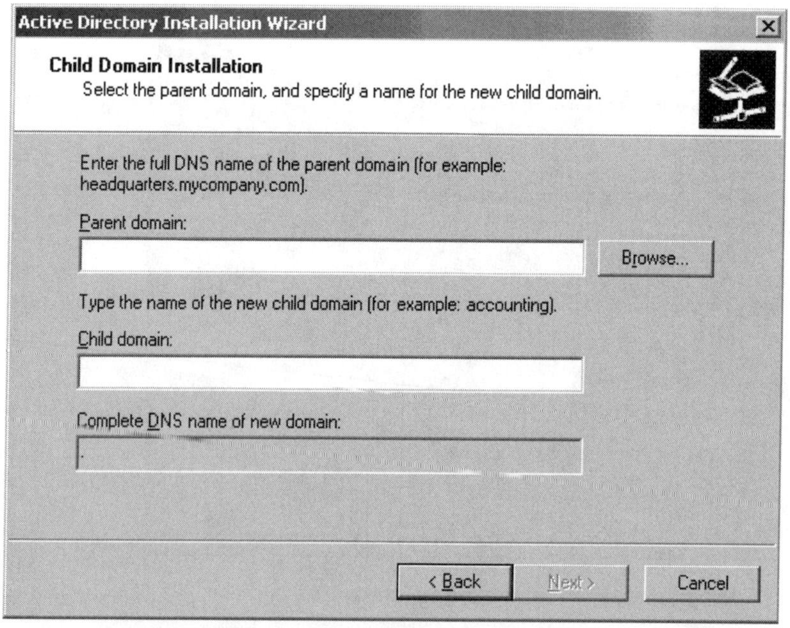

Figure 13.15 Entering the root domain information of the existing forest.

and domain controllers in the forest may be made, and the ADSS console where connections to other forests may be made. The latter is used only in the case of multiple forests. Let's look at some of the management features that pertain to the trees in the forest using the ADDT console.

The ADDT console provides a bird's-eye view of all of the trees in a forest. The console provides some functionality, but is really a leaping-off point to the ADUC console, which we will discuss in more detail in a moment. Why the entire tree structure, or structures, is not available in this console provided in a hierarchical view is still somewhat of a mystery, though a custom console that provides similar functionality to this may be created.

Open the ADDT console from the Administrative Tools group and expand the tree or forest structure (see Figure 13.16).

If you have joined another tree to the forest, there will be multiple root domains represented in the console. Highlight the root object in the console (the Active Directory Domains and Trusts object) and pull down the Action menu (see Figure 13.17). There are a couple of items of interest on this menu: Operations Master and Connect to Domain Controller.

The Operations Master option allows the focus of the server that is the acting Operations Master to be changed to another domain controller in the Active Directory hierarchy. This action should be performed only out of necessity; namely, only in the case that this server

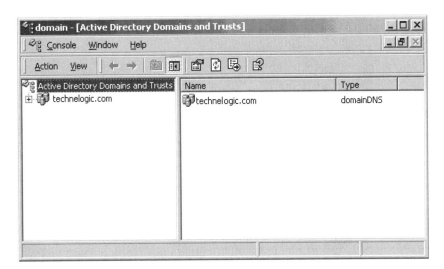

Figure 13.16   The ADDT console.

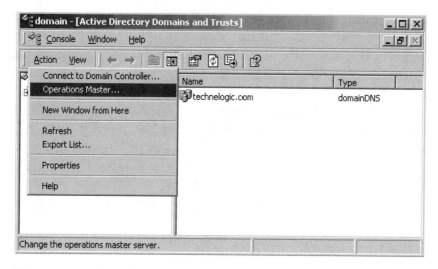

Figure 13.17 The Action menu options of the ADDT console.

has suffered some sort of fatal blow and the service needs to be transplanted to an operation server. This information for specific domains may be accessed from the ADUC console via the same Action menu item of the root object. The authoritative server for FSMO roles of the RID Pool, PDC Emulator, and Infrastructure Master is listed there and is shown in Figure 13.18.

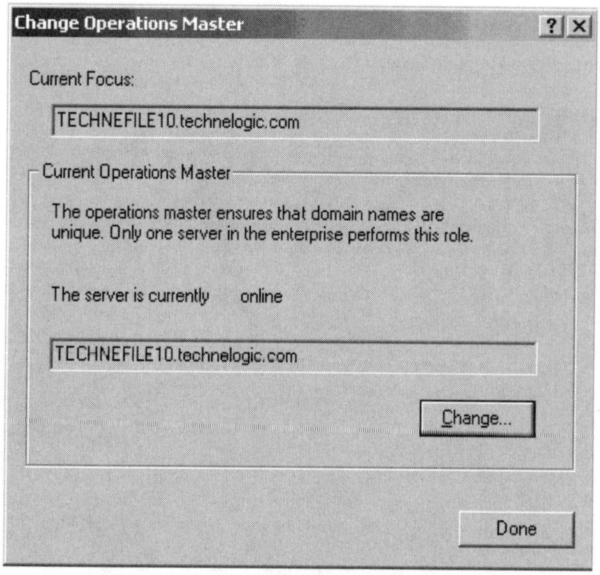

Figure 13.18 Changing the Operations Master role.

The second option, Connect to Domain Controller, launches the ADUC console for a specified domain controller in the directory for further management of the domain at the object level.

The organizational hierarchy of the directory structure and the logical naming structure in place simplifies managing a forest of domains and trees in Active Directory. One console provides enterprise-wide administrative functions to IT departments. The creation of a forest helps to organize large, multinational organizations that may encompass many different companies, but choose to function on a global private network that works seamlessly and is easily managed. The possibility of such structures in Windows 2000 defines its place in the enterprise arena as a scalable and functional alternative to other platforms such as Unix. With the addition of high-availability options found in the Advanced Server and Data center products, Windows will be a formidable opponent to other operating platforms.

Best Practices

The concepts of trees and forests are appealing not only to IT mangers, but also to upper management who seek a seamless solution that is easy to use. Which domain model is right for your particular organization? The use of a multidomain model to create trees and forests over the use of a single domain is a design choice that must be ironed out in the planning phase of a Windows 2000 rollout. The pros and cons must be weighed on a per-case basis, but there are definitely situations in which the multidomain model will work where a single domain will not.

The use of a single domain certainly has its place and holds advantages over multidomain models, but lacks scalability and does not provide an adequate structure for decentralized organizations. The use of such trees is also better suited for organizations that span large geographic locales where site replication can be controlled through the use of sites and site links. One of the first processes of logon is the presentation of the client's IP address and subnet mask to the domain controller that first answers a logon request. If the subnet is discovered to have a domain controller defined by a site with closer proximity to the client, the request is passed to that domain controller for authentication requests. The result is quicker logons (see Figure 13.19). This may be facilitated only through the use of multiple domains and sites.

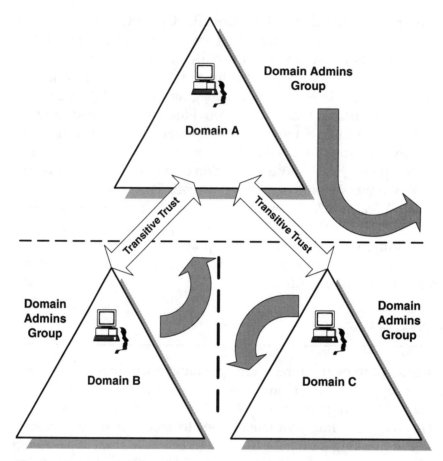

Figure 13.19   Logons are quicker using sites and defined subnets.

In large trees, it is important to log the servers on that are acting in Operations Master roles (see Chapter 12), as these are necessary to the overall function of the directory and network operation. While some operations role failures may go undetected by both users and administrators until certain directory functions are performed, there is one Operations Master role that can cause major headaches should the server housing this service go south. Fortunately, this applies only to mixed-mode networks where Windows NT and 9x clients log on and a Windows 2000 server is acting as a PDC Emulator Master. Failure of this role will cause these clients to fail to authenticate to the network. The role may be seized by another server, as discussed earlier in the chapter. Knowing which servers are acting in these roles will help track down associated problems quickly.

Large-scale implementations of Active Directory that contain super scalar domains containing very large amounts of objects may need a specialized disaster recovery plan to restore the huge amounts of data contained within. Develop a backup strategy for directory databases similar to that of a production database server.

Administrative inheritance is not supported across domains, trees, and forests. This type of access must be explicitly granted by an authoritative party in the other domain(s). If the organization is decentralized, but some administrative functions cross domain boundaries, develop a strategy for creating administrative access, and remember that delegation over specific object containers may be used as well where specific administrative permissions may be granted and controlled.

The use of sites to control replication is imperative in WAN environments. The development of a site strategy may prove challenging in decentralized organizations. Work with the different IT divisions to develop a solid topology and replication schedule. Employ the use of infrastructure members that can offer recommendations about the best use in the routed environment.

Remember, deep domain structures can cause very serious overhead to the directory. Use OUs at the third or fourth level of domains. In the event that an OU becomes too large to manage, split it into other OUs and move the resources using the ADUC console.

Distribute GCSs in a distributed manner and across wide area links to facilitate faster client logons and directory queries. It serves no purpose to have a domain controller local to a client in France when the domain controller has to check Universal group membership in the United States over a 56K link. The same notion holds true for queries.

Summary

The issues surrounding a decision to implement a multidomain model that involves complex tree structures and intricate site creation and management are many. The planning phase of your Active Directory implementation, carefully executed, will result in an architecture that will require little replication of tasks during the build phase. The planning phase is even more critical for larger organizations that face the monumental task of architecting the system to work well over the distributed framework of the existing network infrastructure.

This chapter covered trees and forests from basics to the complex reasoning involved in determining the physical and logical structures. We covered the definition of forests, followed by a brief discussion of trust relationships. We also looked at the issues surrounding complex domain structures and then performed a hands-on to create a second tree structure. The management consoles used to administer trees and forest were explained, and we rounded out the discussion with best practices for large implementations of Active Directory.

Customizing Active Directory Using the Schema

INTRODUCTION

Now that directory services have been enabled and configured, and computers and users are filling the void, it may be necessary to make global changes to the way that objects are defined to the directory and, ultimately, the user. These attributes are defined in the directory schema.

This chapter covers the how and why of the directory schema, the actual definition files, if you will, for objects that exist within. This chapter should serve as an introduction to the schema and schema modification. Discussion of each object class and attribute is not covered, as these subtopics could fill a book in their own right. The references section at the end of the book provides pointers to outside resources. Issues discussed in this chapter include:

- Overview of the Active Directory Schema
- The Active Directory Schema Manager Console
- Modifying the Schema
- Uses
- Best Practices

The Active Directory is said to be both scalable and flexible. The scalability of Active Directory was discussed in earlier chapters. This chapter explores the flexible and configurable nature of the directory through the use of schema modification. The ability to modify the schema is part of managing the Active Directory and is considered an advanced administrative function. There should be tight controls over this action, and customizing the directory using the schema should be planned either in the planning phase or later with the use of a committee or group designated over such actions.

Every object and its related attributes exist in the Active Directory because the schema defines them. This includes domains, services such as DNS, container objects such as an organizational unit (OU) or the Users container, and leaf objects such as computers, printers, users, groups, and so forth. The attributes of an object define characteristics about the object.

One of the most useful features of Active Directory and part of Microsoft's Total Cost of Ownership (TCO) initiative is the ability to query the directory for useful information. In terms of how attributes are used in regard to this principle from a user perspective, LDAP queries to the directory are based on criteria entered into the search mechanism by the user. The criteria are actually certain common attributes that are stored in the Global Catalog (GC) and defined by the schema.

The default set of attributes defined in the schema will often suit the needs of most organizations. For a search that involves people, attributes might include the person's first and last name and associated e-mail address. In the case of printers, attributes may go farther than just a name and define the physical location or special characteristics of the object (see Figure 14.1).

As long as the attribute is defined in the schema and GC, a search may cross over the boundaries of the local domain, spanning the entire tree or forest. If a query contains a search for an object where the criteria are not defined in the GC, the search is limited to the local domain. This is due to the nature of the query mechanism and how it uses the GC to be "aware" of what is in the directory. The local domain controllers store a replica of local object directory information and all attributes. Therefore, local domain controllers are capable of providing more information to the client about local directory object attributes, but searches outside of the domain are limited to the subset of attributes stored on the GC. Directory trees that consist of one domain will provide more information to queries than multidomain models. That is, of course, unless there is a mechanism by which the GC attribute set

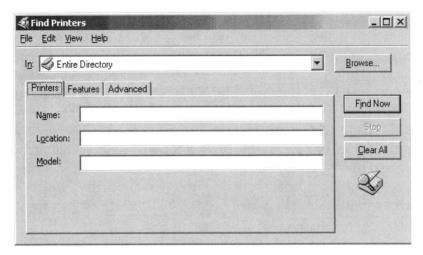

Figure 14.1   Searching for printers.

could be expanded to include other than the default set of attributes installed during creation.

 Those of you who remember all of the warnings and supportability issues surrounding the editing of the registry in Windows NT will feel right at home with the next statement. Use extreme caution when modifying the schema. Misconfiguration of the schema could result in detriment to the directory.

An Overview of Schema Components

Installing Active Directory on the first domain controller in a domain creates the schema, which is stored in the GC. This is why all domains in a tree or forest share the same GC and, ultimately, the same schema. The physical components that make up the schema and facilitate query functions are the Schema Master server (one of the Operations Master roles), the GC that stores a subset of all object attributes in the directory, and the directory data store where the physical data is kept. Additionally, the schema cache is a memory resident copy of the schema residing on each domain controller. This information is stored in physical memory for quick retrieval (kind of like using the #PRE option in LMHOSTS files of old to preload WINS information into physical memory in Windows NT, 9x, or 3.x clients) and is refreshed at given intervals from the physical store.

Logical components of the schema are stored in the directory data store. All objects in the Active Directory are defined through the schema. Because the directory is a hierarchical structure comprised of parent and child objects, it is logical to assume that every object in the directory is further defined by the parent container where it is housed, on up to the root of the tree structure. It is this premise that helps explain the reason for keeping domain and OU levels shallow. The overhead incurred by the operating system from having to drill down through an endless hierarchy of table data to retrieve the attributes of a leaf object can be overwhelming to a server, not to mention the amount of physical memory that it takes to contain such a complex schema cache.

Schema Tools

There are a number of tools that may be used to address the schema information contained in the directory. The Active Directory Schema Snap-in is available natively in Windows 2000, and two other tools, the ADSI Edit and LDP tool, are available in the Windows 2000 Resource Kit. Since many readers will not have a copy of the Resource Kit available, only the native tool is discussed here.

 The Resource Kit is an invaluable tool to administrators of any Windows Server product for two reasons. First, the Resource Kit is full of tools that are not available with the base install of the product, and many of which are not available for download. These tools provide advanced tools for configuring and tuning the operating system. The second reason to obtain and learn the tools in the Resource Kit is purely educational. Tons of documentation are included with the Resource Kit, coupled with the fact that the use of the tools included helps you to understand the inner workings of the operating system. If you want to be considered a "pro," get the Kit!

While the Schema tool is included with Windows 2000, it must be initiated in two steps in order to work. The Active Directory Schema tool must be created and then saved for future use, as it is not part of the base tools set. The following illustrates the procedure:

Since the tool is not part of the native Snap-ins available at installation of the domain controller, the DLL must be registered in the registry for use. Do this by typing the following at a command prompt:

```
Regsrv32 <system_root>\system32\schmmgmt.dll
```

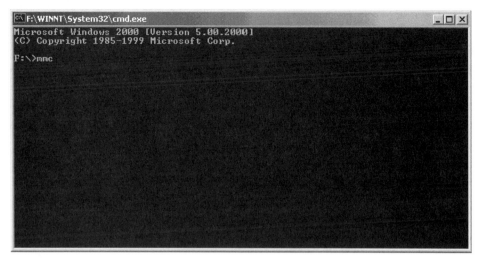

Figure 14.2 Opening the MMC to create the Active Directory Schema tool.

Begin by opening an instance of the Microsoft Management Console. From a command line, type "mmc" and press Enter (see Figure 14.2).

An empty MMC console is displayed. From the Console menu, choose Add/Remove Snap-in (see Figure 14.3).

From the Add/Remove Snap-in window, click Add. Choose the Active Directory Schema Snap-in (see Figure 14.4), and then click Add to use the Snap-in.

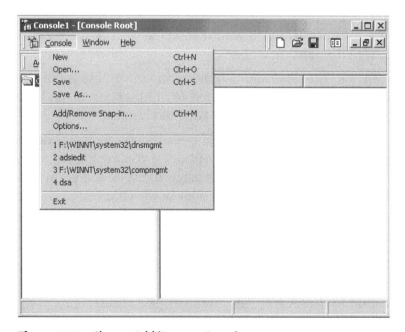

Figure 14.3 Choose Add/Remove Snap-in.

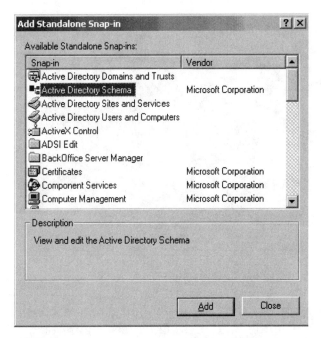

Figure 14.4   Choose the Active Directory Schema Snap-in.

Choose OK to continue. The Snap-in is now installed. Save the console from the Console menu so that it may be used in the future.

Highlight the Active Directory Schema container.

Several options of interest are:

Change Domain Controller. Allows the management of the schema from a different domain controller.

Operations Master. The Operations Master role information may be viewed here. The role may be relocated to another server, and the ability to modify the schema may be adjusted here.

Permissions. The ability to administer permissions to the Schema container are controlled through this option. If you are logged on as administrator, you may receive a message like the one shown in Figure 14.5. More on that is included later in the chapter.

Reload Schema. This reloads the schema cache in to physical memory.

Now expand the Classes container (see Figure 14.6) and notice the various class objects that have been installed with the base schema. Browse the objects to become familiar with these objects.

Repeat this action for the Attributes container (see Figure 14.7).

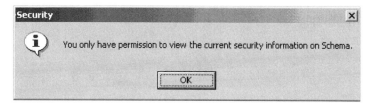

Figure 14.5 Permissions message displayed.

More on the Schema

The schema is installed as part of the base install of the Directory Information Tree (DIT). This "base DIT" and "base schema" contain the basic units necessary to build and configure an Active Directory network. At the beginning of the book we discussed the three parts of the directory that are common to any Active Directory tree or forest: the schema, the GC, and configuration information. All three are replicated throughout between domains and further domain controllers in order to provide unified directory functions. Just as each naming configuration naming context functions as a unit of replication, so does the

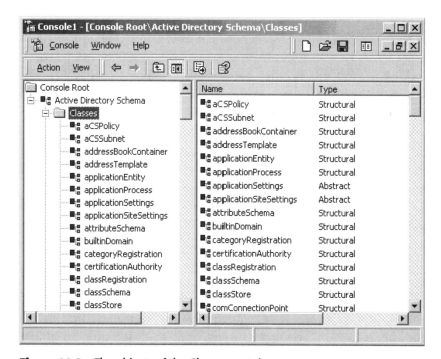

Figure 14.6 The objects of the Classes container.

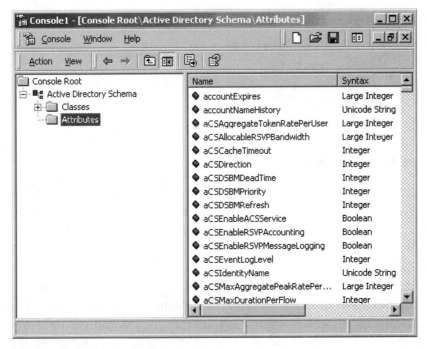

Figure 14.7   The objects of the Attributes container.

schema in order to facilitate directory-wide operation. The entire naming context of the Active Directory is based on X.500 nomenclature, where every object in the directory has a distinguished name (DN). The schema is a container like anything else in the directory, and therefore it may also be addressed by its DN.

Directory information is accessed as a database and uses the Extensible Storage Engine (ESE) as the primary database engine. As in Exchange, this is an implementation of the JET database engine that is optimized for quick retrieval of the data stored in the directory. The information that is accessed through the ADS console is pulled from the physical store of the directory information. The location of the directory database is determined on installation, and the physical file name of the database is NTDS.dit.

The definition of directory containers or entities stored in the schema is referred to as *metadata*. This metadata is further subdivided into two types: *classes* and *attributes*. Classes define a unique object type in the directory and consist of three types: structural, abstract, and auxiliary, the latter of which may be applied to the other two types to extend the attributes (the auxiliary class is a list of additional attributes, if you will, that are applied in bulk to other objects). An example of an object is a user found in the Users container. Attributes actually define the properties of an object. An example of an attribute of a user might be the "last name" property.

Directory Objects Are Based on Standards

The Active Directory is based on directory standards, particularly the X.500 specification. Objects in the directory are not only defined by the attributes associated with them, but also have a unique identifier associated with them called an Object Identifier (OID). This is a number definitively identifying the object class or attribute to the directory service. OIDs are not randomly generated numbers; rather, they are issues based on standards organizations or *issuing authorities*. These numbers help to define the hierarchy and are represented by a dotted decimal notation similar to that used in IP addressing. In order to create unique objects in the directory, organizations may obtain a root OID structure from an issuing authority. Since these are not randomly generated and are meaningful to the directory, it is logical to assume that in order to extend the use of the director, an OID must be obtained first. The American National Standards Institute (ANSI) is the issuing authority for the United States. This further explains the difference in the administrative tasks of creating objects and defining attributes in the directory, and actually modifying the schema to add new class objects. The addition of directory structural components is carried out using the ADUC console, and the schema predefines creation of these objects. Extending the schema to contain unique objects requires the use of OIDs, and is, therefore, not a common task. Randomly assigning OIDs to new object classes has serious repercussions to the directory.

OIDs for object classes are viewed from the ADS console by double-clicking the particular object class as shown in Figure 14.8.

Classes

Classes have a set of flexible and mandatory definitions (attributes) that are applied to the object. Flexible attributes are those that may be changed by that administrator or programs. An example of this might be the format of the phone number attribute of the user object. In

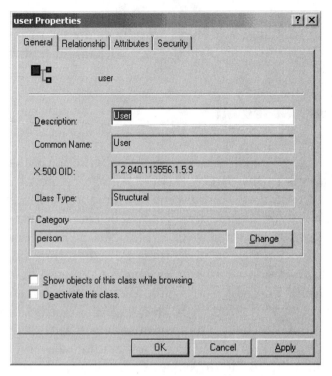

Figure 14.8 The OID is located on the General tab of the Properties page of an object class.

international organizations, a provision for international country codes might be added. Mandatory definitions are those that either must be added or are added by default.

Class objects are defined in the directory by another object that acts as a sort of template called the *classSchema*. The purpose of this object is to maintain unity among object classes in the directory. The following list describes the classSchema object attributes that define what must be entered during class object creation, and it was taken from the Microsoft Windows 2000 Resource Kit:

- The name of the class
- The LDAP display name of the class
- The object identifier for the class
- The GUID for the class
- The attributes that must be present for an instance of the class
- Other attributes that can be present for an instance of the class

- The classes to which the parent of instances of this class might belong
- The superclass from which this class inherits characteristics (Parent)
- Other Auxiliary classes from which this class inherits attributes
- The type of class (Abstract, Structural, or Auxiliary)
- The default hiding state for the class

Objects contained in the Active Directory may be of three types. These object classes are labeled Structural classes, Abstract classes, and Auxiliary classes. When viewing schema information in the ADS console, this information is displayed in the Type column. The structural components are the only type that may be created, and they are represented in the directory tree and may be created as a child of another structure object or abstract object. It may also contain any Auxiliary objects. Examples of this type of object are the OU container or the User container. Abstract classes are not published directory objects; rather, they serve as templates to further define structural objects. A structural object may not be solely derived from this object type. Auxiliary objects are a set of class attributes that act as a sort of add-on module to Structural and Abstract objects. This object type is added to the other two class types in order to further define the object.

To view this information using the ADS console, open the ADS console and expand the Classes container to view all object classes of the schema. Choose the User object class and double-click to view the Properties page (see Figure 14.8).

Notice the four tabs, General, Relationship, Attributes, and Security. The General tab displays a description of the object, the object name, OID, and type. The Category section allows an Auxiliary object type to be associated with the structural object. In this case the "person" object is associated with the user object class, which helps to further define this class.

The Relationship tab displays information about other class definitions pertaining to the object. The *Parent Class* is the parent class object of the object. The Auxiliary Classes are displayed next showing relational auxiliary definitions. The Possible Superior section allows the addition or deletion of possible parent containers where the object might be added (see Figure 14.9).

The Attributes tab contains the defining attributes of the object of which there are two categories, mandatory and optional. Mandatory

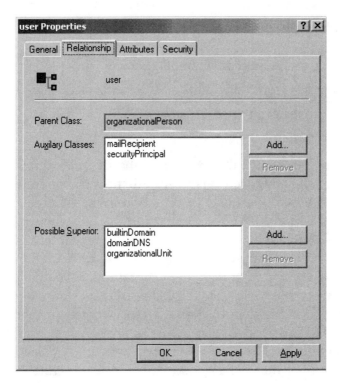

Figure 14.9 The Relationship tab.

attributes must be assigned for certain object classes, and this may be dictated by the relationship of a parent object. Optional attributes are those that are subjectively assigned to the object (see Figure 14.10).

Security for a particular schema object may be defined as well using the Security tab of the object class properties. Notice the extensive list of security definitions for the User object shown in Figure 14.11.

All modification of class objects defined in the schema will take place using this interface. Modifications to these objects should be performed with the greatest care, and the implications fully understood. The schema classes are further defined by attributes, of which there are over 850 defined in the base installation. The next section discusses these further.

Attributes

The object attributes defined by the schema help to further define the properties of directory objects. Attributes are associated with a class object and may be created to further extend the definitions of an object.

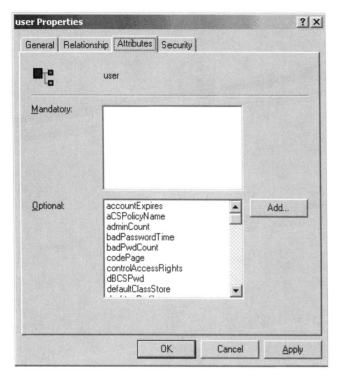

Figure 14.10 The Attributes tab.

Attributes also require an OID for creation, as they are members of the directory structure.

The attributes of the user class object may be viewed using the ADUC console by viewing the properties of a user, and some of these properties are published to the GC in order to locate a user (see Figures 14.12 and 14.13).

Attributes defined in the schema are viewed from the ADS console. Familiarization with these attribute types is beneficial to reduce the possibility of duplication of effort and to further understand which apply to certain class objects.

Attributes may be modified and published through the ADS console. Do this by opening the ADS console and double-clicking an attribute in the Attributes container (see Figure 14.14).

There is only one tab on the Attributes Properties page to configure attribute properties. Figure 14.15 shows the General properties page for an attribute called "department." From here, the description (display name) of the object may be changed; the common name is displayed, as is the OID. Different from the General properties page of object classes is

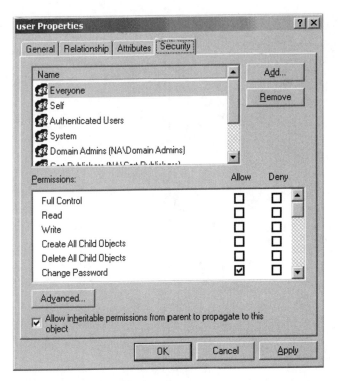

Figure 14.11   The Security tab.

the addition of two checkboxes, "Index this attribute in the Active Directory" and "Replicate this attribute to the Global Catalog." These are important in publishing attribute information about objects. For example, if a new attribute were created and added to the user object to describe employee ID numbers, this information could be published to the catalog and searched across forests. The same process might be used to create more and descriptive search fields for printers or computers. In our example, the department attribute is assigned to the User object, but is not replicated to the GC for querying. This attribute might be helpful in locating users in the directory.

Modifying the Schema

The Active Directory schema defines the set of all object classes and attributes that can be stored in the directory. For each object class, the schema defines where it can be created in a directory tree by specifying the parents of the class object. There are objects that may be modified in

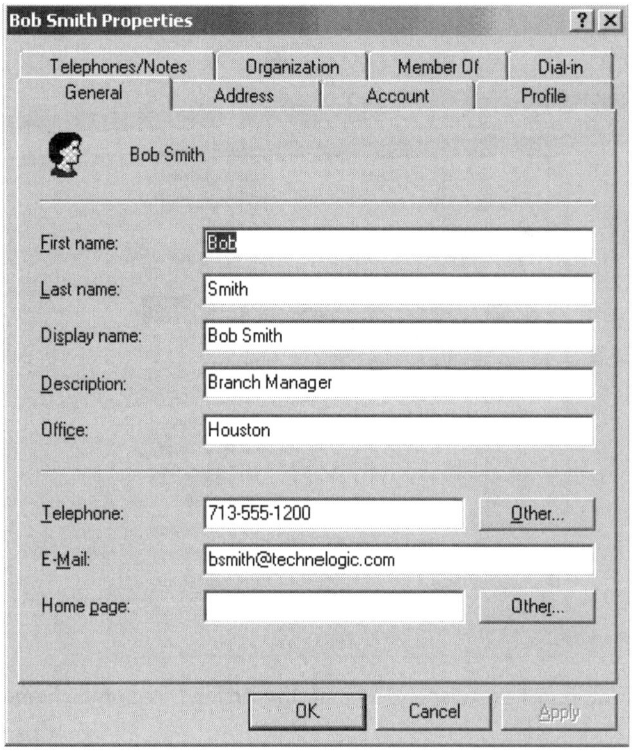

Figure 14.12   User properties shown from the ADUC console.

the schema, and others that may not be, such as system objects. Additionally, there are guidelines that should be followed in determining whether or not to alter the schema. Other issues such as permissions and inheritance affect the decision and modification process.

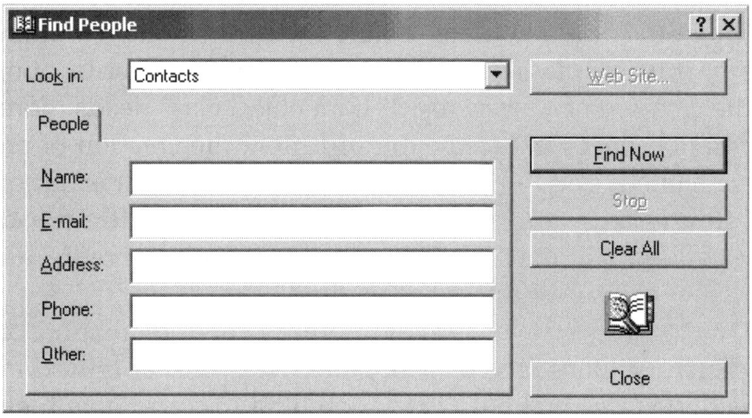

Figure 14.13   User search.

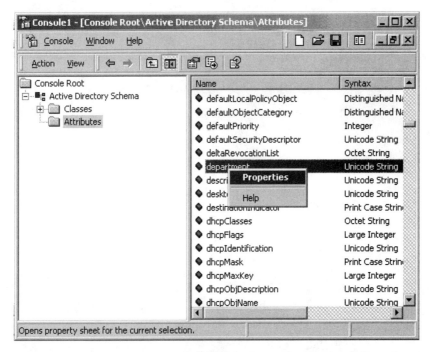

Figure 14.14 Properties of attributes are displayed using the Active Directory Schema console.

When to Extend the Schema

The schema may be modified by either a user or an application that has permission to do so. The decision to do so must not be taken lightly, as the effects are global. There are two functions that may be carried out in relation to schema modification, adding or retiring metadata.

The creation of an object in the schema container is dictated by one of three needs. The need for a new class, where the base implementation does not contain sufficient classes to fulfill the need of the organization, will result in the creation of a class object. If an object class needs more attributes to describe the object to the organization, the creation of an attribute is necessitated. The third decision to create an object is out of the need to create an Auxiliary class object to apply attributes to a broad array of object classes. It may also become necessary to retire an attribute or class when its usefulness has expired.

It is important to note that an OID is required for the creation of objects in the directory. Once an OID is obtained, it is further critical to understand the dotted decimal notation used with OIDs and how they relate to the object hierarchy for your particular tree. The Resource Kit

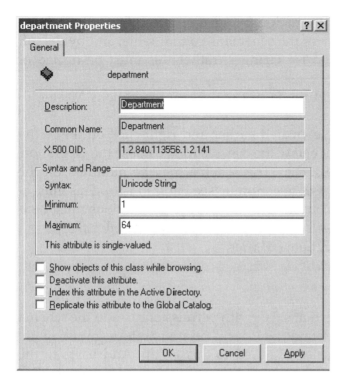

Figure 14.15   The properties page of the Department attribute.

does provide a tool called oidgen.exe that allows the creation of unique OIDs, although the use of this tool will not be covered in this book. See the Resource Kit for more details.

Requirements

Changes to the schema are global and affect the entire forest. This is true because every domain controller in the forest contains a replica of the schema, and changes are replicated throughout the structure. There are additional concerns performing this operation when an organization is widely distributed across WAN links, as schema replication is a separate process from other directory change information.

Active Directory uses the concept of multimaster replication to exchange directory information between members and improve performance. This could present a problem when modifying the schema, as the Schema Master server must be accessed during the operation, thereby preventing replication during modifications. The schema is a replicated container. Replication is halted during schema modification to prevent errors in information being replicated. Only the Schema Operations Master copy of the schema is configurable, and by default, the server is *not* enabled for changes; rather this must be turned on using the ADS console.

In order to enable edit mode of the Schema Operations Master, do the following:

Open the ADS console created earlier and right-click on the Active Directory Schema object below the console root. Choose the Operations Master option and check the "The Schema may be modified on this server" checkbox. Click OK to continue (see Figure 14.16). This must be performed at a server console, and the proper permissions must be in place if this is being performed from a domain controller that is in a domain other than the Schema Master.

Permissions

There is a specific group that exists with permissions to edit the schema, Schema Admins. By default, the local administrators group of the Schema Operations Master is added to this group. Add users to this group who will participate in the editing of the schema. See the "Best Practices" section for more on permissions and strategy on the schema.

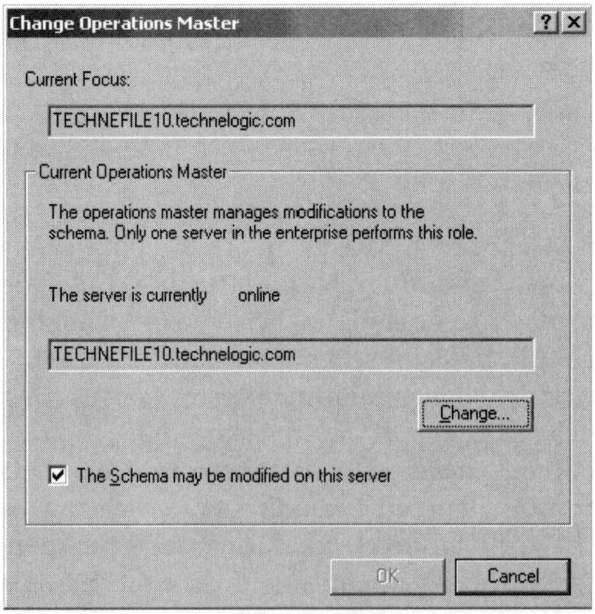

Figure 14.16   Enabling the Schema Master for edit mode.

Inheritance

An important concept that must be understood before undertaking schema modification is *inheritance*. A simple concept, it dictates what class object attributes are mandatory to child objects. That is, if a class object were created as a child object (sometimes referred to as a *subclass*) under the printers object class, which itself had an attribute called "Maker," the child object will also possess this attribute. Therefore, attributes and subclass creation must be well thought out in order to have meaningful child object classes with meaningful attributes.

Adding New Objects

An object definition consists of a name, an OID, a list of mandatory and optional attributes, the list of classes that can be parents of the object, the parent class if any, and a list of any auxiliary classes. Before creating a class object, have all of this information available.

 The creation of objects using the ADS console was not available in the release of the operating system used during the writing of this book. If the feature should become available, updates to the book will be posted on the Wiley Web site at www.wiley.com/compbooks/schwartz.

Modifying Classes

Modifying object classes involves changing one of the following: the description, the category, the list of mandatory and optional attributes, the list of auxiliary classes and possible parents of the object, and security. Use the ADS console created earlier to modify a class object.

Open the ADS console and click on the Classes container. In the results pane, double-click the class object you want to change (see Figure 14.17).

The Object Properties page is displayed. Change the required fields, and click OK to continue (see Figure 14.18).

Adding Attributes

An attribute definition consists of a name, a unique OID, a syntax that defines what kind of data the attribute can hold, and optional range limits. For strings, the value limits set the minimum and maximum length of the string. For integers, the value limits set the minimum and maximum value of the integer.

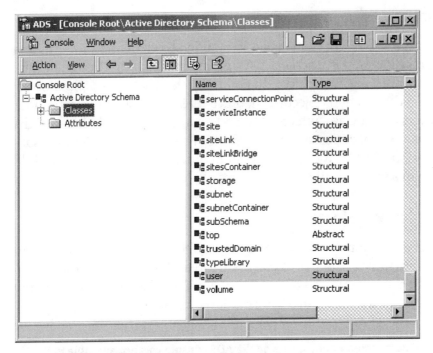

Figure 14.17 Opening the Classes container.

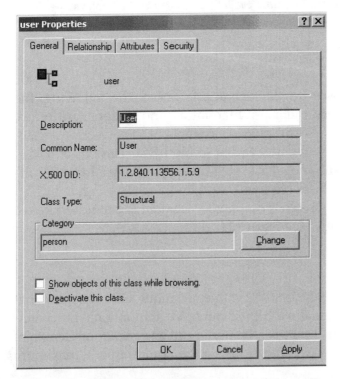

Figure 14.18 Displaying the Properties page to change class options.

As part of the creation of an attribute, it should be determined if the object will be part of the database index to enhance query performance in the Active Directory. When no index is available to satisfy a given query, the LDAP server must read the entire partition of the domain controller to find the information. If the attribute will be frequently used in queries, it is recommended that it be indexed. The downside to this is the cost incurred, as adding an instance to the index consumes physical disk space and affects performance overall. Permanency of the attribute is also an issue in relation to indexing attributes.

Publishing the attribute in the GC also has ramifications. If the attribute is used often, or in several cases, it may be a good idea to publish. Attributes published in the GC will be replicated and stored on other GCs in the forest. This is a cost, and the implications of sizing servers appropriately must be understood.

To add an attribute to the schema, open the ADS console created earlier and right-click the Attributes container. Choose the Create Attributes menu option (see Figure 14.19).

A standard warning is displayed stating that the creation of schema objects is a permanent action, though these objects may be disabled (see Figure 14.20).

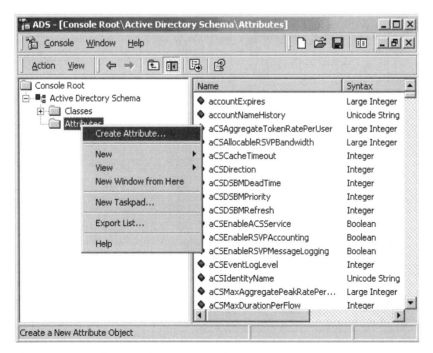

Figure 14.19   Choosing the Create Attribute option.

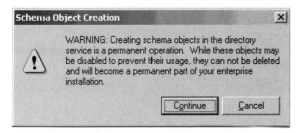

Figure 14.20 Warning message.

The Create New Attribute page is displayed (see Figure 14.21). The Identification section of the page is where object Common Name, LDAP Name, and OID are entered. The Syntax and Range section allows the input of the syntax type and optional string length (or in the case of an integer value, the inter range allowed). Click OK when finished.

Disabling a Schema Object

Disable schema objects when there is no longer a need to use them in the directory. This is used in place of deleting these objects, which is not an available option. Open the ADS console and expand either container (classes or attributes may be disabled). Open an object's properties and check the "Deactivate this <class> or <attribute>" checkbox.

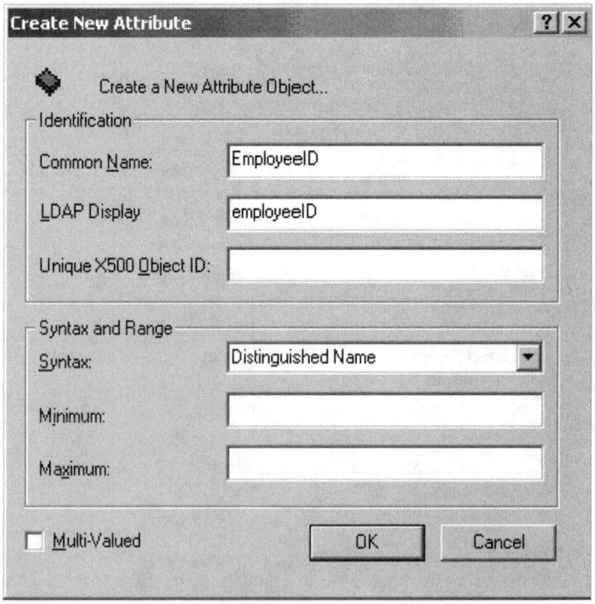

Figure 14.21 The Create New Attribute page.

Best Practices

Modifying the schema is a straightforward process, but the implications must be fully understood. Use the following guidelines to maintain a consistent and error-free use of this technique:

Caution all administrators. It cannot be stressed enough that changing the schema has global repercussions and should be pursued cautiously and by a skilled person. All of the class object and attribute object properties and classes should be thoroughly examined before attempting modification.

Create a group to control the process. A group or individual within the organization should be designated as the schema policy authority. It is from this group that all decisions regarding editing, design, policy, and change control of the schema should originate. The use of a database administrator in such a group might prove a great asset, as the policies regarding the use and modifications of the schema are based on database technology.

Lock down permissions. Use the Schema Admins group with great care. Only add the groups or users who absolutely must have write access to the schema. Enable logging on the Schema container to monitor access, as malicious intent will surely focus on the schema as a target.

Summary

The ability to modify the schema is two-fold, where objects may be created during day-to-day operations or by directly modifying the schema using the Active Directory Schema Snap-in. This ability makes the Active Directory a flexible mechanism for publishing directory information on a global level. This chapter began with a discussion of the schema and schema objects, followed by the tool used in Windows 2000 to view and modify the schema. Schema members were also discussed, covering class and attribute objects in detail. The chapter rounded out with a discussion on modifying the schema and best practices. From here, the discussion moves toward managing the directory where everyday tasks are completed using the Active Directory Users and Computers console, as well as advanced administrative techniques such as batch updates of the directory.

Active Directory Management

INTRODUCTION

So far, the focus has been on creating and managing directory objects at a high level, such as domains and configuring site information, even configuring the Schema and Global Catalog (CG), which are global concepts. What about the lower structural levels to be implemented in the directory, such as Organizational Units (OUs), computers, and users? These objects serve to populate the directory with useful members and structures. This discussion was saved until the later chapters of the book, as focus on the installation of the directory and Active Directory issues themselves predicate managing directory objects.

This chapter discusses the following:

- Tools Used in Managing Directory Objects
- Creating Users
- Creating Groups
- Creating Organizational Units
- Grouping Users, Groups, and Computers
- Managing the Directory Objects with Windows Scripting
- Advanced Administrative Tips

Perhaps the tool most used to manage the directory is the Active Directory Users and Computers console found in the Administrative Tools group. That is, unless you have already mastered the Windows Scripting feature of the operating system. Both of these tools are integral to managing the directory and should be mastered by anyone managing the Active Directory.

The Active Directory Users and Computers Console

The role of the network administrator is a complex one filled with a myriad of duties. One of the most time-consuming tasks (other than putting out the endless fires!) is creating accounts and maintaining groups. The primary tool to perform this function is the Active Directory Users and Computers (ADUC) console by which all accounts that live in the domain are created and modified. Those with experience using the User Manager for the Domains tool of old will find comfort in this new tool for its ease of use and information features.

Creating objects in Windows 2000 is a bit more complex than in previous versions. Each object should have descriptive properties that allow users of the directory to query for this information and in due course find what they are looking for on the directory. The old approach was to drill down endlessly for this information. The point being made here is this: Take the time to fill out user information completely so that queries are meaningful when a response is returned. To get philosophical, you only get out of the network what you put into it. There are many fields to be completed when creating user accounts. Try to be as comprehensive as possible. Microsoft has integrated the Windows Scripting Host (WSH) technology into the operating system to aid in batch processing of all types of information to the directory. It may be prudent to read up on this technology, which uses any number of programming languages to script for the operating system, including Visual Basic and Java. Figure 15.1 depicts a typical ADUC console.

Open the console and notice the root and first-level objects. Figure 15.2 shows the ADUC console and objects. There are four main first-level folders:

- Built-in (Accounts)
- Computers
- Users
- Domain Controllers

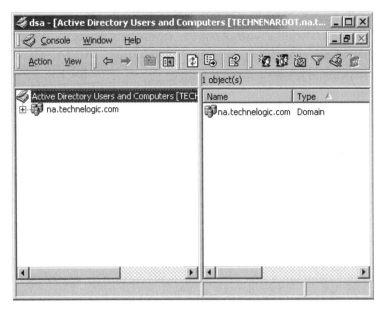

Figure 15.1   The Active Directory Users and Computers console.

Accounts for computers, groups, and users are created, modified, disabled, moved, and deleted from the ADCU console. Domain objects are also "published" to the directory through this console, and OUs within the domain are created here.

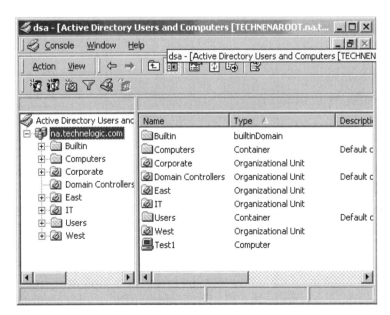

Figure 15.2   The main objects of concern for managing directory objects are the Built-in, Computers, Users, and Domain Controllers containers.

The Built-in folder, like previous versions of the operating system, contains the built-in accounts created by the operating system, which are used primarily to service the operating environment. Add users or groups to these groups who will function as support staff for the local server or domain.

The Computers folder contains computer accounts objects for the domain. This object contains the computer accounts that participate in the domain. Accounts (computer names) may be added prior to joining workstations or servers to the domain to "authenticate" the computer to the domain and bypass having to use an administrator account to join the domain.

The Users container houses, you guessed it, user accounts. Groups are also stored here.

The last container object is Domain Controllers. Inside this container are the domain controllers for the domain, and certain properties of each may be managed from here.

To begin, first double-click the *domain* object, represented by the name of the domain being managed, to expand the first-level objects, and then right-click the domain object to view the choices available (see Figure 15.3). Commonly used menu items here are:

- Delegate control
- Find (common to all objects)
- Connect to Domain
- Connect to Domain Controller
- Operations Master
- New (common to all objects)
- Properties (common to all objects)

Beginning at the top of the list, Delegate control allows a group or user the authority over the domain object (or whichever object was selected in the console hierarchy). This is helpful in delegating authority to domains or domain objects. If this is a child domain, a group from a parent domain may be placed as the delegated authority for the domain, or other such useful functions (see Figure 15.4).

The Find feature allows a search of published objects in the directory to quickly find and manipulate resources. In large domains and trees, this function will be invaluable due the sheer enormity of objects that may exist (see Figure 15.5).

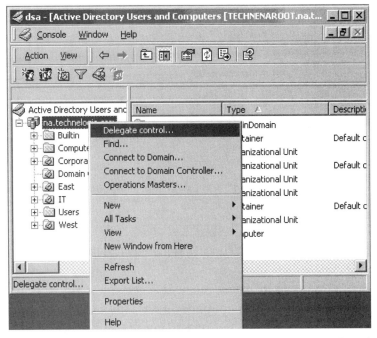

Figure 15.3   The actions that may be performed at the domain object level of the console.

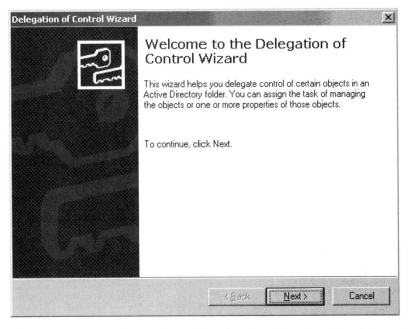

Figure 15.4   The Delegate Control launches the Delegation Wizard to assign control of objects.

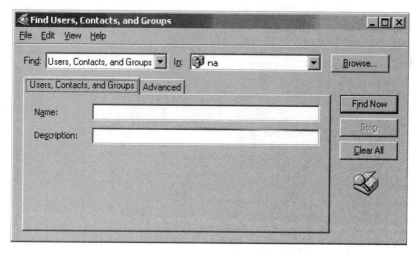

Figure 15.5   The Find feature allows administrators to find what they want, quickly.

The Connect to Domain feature connects the console to a domain (other than the current domain) for management. That is, all domains may be managed through one console, providing the appropriate permissions are in place (see Figure 15.6). As we discussed earlier in the book, domains are islands of security, and management across domains is permitted only by explicit permission.

Connect to Domain Controller allows management of other domain controllers in the domain.

The Operations Master option deserves some special attention and definition. There are five Operations Master roles that a domain controller can fulfill, and all five of these operations must be fulfilled in an Active Directory forest. The five roles are (see Figure 15.7):

PDC Emulator. This domain controller serves to emulate a down-level primary domain controller (PDC) server and handles requests from down-level backup domain controllers (BDCs) and clients regarding legacy logon information, and also handles replicating this data between the Windows 2000 domain controllers and legacy BDCs.

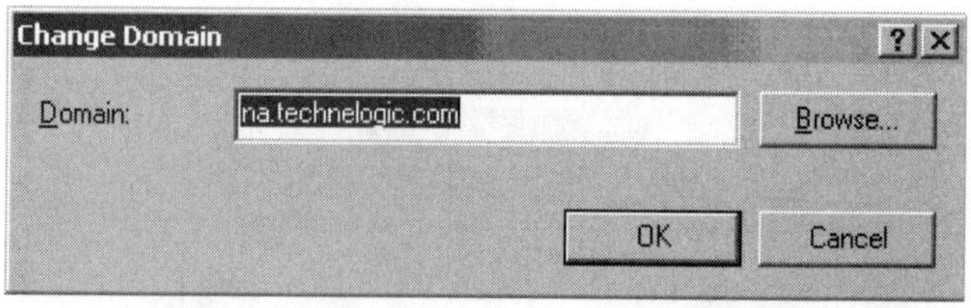

Figure 15.6   Any domain controller (or domain) may be accessed through the ADUC console.

Schema Master. Handles and tracks all updates to the directory schema.

Infrastructure Master. Handles updating information pertaining to domain groups. When group information changes in the directory, the Infrastructure Master updates this information via multimaster replication to the local domain controllers and other domains in the tree.

Domain Naming Master. Tracks the creation or removal of domains in the forest.

Relative ID Master. Tracks and maintains Relative IDs (RIDs) for the domain, which are affixed to Domain Security IDs (DSIDs) of objects to form the SID.

These operations are critical to the health of the domain and Active Directory. Failure of any of the Operations Masters will result in directory failures. The Operations Master role may be moved to another server in the event of network or server failure (promoted, if you will), though this operation is not recommended and is considered a last-ditch effort to rectify problems with the directory.

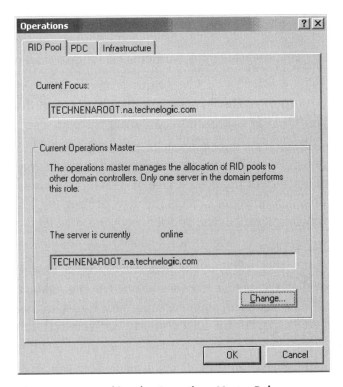

Figure 15.7   Tracking the Operations Master Roles.

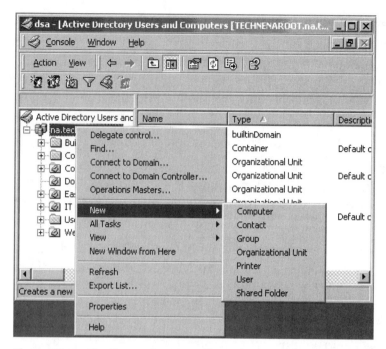

Figure 15.8 The New action Item allows the creation of directory objects such as OUs and users.

The New menu item contains several submenu items (see Figure 15.8):

Computer. This function is used to add a computer account to the domain. Adding a computer to the wrong container, such as at the domain level, will fail. Use the Computers container instead.

Contact. This feature allows a contact person to be added to a container object for reference by the user community, and the information is returned from a query of the object. Use of contacts will help reduce misrouted calls pertaining to objects (broken printer, etc.) or help desk calls by pointing users to the proper resource contact.

Group. Use this option to create a new domain or OU group.

FRS Settings. Turns on File Replication System services for the object. This service is beyond the scope of this book, but for the sake of satisfying curiosity, the FRS provides a mechanism for two-way file or object replication and is part of the Distributed File System (DFS) services.

Organizational Unit. As the name implies, this is the option to select for the creation of OUs. More on this option a little later in the chapter.

Printer. Allows the publishing of down-level printers to the directory. Creating Windows 2000 printers is accomplished through the Add Printer Wizard, and the printers are published to the directory automatically.

User. This option is used to create new user accounts.

Shared Folder. Creates new shares on the server. This may also be accomplished through Windows Explorer or the Computer Management console.

Finally, the last option of the main menu that is of importance is the Properties menu item. Properties of all objects in the console may be displayed and information for each entered. Additionally, the delegation of the object may be arranged here. Now for more hands-on as OUs and users and groups are added to the directory using the ADUC.

Cumulatively, these items will comprise the bulk of the object tasks used in managing the directory. As a rule, when creating objects, it is important to fill out as many fields as possible about objects to aid in the query process. Attributes that you may find useful for searches may be published to the Global Catalog (GC) as outlined in the previous chapter.

Object Management Hands-On

One of the single most important and cumbersome tasks of the administrator is the creation of objects, namely users and groups, but also computers and printers. In this section, the ins and outs of this task are covered beginning with the creation of OUs as containers for grouping our users, groups, and computers.

Step-by-Step Creating Organizational Units

We discussed earlier in the book the theories behind directory structures. Now that the domains are in place, it is time to create OUs to logically group resources in the directory.

Begin by right-clicking on the domain object of the ADUC console and select New and Organizational Unit. A window similar to the one shown in Figure 15.9 is displayed.

Type in the name of the new OU, and then click OK. It really is that simple. The OU is simply a container for grouping resources and delegating control. This step completed, users may be added to the system to populate these containers.

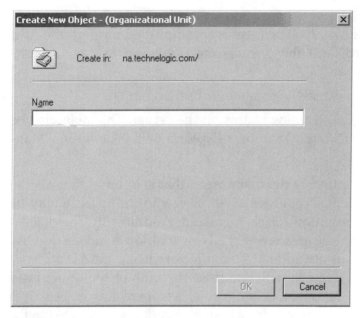

Figure 15.9 The Create New Organizational Unit page.

Step-by-Step Creating Users and Groups

The next logical step is to add users and groups to the directory. Right-click on the User container and select New and then User. The Create New Object (User) page is displayed. Enter the first and last name of the user and the logon name as shown in Figure 15.10. Click Next to continue

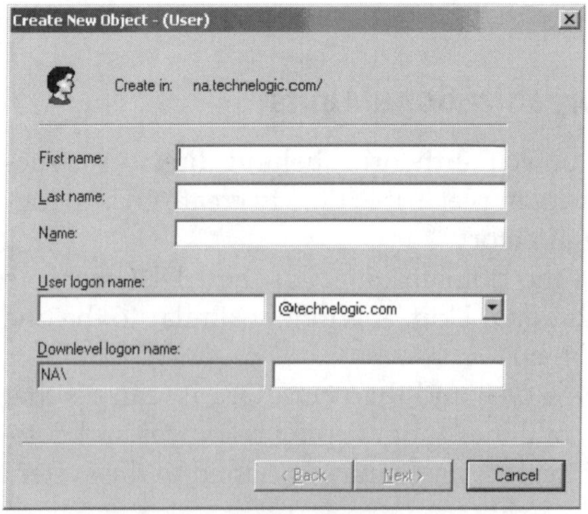

Figure 15.10 The Create New User Object page.

to the password page. Enter a password and confirm, then click Next. A summary page is displayed. Click Finish to complete the operation or Back to change selections.

Moving Resources

If there are member (resource) servers that exist in the domain or at this stage, they can be moved to this new container using the Move command on the main right-click menu. This task is shown in Figures 15.11 and 15.12. Users may be moved into OU containers in the same manner as servers or other resources. While all of the mechanics are new, none of these administrative functions are rocket science, though they are time consuming. Learn WSH and how to use it with Windows 2000. Being able to batch users and all of the properties associated with the account into a single script not only saves time, it also removes the tedium of everyday administrative functions such as this.

Managing User Properties

Now that the user has been created, the user object properties may be added. Right-click on the new user account, and select properties. The Properties page is shown, and user information may be (or rather, should be!) added. Account information may be changed here, profiles assigned, dial-in permissions assigned, and group associations added (see Figure 15.13).

Fill in all of the user information on the General page so that this information will be reflected in the directory, then move to the Address

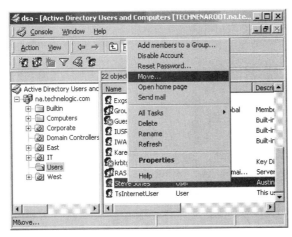

Figure 15.11 Moving resources to an OU.

Figure 15.12 Select the container where the user should be moved.

tab. The information entered here will help users look up snail mail information for users in the directory. Enter all fields here to make the directory helpful to users (see Figure 15.14).

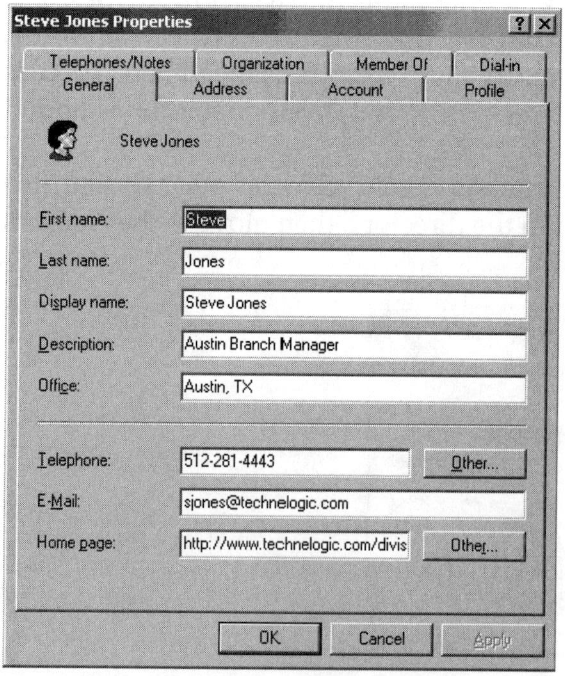

Figure 15.13 A typical User Properties page.

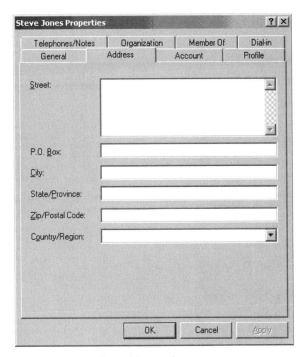

Figure 15.14 The Address tab.

The Account tab is used to configure various aspects of the user account, such as logon name, the suffix, the logon hours, what computer the user may log on to, options for the account, and an expiration date for the account. All of this should look somewhat familiar to veteran Windows NT administrators (see Figure 15.15).

The Profile tab will institute a mandatory profile for the user that follows the user wherever he or she may log on. Additionally, this tab is used to configure the account for use of a logon script, home directory on a file server for personal documents, and a shared folder affinity (see Figure 15.16).

The Telephone/Notes tab allows the input of telephone contact information, a must for administrators! (See Figure 15.17.)

The Organization tab is where information is entered about the user and his or her place in the organization itself, including Job Title, Department, Company, and Manager (see Figure 15.18).

The Member Of tab is used for including users in groups created within the organization (see Figure 15.19).

Last, but certainly not least, is the Dial-in tab, which is used to grant access to the network via external connectivity (see Figure 15.20).

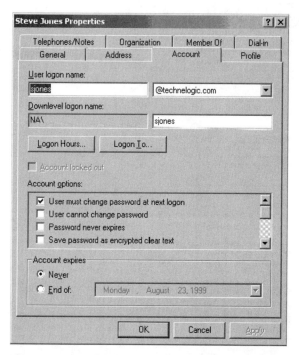

Figure 15.15 The Account tab is used to configure the user account.

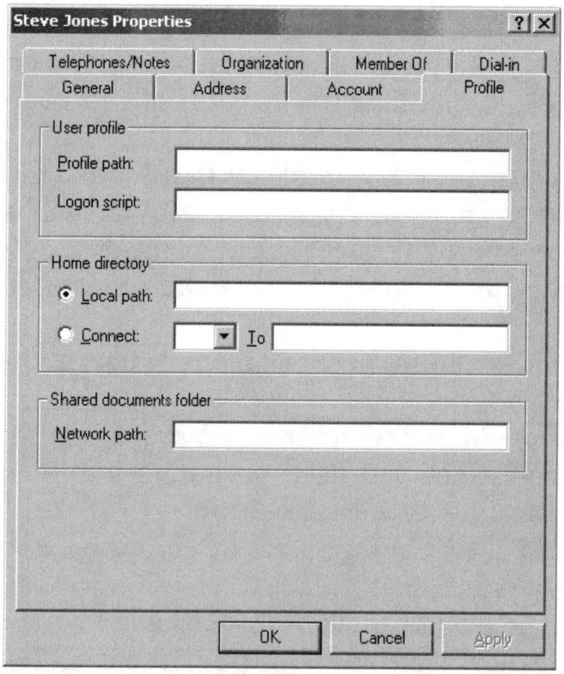

Figure 15.16 The Profile tab.

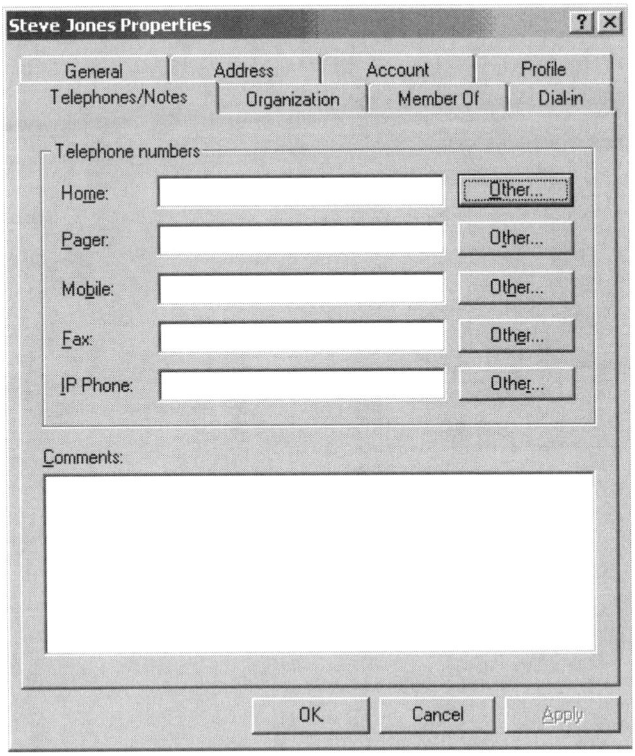

Figure 15.17 The Telephone/Notes tab.

Remote users who dial in to the network should have the Allow Access option selected here, as well as any user who needs to gain access to network resources from a remote location.

That about rounds out user account configuration. Filling out these tabs of information may be laborious and tedious, but a best effort should be made to be as complete as possible. Doing so will help users find resources on the network. This task may be assigned to an HR person, if such a resource exists, where his or her account could be locked down suffi-ciently to simply enter this type of information. As we discover later in the chapter, there are better and more efficient ways of doing this.

Advanced Object Administration Techniques

The directory has many new features offered that may actually consume more of an administrator's time than previous versions of Windows NT. From a technical perspective, this is not your grandma's operation sys-tem! As we have seen, the simple act of inputting user information

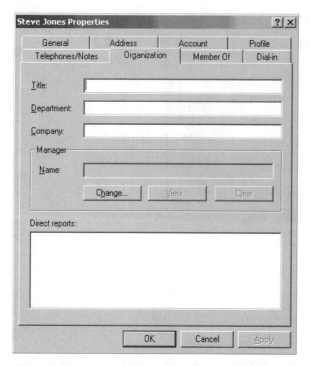

Figure 15.18 The Organization tab.

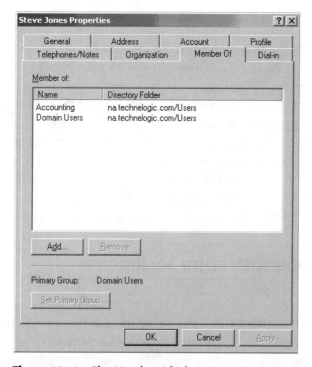

Figure 15.19 The Member Of tab.

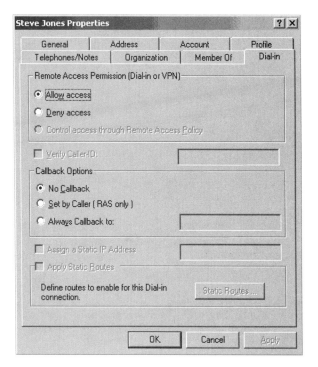

Figure 15.20 The Dial-in tab.

(unless you get lazy) is a task in and of itself. As administrators of Microsoft Exchange Server know, there are ways to ease the administrative burden of user account management through the use of import features. Fortunately, once again due to standards, this ability is inherent in the Windows 2000 operation system in the form of two command-line tools, LDIFDE and CSVDE.

First, a discussion of how these tools work. Active Directory is based on standards, the most prominent of which is Lightweight Directory Access Protocol (LDAP). There are several proposed specifications that exist as addendums to the LDAP specification, one of which supports the bulk import/export of directory information using LDAP as the primary interface to the directory.

LDIFDE is based on this proposed standard of LDIF, or LDAP Data Interchange Format, which supports the addition, removal, and modification in batch of directory information. This works for many leaf and container objects such as users, groups, OUs, printers, and so forth. To start LDIFDE, click Start, then click Run, then type "CMD" and press Enter. At the command prompt, type the command "LDIFDE" and the appropriate parameters. The following summarizes the command format and options for the LDIFDE tool, and is reprinted from the command-line help found by typing LDIFDE -?:

```
LDIFDE [-i] [-f ] [-s] [-c] [-v] [-j] [-t] [-d] [-r] [-p] [-1] [-o] [-g]
[-m] [-n] [-k] [-a ] [- b][-?]
```

Parameters

-i
Specifies import mode. If not specified, the default mode for LDIFDE is export.

-f *filename*
Identifies the import or export file name.

-s *server name*
Specifies the domain controller to perform the import or export operation.

-c *string1 string2*
Replace all occurrences of string1 with string2. Typically is used when importing data from one domain to another and the distinguished name of the export domain needs to be replaced with that of the import domain.

-v
Sets verbose mode.

-j *Directory Path*
Use to set the log file location. The default is the current directory.

-t *Port Number*
Use to specify a LDAP port number. The default LDAP port is 389. The Global Catalog port is 3268

-d *BaseDN*
Use to set the distinguished name of the search base for data export.

-r *LDAP filter*
Use to create a LDAP search filter for data export. For example to export all users with your surname, the following filter could be used:

```
-r "(&(objectClass=user)(sn=yoursurname))"
```

-p *Scope*
Set the search scope. May be one of Base, OneLevel or SubTree

-1 *LDAP attribute list*
Set the list of attributes to return in the results of an export query. If this parameter is omitted, all attributes are returned. For example to retrieve only the distinguished name, common name, first name, surname and telephone number of the returned objects, the following attribute list would be specified:

```
-l "distinguishedName, cn, givenName, sn, telephone"
```

-o
List of attributes to be omitted from the results of an export query.
This is typically used when exporting objects from the Active Directory
and then importing them into another LDAP compliant directory. There may
be some attributes that are not supported by the other directory, so
these attributes may be omitted from the result set using this option.
For example to omit the objectGUID, whenChanged and whenCreated
attributes the following omission would be specified:
-o "whenCreated, whenChanged, objectGUID"

-g
Do not perform paged searches.

-m
Omit attributes that only apply to Active Directory objects such as the
ObjectGUID, objectSID, pwdLastSet, samAccountType attributes.

-n
Do not export binary values.

-k
Skip errors during the import operation and continue processing. Typical
errors that may be skipped include those where the object already
exists.

-a *user distinguished name password*
Sets the command to run using the supplied user distinguished name and
password. (The default is to run using the credentials of the currently
logged on user.) For example:
a cn=yourname,domain controller=yourcompany,domain controller=com
password

- b *username domain password*
Sets the command to run as *username domain password*.(The default is to
run using the credentials of the currently logged on user.)For example:
b yourusername yourcompanydomain password

-?
Use to display Help.

Figure 15.21 illustrates one example of how this utility might be used to export to a file called export.ldif.

The CSVDE utility is quite similar to the LDIFDE tool, with the exception that it imports and exports to a comma-delimited format that is readable and editable through Microsoft Excel as a .csv file. The following shows the command set of the utility, which is similar to the LDIFDE extensions.

A utility program called CSVDE is included in Windows 2000 to support batch operations based on the CSV file format standard. CSVDE is a command-line program that may be run from a command window.

```
CSDVE [-i] [-f ] [-s] [-c] [-v] [-j] [-t] [-d] [-r] [-p] [-l] [-o] [-g]
[-m] [-n] [-k] [-a ] [- b] [-?]
```

Parameters

-i
Specifies import mode. If not specified, the default mode for LDIFDE is export.

-f *filename*
Identifies the import or export file name.

-s *server name*
Specifies the domain controller to perform the import or export operation.

-c *string1 string2*
Replace all occurrences of string1 with string2. Typically is used when importing data from one domain to another and the distinguished name of the export domain needs to be replaced with that of the import domain.

-v
Sets verbose mode.

-j *Directory Path*
Use to set the log file location. The default is the current directory.

-t *Port Number*
Use to specify a LDAP port number. The default LDAP port is 389. The Global Catalog port is 3268

-d *BaseDN*
Use to set the distinguished name of the search base for data export.

-r *LDAP filter*
Use to create a LDAP search filter for data export. For example to export all users with your surname, the following filter could be used:
-r "(&(objectClass=user)(sn=yoursurname))"

-p *Scope*
Set the search scope. May be one of Base, OneLevel or SubTree

-l *LDAP attribute list*
Set the list of attributes to return in the results of an export query. If this parameter is omitted, all attributes are returned. For example to retrieve only the distinguished name, common name, first name, surname and telephone number of the returned objects, the following

```
attribute list would be specified:
-l "distinguishedName, cn, givenName, sn, telephone"

-o
List of attributes to be omitted from the results of an export query.
This is typically used when exporting objects from the Active Directory
and then importing them into another LDAP compliant directory. There may
be some attributes that are not supported by the other directory, so
these attributes may be omitted from the result set using this option.
For example to omit the objectGUID, whenChanged and whenCreated
attributes the following omission would be specified:
-o "whenCreated, whenChanged, objectGUID"

-g
Do not perform paged searches.

-m
Omit attributes that only apply to Active Directory objects such as the
ObjectGUID, objectSID, pwdLastSet, samAccountType attributes.

-n
Do not export binary values.

-k
Skip errors during the import operation and continue processing. Typical
errors that may be skipped include those where the object already
exists.

-a user distinguished name password
Sets the command to run using the supplied user distinguished name and
password. (The default is to run using the credentials of the currently
logged on user.) For example:
a cn=yourname,domain controller=yourcompany,domain controller=com
password

- b username domain password
Sets the command to run as username domain password.(The default is to
run using the credentials of the currently logged on user.)For example:
b yourlogonname yourcompanydomain password

-?
Use to display Help.
```

Complex switches may be used to filter only the data out of the tree that is needed such as only OUs or a specific OU. Figure 15.21 shows an export function from the command line. Figure 15.22 shows the exported user fields that were imported into Excel, and then users added for bulk import to the directory. Fields such as "address" and "manager" are included to reduce the tedium of having to manually

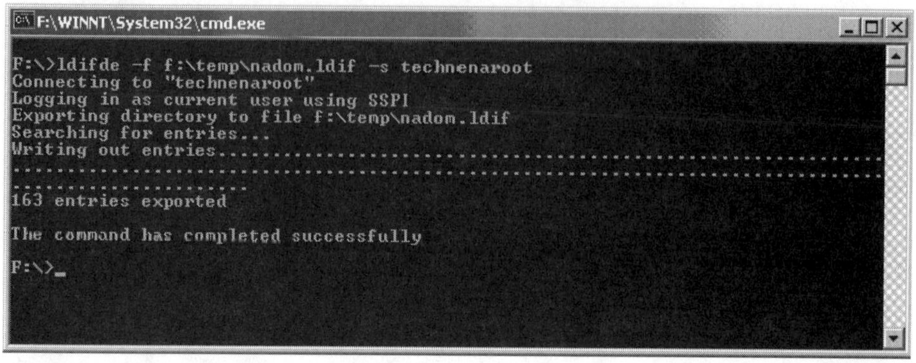

Figure 15.21   An export using the CSVDE utility.

input the data on a case-by-case basis. The fact that a productivity tool may be used to alter the data of the fields means that arbitrary tasks such as creating the comma-delimited file may be done by administrative assistants.

As stated, these tools work for creation, deletion, and modification of many directory object types, and they benefit the administrator by saving time not only through the batch act itself, but offering the ability to outsource the creation of the object file to another source

Summary

The management of directory objects is a crucial and time-consuming aspect of the overall administrative tasks performed by administrative personnel. User accounts, especially in a large environment, are in a constant state of flux. The ability to manage these resources effectively

Figure 15.22   Adding users and properties in bulk.

affects the overall outcome of the network and the amount of help desk calls answered. Fortunately, Windows 2000 provides a robust tool for creating users, groups, computers, and OUs for organizing these resources further. Additionally, there are two command-line tools that can aid in the bulk import and export of directory information. Used in conjunction with the ADUC console, an effective management plan for these resources may be created and utilized. This chapter covered all of these tools and the actual hands-on in performing object creation in the directory, both using the ADUC console and the bulk import tools. Next, we are going to take a look at Group Policy, part of Microsoft's overall TCO strategy to unify desktops.

CHAPTER 16

Group Policy and the Active Directory

INTRODUCTION

This chapter covers one of the main Total Cost of Ownership (TCO) objectives implemented in Windows 2000, Group Policy, which allows an administrator to lock down the desktops of users in order to facilitate standards across the organization. Group Policy is considered a large part of the move toward standardization in most organizations to save growing IT costs. While Policies were part of previous versions of Windows NT, the feature was limited and limited in use. The robust features found in Windows 2000 integrate with the Active Directory and are far more robust. This chapter discusses the implementation of Group Policy using Active Directory. The following items are covered:

- Defining Group Policy
- Uses of Group Policy
- Comparing Group Policy to Previous Versions
- Computer versus User Settings
- Hands-On

It is the nightmare of any administrator, desktop support person, or help desk staff: a stack of v-mails, e-mails, or trouble tickets sitting in the In-box on a Monday morning. It is bad enough that it's Monday to begin with, but you have prepared yourself mentally on the way to work already that it is just going to be another one of those Mondays. The tickets are collected and phone calls made to see if the problem can be resolved over the phone before hitting that path to visit the actual desktop. The first call goes well and the problem is resolved, one down, 29 to go. The next call reveals a similar problem, yet when asked to follow the same "path" to the problem the user states that he or she doesn't don't have that icon or program group on the computer. How can that be? All of the desktops were set up using the same template and installation process. You visit the desktop for further investigation to find a desktop where the icons are 20 times the normal size, groups and application icons are in complete disarray having been dragged to the desktop, and a cute little desktop theme has been installed with tie-dye wallpaper, pink hippie flowers, and a profusion of fuschia undertones. Your immediate thought is to run away in fright, but you remain calm and try to work through the problem. The problem is resolved and you move to the next ticket, another desktop. Same scenario, different desktop, things have been scrambled to the user's liking. Finding anything on the system takes twice as long. Your whole day continues this way.

This type of scenario is played out every day by IT staff everywhere. It seems that users, after a given time, start to think that the workstation they are using somehow belongs to them, and that it must be customized to the point where it looks like the side of a New York subway train. Then when users explore enough to discover the ability to create shortcuts on the desktop by *moving* icons rather than creating a shortcut to the original, the Start menu and Program Groups become mangled and incongruent.

There are, however, measures that may be taken to preclude such activities from happening. It's not that you have to take the fun out of the user's day; rather, it must be equated to dollars and cents, and fun may be saved for around the water cooler. IT departments have been tasked (or taxed as the case may be) with lowering the cost of computing throughout the organization, from the desktop, to the wall, to the server, to the database and applications. The push is to do more with less and streamline the process. It is from this initiative that the Group Policy was born.

Group Policy Defined

The ability to unify the look and feel of desktops and then lock those settings down is a tremendous asset to organizations that are on the road to standardization. The move toward standards equates to lower total cost of systems and operating costs, and the adoption of standards is found throughout Windows 2000 and Active Directory.

Standard hardware configurations allow organizations to drop software loads and programs across the enterprise without having to visit every desktop in the enterprise, a significant cost savings. Applications and operating systems may be bundled as common packages and "pushed" out in this manner to automate the entire process. This, however, is only the beginning of standardization. From a help desk standpoint, troubleshooting a single or a few desktop configurations means quicker problem resolution and ultimately being able to support more desktops with fewer staff.

Group Policy is the vehicle that gives administrators the ability to lock down Windows-based desktops for a consistent look and feel. Very specific settings may be implemented at the desktop and enforced by the Active Directory. This is done using administrative tools such as the Group Policy Snap-in or the Computer Management console (see Figures 16.1 and 16.2).

Group Policy allows the administrator to define and control the behavior of users' desktops. One of the big advances in this feature over previous versions is the ability to apply policy at almost any level of the directory tree, from the user or computer to the OU or domain. Once in place, Group Policy will help to refine and streamline the way that your organization does business internally.

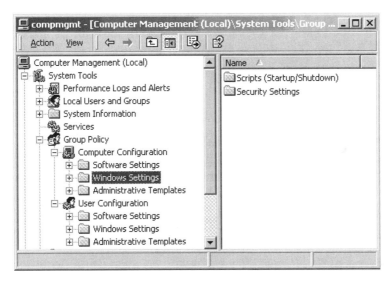

Figure 16.1 The Group Policy feature of the Computer Management console found in the Administrative Tools group.

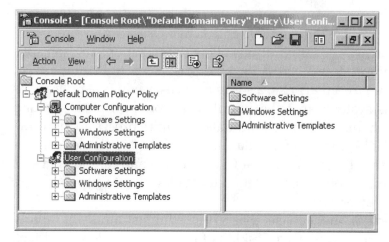

Figure 16.2   A Group Policy console created using the Group Policy Snap-in.

Uses

The following features may be managed using Group Policy:

Registry-based desktop attributes. Any feature of the desktop that involves configuration or customization, including the removal of rights or program groups such as "Games." This may be applied to the user or computer account.

Software installation. Allows programs or groups to be enforced.

Security settings. The ability to enforce security policy at the user or computer level. This feature allows the enforcement of logon hours, password length and duration, and so forth.

Scripts. Logon and logoff scripts may be enforced for a group of users or computers.

Additionally, objects such as printers may have policy associated as well as folder redirection to a common shared folder. These policies may be set at the root of the directory or at the organizational unit (OU) level for greater manageability and flexibility throughout the enterprise.

Comparing New Features to Windows NT

In previous versions of Windows NT version 4.0, policy editing provided a means to accomplish common user or computer policy at the domain level or group or user level. That in and of itself was a limitation. The poledit.exe program was the main tool used to configure these settings. There were a couple of problems with the way in which policy was implemented in Windows NT 4.0, one of which we have already mentioned. Another problem inherent to the way policies were handled involved the registry entries created by the policy editor. When registry settings were applied using the policy editor, the registry retained the changes and were not removable without editing the registry. Security was also an issue, as updates were not provided through a secure channel.

The new Group Policy feature using Active Directory addresses all of these features and allows the policy to be applied at the domain, site, or OU level for finer application. Registry settings are not persistent on workstations, and the application of such policies is performed in a secure manner using Active Directory security features. Policy affects all users in the designated container, though the ability to filter accounts is available.

Group Policy Structure and Functions

The following sections outline the structure and function of Group Policy in Windows 2000. Group Policy uses the concept of templates to construct registry changes made at the client level.

Overview

There are several elements and features that comprise the group policy system, including group policy templates, the group policy object, multiple Group Policy object considerations, and inheritance, all of which affect the policy being implemented.

Templates

Templates are identified by files having the .adm extension, of which there are several included with the base installation. These templates are used to generate the policy files for respective clients and may be used to create specific policies for different user sets such as groups or OUs. These offer support for Windows 2000, Windows NT, and Windows 9x clients. Table 16.1 provides a brief description of the installed templates and their functions.

There are several others that are used to manage Internet Explorer functions and Internet policies that are beyond the scope of this book. Use of these five should cover all desktop policy configuration issues.

Table 16.1 Group Policy Templates

TEMPLATE	FUNCTION
System.adm	Only for use with Windows 2000 clients
Winnt.adm	UI components used with Windows 2000
Windows.adm	UI options in Windows 9x
Common.adm	UI options shared between Windows 2000 and Windows 9x
Shell.adm	Controls features of the Explorer shell (e.g., the Start button, etc.)

By default, all of these templates may not be visible in the console, needing to be added by using the following procedure.

Begin by opening the Computer Management console from the Administrative Tools group in the Start menu (see Figure 16.3).

Next, expand the System Tools object to reveal the Group Policy object and expand it as well (see Figure 16.4).

There are two groups under the Group Policy object: Computer Configuration, which is used to configure computer-based policy, and User Configuration, which is used to configure policy for users objects in the directory (see Figure 16.5).

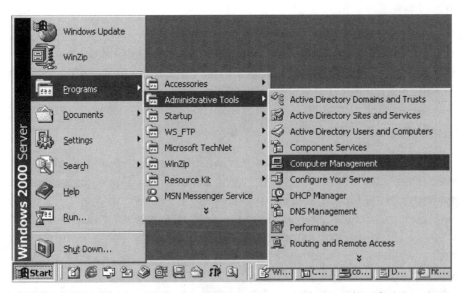

Figure 16.3 Opening the Computer Management console from the Administrative Tools group.

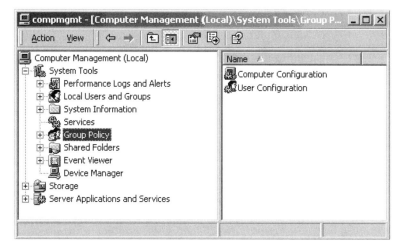

Figure 16.4 Accessing the Group Policy object in the Computer Management console.

Expand the User Configuration object to reveal the three subfolder objects: Software Settings, Windows Settings, and Administrative Templates (see Figure 16.6).

Right-click the Administrative Tools folder and choose Add/Remove Templates (see Figure 16.7).

The Add/Remove Templates window appears and displays a list of templates from which to choose. Select the relevant templates (use Ctrl + click to choose more than one item), and click Add, then Close to continue (see Figure 16.8).

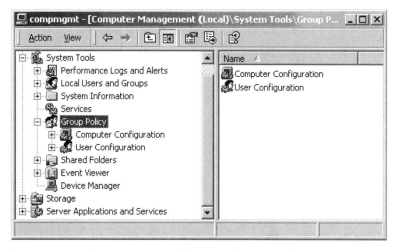

Figure 16.5 The Computer and User Configuration objects.

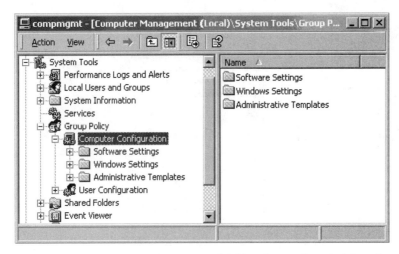

Figure 16.6   The User Configuration subfolders house the Administrative Templates.

Once added, the templates are shown as subfolders under the Administrative Templates folder. These stencils are now ready to use in assigning group policy at the user level.

The Group Policy Objects

The policies created in Windows 2000 are stored in a Group Policy Object (GPO) and further associated with an applicable container

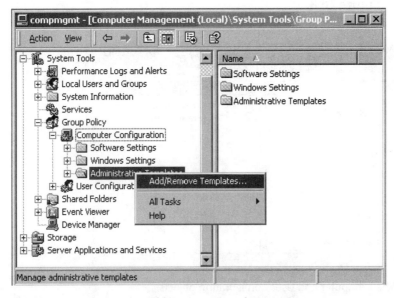

Figure 16.7   Choose the Add/Remove Templates option.

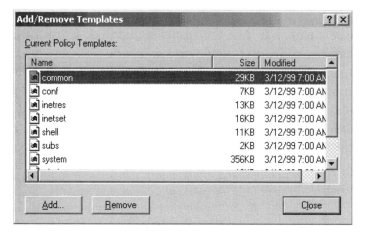

Figure 16.8 The Add/Remove Templates windows allows you to select templates.

object. These are created through the Group Policy Snap-in or the Computer Management console, and they are the net result of creating a policy. This may be thought of as a policy document, if you will. A GPO is either local or nonlocal, meaning it is stored on a domain controller or on the local workstation. This chapter covers only server-based GPOs.

Multiple Group Policy Objects

It is possible to apply more than one GPO to a container. The GPO may then be prioritized for further configuration.

Using Security Groups with GPOs

One important feature of Windows 2000 Group Policy is the ability to add computer accounts to security groups, which then allows specific computer accounts to be filtered from having the Group Policy applied. This is particularly handy in a case where a policy is going to be applied to an OU or domain level, and specific computers (groups or users also) need to be excluded; for instance, high-level company officials or IT staff (ah, privilege!).

Inheritance

It is important to understand the concept of inheritance as it pertains to applying Group Policy. Child objects contained by a parent inherit

Group Policy. Therefore, in the case of applying Group Policy at the root level, all objects underneath will use the policies instated. If multiple GPOs exist, the higher-level Group Policy will supersede policies stated below it. This blanket effect can cause a great deal of confusion in decentralized organizations if communication is not open, or if an administrator gets cavalier. For this reason, it might be a good idea to first fully understand the effects of inheritance and the ability to filter; and second, only designate certain administrators as Policy Admins. Once policy has been reviewed, planned, and implemented, there will usually be little change (see Figure 16.9).

Computer Settings versus User Settings

We have explored the fact that there are two distinct types of policy categories, but what exactly is the difference? Which type will best fit

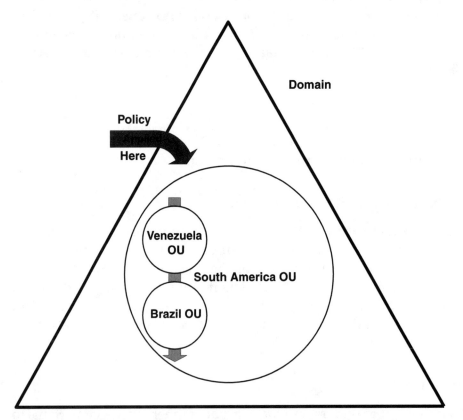

Figure 16.9 An example of how inheritance works in applying Group Policy.

your organization? Are there advantages of one over the other, or are they used in conjunction? The next section explores these questions and more.

Overview

As the names may imply, Group Policy computer settings manage those settings that pertain to Microsoft Windows-based operating systems, and Users settings affect the user and user environment. User policy objects that are applied to containers affect the user at logon, whereas computer policies are instrumented during the startup of the workstation and operating system. Group Policy settings are stored in two hives of the registry on the client machine, HKEY_ CURRENT_ USER and HKEY_LOCAL_ MACHINE. (See Figures 16.10 and 16.11.)

User configuration items that can be controlled include:

- Logon/Logoff scripts
- Security settings
- Locking down Control Panel items
- Locking down desktop items
- Locking down shell items
- Locking down Start menu features
- Locking down configuration options

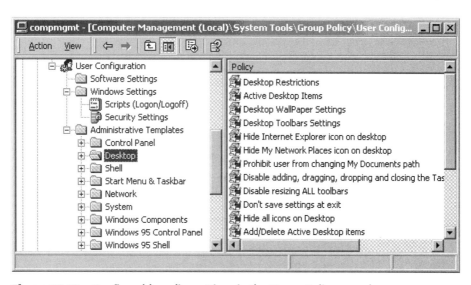

Figure 16.10 Configurable policy settings in the Group Policy console.

Computer configuration items include:

- Logon/Logoff scripts
- Security settings
- System settings (logon, file system, group policy and task scheduler, and others)
- Network settings

The subcategories for each of these are far too numerous to list, but it is advisable to explore all of them and understand each. Set up a test OU, or group and user accounts and computers to test these options before rolling them out. Additionally, software policy is common to both types.

Software Policies

The ability to control which applications are used on a client desktop has several implications. First, the ability to make mandatory the programs displayed on a user desktop means a consistent desktop across

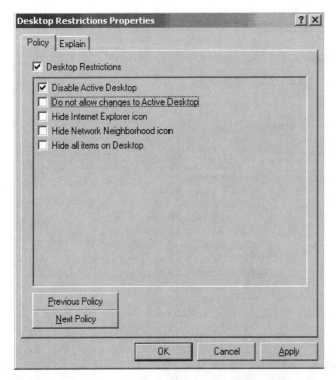

Figure 16.11 An individual policy configuration page.

the enterprise. Second, being able to lock down the workstation sufficiently means that unauthorized programs are precluded from being installed by end users, heading off potential virus infections or unruly products that may cause a system crash.

Software Management

Windows 2000 Group Policy has the additional benefit of being able to push applications to client machines in the form of packages, similar to the method used in Microsoft's Systems Management Server (SMS). Unfortunately, this applies only to Windows 2000 clients. Applications are sent via packages that have a .msi (Microsoft Installer) extension. A share is created on a server in the enterprise to distribute the package. The Software Installation Snap-in is used to configure the entire process. Applications use the Active Directory and Group Policy to distribute software, and this complex feature is beyond the scope of this book. See the Windows 2000 Help Documentation for further instructions, or visit the Microsoft Web site.

Tools

We have already used one of the tools used in configuring Group Policy, Computer Management. The Computer Management console is used to configure many settings other than just Group Policy, so it may not be the best tool to distribute to Group Policy administrators or to use on a workstation. Configuring a custom tool in these cases is just the solution. In this section, we discuss the creation of such a tool, as well as the ins and outs of setting policy with the tool.

Start an instance of MMC from a command line, and select the Add/Remove Snap-in from the Console menu (see Figure 16.12).

Choose Add, then choose the Group Policy Snap-in, and Add. This spawns the Select Group Policy Object configuration page (see Figures 16.13 and 16.14).

Click Browse to select the focus of the console. Notice that a domain, OU, site, or computer may be selected as the focus. If configuration were going to be made at the root level, then that object would be selected. In our example, choose the Default Domain Policy option, and click OK to continue (see Figure 16.15). When returned to the original page, you may opt to select the checkbox that allows the focus of the

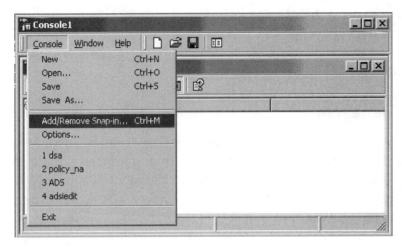

Figure 16.12   Choose the Add/Remove Snap-in option.

tool to be changed at startup. Do this only if the person using the tool will need the ability to change the focus. Click Finish to continue.

The tool has now been created, and the proper extensions and focus set. Since the elements of the console are the same as those found in the Computer Management console, we can jump right into using the

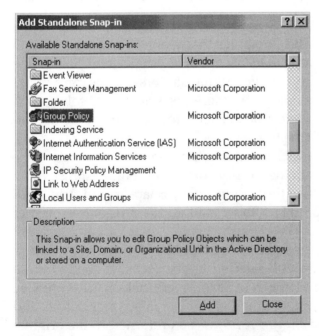

Figure 16.13   Choose the Group Policy Snap-in.

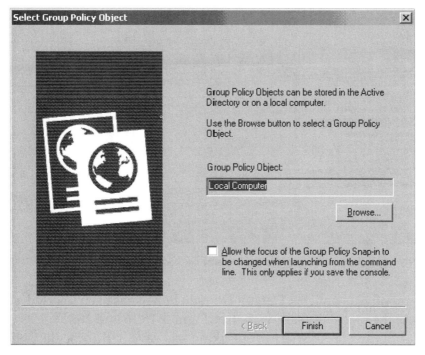

Figure 16.14   The Select Group Policy Object configuration page.

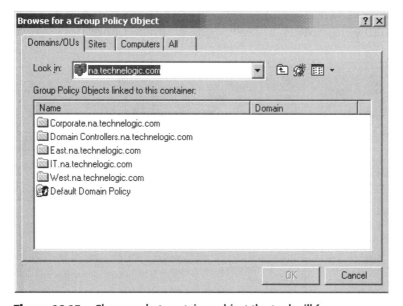

Figure 16.15   Choose what container object the tool will focus on.

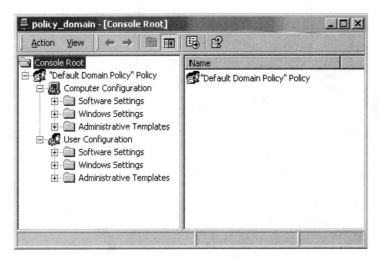

Figure 16.16 Select the option to change focus of the tool at startup.

console to configure policies. Default Domain Policy has been selected, so the focus of the tool is domain-wide (see Figures 16.16 and 16.17).

First, configure the console to your liking and save it. Browse the policies categories and then select the Start Menu & Taskbar subfolder and choose the Remove Run menu from Start Menu policy by double-clicking the object (see Figures 16.18 and 16.19).

Implementing a policy from this page is a little deceiving at first. It appears the option is not changeable, as it is grayed out. Click the checkbox to enable the option, and click OK to finish. Other policies are

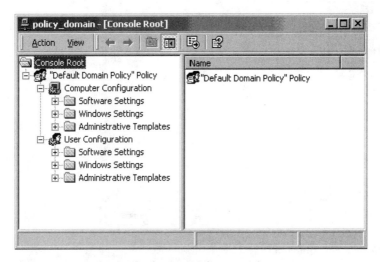

Figure 16.17 The finished Group Policy console.

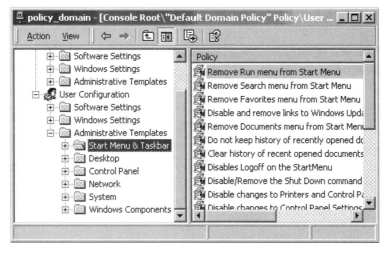

Figure 16.18   Select the Start Menu & Taskbar object.

a bit more complicated with dependencies to be configured, but that really is the long and short of it. Since this console is focused on the domain as default policy, it applies to all users.

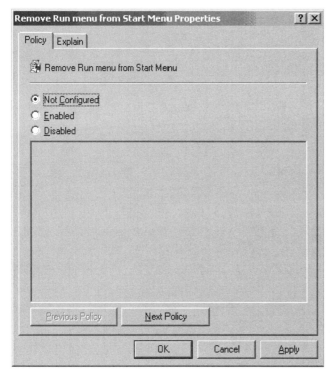

Figure 16.19   The Remove Run menu from the Start Menu policy configuration page.

Summary

Group Policy is a powerful tool that can help organizations streamline the user environment by enforcing mandatory polices on computers and users. User policies follow the user throughout the Active Directory tree. Computer policies are focused on a particular computer contained in a particular container. The main management tool used to configure policies is the Computer Management console, but individual MMCs that utilize the Group Policy Snap-in allow such tools to be passed on to the proper authorities. Configuring Group Policy is a straightforward process that takes little more than a lot of thought and a few mouse clicks.

CHAPTER

17

Coexistence Issues

INTRODUCTION

Windows 2000 fits not only into your existing Windows NT environment, but also into multivendor environments that employ directory services. This chapter covers the issues of both native NT and multivendor directories. The topics discussed are:

- **Mixed-Mode Environments**
- **Mixed-Mode Issues**
- **Directory Standards**
- **ADSI**
- **Comparing Active Directory to Third-Party Directories**

It has only been recently that standardization at the protocol level has introduced true multivendor, multiproduct functionality. This may be mainly due to the standardization of the Internet as the core global network having a trickle-down effect at the vendor level. Then again, it could be that vendors have decided to live together in peace and harmony, working toward a global utopia. Yeah, right! But seriously, the existence of multiple directories within an organization amounts to higher management costs, usability issues, and support costs.

While product interaction has been facilitated in the past using gateways that actually act as a sort of Application layer translator, this process was and still is cumbersome and expensive. If all systems used a common set of protocols for directory communication, then logic would have it that all of these would-be directories would be able to interact (as long as the core networking protocol is the same). Windows 2000 Active Directory, Novell NetWare NDS, and Sun Microsystems Sun Directory Services are all constructed using X.500 standards and LDAP as the primary directory communication protocol. The odd man out is Windows NT, whose "directory services" are nonexistent.

The idea of a unified multivendor environment is very appealing to IT mangers, as existing systems may be leveraged instead of scrapped or converted. The net result is a cost savings overall, not only from inhibiting a migration, but also from using a single interface or API to manage the enterprise (see Figure 17.1).

Mixed Windows NT and Windows 2000 environments (see Figure 17.2) have issues all their own. While the two operating systems exist together well due to provisions made in Windows 2000, using such a

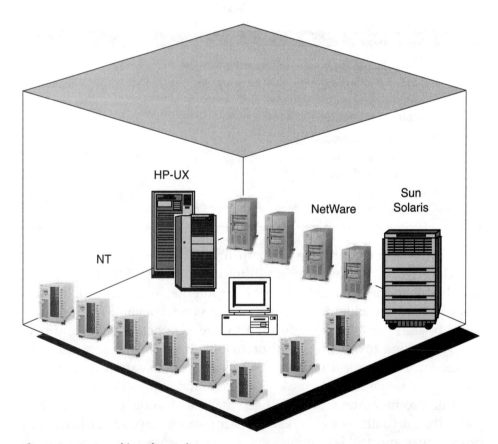

Figure 17.1 A multivendor environment.

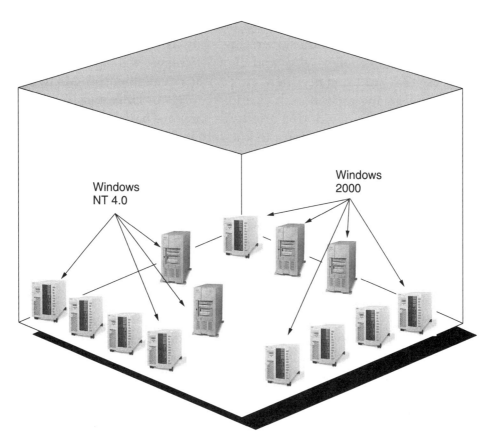

Figure 17.2   A mixed Windows 2000/NT environment.

model may inhibit the Windows 2000 environment from working at its full potential. This chapter explores these and other issues surrounding mixed environments in which Windows 2000 coexists with one or several other operating systems.

Scenarios

Several interoperability scenarios might be encountered during a Windows 2000 and/or Active Directory implementation. These include situations in which legacy NT systems are used in conjunction with Windows 2000, those where third-party operating systems without directory services coexist with Windows 2000, and those where multiple vendor directories exist in the same environment.

Windows 2000 is built to interoperate not only with its down-level relatives, but also with other operating systems that use directory services such as Novell's NDS and Sun Microsystems Sun Directory Services v 3.1. Additionally, there are add-ons available from Microsoft that will allow interaction with various features of Unix and NetWare. These will only be mentioned briefly, as they are beyond the scope of this book, although it is helpful to know that such tools exist to extend the functionality of the enterprise network.

Windows NT

Throughout the book, we have discussed the built-in features of Windows 2000 Server that allow it to interoperate with legacy NT products. This is only partly true. There are serious issues regarding the authentication methods used in the Windows NT 3.x product line that preclude it from working properly with Windows 2000. It is likely that this support will not be added to the release product, and it is therefore the recommendation of Microsoft that NT 3.51 clients and servers not be used in conjunction with Windows 2000. The Resource Kit and Technet are good sources for providing the technical details of this problem. For now, just remember that NT 3.51 and Windows 2000 are oil and water. A mixed NT/2000 environment is called a *mixed-mode* environment, which means that there are two security providers in place, one using Kerberos to authenticate native clients, and one using NTLM to authenticate down-level clients. Figure 17.3 shows a typical coexistence to upgrade scenario.

A mixed environment will either function as a temporary stage where the network is in a state of transition migrating to Windows 2000, or IT organizations may opt to keep member servers as file, print, and application servers to keep costs down. The first approach does limit the functionality of Windows 2000 domains. Because a mix of domain controller types may exist in domains, the limit to domain accounts is held to 40,000. This, however, will not be an issue for most organizations. Figure 17.4 illustrates a scenario where Windows NT 4.0 and Windows 2000 coexist on a permanent basis.

The pecking order for upgrading servers from NT to Windows 2000 starts with Primary Domain Controllers (PDCs), then Backup Domain Controllers (BDCs), then member servers and workstations. Chapter 18 covers this in more detail. This process dictates the need for Active Directory servers to operate in dual roles where once the PDCs of domains have been upgraded, these Windows 2000 servers must act as the PDC to all BDCs in the enterprise and down-level clients.

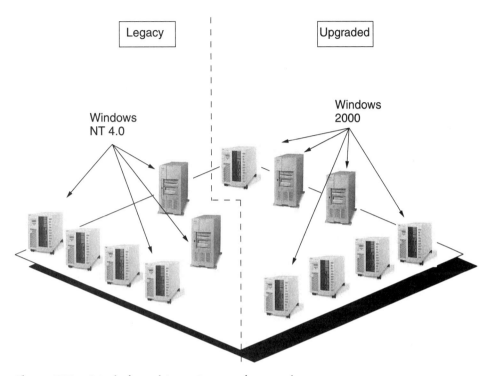

Figure 17.3 A typical coexistence to upgrade scenario.

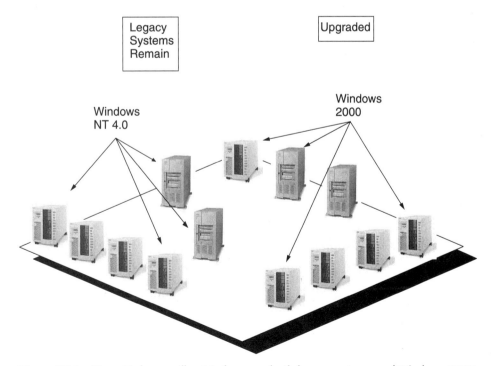

Figure 17.4 Many IT shops will opt to leverage both legacy systems and Windows 2000.

Domain Controller Issues

The first domain controller in a domain promoted in the Active Directory tree functions as the PDC Emulator Single Operations Master, or PDC Emulator. This server in mixed-mode environments performs the following operations:

- **Account database changes and replication to BDCs**. The PDC Emulator acts as the replication provider for both multimaster replication to Windows 2000 domain controllers and NTLM single-master replication to BDCs.
- **NTLM authentication**. All down-level clients will need to be authenticated using NTLM authentication.
- **Browse functionality for Windows NT 4.0 and Windows 9x clients**. Down-level clients use browsing to find network objects rather than a directory.

Interestingly enough, once the entire network is upgraded to Windows 2000 and switched to native mode, the PDC Emulator still functions to process validation of account lockout requests from other DCs in the domain.

In mixed-mode environments where Windows 2000 domain controllers and Windows NT domain controllers coexist, both authentication methods exist and may be used to authenticate either native or down-level clients. Native clients may be authenticated by a BDC using NTLM protocol in the absence of a native domain controller.

Other Issues

Domain controller infrastructure coexistence is built in and should function seamlessly once implemented. There are other services that carry over from Windows NT that will not function properly; namely, the LAN Manager Replication service and the Remote Access service. See Chapter 18 for more information.

Security is another major difference between the two operating systems, and beyond the authentication process lie issues of how system policies and trust relationships interoperate amid the two.

Windows 2000 uses transitive trusts rather than the explicit trust model used in NT. Careful consideration and planning steps must be taken to ensure the proper installation of trusts between Windows 2000 domains and NT domains while preserving the security in place. Additionally, down-level domain controllers will not recognize transitive trusts. Therefore, in a domain of mixed domain controllers, it may be necessary to implement explicit trusts to facilitate cross-domain authentication of clients. This makes a good case for upgrading *all* NT domain controllers to Windows 2000 domain controllers as quickly as possible.

Unix

There is a set of tools available for Windows 2000 that provides NFS client and server software. This add-on product must be purchased separately. This add-on allows Windows 2000 clients to access file and print resources on Unix systems, and it works with most major flavors of Unix. For more information on this product, visit Microsoft's Web site at www.microsoft.com.

Since both systems communicate with the TCP/IP protocol, only security access and services that lie above the Protocol layer need an intermediary to communicate. Windows 2000 provides a native service for Unix application-level interaction in addition to those provided for Macintosh and NetWare. Another new feature to the new operating system is the addition of a Telnet daemon that offers a remote command-line utility for administrators. Unix administrators will find this feature a welcome change, and the service is installed by default.

NetWare

Other than Unix, NetWare and Windows network operating systems share the majority of the market share. The competition between the two is often fierce, as is evident not only by searching one or the other's Web site for information on the competitor (go to www.novell.com and search on Windows 2000, and vice versa), but also in the products each releases to work with the other's products (NDS for NT is a case in point). Microsoft offers several native products that may be installed in addition to the base operating system. Gateway Service for NetWare (GSNW) offers a bridge to NetWare 3.x or 4.x servers, offering logon script processing and file access via the gateway. GSNW installs the Microsoft version of the IPX stack for access to legacy NetWare servers. Most modern NetWare systems and networks run TCP/IP as the core protocol. Another tool, the Directory Service Migration tool (DSM), allows the migration of either bindery or NDS structures and data to a

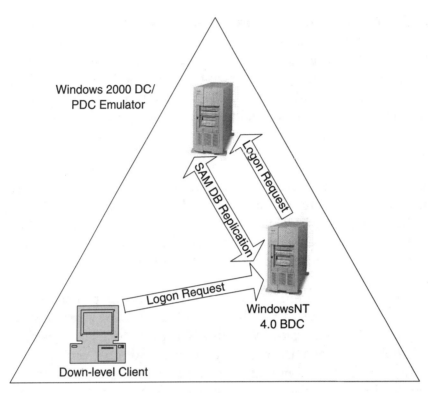

Windows 2000 DC/
PDC Emulator

SAM DB Replication

Logon Request

Logon Request

WindowsNT
4.0 BDC

Down-level Client

Figure 17.5   Interoperation NetWare/Windows NT.

Windows 2000 Active Directory tree. This product is discussed in greater detail in the next chapter. Figure 17.5 illustrates the interoperation between NetWare servers and Windows NT.

In addition to the native tools available, Microsoft offers an add-on tool called File and Print Services for NetWare (FPNW), which allows Net-Ware clients to access file and print resources on a Windows 2000 server.

Directory Services

Novell has offered X.500-based directory services for some time in its NDS product, but others have been somewhat slow to jump on board the directory services train. Part of this may be due to the fact that X.500 directory standards and offshoots such as LDAP were only until recently considered a de facto industry standard.

The adoption of standards by software vendors allows interaction between systems at an application level, rather than having to provide a gateway or bridge between systems. Windows 2000 (and others) uses standards that were born primarily out of military research—what is now Internet standard. Many companies that develop and produce operating systems are making the move toward adding directory services to their products in order to add structure and ease of management. To better understand how directory services integrate, it is essential to grasp these standards and how they work.

Standards—Why Directory Interoperation Is Possible

The foundation of most industry standard directory services is X.500, although the primary directory provider protocol is LDAP rather than its heavier cousin DAP. LDAP is not defined under the X.500 specification at all. Indeed, LDAP is scantily defined by RFC documents and still considered an IETF draft. Beyond directory services, Windows 2000 offers a slew of other standards or proposed standards, including DNS, Kerberos, and the TCP/IP protocol and tools.

The X.500 standard defines the structure of the directory itself. This is important to intra-directory communication because the same type of objects exist between directories, regardless of what they might be called. For example, Novell's NDS contains a logical unit in the directory called an Organization (not an Organizational Unit (OU)) that may be directly translated to a Windows 2000 domain. OUs in NDS factor equivocally to OUs in Windows 2000.

X.500 names also play a large role in the interoperability of these systems. The use of the Distinguished Name specification also allows objects to coexist one to one between directories as long as the two are unique between directories. The DN of a directory object is always unique, as discussed in Chapter 4.

While a directory may follow the X.500 specification, the protocol used to access or query the directory may vary. DAP is the primary protocol used in conjunction with X.500 directories, although it's a featherweight.

Standards alone do not account for all of the interoperability between Windows 2000 and other directory services. Another reason directory interaction is possible between these systems lies in that Microsoft has provided a robust set of tools and APIs for Active Directory titled Active Directory Services Interface, or ADSI, and is the topic of the next section. ADSI provides standards-based development of directory service applications for Windows 2000 and beyond.

ADSI—The Second Part of the Equation

One of the strongest reasons in the past for buying Microsoft products relates to the support that the company has maintained for development tools and developers through the years. With the release of the Windows 2000 product and Active Directory, Microsoft has taken this premise a step further with the introduction of ADSI. ADSI is a set of Component Object Model (COM) interfaces that provide developers with a tool to create cross-directory tools.

ADSI provides developers with access to multiple DS providers, including Lotus Notes, X.500, NetWare Bindery, and NDS, as well as the Active Directory and legacy NT directory services. Much like the ODBC programming specification, ADSI provides an abstract API to program across directories. Used in conjunction with single sign-on, users may be added to all directories and sign on one time to access resources across the enterprise. Additionally, searching across directories to locate resources is a possibility (see Figure 17.6).

From a technical perspective, the client software accesses an object in the namespace via an ADSI/COM interface called a *provider*. Different providers impart access to different levels of directory objects as well as

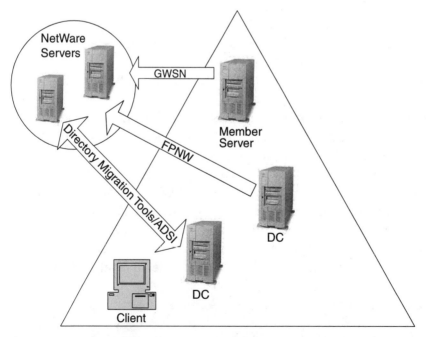

Figure 17.6 ADSI provides a programming methodology that crosses directory boundaries.

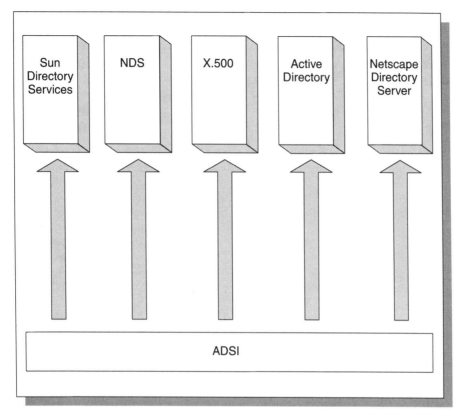

Figure 17.7 Client pieces communicate through COM providers to talk to the directory.

different services such as update or search. Figure 17.7 illustrates the abstraction provided by the COM interfaces.

Comparing Active Directory to Other Directory Services

While both network operating systems offer robust directory services, there are definite differences between the two. Directory services should provide certain requirements in order to entertain scalability and manageability. Table 17.1 is reprinted courtesy of Microsoft and therefore leans in the favor of Windows 2000 Active Directory. However, it does provide an adequate comparison of the two products. Table 17.2 contrasts the two products by role (service).

Table 17.1   Comparing Active Directory to NDS by Requirement

REQUIREMENT	ACTIVE DIRECTORY	NDS
Scalability without complexity	• Partition boundary is a Windows 2000 domain to enable direct access to all objects in a domain. • Partitions use indexed data store for fast retrieval. • Designed to hold millions of objects. • Optimized replication between sites and over slow network links. • Global Catalogs are updated simultaneously with other replication cycles to ensure low latency. • Single data store and access methods for partitions and catalogs.	• Partitions are not indexed. • Novell recommends a maximum of 1000 objects per partition and that partitions should not span WAN links. • Administrators must manage partition sizes and restructure partitions as they fill up. • Searching for objects directly across partitions requires tree walking. • Different data store for partitions and catalogs. • High catalog latency since catalog is rebuilt only at scheduled intervals (default is 24 hours).
Internet standards support	• Implemented as a native LDAP server that requires no request translation. • Consistent interpretation of access control rights when access is through LDAP. • Provides LDAP-based access to all features. • Full name space integration with DNS to simplify object location and access.	• Provides LDAP support by server-based interface that must be installed on NDS servers individually. • LDAP requests must be translated to NDS formats. • Limited LDAP-based access to NDS features. • Different naming syntax for LDAP access versus access by NDS APIs. • Access rights interpreted differently when access is via LDAP versus NDS APIs. • No name space integration with DNS makes object naming and location more complex.
Flexible security services	• Provides support for popular security technologies such as Kerberos and Smart Cards. • Catalog enforces object- and attribute-level security. • No restrictions on security groups that span partitions (domains).	• Lacks support for Kerberos and Smart Cards. • Catalog does not enforce object- and attribute-level security within the catalog database. • Novell recommends that administrators minimize the use of groups that span partitions.

Table 17.1 *(Continued)*

REQUIREMENT	ACTIVE DIRECTORY	NDS
Support for synchronization and consolidation	• Provides the scalability required to consolidate large directories without administrative complexity. • Built-in LDAP-based change history interfaces facilitate use as a meta-directory platform. • Catalog architecture enables fast, efficient query of large numbers of objects. • Will be used by Microsoft products such as Exchange 6.0, MSMQ 2.0, and MCIS 3.0.	• Partition size restrictions limit use for directory consolidation. • Provides no formal way to request change history information; requires customized synchronization agents. • Catalog architecture forces tradeoffs between speed and consistency with underlying partitions. • Not used by Novell's GroupWise product for account management and address book functions.
Comprehensive development environment	• Provides COM-based Active Directory Services Interface (ADSI) for simplified development. • JADSI supports access from Java applications. • Provides the scalability required to ensure that applications can store, access, and manage millions of objects without application-level complexity. • Provides LDAP-based access to all features.	• No ADSI implementation for use by applications running on NetWare. • JNDI supports access from Java applications. • Applications must work within partition limitations. • Limited LDAP-based access to NDS features.

Table 17.2 Comparing Active Directory to NDS by Role

ROLE	ACTIVE DIRECTORY	NDS
User and network resource management	• Provides the scalability required to store, locate, and manage large numbers of objects efficiently and without administrative complexity. • Catalog architecture enables fast, efficient query of large number of objects.	• The number of partitions required by NDS to hold expected numbers of objects slows access and increases management complexity. *Continued*

Table 17.2   Comparing Active Directory to NDS by Role *(Continued)*

ROLE	ACTIVE DIRECTORY	NDS
	• Global Catalogs are updated simultaneously with other replication cycles to ensure low latency. • Designed to optimize replication traffic across wide-area network links.	• Catalog architecture forces tradeoffs between speed and consistency with underlying partitions. • High catalog latency since catalog is rebuilt only at scheduled intervals (default is 24 hours). • Partitions that span wide-area links not recommended by Novell.
Security authentication and authorization services	• Provides support for popular security technologies such as Kerberos and Smart Cards. • Catalog enforces object- and attribute-level security. • Scales to supports large numbers of extranet users. • DNS integration simplifies object naming and location through Internet protocols.	• Lacks support for Kerberos and Smart Cards. • Catalog does not enforce object- and attribute-level security within the catalog database. • Partition size limits complicate extranet use. • Lack of name-space integration with DNS makes object naming and location more complex.
Centralized directory management	• Provides the scalability required to consolidate large directories without administrative complexity. • Built-in LDAP-based change history interfaces facilitate use as a meta-directory platform. • Catalog architecture enables fast, efficient query of a large number of objects.	• Partition size restrictions limit use for directory consolidation. • Provides no formal way to request change history information; requires customized synchro-nization agents. • Catalog architecture forces tradeoffs between speed and consistency with underlying partitions.
Directory-enabled infrastructure and directory-enabled applications	• Strong support from leading vendors. • Windows 2000 provides a rich development environment that is supported by many tools. • Provides the scalability required to ensure that applications can store, access, and manage	• Support from many leading vendors missing. • NetWare provides a limited environment for application developers. • Applications must work within partition limitations. • Limited LDAP-based access to NDS features.

Table 17.2 *(Continued)*

ROLE	ACTIVE DIRECTORY	NDS
	millions of objects without application-level complexity. • Provides LDAP-based access to all features.	

Many are not aware that Sun Microsystems is actively competing in the directory services market as well. Sun's latest version (3.1) is compared in Tables 17.3 and 17.4.

Table 17.3 Comparing Active Directory to Sun's Directory Services by Requirement

ROLE	ACTIVE DIRECTORY	NDS
User and Network Resource Management	• Provides the scalability required to store, locate, and manage large numbers of objects efficiently and without administrative complexity. • Catalog architecture enables fast, efficient query of a large number of objects. • Global Catalogs are updated simultaneously with other replication cycles to ensure low latency. • Designed to optimize replication traffic across wide-area network links.	• Because there is no catalog mechanism, users in different partitions (or data stores) can only be found using LDAP's referral mechanism. • SDS requires big hardware and a greater TCO to overcome dbm's limitations. • Does not easily support enterprise-wide partitions.
Security Authentication and Authorization Services	• Provides support for popular security technologies such as Kerberos and Smart Cards. • Catalog enforces object- and attribute-level security. • Scales to supports large numbers of extranet users. • DNS integration simplifies object naming and location via Internet protocols.	• Lacks support for Kerberos and Smart Cards. • SDS uses the LDAP's referral mechanism complicating extranet use. • Poor name space integration with DNS.
Centralized Directory Management	• Provides the scalability required to consolidate large directories without administrative complexity.	• Data Store size restrictions restrict directory consolidation.

Continued

Table 17.3 Comparing Active Directory to Sun's Directory Services by Requirement *(Continued)*

ROLE	ACTIVE DIRECTORY	NDS
	• Built-in LDAP-based change history interfaces facilitate use as a meta-directory platform. • Catalog architecture enables fast, efficient query of a large number of objects.	• No centralized management. • As there is no catalog architecture in SDS, users rely on LDAP's slower referral mechanism where every extra server must be known beforehand.
Directory-Enabled Infrastructure and Directory-Enabled Applications	• Strong support from leading vendors. • Windows NT provides a rich development environment that is supported by many tools. • Provides the scalability required to ensure that applications can store, access, and manage millions of objects without application-level complexity. • Provides LDAP-based access to all features.	• Little vendor support. • SDS supports only native LDAP APIs. • SDS applications use the cumbersome referral mechanism to span partitions. • Data stores limited to a million objects.

Table 17.4 Comparing Sun's Directory Services by Role

REQUIREMENT	ACTIVE DIRECTORY	SUN DIRECTORY SERVICE
Scalability without Complexity	• Partition boundary is the ability of a Windows 2000 domain to enable direct access to all objects in a domain. • Partitions use indexed data store for fast retrieval. • Designed to hold millions of objects. • Optimized replication between sites and over slow network links. • Global Catalogs are updated simultaneously with other replication cycles to ensure low latency.	• SDS uses the Berkeley Btree database (dbm). • Each dbm partition or data store has a million object limit, but in reality due to dbm limitations, this is likely to be a lot less, leading to large numbers of data stores for enterprise WANs. • SDS has no concept of a catalog or root data store to promote faster retrievals. • SDS uses the slower LDAP referral mechanism

Table 17.4   *(Continued)*

REQUIREMENT	ACTIVE DIRECTORY	SUN DIRECTORY SERVICE
	• Single data store and access methods for partitions and catalogs.	to find a user or entry in other data stores. • Large SDS Data Stores require careful management of indexes and file space. • Does not span data stores.
Internet Standards Support	• Implemented as a native LDAP server that requires no request translation. • Consistent interpretation of access control rights when access is via LDAP. • Provides LDAP-based access to all features. • Full name space integration with DNS to simplify object location and access.	• Faithful LDAP version 3 implementation. • Cumbersome DNS namespace mapping.
Flexible Security Services	• Provides support for popular security technologies such as Kerberos and Smart Cards. • Catalog enforces object- and attribute-level security. • No restrictions on security groups that span partitions (domains).	• Lacks support for Smart Cards. • No Kerberos support. • As SDS does not span partitions, there are no security mechanisms available across multiple platforms.
Support for Synchronization and Consolidation	• Provides the scalability required to consolidate large directories without administrative complexity. • Built-in LDAP-based change history interfaces facilitate use as a meta-directory platform. • Catalog architecture enables fast, efficient query of a large number of objects. • Will be used by Microsoft products such as Exchange 6.0, MSMQ 2.0, and MCIS 3.0.	• Data Stores are limited to 1 million objects. • No global catalog for top level consolidation of objects. • Works with Solaris Internet Mail Server and a Sun calendar program. As yet there are no other third party offerings that are designed to interoperate with SDS.[1]
Comprehensive Development Environment	• Provides COM-based Active Directory Services Interface (ADSI) for simplified development.	• Only standard LDAP APIs are provided for third-party developers to interoperate with SDS. *Continued*

Table 17.4   Comparing Sun's Directory Services by Role *(Continued)*

REQUIREMENT	ACTIVE DIRECTORY	SUN DIRECTORY SERVICE
	• JADSI supports access from Java applications. • Provides the scalability required to ensure that applications can store, access, and manage millions of objects without application-level complexity. • Provides LDAP-based access to all features.	• Applications must work within partition limitations. • No development environment.

[1] Other applications that support the LDAP protocol can work with SDS.

Fortunately, both NDS and SDS are standards-based and should interact quite well with Microsoft's directory offering. This is extremely important in that Microsoft does offer quite a large market share in the networking community, but Novell and Sun are also very heavily leveraged in many server rooms and data centers and are likely to remain. This point in mind, many third-party software vendors are poised to offer integration products that will go beyond the basics of directory integration and offer a true multivendor solution.

Summary

In Chapter 17 we attempted to demonstrate how the Active Directory will integrate with existing and future systems. This was, in fact, one of high-level design goals of the operating system in an effort to reduce IT costs and seamlessly integrate platforms across the board. This obviously is a win/win situation for Microsoft and the user community as well.

Upgrade Issues

INTRODUCTION

It is likely that many companies that are planning to implement Windows 2000 already have a Windows NT infrastructure in place. Other network operating systems may be in use as well, such as Novell's NetWare. Windows 2000 provides an upgrade path for both NT and NetWare, although there are many issues to consider in the upgrade process. These issues and processes must be understood up front in order to facilitate a smooth transition. This chapter discusses these issues and the following scenarios:

- Examining the Existing Domain Structure
- Consolidating Domains
- Upgrade Paths And Issues for NT Networks
- Upgrade Paths and Issues for NetWare Networks
- The Upgrade Process

Windows 2000 was built with an upgrade process for legacy NT networks and with the ability to coexist with legacy systems. Indeed, the latter would need to be true for a migration to occur, lest you be tasked to upgrade the entire network in one weekend! The operating system's ability to coexist with Windows NT means that a staggered migration is possible, and this is the preferred path that Microsoft recommends. The process is not as simple as upgrading servers beginning with the first server in sight. Rather, a logical approach must be used to facilitate the logon process, first by upgrading the primary domain controllers (PDCs), backup domain controllers (BDCs), then member servers, and, ultimately, clients, if that is within the scope of your organization's implementation plan. Figure 18.1 shows a common coexistence scenario.

Besides Windows NT upgrades, Novell NetWare servers also have an upgrade path with Windows 2000, much the way that was provided in NT, although importing from NDS is supported rather than just NetWare 3.x bindery technology. Many organizations are choosing this option to unify the technology in company data centers (see Figure 18.2). This chapter explores these processes and discusses the pitfalls to watch out for.

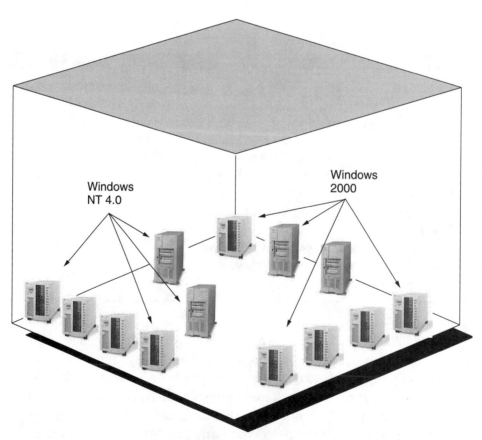

Figure 18.1 Windows 2000 and Windows NT may coexist.

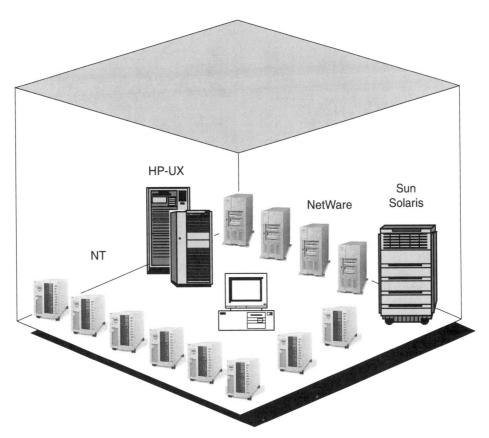

Figure 18.2   A mixed-vendor environment.

Scenarios

Two scenarios are discussed in this chapter. The first section deals with upgrading from Windows NT (Figure 18.3) to Windows 2000. The process involves all of the parts of a new install, with a few added considerations. Domain models are of great importance here as is a solid plan for backing out of the process. Only three of the four Windows NT domain models are discussed, as the fourth model, the complete trust, was never a recommended model to begin with and seldom implemented. Domain consolidation is also important to consider in the overall plan.

The various Operations Master roles of domain controllers in the environment were discussed in previous chapters, particularly the PDC emulator. Therefore, we will not go into detail here regarding their

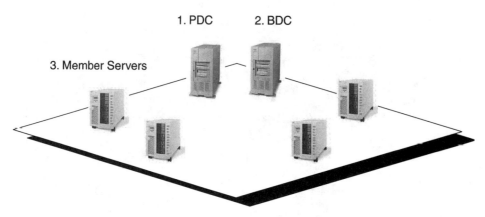

Figure 18.3 Upgrading from NT.

function. It is important to remember that this service is generally found on the first Windows 2000 domain controller installed in the environment.

The second scenario discusses the migration of NetWare servers to Windows 2000 (see Figure 18.4). The process involves converting NDS directory information to an installed domain controller using the Directory Service Migration Tool that is installed optionally under Windows 2000.

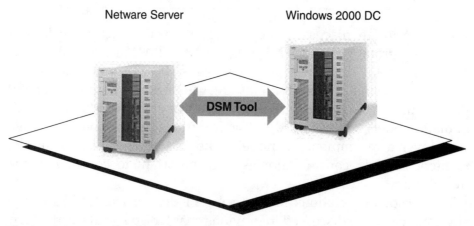

Figure 18.4 Upgrading from NetWare.

Before Beginning

It is understood that the upgrade process must closely follow the process of implementing a fresh install of Windows 2000, where the existing domain structure and model must be considered before upgrading. An example of this might be if an organization has a single-master domain model—the security accounts domain is the likely target to begin the upgrade process—not a resource domain. The root domain would begin here and the subsequent domains would follow.

A back-out plan is paramount to recover in the case of adversity, and an upgrade such as this should never be attempted without such a plan drafted and tested (see Figure 18.5). A thorough assessment should be made on a case-by-case basis to determine what services are running on the particular server in question, and the proper backups implemented. For servers that are running DHCP and WINS, a manual backup should be made of these databases as well. Make two backups to tape instead of just one.

A test environment may be prudent in order to head off any unforeseen circumstances, and these should be well documented. Being prepared ahead of time saves the embarrassment and potential trip to the various Internet job sites to search for a new job. If resources are scarce, beg, steal, or borrow whatever is necessary to complete this step!

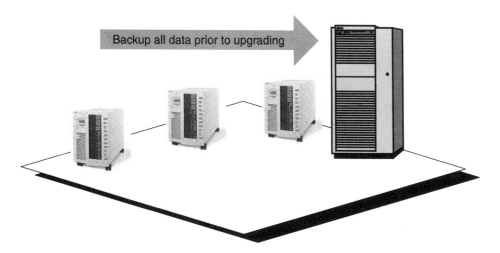

Figure 18.5   Disaster recovery is key.

The test environment should be used to test the upgrade process by mimicking the production environment as closely as possible, and backup and recovery should be tested as well (Figure 18.6). Use a BDC from production as a PDC in the test environment. Once the server is in place on an isolated network, the BDCs in the test environment will replicate the SAM database and other relevant information and the testing can begin. Be sure to document every stage of the process to refer to later. If for some reason there is only a PDC installed in smaller, remote domains, acquire a workstation to use as a temporary BDC, so more than one copy of the SAM database exists.

There are also some special considerations regarding NT-specific services as well, such as the replication service and Remote Access Service

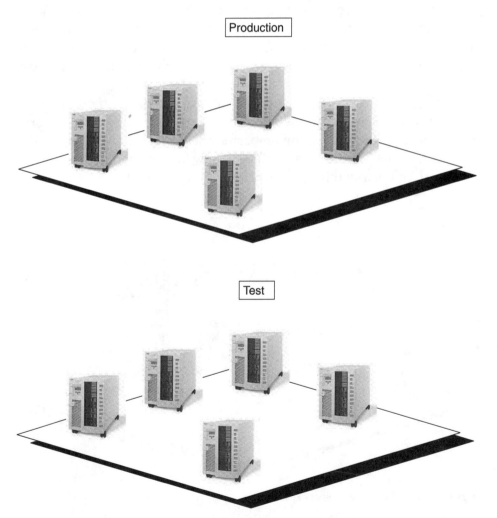

Figure 18.6   Testing environments should closely mimic the production environment.

(RAS). The replication services used in NT are not compatible with those found in Windows 2000. Before upgrading domain controllers, disable the Directory Replication service. In addition, there are issues with using RAS to access objects in the directory. During the upgrade, you may be asked to weaken RAS security for backward compatibility. Doing so depends on your particular situation and dial-in solution.

The Upgrade Path

Okay, so testing and disaster recovery are very necessary steps in the upgrade process—what are the next steps? Logically, it might be best to first determine the existing domain structure and note any special needs. An assessment of the IT infrastructure (centralized versus decentralized) might be a good idea as well. Once a solid document exists, the next step is to decide whether domains will need to be restructured. Once complete, the next step is to examine the DNS infrastructure, and finally the actual process of upgrading the domain controllers begins, followed by member servers or clients if that applies in your given case (see Figure 18.7). The following sections outline these processes.

Determining the Existing Domain Structure

The existing NT domain structure plays a very important role in the resulting upgrade strategy. Three of the four domain models are discussed in this section: the Single Domain, Single Master, and Multiple Master models. Trust relationships must also be mapped and documented, as special one-way trusts may be a concern.

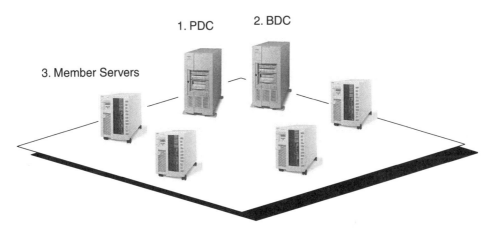

Figure 18.7 The upgrade path for NT.

The simplest upgrade will occur when the existing domain is a Single Domain model because the relationship is one to one. Do not confuse the fact that this one-to-one relationship will affect the staged rollout of the Windows 2000 product. This model may contain up to 40,000 accounts, which in turn means the domain will encompass many domain controllers, member servers, and clients. These may be upgraded in groups to facilitate an incremental rollout. Resources may be grouped into OUs for a more logical structure that was not previously available in the Single Domain model (Figure 18.8).

The Single Master model (Figure 18.9) carries specific guidelines or rather upgrade path that must be followed in order to retain the existing structure. In the Single Master model, the accounts are contained in the master or top-level domain, and lower-level domains are considered "resource" domains. The accounts domain should be upgraded first, followed by lower-level domains. Once the upgrade is complete across all domains, resources such as users, groups, and computers may be moved to organizational units (OUs) or other domains.

In situations where there are Multiple Master domains (Figure 18.10), it must be determined first why this structure was used. Was it used to facilitate a large number of accounts, was it created because of a decentralized IT structure, or was it due to a geographically disparate environment? The answers to these questions will help to determine

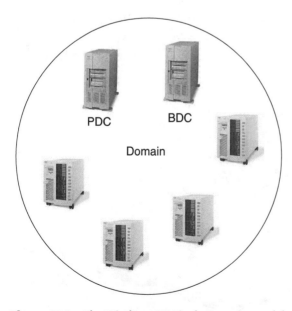

Figure 18.8   The Windows NT Single Domain model.

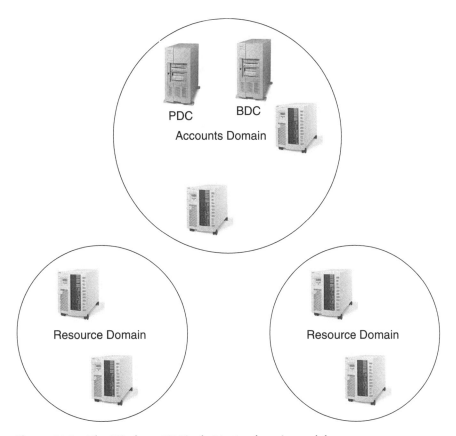

Figure 18.9   The Windows NT Single Master domain model.

whether a single tree will be formed from these domains, or a forest of trees to retain the IT management model.

In the case of a forest approach, two separate tree structures may be used to retain more closely the original structure, though the reason for doing this should be thought through. In the case of geographically separate regions, sites may be used to control replication traffic of domain information. In the case that the domain was "split" in order to facilitate more than 40,000 accounts, Windows 2000 domains will support 25 times that number.

A single-tree approach is also viable for this type of migration. To do this with the least amount of difficulty, create a root domain and then upgrade the accounts domains as child domains to the root. Resources may be moved later to better facilitate the overall design goals determined in the planning stages.

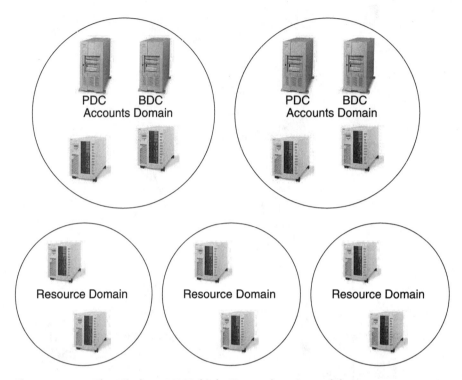

Figure 18.10 The Windows NT Multiple Master domain model.

Where resource domains exist, it is best to migrate the resources from those domains into other domains or the accounts domain, if possible. Overall, the fewer the domains that are present prior to the upgrade, the smoother the upgrade will be. The next section discusses the why and how of migrating to a simpler domain model.

Consolidating Domains

Two consolidation efforts may take place either pre- or post-upgrade. In the case of preliminary restructuring, put simply, the more basic the existing structure, the easier it will be to perform the upgrade. With the Windows NT product, this may be very labor intensive and therefore not appealing to many organizations. This will surely be determined by the complexity of the existing structure. If possible, migrate resource domain objects to the master domain. There are considerations to consolidating these resources, such as group membership and resource ACLs. It may help to develop a list of existing group-to-resource mappings to facilitate such a move.

The second option is to upgrade all existing structures to Windows 2000 and then consolidate resources. There are several reasons that this method is less time consuming. First, a Windows NT domain controller that is upgraded may be demoted or redeployed anywhere in the enterprise. This means that the server will not need to be rebuilt, which equates to a time/resource savings. Second, group, computer, and user accounts may be moved across domains as necessary in order to consolidate resources. Third, policies that have been set for these accounts are moved along with the user and do not have to be recreated. Figure 18.11 shows a consolidation scenario.

Consolidation is not necessary to an upgrade, and there are issues. It should be noted that resource domains need not be eliminated from

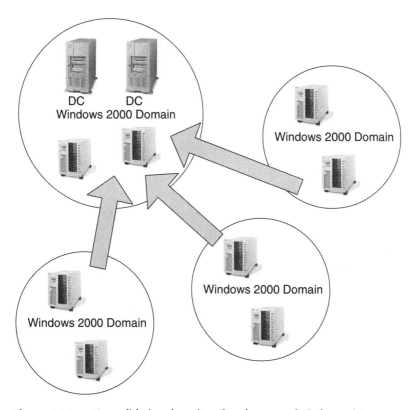

Figure 18.11   Consolidating domains after the upgrade is far easier.

your overall design. Indeed, there may be a need for such structures in an organization. OUs, however, are more flexible and can accomplish the same effect. One of the main issues is time and resources. In the time that passes before an upgrade, eliminate the creation of subsequent resource domains if possible. Also, in regard to moving accounts around from domain to domain, while the process is allowed in Windows 2000, a new Security ID (SID) is created, and the old SID attached to the account from the previous domain is appended to a SID history list. If too many of these SIDs exist, it may cause authentication latency across domains. Another issue involves the number of objects that may be stored in a mixed-mode domain. The limitation is set by the existence of down-level domain controllers and clients where the 40,000 account principle carries over from Windows NT 4.0.

DNS

Active Directory will not function, or install for that matter, without the existence of a DNS infrastructure (Figure 18.12) that supports the use of service resource records (SRV RRs), and while not mandatory, support for dynamic updates (see Chapter 10). When the upgrade process is instigated, the server will attempt to locate a DNS server that supports these options. Many current versions of DNS, including Berkeley's BIND implementation, support both of these options. Check that your particular flavor conforms to these standards, and that the service is configured as such.

Many organizations that do not host their own Internet site or are homogeneous Windows NT environments may not have DNS available at all. This being the case, it is better to use the DNS services of Windows 2000 from the start rather than attempt to integrate the Windows NT 4.0 version of DNS prior to upgrading.

DNS helps to define the Active Directory structure, and is an integral part of the overall system. When designing the upgrade model, it is very important to consider the existing DNS structure and to modify it as necessary to accommodate the design.

Upgrading Domain Controllers

The process of upgrading begins with the PDC and moves logically to the BDC, member servers, and then to clients. The PDC is upgraded first since it is authoritative for all accounts in the domain, possessing a

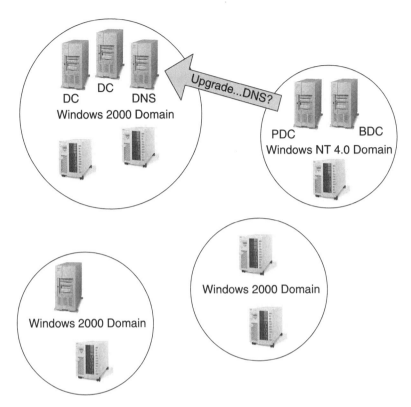

Figure 18.12   DNS is integral to the upgrade.

read/write copy of the SAM database just like Windows 2000 domain controllers.

The upgrade of the PDC also means that the first server will become the PDC Emulator, which will serve requests from down-level BDCs and clients (Figure 18.13). It is important to understand which domain to upgrade first (if there are more than one), as this will become the root structure of the newly formed tree. All other domains will be created as child domains. During the process, all security principles such as Windows NT user and group accounts are migrated to the Active Directory.

Once the PDC of the first domain is created, the strategy recommended by Microsoft in the case of multiple domains is to upgrade the other PDCs of the resource domains; or in the case of a Multiple Master scenario, the other accounts domains first. This will help to facilitate the overall tree structure where replication can occur, and the schema and Global Catalog (GC) established for the tree or forest. Once this has been done, the BDCs are the next target.

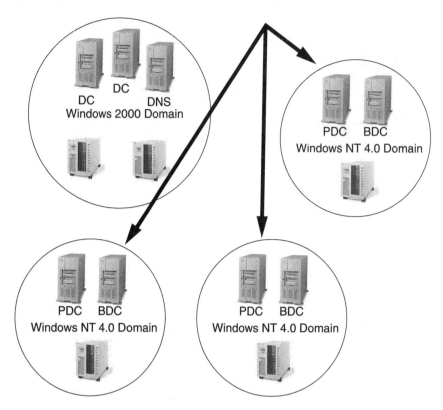

Figure 18.13 All PDCs should be upgraded first.

BDCs should be upgraded quickly in order to maintain redundancy in the domain. Another consideration in migrating BDCs, particularly in smaller or dispersed environments, is the possibility that the BDC may be functioning in other roles (Figure 18.14), such as an application server. This is where the testing that was talked about earlier also comes into play. Make sure that all applications have been tested and work under the new operating system. If the server is multifunctional, its role may be changed after the upgrade process if resources are strained.

Upgrading member servers is straightforward and does not have any stipulations attached to the upgrade process other than it is recommended that they be upgraded after domain controllers. Of course, if the server functions as an application server, all applications should be tested for compatibility.

Workstations will follow the server upgrades and may take place in any order. It may be helpful to wait on upgrading clients until all adjustments have been made to the directory tree (such as consolidation).

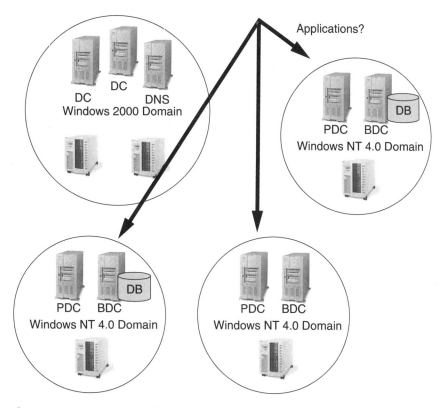

Figure 18.14 BDCs may be functioning in other roles, and this must be considered before upgrading.

Another preferred method might be to wait until the replication topology has been developed through the use of sites, where clients may be upgraded by subnets that fall into one site category or another.

Revisiting Active Directory Design Goals

All of the principals that follow a fresh installation are carried over to the upgrade process with the addition of planning for the upgrade and the rules that must be followed for upgrading. The ultimate success or failure will depend on how tightly you adhere to the upgrade policies, and the thoroughness of the planning and testing phases.

Review the steps outlined in the Preface, which will provide an overall road map for the implementation process as well as when to interject the upgrade process in the overall project plan.

Novell NetWare

The process of upgrading Novell NetWare servers is in reality a migration that involves a multistep process using the Directory Services Migration Tool, available at the time of server installation or later by using the Add/Remove Programs icon on Control Panel. This tool was available in earlier versions of Windows NT, although it lacked the ability to migrate NetWare Directory Service (NDS) information available in the 4.x version of the NetWare product.

Migrating NetWare Servers to NT

The process of migrating NetWare information to Windows 2000 may involve actually migrating an entire NDS tree to a Windows 2000 Active Directory structure or simply migrating the Bindery of a single NetWare 3.x server. The primary tool used to perform the migration is included in the source installation code for Windows 2000 but is not installed by default. The process for using the tool follows several steps that actually involve an indirect process that is non-invasive to the data being exported and is somewhat similar to the directory export utilities discussed earlier in Chapter 15. Figure 18.16 compares the objects between an NDS tree and an AD tree.

The following steps outline the overall process:

1. **The NetWare Directory Tree is mapped.** The NetWare Directory Tree should be mapped to transpose it directly to an Active Directory structure. Each server that acts as an NDS server should correspond to a Windows 2000 domain controller.

2. **Adjust the NDS Tree scheme.** If the architecture of the Active Directory Directory Information Tree (DIT) does not correspond one to one to the NDS structure, then a special adjustment to the project plans must be made to reflect how one structure will correspond to the other.

3. **Testing the migration.** A sample of the production NetWare environment and the Windows 2000 trees should be reproduced in a test environment, and results of the migration documented.

4. **Migration begins using the DSM tool.** The actual migration begins after all planning and testing have been completed to satisfaction.

The actual steps used in the migration process using the Directory Services Migration tool are outlined next to better understand the steps involved, and in the next section, an actual hands-on using the tool is performed.

1. **Install the Directory Services Migration tool (DSM).** The DSM tool is not installed by default and must be installed using the Add/Remove Programs applet in Control Panel.

2. **Create a "project" in the DSM tool.** In this step, a project is named and defined. This is helpful in doing an incremental migration where multiple projects may be defined.

3. **Create a new view.** Once the project has been defined, a new "view" is created to define the source information of the NetWare NDS tree or Bindery. Simply put, this is the target data or container that will be migrated to the Active Directory tree. This data is moved to an offline store (database) for editing. The whole tree may be moved offline and specific branches migrated.

4. **Configure resources to transfer offline.** The next step is to further define what data will be moved to the new tree structure in Active Directory. Items may be added, removed, deleted, and moved between containers. It is important to understand the differences between the structural components of NDS and those found in Active Directory.

5. **Importing the data into Active Directory.** When all relevant data has been configured for import, the next step is to migrate the data to Active Directory. An import container is chosen for the data, which may be a domain, OU, or other container such as users or groups. File or application objects are also targets for migration, and there is a special provision for moving data built in to the tools.

6. **Verify the migration.** Once the migration operation completes, check the data against the original on the NetWare server for verification. Test user logons and data or directory access.

The migration process is straightforward and allows the operation to be performed on the data offline to provide a noninvasive method for replicating data from one system to another. While Novell's NetWare and NDS products are standards based and will work together (with some customization or with third-party tools) with the Active Directory, many IT departments have turned away from the idea of using multiple vendors in their server rooms and data centers in order to streamline costs. The Directory Services Migration tool provides a simple and effective tool for accomplishing this.

The Directory Services Migration Tool

The first step in migrating from NetWare to Windows 2000 is to actually install the tool itself. Begin by opening the Control Panel from the Start menu and then Settings. Locate the Add/Remove Programs icon and double-click (Figure 18.15).

For those of you familiar with previous versions of this applet, this will look a little different. The interface is three-part, of which the Add/Remove Windows Components should be selected (Figure 18.16).

The Windows Component Wizard is launched that will display a list of installable programs. Click Next to continue past the welcome page (Figure 18.17).

The next page displays a list of components that may be added or removed. The particular section of interest here is the Management and Monitoring Tools, which should be highlighted, and the Details button depressed (Figure 18.18).

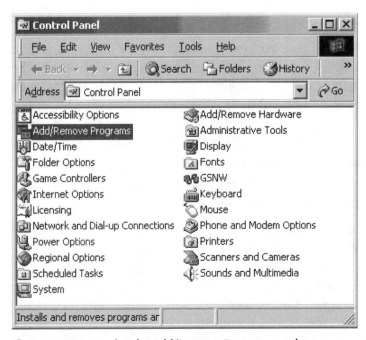

Figure 18.15   Starting the Add/Remove Programs applet.

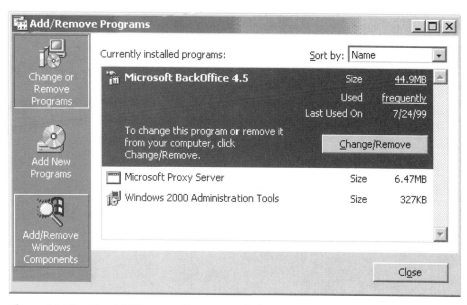

Figure 18.16 The Add/Remove Programs window.

Figure 18.17 The Windows Components Wizard is launched from the Add/Remove Programs applet.

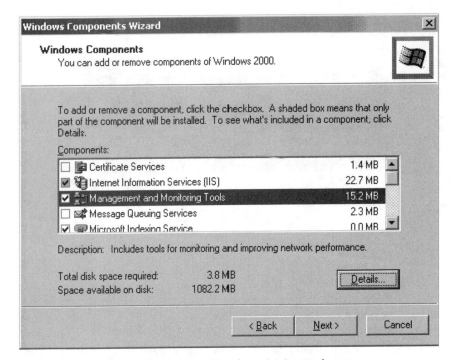

Figure 18.18 Select the Management and Monitoring Tools group.

There are four choices within this group, one of which is the DSM tool (Figure 18.19). Choose this component, and click OK.

The Wizard begins the installation and configuring of the selected components. Once finished, click Finish to complete the task. Control is returned to the Add/Remove Programs applet. Installation is complete. Since the tool installs the IPX protocol that must be bound to the NIC in the server, the system must be rebooted. Do so to complete the installation.

 When the system comes back up, after you log on to Windows 2000, you will be asked to select and log on to the NDS tree. You should be logged on with administrative credentials to perform the following functions. The server that is acting as the import server should have Active Directory installed and configured properly.

To launch the tool after rebooting, click Start, then Programs, then Administrative Tools, then the DSM tool.

Once open, begin by defining the project. Highlight the console root, and from the Action menu, choose New and then Project (Figure 18.20).

Give the project a name, and click Finish. Enter the project information, and click OK to continue (Figures 18.21 and 18.22).

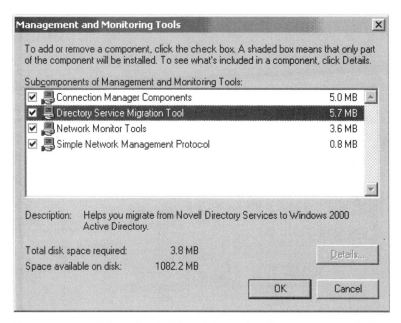

Figure 18.19   Select the DSM tool from the Management and Monitoring group of components.

To create a new view, right-click the newly created project and select New from the resulting menu, and then View from NetWare (Figure 18.23).

The program will use the client for NetWare to log on to NetWare and download the directory information. Once complete, this information is

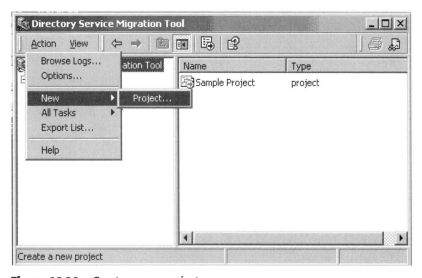

Figure 18.20   Create a new project.

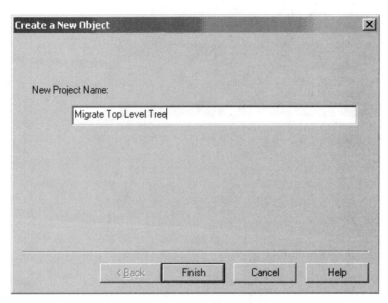

Figure 18.21 Name the project.

now stored in a local database for manipulation. Because the data is offline and not the "live" data, there is no fear of corrupting the NetWare

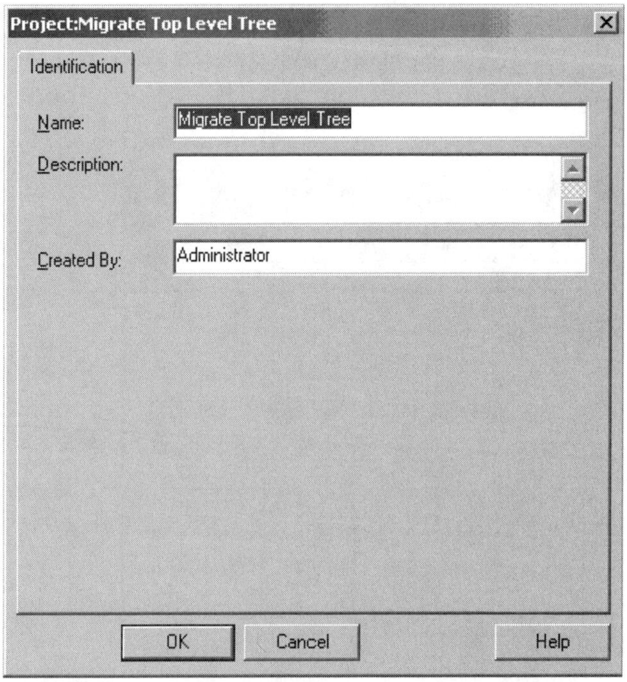

Figure 18.22 Enter information about the project.

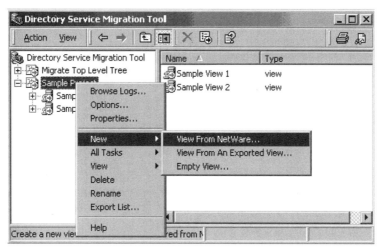

Figure 18.23 Creating a new view.

data. Select the information that will be migrated to the Active Directory tree, and delete that information that will not be migrated. When editing is complete, right-click the level of the structure from which the migration will start (e.g., the root Organization container or an OU) and choose the Configure Object to NTDS option, which starts the Configure Objects to NTDS Wizard. The only step necessary in the Wizard is to choose the recipient container. Finish the migration and check the resulting data using the NDS tree as a guide.

 There are a couple of important points here. First, it may be necessary to actually create a receiving container such as an OU prior to the migration. Second, in NetWare there are containers called Organizations, which would be equated to the domain level, and OUs that correspond to, of course, OUs. This is important to remember in migrating objects between NDS and Windows 2000, as Organizations will not migrate to the OU level.

With test migration complete, there are a couple of items that should be reviewed before the real migration takes place. Several configuration options may be set prior to running the migration. Right-click on the root object in the console, and select properties (this may also be set at the project level). The following is a brief synopsis of the configuration options.

The General tab is used to relocate the database file directory (see Figure 18.24).

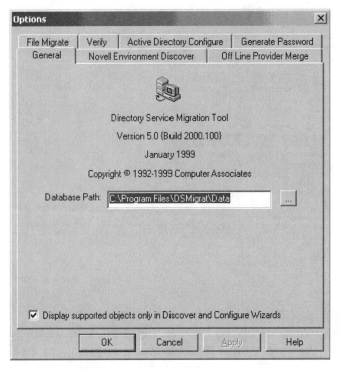

Figure 18.24   The General configuration tab.

The next tab in line, Novell Environment Discover, is used to configure the discovery of objects in the NetWare environment and the maximum number of objects allowed per view (see Figure 18.25).

The Offline Provider Merge tab is used to set options to append multivalued properties or replace them (see Figure 18.26).

The File Migrate tab is used to configure overwrite properties for directory or file duplicates (see Figure 18.27).

The Verify tab allows maximum parameters to be set for various object types, including DN length and the number of objects in a container. These are scanned prior to migrating to constrain lengthy or unruly objects (see Figure 18.28).

Next is the Active Directory Configure tab with options for overwriting existing properties for single or multivalued objects. This would apply only if the object type property already exists in the directory, and using these options should be understood prior to their use. See the Windows 2000 help file for more information on using this feature (see Figure 18.29).

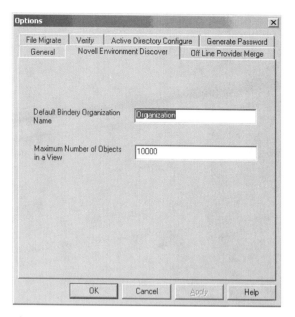

Figure 18.25   The Novell Environment Discover tab.

The last option to configure is the way that the migration will handle passwords from one system to the other. Use simple settings such as the "set to the users logon name" to make the logon process easy for users,

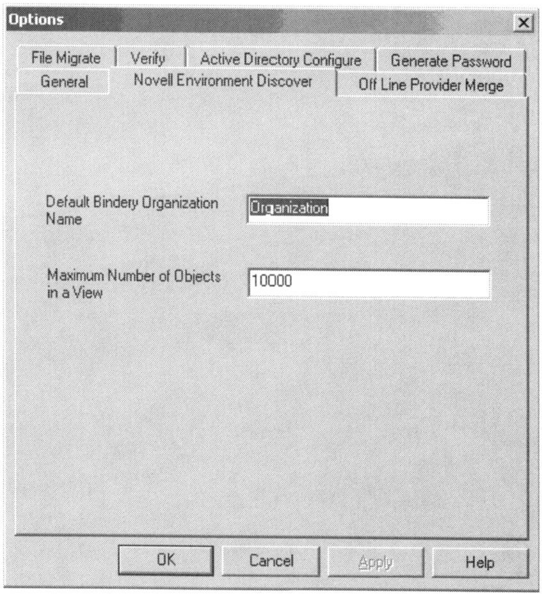

Figure 18.26   The Offline Provider Merge tab.

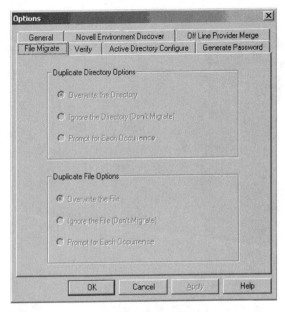

Figure 18.27 The File Migrate tab.

and then enforce the "user must change password at next logon" option for tighter security. E-mail instructions can help this process along as well (see Figure 18.30).

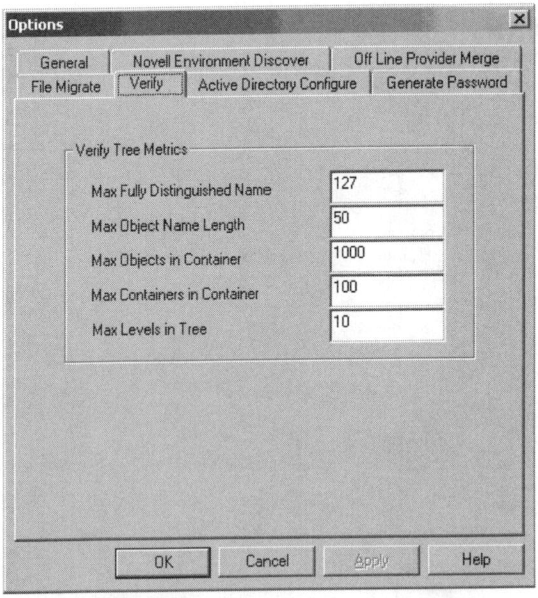

Figure 18.28 The Verify tab.

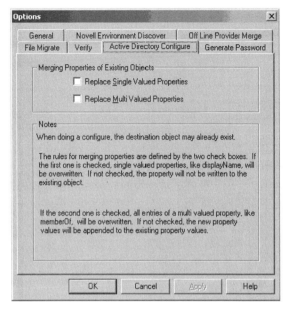

Figure 18.29 The Active Directory Configure tab.

Finally, objects may be individually configured on a case-by-case basis by double-clicking the object in the console and modifying the

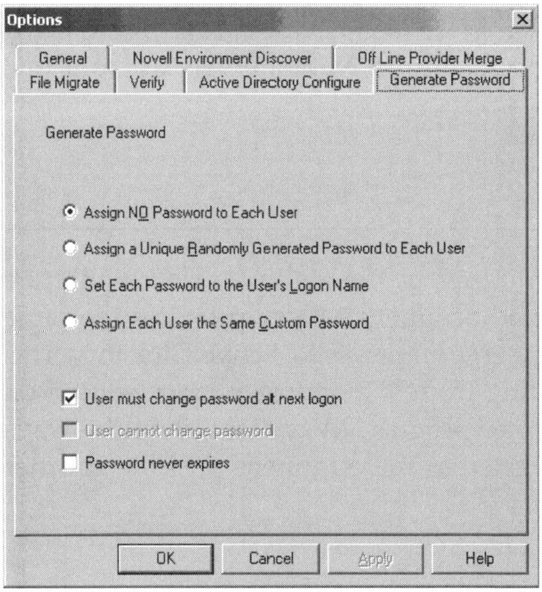

Figure 18.30 The Generate Password tab.

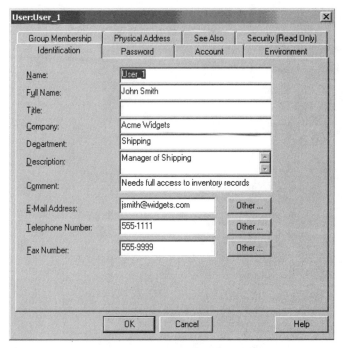

Figure 18.31   Configuring an exported user object.

information as needed. This may prove time consuming, and you would be better served to do the migration first, then export the data to a CSV file for manipulation in Excel (see Chapter 15). Figure 18.31 shows a typical configuration screen for a NetWare user account that was exported to the DSM tool.

Summary

Windows 2000 allows the administrator the ability to slowly migrate legacy NT systems over a period of time, and also provides the same option to migrate from NetWare environments to Active Directory. This chapter dealt first with migrating from NT, and then later focused on migrating from Novell's NetWare product. Migrations should always be meticulously planned and tested as thoroughly as possible in order to ensure smooth transition.

Glossary

access control list (ACL). A set of data associated with a file, directory, or other resource that defines the permissions that users and/or groups have for accessing it. In the Active Directory directory service, an ACL is a list of access control entries (ACEs) stored with the object it protects. In Windows NT, an ACL is stored as a binary value, called a *security descriptor*.

access control entry (ACE). Each ACE contains a security identifier (SID), which identifies the principal (user or group) to whom the ACE applies, and information on what type of access the ACE grants or denies.

Active Directory. A structure supported by Windows 2000 that lets any object on a network be tracked and located. Active Directory is the directory service used in Windows 2000 Server and is the foundation of Windows 2000 distributed networks.

Active Directory Service Interface (ADSI). ADSI is a client-side product based on the Component Object Model (COM). ADSI defines a directory service model and a set of COM interfaces that enable Windows NT and Windows 95 client applications to access several network directory services, including Active Directory. ADSI allows applications to communicate with Active Directory.

ADSI provides the means for directory service clients to use one set of interfaces to communicate with any namespace that provides an ADSI implementation. ADSI clients gain a simpler access to a namespace's services by being able to use ADSI in place of the network-specific application programming interface (API) calls. ADSI conforms to and supports standard COM features. ADSI also supplies both automation-compliant interfaces for use by name-bound controllers, such as Java, Visual Basic, and Visual Basic, Scripting Edition, and also nonautomation interfaces for language environments such as C and C++ that can optimize for performance. In addition, ADSI supplies its own OLE database provider.

attribute. A single property of an object. An object is described by the values of its attributes. For example, a car can be described by its make, model, color, and so on. These are the attributes of the car. The term *attribute* is often used interchangeably with *property*, which means the same thing. Attributes are also data items used to describe the objects that are represented by the classes defined in the schema. Attributes are defined in the schema separately from the classes; this allows a single attribute definition to be applied to many classes.

authentication. Verifying the identity of a user who is logging on to a computer system, or verifying the integrity of a transmitted message.

backup domain controller (BDC). In a Windows NT Server 4.0 or earlier domain, a computer running Windows NT Server that receives a copy of the domain's directory database, which contains all account and security policy information for the domain. The copy is synchronized periodically and automatically with the master copy on the primary domain controller (PDC). BDCs also authenticate user logons and can be promoted to function as PDCs as needed. Multiple BDCs can exist on a domain.

In a Windows 2000 domain, BDCs are not required; all domain controllers are peers, and all can perform maintenance on the directory. Windows NT 4.0 and 3.51 BDCs can participate in a Windows 2000 domain when it is running in mixed mode.

bridgehead server. A bridgehead server is a strategic server used to funnel all site traffic generated by site links in a multisite Windows 2000 implementation. Bridgehead servers will host all of the site links within a site in order to maintain communication between sites.

container. A special type of Active Directory object. A container is like other directory objects in that it has attributes and is part of the Active Directory namespace. However, unlike other objects, it does not usually represent something concrete. It is the container for a group of objects and other containers.

cost. A term used in routing that associates a numeric value to a particular route to create route affinity.

database layer. An architectural layer of Active Directory that isolates the upper layers of the directory service from the underlying database system by exposing application programming interfaces (APIs) to the Directory System Agent (DSA) layer so that no calls are made directly to the Extensible Storage Engine (ESE).

delegation. Delegation allows a higher administrative authority to grant specific administrative rights for containers and subtrees to individuals and groups. This distributed model of administration alleviated the need for administrators to monitor or service requests from the enterprise, and empowers users to take control of delegated segments of the network. Delegation is usually applied at the organizational unit (OU) level.

distinguished name. Every object in the Active Directory has a unique distinguished name. The distinguished name identifies the domain that holds the object, as well as the complete path through the container hierarchy by which the object is reached. A typical distinguished name might be: CN=JohnSmith,CN=Users,DC=Technelogic, DC=Com. This distinguished name identifies the "James Smith" user object in the Microsoft.com domain.

domain. A logical group of resources contained by a set of security boundaries and unique security identifiers (SIDs).

domain controller. A Windows NT Server holding a partition of the Active Directory.

domain local group. A domain local group can only be used on ACLs in its own domain. A domain local group can contain users and global groups from any domain in the forest, universal groups, and other domain local groups in its own domain.

Domain Name System (DNS). Hierarchical distributed database used for name/address translation and client-server rendezvous. DNS is the namespace used on the Internet to resolve computer and service names to TCP/IP addresses. Active Directory uses DNS as its location service, and so clients find domain controllers via DNS queries.

Extensible Storage Engine (ESE). The Active Directory database engine. ESE is a newer version of the Jet database that is used in Microsoft Exchange Server versions 4.x and 5.x. Much like a SQL database, the ESE uses a transaction database system, which means that it uses log files to ensure that committed transactions are safe.

first-layer domains. Refers to a domain or domains under the root domain, and are typically set up as geographical representations in a Windows 2000 network.

forest. A group of one or more Active Directory trees. All trees in a forest share a common schema, configuration, and Global Catalog (GC). The trees do not form a contiguous namespace. All trees in a given forest trust each other via transitive trusts.

global catalog (GC). The GC contains a partial replica of every Windows 2000 domain in the directory. The GC lets users and applications find objects in an Active Directory domain tree given one or more attributes of the target object. It also contains the schema and configuration directory partitions. This means the GC holds a replica of every object in the Active Directory, but with only a small number of their attributes. The attributes in the GC are those most frequently used in search operations (such as a user's first and last names, logon names, and so on), and those required to locate a full replica of the object. The GC allows users to quickly find objects of interest without knowing what domain holds them and without requiring a contiguous extended namespace in the enterprise. The GC is built automatically by the Active Directory replication system.

global catalog server (GCS). A Windows 2000 domain controller that holds a copy of the GC for the forest.

global group. A global group can appear on ACLs anywhere in the forest, and may contain users and other global groups from its own domain.

Group Policy. Refers to applying policy to groups of computers and/or users contained within the Active Directory containers. The type of policy includes not only registry-based policy found in Windows NT Server 4.0, but is enabled by Directory Services to store many types of policy data; for example, file deployment, application deployment, logon/logoff scripts and startup/shutdown scripts, domain security, Internet Protocol Security (IPSec), and so on. The collections of policy are referred to as Group Policy Objects (GPOs).

Group Policy Object (GPO). A virtual collection of policies. It is given a unique name, such as a globally unique identifier (GUID). GPOs store group policy settings in two locations: a Group Policy Container (GPC) (preferred), and a Group Policy Template (GPT). The GPC is an Active Directory object that stores version information, status information, and other policy information (for example, application objects). The GPT is used for file-based data and stores software policy, script, and deployment information. The GPT is located on the system volume folder of the domain controller. A GPO can be associated with one or more Active Directory containers, such as a site, domain, or organizational unit (OU). Multiple containers can be associated with the same GPO, and a single container can have more than one associated GPO.

Hostname. A DNS term that refers to the name given a particular device on an IP network. The hostname may refer to a workstation, server, router, and so forth.

Inheritance. The effect of propagating an object's properties to its child or subtree members.

Kerberos. Developed by MIT, Kerberos is a security system used to authenticate users. The Kerberos protocol is the primary authentication mechanism in the Windows 2000 operating system.

Knowledge Consistency Checker (KCC). The KCC is a built-in service that runs on all domain controllers and automatically establishes connections between individual machines in the same site. These are known as Windows 2000 Directory Service connection objects. An administrator may establish additional connection objects or remove connection objects. At any point, though, where replication within a site becomes impossible or has a single point of failure, the KCC will step in and establish as many new connection objects as necessary to resume Active Directory replication.

Lightweight Directory Access Protocol (LDAP). A protocol used to access a directory service. LDAP support is currently being implemented in Web browsers and e-mail programs, which can query an LDAP-compliant directory. LDAP is a simplified version of the Directory Access Protocol (DAP), which is used to gain access to X.500 directories. It is easier to code the query in LDAP than in DAP, but LDAP is less comprehensive. For example, DAP can initiate searches on other servers if an address is not found, while LDAP cannot in its initial specification. LDAP is the primary access protocol for Active Directory.

Logical structure. The elements of Active Directory that overlay the physical structure of the directory and help to unite all elements. Examples include the schema and DNS.

multi-master replication. The Active Directory provides multi-master replication. Multi-master replication means that all replicas of a given directory partition are writeable. This allows updates to be applied to any replica of a given partition. The Active Directory replication system propagates the changes from a given replica to all other replicas. Replication is automatic and transparent.

Active Directory multi-master replication propagates every object (such as users, groups, computers, domains, organization units (OUs), security policies, and so on) created on any domain controller to each of the other participating domain controllers. If one domain controller in a domain slows or fails, other domain controllers in the same domain can provide the necessary directory access because they contain the same directory data.

namespace. A name or group of names that are defined according to some naming convention; any bounded area in which a given name can be resolved. The Active Directory is primarily a namespace, as is any directory service. A telephone directory is a namespace. The Internet uses a hierarchical namespace that partitions names into categories known as top-level domains, such as .com, .edu, and .gov, which are at the top of the hierarchy.

name resolution. The process of translating a name into some object or information that the name represents. A telephone book forms a namespace in which the names of telephone subscribers can be resolved to telephone numbers. The Windows NT file system forms a namespace in which the name of a file can be resolved to the file itself. The Active Directory forms a namespace in which the name of an object in the directory can be resolved to the object itself.

NetBIOS. Short for Network Basic Input Output System, NetBIOS is an API based on Server Message Block communication format, and extends operating system network functionality.

object. An object is a distinct, named set of attributes that represents something concrete, such as a user, a printer, or an application. The attributes hold data describing the thing that is identified by the directory object. Attributes of a user might include the user's given name, surname, and e-mail address.

object identifier. An object identifier is a number identifying an object class or attribute in a directory service. Object identifiers are issued by issuing authorities and form a hierarchy. An object identifier is represented as a dotted decimal string (for example, "1.2.3.4"). Enterprises (and individuals) can obtain a root object identifier from an issuing authority and use it to allocate additional object identifiers. For example, Microsoft has been issued the root object identifier of 1.2.840.113556. Microsoft manages further branches from this root internally. One of these branches is used to allocate object identifier for Active Directory classes, another for Active Directory attributes, and so on.

Most countries in the world have an identified National Registration Authority (NRA) responsible for issuing object identifiers to enterprises. In the United States, the NRA is the American National Standards Institute (ANSI). An enterprise can register a name for the object identifier as well. There is a fee associated with both root object identifiers and registered names.

operations master. Active Directory operations that are single-master; that is, not permitted to occur at different places in the network at the same time. Examples of these operations include:

- relative identifier (RID) allocation
- schema modification
- primary domain controller (PDC) election
- certain infrastructure changes

organizational unit (OU). A container object that is an administrative partition of the Active Directory. OUs can contain users, groups, resources, and other OUs. OUs enable the delegation of administration to distinct subtrees of the directory.

partition (1). A complete unit of replication within the store.

partition (2). The Active Directory is made up of one or more directory partitions. A directory partition is a contiguous subtree of the directory that forms a unit of replication. So, a given replica is always a replica of some directory partition. In the Active Directory, a single server always holds at least three directory partitions: the schema, the configuration, and the directory partition(s). The schema and configuration are replicated to every domain controller in a given forest. The per-domain directory partition is replicated only to domain controllers for that domain.

policy. The set of rules that govern the interaction between a subject and an object. For example, when an Internet Protocol (IP) security agent (the subject) starts on a given computer (the object), a policy determines how that computer will participate in secure IP connections.

policy engine. Software that executes at decision points to perform policy selection, to evaluate conditions, and determine what actions must be performed. The concept of the policy engine is quite diffuse; policy engine functionality will often be spread through many parts of the distributed system. For example, Windows 2000 provides a policy infrastructure that includes a policy store (Group Policy Object), a policy engine that runs as part of user logon (WinLogon), and an API for services to invoke the policy selection process on demand (GetGPOList). Some applications and services will use WinLogon integration to apply their policies to users; others will use GetGPOList to implement their own policy decision and enforcement points.

primary domain controller (PDC). In a Windows NT Server 4.0 or earlier domain, the computer running Windows NT Server that authenticates domain logons and maintains the directory database for a domain. The PDC tracks changes made to accounts of all computers on a domain. It is the only computer to receive these changes directly. A domain has only one PDC. In Windows 2000, one of the domain controllers in each domain is identified as the PDC for compatibility with down-level clients and servers.

primary domain controller emulator. PDCs are the first servers that are upgraded in a Windows 2000 migration. Once Windows 2000 and Windows NT servers exist together in an environment, it is known as a *mixed-mode* environment. In a mixed-mode Windows 2000 / Windows NT environment where down-level domain controllers such as BDCs exist, it is necessary to have a server that functions in the role of the PDC to handle authentication requests and SAM updates. The PDC Emulator functions in this role and is typically the first domain controller in a Windows 2000 domain. The PDC emulator role may be moved if necessary.

profile. A collection of information selected and applied to the interaction between a subject and an object by an action that is the outcome of evaluation of policy conditions. The content of a profile is specific to the subjects and objects in question. Profiles can further simplify administration by reducing the total number of policies. For example, a given server application may have a large number of configuration parameters. A policy for that application can reference the profile; this is simpler than using multiple policies to accomplish the same thing.

query. A request for information given some type of attribute for the information requested, such as a name. In Windows 2000, queries are LDAP based and are based on the presence of objects in the directory.

relative distinguished name. The RDN of an object is the part of the name that is an attribute of the object itself. The attribute that provides the RDN for an object is referred to as the *naming attribute.*

replication. In database management, replication is the function that keeps distributed databases synchronized by routinely copying the entire database or subsets of the database to other servers in the network. There are several methods of replication, including: primary site replication, shared or transferred ownership replication, symmetric replication, (also known as update-anywhere or peer-to-peer replication), and fail-over replication. The Active Directory provides multi-master replication. Multi-master replication means that all replicas of a given partition are writeable. This allows updates to be applied to any replica of a given partition. Replication is automatic and transparent.

root. Typically refers to the root of a tree hierarchy, which may be a domain tree, a directory tree, or a DNS tree.

root domain. The root of a domain tree structure or hierarchy. The root domain in Windows 2000 is the first domain installed and is defined by the root DNS namespace as well.

schema. The definition of an entire database; the universe of objects that can be stored in the directory is defined in the schema. For each object class, the schema defines what attributes an instance of the class must have, what additional attributes it may have, and what object class can be a parent of the current object base.

SID. Security identifier. Used in NTLM authentication practices, the SID is unique to domains and security accounts. Used in conjunction with ACLs, the SID is checked against a the list to approve or deny access. The preferred method of authentication in Windows 2000 is Kerberos.

site. A location in a network holding Active Directory servers. A site is defined as one or more well-connected TCP/IP subnets. Well-connected means that network connectivity is highly reliable and fast (LAN speeds, 10 MM bits-per-second or greater). Sites play a major role in the Active Directory replication service, which differentiates between replication using a local network connection (intra-site replication) and replication over a slower WAN link (inter-site replication). Administrators use the Active Directory Sites and Services Manager Snap-in to administer replication topology for both intra- and inter-site replication.

site connector. Used to connect two sites and are denoted usually segmented by subnet.

slave server. Refers to a DNS server that updates its database via a push/pull mechanism initiated by another DNS server.

store. The physical storage for each replica of the Active Directory. When an object is stored in Active Directory, the system will select a copy of the Store and write the object there. The replication system will replicate the object to all other replicas. The Store is implemented using the Extensible Storage Engine (ESE).

transitive trust. A trust relationship formed between parent and child domains where the trust relationship flows across to adjacent child domains and are bidirectional. An example of this is illustrated in a domain tree where the root domain A has two child domains beneath it, B and C. Transitive trusts exist between domain A and B, and A and C. Due to the nature of transitive trusts, domains C and B trust each other as well.

topology. The "shape" that a network takes.

tree. A domain tree is a set of Windows NT domains connected together via transitive, bidirectional trust, sharing a common schema, configuration, and global catalog (GC). The domains must form a contiguous hierarchical namespace, such that if a.com is the root of the tree, b.a.com is a child of a.com, c.b.a.com is a child of b.a.com, and so on.

Trust relationship. A partnership between two NT domains. The implementation of a trust allows resources between two domains to be shared.

universal group. The simplest form of group. Universal groups can appear in ACLs anywhere in the forest, and can contain other universal groups, global groups, and users from anywhere in the forest. Small installations can use universal groups exclusively and not concern themselves with global and local groups. Windows NT used global and domain local groups, but did not have universal groups.

Zones. On a DNS server, the zone is dictated by the presence of a zone file, and the presence of that file on the server means the server hosts that particular zone.

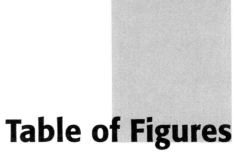

Table of Figures

References

Windows 2000

Overview

Installing and Configuring Microsoft Windows 2000 (MOC Instructor's Guide). Microsoft Corporation: 1999

Microsoft Windows Active Directory: An Introduction to the Next Generation Directory Services; White Paper. Microsoft Corporation, 1999

Active Directory Technical Summary; White Paper. Microsoft Corporation, 1999

Microsoft TechEd Conference Notes. 1998 and 1999

Microsoft Technet CD Subscription. 1998–1999

Planning

Designing a Microsoft Windows 2000 Directory Service Infrastructure (MOC), Instructor's Guide. Microsoft Corporation, 1999

Draft of the Active Directory4 Design and Deployment Considerations; White Paper. Microsoft Corporation, 1999

Planning for a Global Directory Service; White Paper. Microsoft Corporation, 1999

Deployment

Designing a Microsoft Windows 2000 Directory Service Infrastructure (MOC), Instructors Guide. Microsoft Corporation, 1999

Draft of the Active Directory4 Design and Deployment Considerations; White Paper. Microsoft Corporation, 1999

Active Directory

Installing and Configuring Microsoft Windows 2000 (MOC Instructors Guide). Microsoft Corporation, 1999

Microsoft Windows Active Directory: An Introduction to the Next Generation Directory Services; White Paper. Microsoft Corporation, 1999

Designing a Microsoft Windows 2000 Directory Service Infrastructure (MOC), Instructor's Guide. Microsoft Corporation, 1999

Draft of the Active Directory4 Design and Deployment Considerations; White Paper. Microsoft Corporation, 1999

Active Directory Technical Summary; White Paper. Microsoft Corporation, 1999

Microsoft TechEd Conference Notes, 1998 and 1999

Microsoft Technet CD Subscription, 1998–1999

DNS

DNS FAQ; www.intac.com/~cdp/cptd-faq

IP Works Resource Center. Process Software Corporation, www.process.com

DNS and BIND; Web Review Magazine, Aug 4, 1998. webreview.com

Microsoft DNS White Paper. Technet CD Subscription, Feb 1999

Group Policy

Introduction to Windows 2000 Group Policy; White Paper. Microsoft Corporation, 1999

Designing a Microsoft Windows 2000 Directory Service Infrastructure (MOC), Instructor's Guide. Microsoft Corporation, 1999

Group Policy Walkthrough; White Paper. Microsoft Corporation, 1999

Management

Microsoft Management Console Walkthrough; White Paper. Microsoft Corporation, 1999

Introduction to Windows Management Services; White Paper. Microsoft Corporation, 1999

Administering Windows 2000 (MOC Instructor's Guide). Microsoft Corporation, 1999

Migration

Planning Migration from Windows NT to Windows 2000; White Paper. Microsoft Corporation, 1999

Installing and Configuring Microsoft Windows 2000 (MOC Instructor's Guide). Microsoft Corporation, 1999

Standards

X.500

Drilling for Data; Network Computing; Christy Hudgins-Bonafield. Sept 24, 1996

OID Description of X.500 Directory Services. June 19, 1999; www .alvestrand.no/objectid/2.5/html

Understanding X.500; D. W. Chadwick, 1994; www.salford.ac.uk/ its024/Version.Web/contents.htm

Directories and X.500: An Introduction. Barbara Shuh, Information Technology Services—National Library of Canada; March 14, 1997; www.nlc-bnc.ca

DNS

How Dynamic Addressing Is Made Usable with DDNS; Network Computing; James R. Stromski. July 31, 1997; www.nwc.com/816/816r1side.html

The DNS Resources Directory. www.dns.net

DNS FAQ. www.intac.com/~cdp/cptd-faq

IP Works Resource Center; Process Software Corporation. www.process.com

DNS and BIND; Web Review Magazine. Aug 4, 1998; webreview.com

LDAP

An LDAP Roadmap and FAQ. www.kingsmountain.com/ldaproadmap.shtml; Jeff Hodges; Jul 12, 1999

A Scalable Directory Schema in LDAP for Integrated Conferencing Services; White Paper. Andrew Sears, Massachusetts Institutes of Technology; www.isoc.org/inet97/proceedings/A3/A3_3.htm

LDAP Documentation Page. University of Michigan; www.umich.edu/~dirsvcs/ldap/doc/

RFCs

Internet Requests for Comments (RFC). Ohio State University Computer and Information Technology Department; www.cis.ohio-state.edu/hypertext/information/rfc.html

1101 DNS Encoding of Network Names and Other Types. P.V. Mockapetris. Apr 1, 1989. (Format: TXT=28677 bytes) (Updates RFC1034, RFC1035) (Status: UNKNOWN)

1183 New DNS RR Definitions. C. F. Everhart, L. A. Mamakos, R. Ullmann, P.V. Mockapetris. Oct1, 1990. (Format: TXT=23788 bytes) (Updates RFC1034, RFC1035) (Status: EXPERIMENTAL)

1348 DNS NSAP RRs. B. Manning. July 1992. (Format: TXT=6871 bytes) (Obsoleted by RFC1637) (Updates RFC1034, RFC1035) (Updated by RFC1637) (Status: EXPERIMENTAL)

1383 An Experiment in DNS Based IP Routing. C. Huitema. Dec 1992 (Format: TXT=32680 bytes) (Status: EXPERIMENTAL)

1535 A Security Problem and Proposed Correction with Widely Deployed DNS Software. E. Gavron. Oct 1993 (Format: TXT=9722 bytes) (Status: INFORMATIONAL)

1536 Common DNS Implementation Errors and Suggested Fixes. A. Kumar, J. Postel, C. Neuman, P. Danzig, S. Miller. Oct 1993. (Format: TXT=25476 bytes) (Status: INFORMATIONAL)

1537 Common DNS Data File Configuration Errors. P. Beertema. Oct 1993. (Format: TXT=19825 bytes) (Obsoleted by RFC1912) (Status: INFORMATIONAL)

1637 DNS NSAP Resource Records. B. Manning, R. Colella. Jun 1994. (Format: TXT=21768 bytes) (Obsoletes RFC1348) (Obsoleted by RFC1706) (Updates RFC1348) (Status: EXPERIMENTAL)

1912 Common DNS Operational and Configuration Errors. D. Barr. Feb 1996. (Format: TXT=38252 bytes) (Obsoletes RFC1537) (Status: INFORMATIONAL)

1959 An LDAP URL Format. T. Howes and M. Smith. Jun 1996. (Format: TXT=7243 bytes) (Status: PROPOSED STANDARD)

1960 A String Representation of LDAP Search Filters. T. Howes. Jun 1996. (Format: TXT=5288 bytes) (Obsoletes RFC1558) (Obsoleted by RFC2254) (Status: PROPOSED STANDARD)

2164 Use of an X.500/LDAP Directory to Support MIXER Address Mapping. S. Kille. Jan 1998. (Format: TXT=16701 bytes) (Obsoletes RFC1838) (Status: PROPOSED STANDARD)

2247 Using Domains in LDAP/X.500 Distinguished Names. S. Kille, M. Wahl, A. Grimstad, R. Huber, S. Sataluri. Jan 1998. (Format: TXT=12411 bytes) (Status: PROPOSED STANDARD)

2255 The LDAP URL Format. T. Howes, M. Smith. Dec 1997. (Format: TXT=20685 bytes) (Status: PROPOSED STANDARD)

2256 A Summary of the X.500(96) User Schema for Use with LDAPv3. M. Wahl. Dec 1997. (Format: TXT=32377 bytes) (Status: PROPOSED STANDARD)

1274 The COSINE and Internet X.500 Schema. P. Barker, S. Kille. Nov 1991. (Format: TXT=92827 bytes) (Status: PROPOSED STANDARD)

1275 Replication Requirements to Provide an Internet Directory Using X.500. S.E. Hardcastle-Kille. Nov 1991. (Format: TXT=4616, PS=83736 bytes) (Status: INFORMATIONAL)

1276 Replication and Distributed Operations Extensions to Provide an Internet Directory Using X.500. S.E. Hardcastle-Kille. Nov 1991. (Format: TXT=33731, PS=217170 bytes) (Status: PROPOSED STANDARD)

1279 X.500 and Domains. S. E. Hardcastle-Kille. Nov 1991. (Format: TXT=26669, PS=170029 bytes) (Status: EXPERIMENTAL)

1292 A Catalog of Available X.500 Implementations. R. Lang, R. Wright. Jan 1992. (Format: TXT=129468 bytes) (Obsoleted by RFC1632, FYI0011) (Status: INFORMATIONAL)

1308 Executive Introduction to Directory Services Using the X.500 Protocol. C. Weider, J. Reynolds. Mar 1992. (Format: TXT=9392 bytes) (Status: INFORMATIONAL)

1309 Technical Overview of Directory Services Using the X.500 Protocol. C. Weider, J. Reynolds, S. Heker. Mar 1992. (Format: TXT=35694 bytes) (Status: INFORMATIONAL)

1330 Recommendations for the Phase I Deployment of OSI Directory Services (X.500) and OSI Message Handling Services (X.400) within the ESNET Community. ESCC X.500/X.400 Task Force, ESnet Site Coordinating Committee (ESCC). May 1992. (Format: TXT=192925 bytes) (Status: INFORMATIONAL)

1430 A Strategic Plan for Deploying an Internet X.500 Directory Service. S. Hardcastle-Kille, E. Huizer, V. Cerf, R. Hobby, S. Kent. Feb 1993. (Format: TXT=47587 bytes) (Status: INFORMATIONAL)

1487 X.500 Lightweight Directory Access Protocol. W. Yeong, T. Howes, S. Kille. July 1993. (Format: TXT=44947 bytes) (Obsoleted by RFC1777) (Status: PROPOSED STANDARD)

1488 The X.500 String Representation of Standard Attribute Syntaxes. T. Howes, S. Kille, W. Yeong, C. Robbins. Jul 1993. (Format: TXT=17182 bytes) (Obsoleted by RFC1778) (Status: PROPOSED STANDARD)

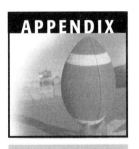

ISO Recommendations for Container Nomenclature

ISO Country Codes

Country	A 2	A 3	Number
AFGHANISTAN	AF	AFG	004
ALBANIA	AL	ALB	008
ALGERIA	DZ	DZA	012
AMERICAN SAMOA	AS	ASM	016
ANDORRA	AD	AND	020
ANGOLA	AO	AGO	024
ANGUILLA	AI	AIA	660
ANTARCTICA	AQ	ATA	010
ANTIGUA AND BARBUDA	AG	ATG	028
ARGENTINA	AR	ARG	032
ARMENIA	AM	ARM	051
ARUBA	AW	ABW	533
AUSTRALIA	AU	AUS	036
AUSTRIA	AT	AUT	040
AZERBAIJAN	AZ	AZE	031
BAHAMAS	BS	BHS	044
BAHRAIN	BH	BHR	048
BANGLADESH	BD	BGD	050

BARBADOS	BB	BRB	052
BELARUS	BY	BLR	112
BELGIUM	BE	BEL	056
BELIZE	BZ	BLZ	084
BENIN	BJ	BEN	204
BERMUDA	BM	BMU	060
BHUTAN	BT	BTN	064
BOLIVIA	BO	BOL	068
BOSNIA AND HERZEGOWINA	BA	BIH	070
BOTSWANA	BW	BWA	072
BOUVET ISLAND	BV	BVT	074
BRAZIL	BR	BRA	076
BRITISH INDIAN OCEAN TERRITORY	IO	IOT	086
BRUNEI DARUSSALAM	BN	BRN	096
BULGARIA	BG	BGR	100
BURKINA FASO	BF	BFA	854
BURUNDI	BI	BDI	108
CAMBODIA	KH	KHM	116
CAMEROON	CM	CMR	120
CANADA	CA	CAN	124
CAPE VERDE	CV	CPV	132
CAYMAN ISLANDS	KY	CYM	136
CENTRAL AFRICAN REPUBLIC	CF	CAF	140
CHAD	TD	TCD	148
CHILE	CL	CHL	152
CHINA	CN	CHN	156
CHRISTMAS ISLAND	CX	CXR	162
COCOS (KEELING) ISLANDS	CC	CCK	166
COLOMBIA	CO	COL	170
COMOROS	KM	COM	174
CONGO	CG	COG	178
CONGO, THE DEMOCRATIC REPUBLIC OF THE	CD	COD	180
COOK ISLANDS	CK	COK	184
COSTA RICA	CR	CRI	188
COTE D'IVOIRE	CI	CIV	384
CROATIA (local name: Hrvatska)	HR	HRV	191
CUBA	CU	CUB	192
CYPRUS	CY	CYP	196
CZECH REPUBLIC	CZ	CZE	203
DENMARK	DK	DNK	208
DJIBOUTI	DJ	DJI	262
DOMINICA	DM	DMA	212
DOMINICAN REPUBLIC	DO	DOM	214
EAST TIMOR	TP	TMP	626
ECUADOR	EC	ECU	218
EGYPT	EG	EGY	818
EL SALVADOR	SV	SLV	222
EQUATORIAL GUINEA	GQ	GNQ	226
ERITREA	ER	ERI	232
ESTONIA	EE	EST	233
ETHIOPIA	ET	ETH	231

FALKLAND ISLANDS (MALVINAS)	FK	FLK	238
FAROE ISLANDS	FO	FRO	234
FIJI	FJ	FJI	242
FINLAND	FI	FIN	246
FRANCE	FR	FRA	250
FRANCE, METROPOLITAN	FX	FXX	249
FRENCH GUIANA	GF	GUF	254
FRENCH POLYNESIA	PF	PYF	258
FRENCH SOUTHERN TERRITORIES	TF	ATF	260
GABON	GA	GAB	266
GAMBIA	GM	GMB	270
GEORGIA	GE	GEO	268
GERMANY	DE	DEU	276
GHANA	GH	GHA	288
GIBRALTAR	GI	GIB	292
GREECE	GR	GRC	300
GREENLAND	GL	GRL	304
GRENADA	GD	GRD	308
GUADELOUPE	GP	GLP	312
GUAM	GU	GUM	316
GUATEMALA	GT	GTM	320
GUINEA	GN	GIN	324
GUINEA-BISSAU	GW	GNB	624
GUYANA	GY	GUY	328
HAITI	HT	HTI	332
HEARD AND MC DONALD ISLANDS	HM	HMD	334
HOLY SEE (VATICAN CITY STATE)	VA	VAT	336
HONDURAS	HN	HND	340
HONG KONG	HK	HKG	344
HUNGARY	HU	HUN	348
ICELAND	IS	ISL	352
INDIA	IN	IND	356
INDONESIA	ID	IDN	360
IRAN (ISLAMIC REPUBLIC OF)	IR	IRN	364
IRAQ	IQ	IRQ	368
IRELAND	IE	IRL	372
ISRAEL	IL	ISR	376
ITALY	IT	ITA	380
JAMAICA	JM	JAM	388
JAPAN	JP	JPN	392
JORDAN	JO	JOR	400
KAZAKHSTAN	KZ	KAZ	398
KENYA	KE	KEN	404
KIRIBATI	KI	KIR	296
KOREA, DEMOCRATIC PEOPLE'S REPUBLIC OF	KP	PRK	408
KOREA, REPUBLIC OF	KR	KOR	410
KUWAIT	KW	KWT	414
KYRGYZSTAN	KG	KGZ	417
LAO PEOPLE'S DEMOCRATIC REPUBLIC	LA	LAO	418
LATVIA	LV	LVA	428
LEBANON	LB	LBN	422

LESOTHO	LS	LSO	426
LIBERIA	LR	LBR	430
LIBYAN ARAB JAMAHIRIYA	LY	LBY	434
LIECHTENSTEIN	LI	LIE	438
LITHUANIA	LT	LTU	440
LUXEMBOURG	LU	LUX	442
MACAU	MO	MAC	446
MACEDONIA, THE FORMER YUGOSLAV REPUBLIC OF	MK	MKD	807
MADAGASCAR	MG	MDG	450
MALAWI	MW	MWI	454
MALAYSIA	MY	MYS	458
MALDIVES	MV	MDV	462
MALI	ML	MLI	466
MALTA	MT	MLT	470
MARSHALL ISLANDS	MH	MHL	584
MARTINIQUE	MQ	MTQ	474
MAURITANIA	MR	MRT	478
MAURITIUS	MU	MUS	480
MAYOTTE	YT	MYT	175
MEXICO	MX	MEX	484
MICRONESIA, FEDERATED STATES OF	FM	FSM	583
MOLDOVA, REPUBLIC OF	MD	MDA	498
MONACO	MC	MCO	492
MONGOLIA	MN	MNG	496
MONTSERRAT	MS	MSR	500
MOROCCO	MA	MAR	504
MOZAMBIQUE	MZ	MOZ	508
MYANMAR	MM	MMR	104
NAMIBIA	NA	NAM	516
NAURU	NR	NRU	520
NEPAL	NP	NPL	524
NETHERLANDS	NL	NLD	528
NETHERLANDS ANTILLES	AN	ANT	530
NEW CALEDONIA	NC	NCL	540
NEW ZEALAND	NZ	NZL	554
NICARAGUA	NI	NIC	558
NIGER	NE	NER	562
NIGERIA	NG	NGA	566
NIUE	NU	NIU	570
NORFOLK ISLAND	NF	NFK	574
NORTHERN MARIANA ISLANDS	MP	MNP	580
NORWAY	NO	NOR	578
OMAN	OM	OMN	512
PAKISTAN	PK	PAK	586
PALAU	PW	PLW	585
PANAMA	PA	PAN	591
PAPUA NEW GUINEA	PG	PNG	598
PARAGUAY	PY	PRY	600
PERU	PE	PER	604
PHILIPPINES	PH	PHL	608
PITCAIRN	PN	PCN	612

POLAND	PL	POL	616
PORTUGAL	PT	PRT	620
PUERTO RICO	PR	PRI	630
QATAR	QA	QAT	634
REUNION	RE	REU	638
ROMANIA	RO	ROM	642
RUSSIAN FEDERATION	RU	RUS	643
RWANDA	RW	RWA	646
SAINT KITTS AND NEVIS	KN	KNA	659
SAINT LUCIA	LC	LCA	662
SAINT VINCENT AND THE GRENADINES	VC	VCT	670
SAMOA	WS	WSM	882
SAN MARINO	SM	SMR	674
SAO TOME AND PRINCIPE	ST	STP	678
SAUDI ARABIA	SA	SAU	682
SENEGAL	SN	SEN	686
SEYCHELLES	SC	SYC	690
SIERRA LEONE	SL	SLE	694
SINGAPORE	SG	SGP	702
SLOVAKIA (Slovak Republic)	SK	SVK	703
SLOVENIA	SI	SVN	705
SOLOMON ISLANDS	SB	SLB	090
SOMALIA	SO	SOM	706
SOUTH AFRICA	ZA	ZAF	710
SOUTH GEORGIA AND THE SOUTH SANDWICH ISLANDS	GS	SGS	239
SPAIN	ES	ESP	724
SRI LANKA	LK	LKA	144
ST. HELENA	SH	SHN	654
ST. PIERRE AND MIQUELON	PM	SPM	666
SUDAN	SD	SDN	736
SURINAME	SR	SUR	740
SVALBARD AND JAN MAYEN ISLANDS	SJ	SJM	744
SWAZILAND	SZ	SWZ	748
SWEDEN	SE	SWE	752
SWITZERLAND	CH	CHE	756
SYRIAN ARAB REPUBLIC	SY	SYR	760
TAIWAN, PROVINCE OF CHINA	TW	TWN	158
TAJIKISTAN	TJ	TJK	762
TANZANIA, UNITED REPUBLIC OF	TZ	TZA	834
THAILAND	TH	THA	764
TOGO	TG	TGO	768
TOKELAU	TK	TKL	772
TONGA	TO	TON	776
TRINIDAD AND TOBAGO	TT	TTO	780
TUNISIA	TN	TUN	788
TURKEY	TR	TUR	792
TURKMENISTAN	TM	TKM	795
TURKS AND CAICOS ISLANDS	TC	TCA	796
TUVALU	TV	TUV	798
UGANDA	UG	UGA	800
UKRAINE	UA	UKR	804

UNITED ARAB EMIRATES	AE	ARE	784
UNITED KINGDOM	GB	GBR	826
UNITED STATES*	US	USA	840
UNITED STATES MINOR OUTLYING ISLANDS	UM	UMI	581
URUGUAY	UY	URY	858
UZBEKISTAN	UZ	UZB	860
VANUATU	VU	VUT	548
VENEZUELA	VE	VEN	862
VIETNAM	VN	VNM	704
VIRGIN ISLANDS (BRITISH)	VG	VGB	092
VIRGIN ISLANDS (U.S.)	VI	VIR	850
WALLIS AND FUTUNA ISLANDS	WF	WLF	876
WESTERN SAHARA	EH	ESH	732
YEMEN	YE	YEM	887
YUGOSLAVIA	YU	YUG	891
ZAMBIA	ZM	ZMB	894
ZIMBABWE	ZW	ZWE	716

----

* USA: Each State follows standard nomenclature.

Index

WWW. *See* World Wide Web.

X
X.400, 72, 167
X.500, 1, 64, 65, 392
  compliance, 72
  DAP, 63, 71
  data, 76
  definition, 65–68
  future, 77
  gateways, 81
  method, 122
  models, 71–72
  name tree, 134
  naming, 116
  nomenclature, 324
  protocols, 68
  specification, 9, 17, 391
  standards, 64, 66, 68–70, 76–79, 216,
    384, 391
  vendors, 72, 77
  version 3 certificates, 75
X.500 directories, 14

specification. *See* ISB X.500 directory
    specification.
  standard, 3, 16, 167
X.500-based directories, 67
X.500-based directory services, 390
XDS. *See* eXchange Directory Service.

Z
ZAK. *See* Zero Administration Kit.
Zero Administration initiatives, 276
Zero Administration Kit (ZAK), 60
Zone files, 85, 90, 93, 96, 107
Zone information, 91
Zone properties, viewing, 229–232
Zone transfer considerations,
    104–106
Zone types, 224. *See also* Domain
    Name Service zone types.
  changing, 228–229
  choice, 225
Zones, 85, 90–100, 222. *See also*
    Domain Name Service; Primary
    zones; Secondary zones.

What's on the CD-ROM?

This book includes a companion CD-ROM, which provides the reader with all the text of the book, including figures, in PDF format for ease of use.